James H. Cone and Black Liberation Theology

James H. Cone and Black Liberation Theology

by

RUFUS BURROW, JR.

with a foreword by
DR. WILLIAM W. HANNAH

McFarland & Company, Inc., Publishers
Jefferson, North Carolina, and London

British Library Cataloguing-in Publication data are available

Library of Congress Cataloguing-in-Publication Data

Burrow, Rufus, 1951–
    James H. Cone and Black liberation theology / by Rufus Burrow, Jr.
    p. cm.
    Includes bibliographical references and index.
    ISBN 0-89950-900-2 (lib. bdg. : 50# alk. paper) ∞
    1. Cone, James H.   2. Black theology — History of doctrines.
    3. Liberation theology — History of doctrines.   I. Title.
    BX4827.C65B87   1994
    230'.092 — dc20   93-41759
                                                                              CIP

Manufactured in the United States of America

McFarland & Company, Inc., Publishers
  Box 611, Jefferson, North Carolina 28640

TO THE MEMORY OF L. JOYCE MONTGOMERY-FOULKES.
AFRICAN AMERICAN QUEEN AND BEARER OF THE GOOD
NEWS OF LIBERATION. COOL, CALM, COURAGEOUS,
CHRIST-LIKE. SHE FOUGHT THE GOOD FIGHT, AND
WON THE MORE ABUNDANT LIFE! BUT BEFORE SHE LEFT
THIS WORLD SHE TAUGHT MANY WHAT IT REALLY
MEANS TO "KEEP ON KEEPING ON" NO MATTER WHAT
OBSTACLES ARE SET IN ONE'S PATH.

CONTENTS

ACKNOWLEDGMENTS   ix

FOREWORD (by Dr. William W. Hannah)   xiii

INTRODUCTION   xvii

Part One: Foundations of Black Theology

1. THE ORIGINS OF BLACK THEOLOGY   1

   The Historical Origins   3
   Were There Strands of Black Theology During Slavery?   10
   There Is No Bifurcation of Reality   12
   The Contemporary Development of Black Theology   13

2. THE MEANING AND METHODOLOGY OF BLACK
   THEOLOGY   22

   An Early Attempt to Define Black Theology   23
   The Changing Meaning of Black Theology in Cone's Work   26
   The Methodological Components of Liberation Theology   30
   Commitment and Involvement: The First Step   32
   Cultural Identity   36
   The Role of the Social Sciences   38
   Praxis   41
   The Frame of Reference   44
   The Hermeneutic of Suspicion   47
   The Black Experience and Liberation Methodology   49
   Taking the Lived-Story of Blacks Seriously   49
   Passionate Language   50
   The Significance of Reason   51
   The Contextual-Dialectical Method   51

Part Two: Transitions in Cone's Theology

3. FOR MY PEOPLE   57

   Writing for Black People: The Early Period   67
   Writing for Black People: The Middle and Later Periods   70
   For My People, No Matter What!   71

4. SOCIOECONOMIC ANALYSIS IN CONE'S THEOLOGY   78

    Anger and Social Analysis in the Early Period   79
    An Early Awareness of a Need for Social Analysis   87
    The Early Attitude Toward Marxism   91
    Social Analysis and the NCBC   93
    Evidence of Social Analysis in the First Stage   97
    Is There Social Analysis in *Black Theology and Black Power?*   98
    Is There Social Analysis in *A Black Theology of Liberation?*   101
    The Necessity of Socioeconomic Analysis   105

5. DEVELOPING PERSPECTIVE ON OPPRESSION   111

    The Significance of Physiological and Ontological Blackness   114
    Awareness of Other Forms of Oppression: The Early Period   125
    Black Theology and Classism   128
    Black Theology and Sexism: The Great Challenge   132
    An Expanding View of Oppression   139

6. CONE AND THE BLACK CHURCH   146

    The Antebellum Black Church   148
    The Post–Civil War Black Church   153
    A Changing Perspective on the Black Church   159
    Cone's Love for the Black Church   169

Part Three: Some New Directions for Black Theology

7. BLACK THEOLOGY: TOWARD THE YEAR 2000   173

    Black Theology and the Folk   177
    The Truth About Sexism   180
    Speaking the Truth to Black Youth   182
    Doing It for Our People   186
    The Development of "Race Persons," or Doing Our First
        Works Over   189
    The Relations between Blacks and Native Americans   190
    The Relations between Blacks and Latinos   192
    Two-Thirds World Theology-in–Black   194
    Black Theology and Metaphysics   196

NOTES   203

SELECT BIBLIOGRAPHY OF LITERATURE
    BY AND ABOUT JAMES H. CONE   237

APPENDIX: SOME SAMPLES OF JAMES H. CONE'S USE
    OF SCRIPTURE   247

INDEX   251

ACKNOWLEDGMENTS

MOST OF the encouragement and support I received along a sometimes lonely and torturous road did not come from professional colleagues. Rather it came from *the folk*, those common, everyday, ordinary people from many different walks of life, among whom are the most bruised and beaten. It was they who stood with me and helped sustain me both when I entered and exited my "torture chamber" to work on this text. It was some of these who read various versions of the manuscript and provided sharp, helpful critiques and suggestions for improvement.

My pastor, Dr. William W. Hannah, who is on the faculty at Martin University, read the very first draft of the manuscript in the late eighties when no one else would make the time. His very thorough critique and advice forced me back into the chamber to grapple further with issues he raised. The breadth and depth of his knowledge of black liberation theology and his sense of its significance for the black church and the African American community give lie to the oft-made categorical criticism that black pastors know little or nothing about black theology. His support at that early stage racks up one for the black church, for it was one of its own who initially supported this project.

Professor Lewis V. Baldwin of Vanderbilt University proved a steady, supportive colleague and mentor. I am forever indebted to him for ideas he offered which made this a much better book than might otherwise have been the case. Professor Baldwin was a very incisive and diplomatic critic.

My colleague, Ursula Pfafflin, read the entire manuscript and provided helpful suggestions. Another colleague, Karen Baker-Fletcher, a rising star in womanist theology (now on the faculty at Claremont School of Theology), was able through her passion, witness, writing, and lectures to help me to a greater appreciation of the contributions of such nineteenth-century African American "sheroes" as Anna Julia Cooper and Maria Stewart. She helped me to see what their witness means for the total liberation of *all* persons from massive, systemic forms of oppression.

L. Susan May, a professor of homiletics at Lexington Theological Seminary, and Beth Meyerson, both former students, read early and later drafts of the manuscript and contributed significantly to the refining of style as well as substantive changes. Along the same lines, another student, Seana

Murphy ("Murph"), made invaluable suggestions for the use of the late Audre Lorde's work. In addition, she kept before me the overwhelming sense of nihilism within the African American community and its effect on black youth. The present version of the manuscript has been christened with Murph's tears over the murders of nearly two dozen black youths (committed by other black youths!) in Indianapolis over a recent eighteen-month period.

The Rev. Jane Ferguson ("Fergie") was vigilant in ministering to me through the mail, on the telephone, and through periodic visits from Illinois as I worked through this and other projects. A European American woman and former student, Fergie's witness was a constant reminder to me that God intends the total liberation of all persons, not next week or next year, but right now!

Saderia Means, owner of Abba Christian Bookstore in Indianapolis, was always generous in sharing with me the vast wealth of her knowledge about the African American religiocultural heritage. She was both forthright and tender in her critiques of my writing and teaching. She is a true unsung shero who loves the black church enough to be among its staunchest critics, regardless of personal cost.

Carroll Avon Watkins Weaver, a doctoral candidate at Iliff School of Theology and a very able and knowledgeable critic, impressed upon me time and again that at bottom the purpose of this "labor of love" must be to contribute to the liberation of African Americans and all systematically oppressed people. James L. Kirby, a professor of theological social ethics at Lexington Theological Seminary, and Lawrence A. Burnley, a doctoral candidate at the University of Pennsylvania, frequently phoned and wrote words of encouragement when I did not believe I could complete the project. Both are promising, burgeoning black scholars and Personalists in the best sense. Reginald Carl Holmes, senior minister of Park Hill Christian Church in Denver, also a former student, was relentless in reminding me of the importance of this work and the need to "press on no matter what." Like Dr. Hannah and Fergie, he too has been pastor to me on the way to completion of this book.

Yet another former student, the Rev. Livingston R. Malcolm, chairman and general superintendent of the Leeward Islands of the Methodist Church in the Caribbean and the Americas, so believed in me and the importance of this project that he provided a substantial gift that made it possible for me to hide away at a retreat center to complete the first draft.

I would be remiss if I did not mention Heimo Ponnath, whom I have never met, but who, from his home in Germany, made a significant technical contribution. Mr. Ponnath, through my colleague, Ursula Pfafflin, converted my disks so they could be used on IBM compatible computers.

Two million thanks and more to "Lady" Mary Cunningham and

Reubenia ("Beno") Jackson, my ever present comrades in a sometimes unfriendly and hostile environment, and to Kenny Hardin and Dennis Lewis, members of the evening maintenance staff at Christian Theological Seminary who often stopped by my office to "talk about how it really is," as a way of reminding me for whom I must always do my work.

The administration and board of trustees at Christian Theological Seminary made available to me small grants that made it possible to do uninterrupted work on the manuscript at two critical periods. In addition, funds were made available to compensate an outside reader. Needless to say, this was a significant source of support.

Theodore ("Ted") Baker, Sr., of Anderson University has been a constant source of inspiration since my college days there in the early seventies. He followed my academic journey from college to seminary, to graduate school, to seminary professor. He has truly been like the wind beneath my wings. No man has been more of a fan and big brother to me than he.

Finally, I need to mention one more group of people who prepared me to meet the challenges of the mountains and valleys I have encountered. These are the people, who, along with my parents, Fannie B. Burrow (my Rock of Gibraltar!) and the late Rufus Burrow, Sr., instilled in me at a very early age what Garth Baker-Fletcher calls "a sense of somebodyness"; a sense that I am as good as anybody, because God called me into existence. These are the people who taught me that nothing can take the place of excellence and doing one's best. These are my elementary and junior high school teachers in Pontiac, Michigan, all of whom are African Americans and all of whom believed in "the kids from the projects." They include Frederick Douglass Smith, Annie Pearl Moss (who bought me a new pair of brown shoes in the third grade at a time my parents could not afford to), Richard Craig, Sr., Harriet Brooks, Fredeane Sloan, Robert Newby, and William P. Counts.

My wife, Eugena, and our teenage daughter, Sheronn, had the awful task of reminding me over and over again that life cannot be lived to the fullest in the torture chamber. No amount of thanks is adequate to ease what they have endured. None, except they, know better than I how difficult it was for them to put up with me on the way to completing this book.

Rufus Burrow, Jr.
Christian Theological Seminary
Indianapolis, Indiana
Summer 1993

FOREWORD

by Dr. William W. Hannah

PROFESSOR Rufus Burrow, Jr., has demonstrated an uncanny intellectual insight into the work of James H. Cone, particularly with reference to the continuities and changes in his theological project. Cone, the godfather of the development of black liberation theology in its systematic form, powered his way onto the theological scene with the publication of a seminal and controversial text, *Black Theology and Black Power,* in 1969. Burrow has provided a much needed commentary on Cone's approach to black theology and has made clear the connections between its African and African American origins, as well as methodological similarities and dissimilarities that exist among liberation theologies. I consider this work a further legitimization of black theology and its continued viability as a theological option as we approach the year 2000. This in itself is a significant contribution.

For a long time there has been a gap between the systematic study and application of black theology and the black churches. There has especially been a wide chasm between black theologians and black pastors. The theologians have accused the pastors of failing to take seriously enough the liberation-empowerment motif of the Gospel, while the pastors have accused the theologians of having left the church and not taking seriously enough the day to day concrete problems with which the pastor must contend. J. DeOtis Roberts pointed to this rift in both *A Black Political Theology* (1974) and *Black Theology in Dialogue* (1987). This same concern (among other important issues) was raised in the massive study by C. Eric Lincoln and Lawrence Mamiya, *The Black Church in the African American Experience* (1990). The issue is also apparent in Part Two of James Cone and Gayraud S. Wilmore, eds., *Black Theology: A Documentary History, Volume Two 1980–1992.* Indeed, a special issue of the theological journal *Encounter,* of which Burrow and the Rev. Gloria Jean Tate are guest coeditors, also focuses on this troublesome problem. At any rate, it is clear that because of this unfortunate cleft between black theology and the black churches many of the latter continue to be in bondage to Eurocentric evangelical models of theology that have rendered the African American church almost powerless and uncertain of its true identity.

With the publication of Burrow's book, with its conversational and

xiv   **Foreword (Dr. Hannah)**

engaging style, we have an important resource to assist both black theologians and black pastors in further developing an intellectual and functional partnership for the benefit of the whole church and African American community. In addition, this text should go a long way toward liberating well meaning white pastors and theologians from their propensity to think that only Europeans and European Americans can generate authentic theology, and that African Americans cannot possibly produce good theology. Burrow has taken seriously the task of black theology, and suggests some new directions if it is to enhance and maintain its relevance in the black churches and black community.

I was a pastor in Cleveland, Ohio, and very much influenced by the emerging black consciousness movement when Gayraud Wilmore and the black clergy radicals of the National Committee of Negro Churchmen (NCNC) published its statement on Black Power. Subsequently, that committee issued several important statements. It was not long before the group, influenced by the black power movement, changed its name to the National Committee of Black Churchmen (NCBC). Indeed, the group was "pushed" by Black Panthers and black nationalists into what came to be known as black theology. I had been sent by my denomination, the Christian Church (Disciples of Christ), to some of the early meetings in Oakland, California. It was clear from the beginning that Black Panthers and nationalists were fed up with the black church's failure to get radically involved in the violence and injustice being done to the black community. There was clearly an atmosphere of anger and disenchantment with the black church. Many of those who ultimately got involved with the newly emerging black theology were carried or pushed by the tide of discontent, although some of us went willingly. What we were initially lacking was a theology to ground our new found commitment to the liberation of black people. The committee struggled long and hard with this. Little did the members know that there was an unknown black religious scholar at Adrian College in Michigan who was working on the foundations of black theology. This was truly an exciting period.

When the committee voiced its support of the Black Manifesto which was presented by James Forman to Riverside Church in New York City in May 1969, I knew that something revolutionary — something we had not witnessed in the black church community in a long time — was about to be born. It was around this same time that James Cone's book, *Black Theology and Black Power*, appeared. The book catapulted Cone into ultrahot theological limelights. In a relatively short period Cone became the "resident theologian" for the NCBC and played a significant role in the writing of the statement on black theology in June 1969. Little did I know what powerful liberative forces would be unleashed for African Americans.

The designation "black theology" was disagreeable to many people, especially white liberals and African Americans who uncritically adhered to the value system of white middle class America. Yet there were large numbers of African Americans, including myself, who resonated with this "strange" sounding theology. It felt right then and it feels even better now. Many of us jumped for joy and shouted *"Amen!"* when Cone's first book appeared, for it gave us a way of thinking theologically about our longtime belief that we are God's special people and coworkers with God in the struggle for complete liberation.

Professor Burrow has given us a systematic analysis of some of the major transitions or shifts in Cone's theological project since 1969. The transitions include (1) Whom Cone writes and does theology for, (2) social and economic analysis in his theology, (3) Cone's expanding view of oppression, and (4) Cone and the black church. The author's insight into the changes in Cone's theology, both subtle and pronounced, are stimulating, challenging, and helpful in following the development of Cone's version of black theology, which spans the period of the publication of *Black Theology and Black Power* (1969) to *Martin & Malcolm & America* (1991).

In discussing the transitions it is not the author's intention to suggest that Cone *changes* his mind either about his views regarding white theology or his earliest fundamental theses in black liberation theology. Instead, what Burrow does so admirably is to show us how Cone's later, more developed views are an outgrowth and expansion of ideas that appeared in embryonic form in his early writings. For example, around the middle period of his development Cone took a public stance against sexism in the black community and the black church. Burrow argues convincingly that even in Cone's early works he exhibited at least an awareness of discontent among women; he was aware of the women's movement, and knew that blacks were not the only victims of oppression. Burrow does not argue, however, that Cone showed awareness of discontent among African American women in the early stage of his theology, for he did not. In addition, Burrow argues persuasively that Cone's theology was never as narrow and provincial as some early and later critics claimed. Rather, he shows that there has always been a good balance between the universal and particular in Cone's theology. This text also helps us gain insight both into the so-called new racism and its impact on African Americans and other people of color, and the European American practice of denial and explaining everything away, including racism, sexism, and classism.

This book has the distinction of being the first to be published on James Hal Cone. It is one way that the author both honors and thanks a truly great theologian for the example and commitment he has evidenced in his theological journey. Burrow provides a clear picture of Cone's theology as it is worked out in the context of our violent history. His book points to a black theology that includes survival, hope, liberation, and total empowerment. Burrow makes available to African Americans a view of a theology that is affirming of their personhood and the value of the contributions that were made by their slave foreparents to the task of theology, a theology that grabs them at every turn of their life. All of this will help see African Americans through the storm of hostility and oppression. In addition, it reminds us of the God of our mothers and fathers who is always present and active in the lives of the systematically dispossessed and bruised. It reminds us of our inestimable worth as people of God.

One of the most important transitions centers on Cone's developing attitude toward the black church. Burrow explicates Cone's love-hate relationship with the black church and his insistence on speaking the truth to that institution and its leadership despite the heavy price he has sometimes had to pay. He helps us to see that although many problems and limitations continue to exist in the black church, it continues to be the most important vehicle for social change and liberation in and beyond the black community.

Burrow has made a major contribution not only to the black church and the African American community, but to the global community. This book addresses a great need as students, pastors, and white theologians continue to struggle with the meaning and task of black theology, and where it is headed. It will also further enable African Americans to articulate and live out a more functional, practical theology that affirms the personhood of the depressed and oppressed in our community.

The author has included extensive explanatory endnotes, which, in themselves form a commentary on much that is happening in black theological circles, the black community, and other areas of culture in this part of the world. In addition, the endnotes give the reader a good sense of some of the author's deepest sociopolitical and religious concerns regarding his own people as well as others outside the African American community. It is also here that the reader finds some of the author's sharpest critiques of those who have been critical of black liberation theology without having first steeped themselves in the literature.

Many of us have been waiting a very long time for the publication of this book. I highly recommend it to religious scholars, pastors, college, seminary, and graduate students, and laypersons. Any future study of the theology of James Cone will have to reckon with the argument in this book.

Dr. Hannah teaches at Martin University and is senior pastor of University Community Christian Church, Indianapolis, Indiana. This foreword was written July 30, 1993.

INTRODUCTION

J AMES HAL CONE is among the most creative and pace-setting contemporary black theologians. He has been writing major theological treatises since 1968. Although there has until now been no book-length study of his work, there have been at least a dozen dissertations written on his theology since 1974 (some of which are comparative studies)[1]*; a not so impressive number of articles on his work; and some discussion of aspects of his writings by a few theologians in various texts, etc.[2] Cone was criticized most by white theologians, although not many of them have taken either him or the black religiocultural experience seriously enough to be able to write effectively about them. This has been the case despite the fact that Cone was the first to write in a systematic and deliberate way on the subject of black theology. It was Cone who initially made systematic black theology a going concern and developed a viable theology expressing what black clergy radicals influenced by the black power movement were experiencing but were unable to express theologically. It was essentially Cone's groundbreaking work to which other black theologians were compelled to respond.

The twentieth anniversary edition of Cone's first book, *Black Theology and Black Power*, was issued in 1989, along with a celebration to commend his contributions. The present work argues that there is a real need to look seriously and critically at Cone's theology. There are few theologians who have been more misunderstood, and yet who have made the quality of contributions to the fields of theology and ethics in the past two decades as Cone. In part, the failure to understand Cone's theological project is due to the difficulty that many have had in getting beyond the sharp rhetoric and polemic of his first two books. This has led to a misunderstanding of Cone's work and intentions. This study attempts to correct this by demonstrating Cone's influence on black theology and to open a door to an understanding and appreciation of the significance and passion of his work.

This study identifies and discusses some of the significant transitions in the major writings of Cone from the appearance of his first essay, "Christianity and Black Power" (1968)[3] and the further development of its thesis in his first book, *Black Theology and Black Power* (1969), to the publication of *Martin*

*See Notes, beginning on page 203.

& *Malcolm & America* (1991). This last text is particularly important because
from the inception of his theological project Cone was influenced by both
Martin Luther King, Jr., and Malcolm X. In this 1991 book one can see
various shifts in Cone's thinking. For example, in his earlier writings Cone
was closer to Malcolm X on the issue of retaliatory violence. By the publication of *Martin & Malcolm & America* it is clear that he supports Malcolm's view
on the subject philosophically, but practically he is closer to King. So Cone's
last book, commended to me so highly by Lewis V. Baldwin, is very important for my study.

I demonstrate that some of Cone's more recent theological postures,
e.g., his stance on sexism in the black community and church, are not as
novel as appears at first glance. Upon closer examination one can see that
Cone's major works reveal that some of his present views actually appeared
in embryonic form in his early writings. I suggest that there is more continuity than discontinuity in his work. Ideas that were only implicit in his early
works are made explicit as he writes, dialogues, and travels throughout the
United States, Africa, Latin America, and Asia.

For example, although there was no conscious or intentional effort to include socioeconomic analysis in his first two books, I propose that Cone was
at least aware of the need for this in his theological project. That he was not
then well versed in Marxist social analysis does not mean that either social
analysis or his awareness of its significance was absent. Indeed, Marxist
analysis is not the only form of social analysis! Furthermore, Cone was
primarily concerned with white racism and its brutalizing effects on black life-
chances in a racist-capitalist system. Yet he was from the beginning aware
that there were other serious forms of oppression in the United States which
dehumanized and crushed other groups. He did not name these, but there
is evidence that he knew that racism was not the only major social problem.
Cone acknowledged, for example, that in terms of actual numbers more
whites than blacks are victims of poverty. To be sure, it was not until some
years after his early publications that he explicitly made the connections
between racism, sexism, classism, and capitalism. The position advanced in
the present work is that the early Cone (approximately 1968–1975) was further
along in this regard than many white socialist scholars who tended to subsume all social evils, including racism, under the rubric of class. Unlike
Cone, they did not recognize that though racism, like most social evils, is connected with other social problems, it is also unique in itself, and therefore is
irreducible to sexism, classism, or some other social evil. Cone knew that
racism has structural and systemic forms. A social evil of such complexity and
magnitude needed to be addressed both as a separate issue, and in relation
to others. Cone was able to see this early in his theological development,
although he did not then possess ample tools for social analysis to see all of
the ramifications of this.

Since Cone wrote his earlier books in the crucible of the black struggle for civil and human rights in the late sixties and early seventies, he did not believe it necessary, nor did he have the peace of mind or distance of time to engage in the systematic development of such themes as social and economic analysis, black sexism, a blueprint for social reconstruction, the relation between black, feminist, and so-called third-world theologies, and so on. Indeed, because of the state of emergency in the black community the object in those earlier writings was not to present a balanced, objective, and dispassionate statement on black-white relations. To the contrary, it was not possible, he believed, to overstate his case, no matter what white critics (and black ones) said.[4] Rather, Cone believed that it was more important to expose white racism in white theology, white churches, and other white structures,[5] and to do so passionately.

Cone felt obligated to do this. It was an important part of his early witness. He made no secret of his own rage and anger at contemporary forms of white racism, the historic and contemporary brutality and inhumane treatment of blacks, and the silence of white religionists and theologians on this issue.[6] He contended that theology in general, and white theology in particular, was too cool, detached, and uninvolved in the concrete dehumanizing events that have been part of the destruction of black personhood. Although it acknowledged and pointed to the lofty ideals of the Christian faith, traditional theology did not claim them in any committed sense, i.e., through liberating actions on behalf of and with the oppressed. It was time, Cone believed, for somebody to get upset and have the courage and the guts to express the anger that was so pervasive throughout the African American community.[7] He has always maintained that he knew whose side he was on, and felt compelled to say something from a theological perspective that would take seriously the sacrifices made by his parents and other black ancestors, and the systematic degradation they suffered both in and outside the churches.[8]

I have chosen to discuss four of the transitions in Cone's theology in some detail. They are (1) writing and doing theology for his people, (2) social analysis during the early period of his development, (3) developing or expanding perspective on oppression, and (4) attitudes toward the black church. These are by no means all of the important shifts in Cone's theology, but a discussion of them will lead to a better understanding and appreciation of the work and struggles of this still developing theologian.

In order to set the stage I begin with a discussion of the origin of black theology and its early roots in the interior of West Africa. This is followed by an elaboration of the meaning of black theology and the methodology it shares in common with much of liberation theology; shifts in Cone's theology; and consideration of some proposed transitions. I have therefore divided the book into three parts: Foundations of Black Theology; Transitions in Cone's Theology, and Some New Directions for Black Theology. The latter considers

some new directions for black theology that will insure its continued viability
and development as we move toward the twenty-first century.

It would be impossible in a single volume to present a comprehensive
analysis and critique of Cone's entire theological project. It is evident that
whole books can be written on several aspects of Cone's thought, e.g., his
God-concept and the theodicy question; his view of metaphysics and its relation to liberation theology; his concept of violence and reconciliation; and his
theological method. It is my hope, however, that this study will be a significant contribution to the literature on liberation theology in general, and more
specifically, black theology. If this work prompts black scholars and others
who are "black enough" to devote more energy and attention to critical reflection, writing, and discussion of the black religious and cultural experience
and its meaning for the struggle for total liberation and empowerment, my
purpose will have been accomplished.

I believe that every openminded person will benefit from a better
understanding of James Cone, the nature of the black theological enterprise,
and what it means to be African American in a racist-sexist-classist nation.
However, I am primarily concerned about its effect upon African Americans
and their quest for liberation and empowerment. As long as the current social
and economic emergency exists in the black community, African Americans
cannot—indeed must not—worry about what those who oppress them think
about what they say and write. Blacks must—with James Baldwin—make up
their own minds about what they should write as they try to be witnesses to
the truth about their experiences in the United States.[9] In addition, they must
be witnesses to all that has happened and to all that can be if they are faithful
to God and committed to enhancing the lives of the systematically oppressed.
White theologians have benefited and continue to benefit from the wealth that
this country has amassed as a result of the stolen labor of African Americans.
As the posterity of white slave masters and overseers, many white theologians
still share the same mentality of their ancestors. To a large extent this contributes to their unwillingness to hear and accurately interpret the message
of black theology.

Concerned that some black religious scholars are more interested in being accepted by white colleagues than speaking the truth to their people and
participating in their struggle for liberation, Gayraud Wilmore writes that
"some have been distracted beyond recall by the rewards of doing theology
in conventional, majoritarian ways."[10] The mission is first and foremost to
join forces with Jesus Christ and other liberators of humanity to liberate and
empower black people and others who are victims of massive, systematic
forms of oppression.

It is hoped that this book will lead to a deeper understanding and appreciation of the theology of James Cone. This will help to move all with
"sighted eyes and feeling hearts" towards the development of a society which

focuses on making the most of all persons, regardless of race, gender, class, sexual preference, age, or health. More than anything I hope that this study will promote further interest in and discussion of all aspects of black theology.

The reader should be aware that when quoting the writings of others I do not alter the language to comply with more recent usages of inclusive language. I think this can be a constant reminder of the blindness or limitation of many writers of both present and bygone eras. In my own writing, however, I adhere strictly to the use of inclusive language.

1. The Origins of Black Theology

A LTHOUGH ONE need not be a *Conean* in order to enter the debates on black theology in an intelligent way, it is absolutely essential at some point to grapple with the thought of James Hal Cone. This is necessary despite the tendency of many theologians to disparage his work (although many have not read him critically and systematically, and with a view to trying to see through his eyes). Many white theologians and some black ones are often quick to say that one must recognize that "Cone's is not the *only* version of black theology," or, "But there are other black theologians that should be considered as well!" Often they begin their response long before one can get Cone's full name out of his or her mouth. The responses are given in such a way that one can detect both anger — possibly because of Cone's forthrightness in articulating his views — and the subtle implication that he is not the top-notch theologian that some seem to think. Cone's greatest nemesis in black theological circles, J. DeOtis Roberts, makes the point that Cone's is not the normative black theology. "It is unfortunate," he writes, "that most observers of black theology consider James Cone's thought as the norm for all black theology."[1] In addition, the tone that many white scholars use when making similar statements often reveal their patronizing attitude toward black theology in general, and their disdain for the theological project of James Cone in particular. This notwithstanding, Cone has been more favorably characterized by African American colleagues as "the leading exponent of black theology"[2]; "the 'father' of Black Theology"[3]; "the premier Black Theologian,"[4] and the like. Cone has clearly influenced the development of numerous second generation black theologians.[5]

Black theologians are no longer disturbed by the negative attitudes of whites and seldom give them much thoughtful consideration. Having attained academic credibility during the second stage of the development of contemporary black theology (roughly 1972–1976), black theologians no longer expend precious time and energy debating the idea of a universal, neutral theology with those who continue to be their oppressors.[6] This is understandable in light of the long history of black suffering that has resulted from racism. Many blacks are not optimistic that whites will ever treat them with the dignity and respect that all human beings deserve. Black theologians have come to believe that they do not contribute to their struggle for liberation as long as they debate with whites about black religion and culture. The credibility of black religion and culture does not stand or fall with the approval or disapproval of white religionists. Blacks must decide whom they will listen to.

Alfred N. Whitehead said that all European philosophic systems are but a footnote to Plato![7] Similarly, it can be said that all contemporary black theology is a footnote to James H. Cone! Although Cone has not pretended to give all of the answers nor to have raised all the essential questions, he has contributed much to the foundation for the future development of black theology. One should not expect to master the fundamentals of black theology if serious attention is not given Cone's work.

Theo Witvliet contends that Martin Luther King, Jr., was an important pioneer of contemporary black liberation theology.[8] There is strong evidence of King's influence on Cone, although he was also deeply impacted by Malcolm X.[9] Indeed, these two men became favorite conversation topics for Cone, who sees them moving toward each other as well as complementing and correcting each other.[10]

Joseph Washington's controversial text *Black Religion*[11] preceded Cone's first book by five years. However, it was not Washington who actually introduced black liberation theology. J. DeOtis Roberts and Major Jones both wrote books on black theology, each intentionally emphasizing the liberation motif as their point of departure. Yet each of these men were essentially responding to the theological project of Cone.

There are many points of entrance into the dialogue with proponents of black theology. One such point of entry is to review the origin and development of black theology. Is it a recent, or contemporary phenomenon? Does it antedate the sixties? What are some crucial elements in the origin of black theology? A critical consideration of the meaning and methodology of black theology is also essential. This will be the subject of Chapter 2.

Both the present and the next chapter will provide the foundation needed to identify and understand the transitions in Cone's theology. Since the appearance of his first essay in 1968, "Christianity and Black Power," Cone has produced eight books (including two anthologies with Gayraud Wilmore), and several dozen articles. One who reads Cone carefully and systematically will notice shifts or transitions in his thinking from 1968 to the present. To the novice these transitions may appear to be pronounced, but in some instances it can be shown that they are merely a matter of changes in focus or emphasis. In other cases, however, the shifts are more significant. An examination of Cone's earlier writings reveal at least an awareness of some of the issues that he later formulated more forthrightly.

Cone and other first generation black theologians generally contend that black theology was born during the struggle for civil and human rights in the sixties.[12] This is not an inaccurate statement, but it does not go far enough.

Systematic efforts to develop black theology may be dated to the the late sixties and the seventies, but the birth of black theology roots much deeper in black history. Cone contends that the publication of the "Black Power Statement" on July 31, 1966 (by the National Committee of Negro Churchmen, or NCNC),[13] may have been the first conscious effort of black religionists to develop a black theology "in which black ministers consciously separated their understanding of the Gospel of Jesus from white Christianity and identified it with the struggles of the black poor for justice."[14] However, black theology, like the black church, was born in protest — protest which began long before black ancestors were torn from the African homeland and forced into dehumanizing slavery in the Americas. A consideration of the historical origins of black theology further substantiates this claim.

The Historical Origins

Since the black church and black theology were born in protest, the rudiments of contemporary black theology are found where black protest against human captivity first began. Cone tells us that black protest and resistance began on the slave ships, and continued on the auction blocks and plantations in the West Indies, and the Colonies. "It began when the first black person decided that death would be preferable to slavery."[15] Cone is right as far as he goes. What he only implies, however, should be said explicitly. Black protest — the protest that led to the development of the black church in the eighteenth century, and systematic black theology in the early seventies — actually began long before resistance on the slave ships, the auction blocks, and the plantations. The resistance to captivity actually began in the interior of West Africa, where most Africans were captured. Black protest began inland, far from the shores of the Atlantic Ocean. This is where we find the rudiments of the struggle that ultimately led to the cries for "black power" in the sixties and the emergence of black theology. If black theology was born in protest, technically it is a phenomenon of the sixties only in the sense that it began to receive systematic formulation during that period. Since African Americans have always adapted the Christian faith to their particular sociocultural context it would not be completely accurate to say that black theology is a "new" or recent phenomenon. That a people do not have the equivalent of a systematized theology at a given period is not the same as having no theology at all.

There is no evidence that a significant number of Africans went willingly with the white slavers who invaded the West African coast. The Portugese established slave trading posts in West Africa by the late fifteenth and early sixteenth centuries, and the flow of slaves to the Iberian peninsula and the so-called New World had begun. The English did not reach the shores of West Africa until nearly a century later.[16] Ripped from family, friends, and culture, Africans endured many battles for freedom enroute even to the African shores of the Atlantic, before they were forced to board the ships that bore peculiar names such as *Brotherhood, John the Baptist, Justice, Integrity, Gift of God, Liberty,* and even *Jesus*.[17] What is most interesting is that many of these inland battles were only indirectly between the white slavers and the Africans.

Since the African rulers of the coastal areas seldom allowed the slavers to enter the interior to march their captives to the seashore, this meant that African collaborators did the dirty deed for a price. For the part they played they were often given weapons, which enabled some of the better known slave-trading African kingdoms, e.g., Dahomey and Ashanti, to develop into military powers.[18] Although white slavers invaded the interior and forcibly removed Africans from their villages, much of the trade was in black hands. Many of those captured by white slavers or African collaborators were already victims of tribal raids or wars. Upon capture they were forcibly marched to the shores of the Atlantic, where the white slavers waited. The struggles or protests that took place during the grueling march to permanent captivity for most was therefore often between Africans.

But in the final analysis it does not matter who the captured Africans fought against during the march from the interior. What matters is that they did not go willingly and without a fight, which was often to the death. It is important to note that as the enchained Africans fought their African captors they were indirectly fighting those white men who initiated the process that led to their captivity. The Africans were not fools. They knew of the coastal towns or European settlements and often observed their fellow Africans being kidnapped, never to return. Many therefore learned not to go unarmed near the coast when the large ships were near by. Benjamin Brawley has written of the suspicions of the Africans, and of the many "hand-to-hand encounters"[19] with the white slavers. That the Africans did not go willingly with their captors is a great legacy for African Americans.

Black protest began long before many African captives reached the beach compounds where they were caged like animals until departure to the Americas. Upon arrival to the beach areas many attempted suicide as a final assertion of their humanity and desire to remain free. Historian Vincent Harding writes that "it was on the edges of our continent—where some of us gulped down handfuls of sand in a last effort to hold the reality of the land—that the long struggle for black freedom began."[20] The struggle for freedom was inevitable, relentless, and took place from the time of capture in the interior of Africa. The resistance continued throughout the long and hazardous march to the ocean; aboard the slave ships with the peculiar names; and upon arrival in the Americas.

Some African captives were undoubtedly so baffled, afraid, and awed by the strange appearance and brutality of their white captors[21] that they put up little resistance. However, there are many accounts of those who "resisted enslavement at every step in their forced emigration. Conscious of the wrongs they suffered, they began trying to escape on the long march to the coast."[22] Many of those who could not negotiate their escape by any other means committed suicide, both while still near the shorelines of their native Africa, and many miles out to sea. In the account of his own capture and initial desire to jump overboard when first put on the slave ship, Olauda Equiano (1745–1797) wrote of such an incident.

> One day, when we had a smooth sea and moderate wind, two of my wearied countrymen who were chained together, (I was near them at the time,) preferring death to such a life of misery, somehow made it through the nettings and jumped into the sea: immediately, another quite dejected fellow, who, on account of his illness was suffered to be out of irons, also followed their example; and I believe many more would very soon have done the same, if they had not been prevented by the ship's crew, who were instantly alarmed.[23]

Often those who either attempted to jump overboard or who managed to do so but were rescued, were beaten unmercifully, as happened to one of the three Africans that Equiano reported on.[24] In such cases the captives were not even allowed to prefer death to enslavement, nor the right to decide how they would die! But whenever there was an opening they succeeded in dying rather than living a life of dehumanizing enslavement. In addition, their weapons were no match for their white captors, but the Africans often attempted mutinies on the ships, and were sometimes successful. Historians report that mutinies were so frequent that companies began taking out a special "insurrection insurance"![25]

To be sure, there were numerous black protests in the Americas as well. Revisionist historian Herbert Aptheker has done an admirable job of refuting the claim of many early white historians that slave rebellions were rare in the colonies, and that the black slaves were docile, disinterested, or indifferent to freedom. Neither slave songs nor folklore indicate "on balance" that blacks either liked or were indifferent to slavery.[26] Black ancestors took advantage of every opportunity to make it clear that they were not created for enslavement. Aptheker has written both of the frequency and the more than two hundred and fifty "reported Negro conspiracies and revolts."[27] In addition, there is no way to determine the large number of individual escapes and attempted escapes from slavery.

African captives not only had a deep sense of the grave injustice being perpetrated against them, but their love of self, their land, and culture caused them to rebel repeatedly. It is not that some of the captives knew nothing of human slavery before the arrival of the white man. It was not the institution of slavery itself, but the nature of the enslavement practiced by the white captors that was a novelty for the Africans. One scholar observes:

> But African slavery was a far cry from the institution introduced into the
> New World. African slaves were usually considered part of the family for
> which they worked. They had the right to own property, purchase their
> freedom, and marry freemen. Slaves were more often engaged in household
> work than field labor, and slavery was peripheral to the economies of most
> African states.[28]

The European form of slavery, on the other hand, was a total violation of
human dignity and was intended to instill in Africans a sense of being nonpersons, or a means to the comfort of whites. Is it no wonder that African captives preferred the form of slavery practiced in Africa to that of their white
captors?

Contrary to what early white historians wrote, Africans did rebel in the
American colonies — and often! By the time they reached the colonies they
were experienced rebels (for liberation!). Though it really defies description,
a review of what came to be known as the "dreaded Middle Passage" may be
helpful, since it will provide a clearer picture and a better way to remember
the extent of the degradation suffered by the Africans and their determination
to be fully human and free.

The question is, What people subjected to the kind of dehumanizing
treatment the Africans experienced on the slave ships would not have fought
against their captors in an attempt to free themselves literally by any means
necessary? The experience of the Middle Passage was so horrendous and
devastating to African humanity that the consequences are still forthcoming!
Kenneth Goode describes that experience in gory detail.

> After being taken aboard in chains, which were usually not removed until
> the slaver was two or three days at sea, slaves found themselves packed in
> the holds of ships having not as "much room as a man in his coffin" either
> in length or breadth. The men were separated from the women and children
> but they were also wedged in like sardines in a can. . . . The heat was stifling,
> and many slaves found themselves chained to others who had died of suffoca-
> tion. Sanitary conditions, if existing at all, were indescribable. Unable to
> prevent the necessities of nature from occurring, slaves relieved themselves
> as they lay shackled together in "spoon fashion." Oftentimes, stench emanat-
> ing from a slaver could be smelled several miles downwind.
>   Disease was rife aboard ship. Smallpox was worst, but fevers and fluxes
> also caused the death of many. Measles, yellow fever, malaria, dysentery,
> and various viruses were fatal as well. Still others died from "fixed melan-
> choly," or they committed suicide. "The Middle Passage was a crossroads
> and marketplace of diseases."[29]

Basil Davidson recounts the description of the Middle Passage given by an
Englishman named Walsh in 1829. Walsh told of the crew that literally threw
55 Africans overboard during the crossing of the Atlantic.

> . . . and these slaves "were enclosed under grated hatchways, between decks.
> The space was so low that they sat between each other's legs, and stowed so

close together, that there was no possibility of lying down, or at all changing their position, by night or by day. As they belonged to, and were shipped on account of different individuals, they were all branded like sheep, with the owners' marks of different forms. These were impressed under their breasts, or on their arms, and, as the mate informed me with perfect indifference, burnt with a red hot iron...."[30]

Naval friends of Walsh's informed him that this particular slave ship was one of the best they had seen in terms of upkeep and space for the human cargo! The Middle Passage generally took about three weeks. The souls of generations of black people were scarred during the crossing of the Atlantic. Who knows the effects of that brutal experience on the lives of blacks even today? Is it no wonder that black ancestors could sing, "Nobody knows the trouble I've seen. Nobody knows but Jesus."

As if the inhumane accommodations were not enough, the Africans were often forced to sing and dance on the slave ships. This practice was often for therapeutic purposes, e.g., for the relief of melancholia. Forced to dance while still in chains, their ankles were often badly cut and bled profusely. Many of the sorrow songs emerged during this experience.[31] Eric Foner estimates that some 10 to 40 percent of any given cargo of Africans succumbed to disease and sickness during the seemingly endless voyage.[32] John W. Blassingame reports that the mortality rate from disease in the holds of the slave ships was around 16 percent.[33] Only God knows for certain how many Africans were lost during the four-hundred year period of the European slave trade which began around 1444. However, some scholars have estimated the number to be as high as forty million, with twenty million being transported to the Americas, and unknown thousands more lost while in captivity in Africa enroute to the shores of the Atlantic to board the slave ships. In addition, it is not known how many thousands more were lost and unaccounted for on the plantations.[34]

What is both peculiar and instructive about the events of the Middle Passage is that in spite of the many precautions taken by the white slavers there were frequent attempts at mutiny by the Africans. The many acts of suicide were also ways of rebelling against captivity. These were ways of saying that any fate is better than being chained like animals. It was a way of saying: "If I must die, I will choose the means. Rather than live in captivity and be subjected to heretofore unknown brutality I will die like a man or woman — a human being!" This, despite the fact that any failed attempt to exercise the freedom to die as they chose would lead to a severe beating.

It is imperative that African Americans be aware that this spirit of resistance to injustice has been pervasive in their history. On balance, their ancestors never accepted dehumanizing treatment at the hands of white slavers without a fight. This spirit of "relentless surge toward freedom" did not begin on the slave ships and on the auction blocks, but in the interior of the African coast during the forced march to the ocean. Harding makes the point well:

> . . . by the time Integrity and Liberty and Black Boy arrived at Whydah and Malemba — the issues and nature of those early stages of black struggle were starkly defined. At that moment in our history, as the ominous shadows hovered near the coasts, we fought to remain in our homeland. . . . Our struggle was to resist the breaking of our nations, our families, and the chain of our existence.[35]

From the very beginning there was only one issue for the Africans in captivity — *freedom!* They fought with sticks and spears against guns and cannons. They committed suicide through the slitting of their wrists or throats. There were self-induced starvations. Many captives leaped into a sea of hungry sharks. These are all instances of the earliest forms of "black radicalism," "the Great Tradition of Black Protest,"[36] or what Manning Marable has so aptly described as "blackwater." It should be remembered that both men and women participated in these acts of resistance. Because they were often given more freedom of movement on the ships, African women played important roles in the planning and execution of rebellions and mutinies.[37]

The white slavers were no respecter of persons. No gender or class of Africans was exempt from enslavement and degradation. There were artisans, farmers, fishermen/women, blacksmiths, weavers, workers in precious metals, chiefs and kings. Priests and musicians were also captured and held in makeshift forts near the ocean. The presence of these was significant, since they were among the most natural leaders in the group, and were more capable than many others in organizing for resistance. The musicians may have provided songs of deliverance.[38] In this sense the slavers got more than they bargained for.

Surely the priests did not hesitate to call upon their God to deliver them from the hands of the white slavers. It is difficult to imagine these religious leaders praying and calling on their God for anything but liberation from bondage. No doubt they did what they could to arouse their fellow captives to the point of rebellion. Some of these religious leaders made it to the Americas, and there is every reason to believe that they carried the spirit of rebellion with them, passing it on to the next generation. It was likely this first generation of African slaves that posed the greatest threat of insurrection in the Americas.

> Africans played a more important role in revolts until the 1830s than did native-born slaves. African-born conjurors usually prepared potions designed to make the slaves feel immune to injury by whites, and the rebels used drums to signal the start of uprisings in New York in 1712, in Stono, South Carolina, in 1739, and in Charleston's Denmark Vesey conspiracy in 1822.[39]

Brawley also paints a picture of the pure blooded African who was likely to rebel against captivity.

> The Negroes who came to America directly from Africa in the eighteenth century were strikingly different from those whom generations of servitude later made comparatively docile. They were wild and turbulent in disposition and were likely at any moment to take revenge for the great wrong that had been inflicted upon them.[40]

Aware of this, plantation owners lived in fear, and in order to compensate they did not hesitate to subject the Africans to the most cruel treatment in order to keep them in subjection. Punishment included both "crucifixion and burning," which were legalized in some of the early slave codes. What is important here is that the first generation of African slaves did not calmly accept enslavement and did not hesitate to rebel against their white captors. Such rebellion was more likely to occur during the first two years of captivity. Of all immigrant groups that experienced servitude in the Americas the Africans were the chief resisters.

It is also important to point out that many of the conjurors and medicine men were among the Africans who were torn from Dahomey (former name of present-day Benin) and Togo. It is conceivable that the earliest black preachers in the Americas emerged from the ranks of the conjurors and medicine men before they were subjected to "Christian" teachings.[41] Though often thought of as being involved in "bad" or "evil" magic, the conjurors were significant as religious specialists, since in Africa the people often turned to them when there was a desire to have an evil spell cast upon someone, or if one wanted something bad to happen to an enemy. One can imagine how these African-born conjurors may have been called upon by slaves in order to inflict a spell upon their white captors in an attempt to either incapacitate or kill them. These conjurors may have led, or at least stirred up, many of the early slave rebellions.

When black ancestors engaged in violent rebellions for freedom, these were not isolated acts. Rather, they were all part of what Harding has called "the everflowing river of black struggle."[42] We may similarly characterize the black struggle of the sixties, and its relation to the rise of black theology. The struggle of the sixties was a continuation of the long movement of the history of black struggle dating back to the dreadful events on the shores of West Africa during the middle of the fifteenth century. Although the African religious leaders of that period knew nothing of a systematic black liberation theology, what they did know mandated their participation in the fight for deliverance from human bondage.

Therefore, the seeds of black theology were planted long before Africans actually boarded the slave ships. In this sense it can be said that there has been no break in the ever-flowing river of black struggle. Mary Berry and John

Blassingame report that "blacks protested against their conditions and treatment in every period of our history."[43] With this in mind it is possible to say
that the struggles of the sixties were merely a continuation of the struggle that
actually began in the interior of West Africa over four hundred years ago.
There have not been periods in American history when the wheel of black
struggle has not been turning in the direction of freedom. It has been one
long, continuous struggle from the first to the present generation of blacks.
It is therefore possible for present day African Americans to say that their
struggle against racist oppression began long before they were born!

Were There Strands of Black Theology During Slavery?

Theo Witvliet writes that "black theology owes its origin to Black Power.
The struggle for Black Power arose out of the concern of black people to take
matters into their own hands, to be the subjects of their own history."[44] Since
Witvliet did not proceed to give some of the deeper historical context of the
origin of black theology, it must be said that he, like Cone, did not go far
enough. His statement is therefore misleading.

Blacks during slavery were religious people (long before they came to the
Americas), and rebellion against the institution of slavery was not a rare
event. This should prompt us to wonder whether strands of black theology
existed during American slavery. Were there black preachers and other
religious leaders of the period, for example, who deliberately sought through
words and actions to relate Christianity and the Gospel to the experience of
black pain and suffering, as well as to blacks' strong desire for sociopolitical
liberation? Not a few contemporary black religious scholars have given an
affirmative response to this question. Henry J. Young is a representative
scholar.

Young was disturbed that so many scholars argued that black religion
was historically an otherworldly religion, i.e., concerned chiefly about liberation beyond this world. They portrayed black religion as primarily emotional
and accommodationist, with little or no concern for the radical transformation of sociopolitical and economic institutions that made life unbearable for
blacks. Young set out to examine this train of thought more closely by considering the theology of major black religious leaders from 1755 to the 1970s.[45]
He observed that Gunnar Myrdal, author of the massive and landmark study
on blacks in American society, *An American Dilemma* (1944), was one of the
scholars who advocated the view that black religion primarily has an emotional and otherworldly character, and that proponents of this religion seldom
express serious concern about the socioeconomic and political liberation of
blacks from oppression. "Negro frustration," Myrdal contended, "was sub-

limated into emotionalism, and Negro hopes were fixed on the afterworld."[46] Young wanted to know whether such a description could categorically be made of the early black church and its spiritual leaders. Or, is it more likely that this emotionalism and otherworldliness of which Myrdal wrote actually existed alongside another tradition, viz, one which was always concerned about sociopolitical salvation in this world? Had the black church only been otherworldly in its outlook historically, or had it also been this-worldly in its understanding of salvation? How did it understand the idea of spiritual salvation? Is it possible that black religionists understood spiritual salvation to be a holistic concept which necessarily included salvation from sociopolitical systems that degrade persons? Generally, this has been the view of blacks, who inherited the idea from their African ancestors.

When Young considered black religious leaders like Nathaniel Paul, Richard Allen, David Walker, Nat Turner, Daniel Payne, James Pennington, Henry Highland Garnet, Henry McNeal Turner, and others, he concluded that Myrdal was wrong.

> Historically, black religion has been concerned with freedom, liberation, humanization, and the eradication of social evils in this world. Therefore, as opposed to being fixated exclusively with spirituality and heaven, the black church has been the vanguard of social, economic, and political activism within the black community.[47]

Although Young did not include in his study some of the major black women leaders of the period covered in his book, e.g., Harriet Tubman, Sojourner Truth, Jarena Lee, Amanda Berry Smith, Ann Plato, Anna Julia Cooper, etc., had he done so his conclusion can only have been that they too contributed immensely to the prophetic tradition of the black church. In other words, historically black church leaders — whether men or women — were never exclusively concerned about an otherworldly heaven. There was always an element of concern for a new earth in their conception of spirituality. Black religion was not merely the passive, compensatory religion we read about in many American history textbooks.

Black religion has often been prophetic and radical, which is quite distinct from the religion of the white church. For example, Gayraud Wilmore has written of the radicalism of black religion, describing it as the quest for independence from white control, the revalorization of the image of Africa, and the acceptance of protest and agitation as theological prerequisites for black liberation and the liberation of all oppressed peoples.[48] As a more radical religion, "there has been and continues to be a significant difference between black religion and white religion in their approaches to social reality and social change...."[49] This is not to say that every black religious gathering during the days of slavery or since was "a seedbed of revolution," nor that every black preacher was a Nat Turner, Denmark Vesey,

or Gabriel Prosser in disguise. Yet there is considerable evidence that, historically, black religion was more involved in sociopolitical campaigns for black
liberation than previously thought.[50] Blassingame has written of a black religion during slavery times that was more socially and politically conscious
than many scholars initially believed.

> The slave's religious principles were colored by his own longings for freedom
> and based on half-understood sermons in white churches or passages from
> the Old Testament describing the struggles of the Jews, beautiful pictures
> of future life, enchantment and fear, and condemnation of sin.[51]

In order to survive, slaves often had to pretend that they enjoyed and accepted the sermons white ministers preached on obedience to the slave
master. As a rule, however, they were not fooled. Their hearts always burned
for freedom and for the divine punishment of white slave masters. The slaves
may have had otherworldly concerns and thoughts about getting to a spiritual
heaven after death, but the deeper concern was for earthly liberation. Blacks
have always had a strong predilection for liberation from oppressive structures in this world.

There Is No Bifurcation of Reality

Young has shown convincingly that black religious leaders from the middle of the eighteenth century shared similar beliefs with their African ancestors. For example, unlike much of traditional Western Christianity, black
religious leaders have always rejected the idea of the bifurcation of reality.
That is, they did not make a sharp distinction between sacred and profane
in the sense of supposing that there is some aspect of reality about which
neither God nor Christians should be concerned. Rather, reality, for blacks,
has always been perceived as "interconnected, interwoven, and interlocked."
On such a view spiritual liberation is not to be perceived as something that
is separate from political and economic liberation. What is often viewed as
"spiritual" and "physical" are really two moments or dimensions of a single
process. God has created persons so that they are a unity of mind and body.
Inasmuch as God is concerned about the well-being of whole persons, any
aspect of the socioeconomic and political order that causes pain and suffering
to persons must be eradicated, and more humane structures constructed.
Black religious leaders did not set up a dualism between spiritual and physical,
sacred and profane.[52]

There have always been black religious leaders who expressed concern
about heaven and the saving of souls for Christ. But there have been many
others who have exhibited a deep concern for the sociopolitical and economic
liberation of persons in this world. When they preached and talked about a
new heaven and a new earth they often did not do so in traditional spiritual

terms, in the sense of separating the spiritual from the more earthy political and social issues. Many black religious leaders saw no meaning in the idea of a new heaven and a new earth if it had no relevance to a radically transformed society on earth. Though such a society is not identical with the Kingdom of God, it is consistent with what the Kingdom requires.

The Contemporary Development of Black Theology

Black religionists knew nothing of a systematic black theology prior to its appearance in the late sixties and the early seventies. As for the contemporary development of black theology it will be instructive to look briefly at Cone and Wilmore, since each has written of three stages in the origin of this new way of doing theology.[53] Cone made the first conscious effort to develop black theology systematically.

Cone provides some of the historical background on the appearance of the term, "black theology." There is no unanimity of agreement as to who actually used the term first. However, many black religious scholars agree that it was first used in documents of the National Committee of Black Churchmen as the counterpart to "black power."[54] Wilmore made several references to the term "black theology" in a theological commission project in 1968. Cone's book *Black Theology and Black Power* was the first major publication to include that particular nomenclature in the title of a book.

As for contemporary black theology itself, Cone traced its development through three stages. It is easy to link the publication of the "Black Power Statement" of 1966, with phase one. But the issuance of that statement occurred in the context of the civil rights movement It was actually initiated by what Wilmore described as "hungry black pastors," rather than through the deliberate efforts of black theological professors of the period. It would therefore be more accurate to say that phase one began around 1964. In any event, it was black pastors who took the first steps toward developing a theology of the people. They were not content with spending inordinate amounts of time meditating on theological issues while black people were suffering.

It is not difficult to understand this move on the part of black pastors during the middle to late sixties. Most pastors have a special relationship with their parishioners and tend to be closer to them than do academic theologians. It is important to understand that during the sixties black pastors were confronted with a particularly challenging phenomenon.

By the mid-sixties black youths—many of them Christians—had come under the influence of black nationalism and the black power movement. Consequently, many of them began asking tough questions about the relationship between the black church and black suffering. Most pastors found it difficult to give adequate answers. Many discovered that there were no acceptable responses as long as they espoused traditional Christian perspectives. Black pastors could not satisfy black youths as long as they asked the same kinds of questions that their white counterparts in ministry were asking. Some of these black pastors gradually began to see that because their sociocultural situation and their experience of oppression was unlike anything white pastors ever experienced; because white youths did not suffer in quite the same ways nor to the same degree as black youths, they had to begin asking different questions. This was their only hope of giving relevant answers to black youths. Such a step might reverse the tendency of large numbers of black youths to leave the churches. However, many did leave, and not only did they fail to return, but they neither attend as adults nor encourage their children to attend. This partly helps to explain why there is low church attendance on the part of black youths today.

Anticipating a crisis, black pastors began to take the message of black power advocates and the questions raised by black youths much more seriously. During the early and mid-sixties black religious scholars were not yet thinking "black enough" to relate the Gospel to the black struggle for liberation in a significant way. Because of his genuine commitment to the liberation of black and other oppressed peoples, and his consistent and conscious efforts to apply the Gospel to local, national, and global problems, Martin Luther King, Jr., was a black theologian in the best sense of the term.[55] Indeed, Cone shows that the faith of the black church and its historic involvement in the fight for social justice was the decisive influence on King's development from childhood. This was evident in his sermons and speeches to blacks. The white, liberal, Protestant theology he learned in seminary and graduate school provided him the intellectual resources to communicate effectively with white audiences in the spoken and written word.[56] Cone contends that King was a liberation theologian long before the term came into vogue.[57] Indeed, he might have described Malcolm X similarly, although he did theology from an Islamic rather than a Christian perspective.

It was during this first period of the development of contemporary black theology that Joseph Washington's controversial text *Black Religion* appeared. Washington made some strong points, but he mistakenly held that black religion was not authentically Christian since it was a participant in the secular struggle for civil rights. He seemed to reason that since black religion is not authentically Christian it cannot have a Christian theology. This stance elicited a deluge of strong criticism from black religious scholars. Understandably, Washington's book was well received by many white religionists. However, Blacks argued that if there were any authentic version of Christianity in existence at the time, it was that advocated by black religion. The latter, it was held, is authentically Christian because unlike white religion it identified the Gospel with the struggle for liberation and justice, and with the lowly and disinherited.

When Washington's book appeared, Cone was teaching at Adrian College in Michigan. Although it was at Adrian that the first "clear outline of a black theology began to emerge in [his] theological consciousness,"[58] he was not then able to provide the kind of critique of Washington's text he believed was warranted. What he did recognize was that there was much more at stake than met the eye.

> Existentially I was against Washington, but intellectually I did not know at the time how to refute him. If I accepted the definition of Christianity as taught in graduate school, then Washington had a strong case. Although I did not like his conclusions anymore than any black person, they seemed logical, given his premises. In order for me to challenge Washington, I had to challenge the entire white theological establishment, and I was not ready to do that. But the problems he raised stayed on my mind constantly, and I knew that I would have to challenge his identity of the Christian faith with the faith of white churches.[59]

An adequate response required turning the entire Western theological enterprise on its head. The whole problematic had to be stated differently. It was not simply a matter of presenting a new set of norms within the already existing theological structure.

In part, Washington's book had the effect of prompting major theological treatises first by Cone, then by J. DeOtis Roberts and Major Jones. It can be said that Cone's first book was, to a large extent, a response to Washington's argument. The works of other black theologians of the period were primarily responses to Cone.

There were other crucial events during the first period that helped give birth to contemporary black theology. The year after the appearance of Washington's book, Malcolm X was assassinated. Cone assesses the influence of Malcolm on the first and succeeding stages of the development of black theology and on the emergence of black power and concludes that his contribution was significant. One of his chief contributions was the method of looking at the world through his experience at the bottom of American society and through his deep commitment to the liberation and empowerment of his people. Malcolm combined this "with historical research and native intelligence — all of which made him deeply suspicious of Christianity and the Bible as they were interpreted and practiced in the white community."[60] In this one can see several elements which anticipated liberation methodology and was later appropriated by Cone, e.g., the importance of social location, context, and the hermeneutic of suspicion. Malcolm was suspicious of the moral-religious values of whites. He also anticipated the liberation emphasis on social analysis and the unmasking of hidden assumptions. "One of his chief concerns was to uncover the role of European Christianity in the politico-economic exploitation and culturo-spiritual degradation of black people."[61]

In addition, like King, Malcolm was in solidarity with the masses of poor blacks, although they primarily represented the poor in the South and the northern ghettos, respectively. Malcolm was not an academic theologian, and had not, like King, been formally trained in theology. Instead, he was self-taught, and "a grass-roots activist whose critique was defined by his solidarity with the victims of white Christianity."[62]

Malcolm did more than any person of his day to instill in African Americans a sense of self-worth or "somebodyness." He believed this to be the most important key to black liberation. He rejected the negative images of blackness portrayed by white Christianity and claimed that Islam stood for everything positive for blacks, while Christianity proclaimed the opposite. Malcolm was adamant about the need for blacks to love themselves and to be proud of their heritage. More than any other leader he stressed the importance of black culture and black consciousness. King emphasized these as well, but Malcolm clearly dominated in this regard.[63] Malcolm taught blacks to love and respect themselves. It was not as important to him what whites think about blacks as what the latter think about themselves. "We have to change our own mind. You can't change his [the white man's] mind about us. We've got to change our own minds about each other. *We have to see each other with new eyes.* We have to see each other as brothers and sisters"[64] (emphasis added). It is impossible for blacks to be too extreme or radical in their bid to regain their sense of dignity. Extremism in defense or pursuit of human dignity and freedom is a virtuous, not a sinful act. An act of moderation in pursuit of these, on the other hand, is sin.[65]

Malcolm made many other contributions to black theology. Yet his emphasis on black self-love was powerful. In light of the tragic phenomenon of self-inflicted genocide among African American youths today, Malcolm's philosophy of black self-worth is the most potent antidote available. This is a point that black theologians need to stress more frequently and forcefully than ever before if the African American community is to avoid a head-on collision with self-destruction.

The awakening of black consciousness also occurred during the first stage of black theology. In addition to the life and teachings of Malcolm X, the march to Greenwood, Mississippi, gave impetus to the emergence of the black consciousness movement. James Meredith was ambushed in Greenwood in June 1966. King, Stokley Carmichael, Floyd McKissick, and other civil rights leaders agreed to continue the march from the point where Meredith was shot. By the time they reached Greenwood, the birth of the black power movement was complete. The call for "black power" was first uttered by Willie Ricks. On July 31, 1966, the National Committee of Negro Churchmen issued a statement on black power. This had strong implications for relating the Gospel to black power.

The birth of contemporary black theology was not the result of a single event during the sixties. However, it is conceivable that the appearance of Cone's *Black Theology and Black Power* (1969) did more to complete that birth than any other single event of the period. It had the effect of an exploding bombshell in the theological arena. There were many white casualties (and some black ones too!). Many theologians undoubtedly were horrified when they read the book. No white nor traditionally thinking black person could read the book and not feel uneasy. The book also exposed the hypocrisy of many good white liberals.

Cone wrote a new page into the annals of theological history. He came into prominence during the second stage of black theology. Phase one extended roughly from 1964 to 1969. In addition to the assassination of Malcolm X during the first stage, King was brutally murdered. Cone argued in his first book that with the assassination of King, no blacks had reason to believe that whites would ever listen to them or take them seriously.[66]

During the second period of the development of black theology, roughly 1970 to 1976, Cone often found himself in shouting matches with white theologians. He demanded that they be quiet and listen to what blacks were saying.[67] Black theology emerged as an academic discipline during this stage. Yet many white theologians did not take it seriously — neither then nor today. The evidence for this view is found in the fact that minuscle attention is given the works of major black theologians like Cone, when courses on contemporary and systematic theology are offered in white seminaries. There continue to be numerous white theologians who insist that "there is no such thing as black theology." They go right on teaching and writing their ostensibly universal theologies while excluding the religiocultural experiences of all blacks, Latinos, Native Americans, Asians, and European American women. As troubled as white scholars are about black theology, they do not seem to be as disturbed about Swedish, Neo-Orthodox, German, British, Liberal, Crisis, and Existentialist theologies, all of which present difficult challenges to white Protestant traditional beliefs.

During the second phase, black theologians distinguished themselves as scholars. Wilmore referred to this period as a time of "credentializing and legitimizing black religion." This led to the development of the Society for the Study of Black Religion in 1970, under the leadership of Shelby Rooks. The period also saw the beginning of dialogues among black theologians and African and Latin American liberation theologians. Unfortunately the influence of the NCBC declined significantly during this stage. The reaffirmation of the "Statement on Black Theology" (first issued in 1969) brought the period to a close.

When Wilmore outlined the three stages of black theology at the Black Theology Project (February 5–8, 1986), he said that the third phase began in the mid–seventies. It was during the third period that black theology began to emphasize a more global perspective and the importance of dialogue with third world liberation theologians. In addition, social and economic analysis, classism, and sexism were key issues addressed by black theologians.

Theology in the Americas (T.I.A.) also came into existence during the third stage. Initially, T.I.A. brought Latin American and white North American theologians into dialogue, a strategy which made black theologians furious. However, no amount of protesting altered the plan to bring Latins and white North American theologians together to engage in theological reflection. It was as if black theologians did not exist![68]

A pioneer in introducing black theology on the American scene, and the victim of many vitriolic verbal attacks, Cone, significantly, during the third phase of the development of black theology, came again to play the role of maverick. During this stage he took a public stance in favor of black and other forms of feminist theology. He made an effort to turn the corner on this issue as early as the publication of *God of the Oppressed* (1975). Inclusive language appears in this text, although not consistently. There is also evidence of his frustration with the accepted patriarchal tradition. Cone expressed frustration with the practice of the subordination of women to men.[69] He did not consistently make such claims throughout *God of the Oppressed*, but it is important to observe that by this time, Cone was beginning to grapple with the issue of sexism. However, he did not express concern about sexism in the black church and community. This focus came about a year later, when he was invited to deliver a speech at a black women's conference in October 1976 at Garrett Evangelical Theological Seminary.

This was the period which saw the ascendancy of black feminist theologians, ethicists, biblical scholars, and sociologists of religion, e.g., Jacquelyn Grant, Delores Williams, Katie Cannon, Kelly Brown, Cheryl Gilkes, and others who began making important contributions to the literature on black theology. These women began providing a needed critique from the perspective of black women's experience of racism, sexism, and classism. Grant and Cannon are among the leaders in what is known as *womanist theology*, although new contributors are emerging, such as Karen Baker-Fletcher. At the Black Theology Project in 1986, Grant was described as "the mother of black feminist theology."

The third stage of the development of black theology also saw an intensification of dialogue with Marxism and the development of a meaningful relationship with the Ecumenical Association of Third World Theologians (EATWOT). In addition, there was an emphasis on "the names of black ancestors." Wilmore contends that when the names of black ancestors are called they come back to us. Blacks needed to recapture the memory of (what Gustavo Gutiérrez described in another context as) "the beaten Christs" of their history of struggle.

According to Wilmore the third phase ended with Theology in the Americas II in Detroit in 1980. Of course, there have been other important events since that time which signal the need to move beyond the third stage. In Part Three, I will suggest some new directions for black theology if it is to remain vital and viable for African Americans in the twenty-first century.

This chapter has made the point that black theology, like the black church, was born in protest. Black theology is not a new phenomenon. Rather, black protest and the rudiments of black theology extend back more than five hundred years. In this sense black theology is at least as old as Africans' contact with white Christians who sought to enslave them. Allan Boesak makes this point in the South African context, claiming that black theology is not new, and that its "content is as old as the attempts of white Christians to bring the Gospel to blacks."[70] There has never been a time when blacks did not possess their own distinct understanding of Christianity and the Gospel.

Boesak rejects both the idea that black theology is new in the sense of having come into existence in the mid-sixties, and the idea that it is legitimate only if spawned by what white theologians were then calling "the theology of revolution." His statement that black theology in some form has existed as long as white Christians have been preaching to blacks is important, because it implies that Africans in some parts of the continent were introduced to Christianity before they were torn from their homeland and forced to the Americas. Boesak also makes the important point that one of the chief differences between black theology in South Africa and the United States is one of context. In the case of South Africa there are a few black historical documents regarding black history and black theology. This is not as serious a problem for African Americans. Though much of their heritage was preserved through the "oral tradition," a significant amount of this has now been recorded, and in addition a substantial amount of writing remains from the hands of free blacks during American slavery. In addition, there are records of slave and ex-slave narratives. It is therefore not as difficult to remember the history of the struggle for liberation. It is also less difficult to remember that resistance, protest, and rebellion have a place of prominence in the black religiocultural tradition.

Some may wonder why I found it necessary to devote so much attention to connecting contemporary black theology with the historical black experience of protest against oppression. What is the importance, the reader may inquire, of making the point that as a theology born in protest, black theology is not just a phenomenon of the sixties, but roots deeply in the religious and cultural history of African Americans? For many blacks, this question is not different from similar questions raised by numerous whites in universities and seminaries, such as, "Why do blacks keep bringing up slavery and discrimination? Why don't they just leave those things in the past and live their lives from where they are today?" It is important to respond to these questions before proceeding to the next chapter.

In the first place, Eric Foner's claim in 1970 that "many Americans still believe that blacks are a people without a past,"[71] continues to be true today. In the early seventies white Americans finally came to the realization — forced upon them by the civil rights struggles and the black power movement — that they knew very little about the history and culture of blacks, and that it was time to rectify this. It was not long, however, before there was a return to business as usual. But it was good while it lasted! Funding became available for the publication of long out-of-print black manuscripts; research into the African American past by digging into dusty archives; black history classes in secondary schools; the development of black studies programs in colleges and universities; the production of expensive media documentaries on black history; and many more activities that gave the impression that recapturing this history was important for all Americans.

Today, however, the situation is almost completely reversed. It is more difficult to get funding to engage in anything "black." This is evidenced by the increasing difficulty that black scholars experience when seeking research grants to pursue their interests in the area of the black religious and cultural heritage.

Unlike the late sixties, it is evident today that few whites have an adequate grasp of black history. There is no evidence that this trend is being abated or reversed. Even in white seminaries, where students are trained to minister to "all" people, very little attention is given the religious and cultural experience of African Americans. Works by black scholars are seldom included in course bibliographies, and when they are, they are not often required reading. When white seminarians are required to read works by black scholars they often appear puzzled, and do not hesitate to ask why it is even necessary to read "black stuff," when it is obvious that they will primarily be ministering to whites. These students cannot begin to imagine how black students in white seminaries must feel when, daily, over a period of several years of ministerial preparation, they are indoctrinated with white-informed concepts of ministry.

On a more positive note, it is imperative that we keep recalling the long history of black suffering and the struggle against it, because a people without a past has a questionable present and future. Many otherwise good white people appear to express a sense of pain and alienation when blacks begin to chronicle their history. Many, like Anne Wortham, admonish blacks to let bygones be bygones! She contends in essence that since we cannot change the past, and since legislation has eliminated discrimination, blacks need to forget about the past and make the best of the present.[72] This advice is as absurd as asking Jewish sisters and brothers to forget their Holocaust. Blacks would do well to be suspicious of all who advise them to forget about past injustices and suffering heaped upon them, especially since these continue today.

For too long African Americans have been the "absent of history," to use a phrase coined by Latin American liberation theologians.[73] Gutiérrez rightly contends that "human history has been written 'by a white hand' from the dominating sectors."[74] It is therefore understandable why blacks' experience has often been absent from the textbooks (and inadequately presented when present) and why such great efforts have been made to encourage them to forget their history and experience of oppression and struggle. To require this of oppressed people is to "deprive them of a source of energy, of historical will, of rebellion."[75] Much of the motivation to continue the black struggle for total liberation may come from the recognition that there is a long historical precedent for such struggle. It is therefore crucial that blacks recapture the memory of the "beaten Christs" of their race. Having done this, they will need to remake and rewrite their history from their own context.

If a people forget their history, they have no guideposts for present and future. They must never forget! A saying of Marcus Garvey's is apropos here: "A people without the knowledge of their past history, origin and culture is like a tree without roots."[76] The continued existence of a people is jeopardized when they are not familiar with their past. It is necessary for blacks to continue recalling and rewriting their history. Malcolm X was instructive on this point.

> And now it is important for us to know that our history did not begin with slavery's scars. We come from Africa, a great continent and a proud and varied people, a land which is the new world and was the cradle of civilization. Our culture and our history are as old as man himself and yet we know almost nothing of it. We must recapture our heritage and our identity if we are ever to liberate ourselves from the bonds of white supremacy. We must launch a cultural revolution to unbrainwash an entire people.... This cultural revolution will be the journey to our rediscovery of ourselves. History is a people's memory, and without a memory man is demoted to the lower animals. Armed with the knowledge of the past, we can with confidence charter a course for the future.[77]

No people without a sense of their history has a foundation upon which to build either a meaningful present or future. No viable black theology is possible without recapturing and internalizing the black historical, religious, and cultural heritage.

2. The Meaning and Methodology of Black Theology

THIS CHAPTER examines both what Cone means by black theology as a form of liberation theology, and some of its crucial methodological components. In keeping with the theme of this book, I also consider how Cone's thought on the subject has shifted or developed. Since many liberation theologians are agreed that the Latin Americans have done much in the area of the development of liberation methodology, we will frequently find ourselves in conversation with representative Latin American liberation theologians.

One crucial point needs to be made before proceeding further. From their inception in the early seventies, liberation theologies (and especially black theology) have been criticized as not being "real" theologies. Critics have said that they are at best offshoots or spinoffs of political or liberal theologies in the West. Or, the claim has been made that they are closer to being ideology or social ethics. Robert McAfee Brown even points to a Spanish theologian who contends that liberation theology is closer to being testimony and witness than theology proper.[1]

In this study liberation theology is taken to be theology in the best sense of the word. *All theology worthy of the name is liberation theology!* If a theology is not concerned about liberating the minds *and* bodies of persons it is not good theology. Liberation theology proposes a worldview, or way of thinking about God, created persons, nature, and the world, and how they relate to each other. At bottom it is concerned about the way persons live together in God's world. Unlike many prevailing theologies, liberation theology does not, however, seek to conceal its fundamental interest, viz, the liberation of oppressed peoples. Unlike traditional theologies it does not make claims to being a "neutral" theology.

The present work does not underestimate nor seek to undermine liberation theology. Rather, it makes the case that liberation theology is as much a bona fide theology as any in existence. Albert C. Winn's description of liberation theology is instructive in this regard:

> ... we are not dealing here with a mere "regional variant" that we can observe comfortably from a distance.... Nor are we dealing with "political

ideology" or "an ethical reduction of the Gospel." *We are dealing with a genuine theology.* It has its own theological method, gives an account of its own path to truth. It produces its own understanding of God, of salvation, of the church, of eschatology. . . . Above all, it takes Scripture seriously[2] [emphasis added].

White feminist theologians like Susan Brooks Thistlethwaite have a similar understanding of liberation theology.[3]

An Early Attempt to Define Black Theology

The term *black theology* appeared (for what may have been the first time) in a *Time* magazine article in 1968 entitled, "Is God Black?"[4] Grant Shockely, a black scholar in the field of Christian education, attempted to connect the origin of the term with the NCBC.[5] As noted in Chapter 1, we do not know who first introduced the term, although black theologians generally agree that it was first used in NCBC documents as the counterpart to "black power."[6]

One of the best characterizations of black theology appears in the Black Theology Statement of June 13, 1969.

> Black Theology is a theology of black liberation. It seeks to plumb the black condition in the light of God's revelation in Jesus Christ, so that the black community can see that the Gospel is commensurate with the achievement of black humanity. Black Theology is a theology of "blackness." It is the affirmation of black humanity that emancipates black people from white racism, thus providing authentic freedom for both white and black people. It affirms the humanity of white people in that it says No to the encroachment of white oppression.[7]

This early definition of black theology sought to relate the black struggle against racial and economic oppression to the Gospel. Black theology has always been concerned with the well-being of the whole person, thereby transcending the traditional Western dualism of spirit and body. It has never minimized the significance of spiritual health, even when its explicit emphasis has been on sociopolitical liberation. Nor has it been unmindful of the interconnection between a healthy mind and a healthy body.

Black theology seeks coherence between the metaphysical freedom of persons as such, and the concrete sociopolitical freedom that makes it possible for them to live fully human lives. Black theology has always demanded the genuine freedom of both the oppressed and the oppressor. In this sense black theology has always had both a *particular* and a *universal* dimension, and has tried to hold these in creative tension. Although fundamentally a theology of blackness, it takes seriously the universal aspect of the Gospel. This universal dimension requires both that all oppressed peoples be liberated, and that the oppressors themselves be liberated from practices of domination and subjugation. Such practices depersonalize both the oppressed and the oppressor. Jesus Christ came not merely to deliver blacks, but to set at liberty captives everywhere! Although black theology insists upon preference for "the least of these," which, in itself, does not imply exclusivity, it also maintains that the Gospel is for everybody.

That the initial emphasis of black theology was on the liberation of black people from white oppressors did not mean, for Cone, that blacks were the only oppressed people in the United States or any other part of the world. Neither did it mean that God's love extends only to African Americans. Those who concluded otherwise simply misunderstood what black theologians in general, and James Cone in particular, wrote. Cone made the point, even in his early writings, that God is not just concerned about blacks. He always believed the Gospel of liberation was applicable to all persons, despite the "either-or" approach we find in *Black Theology and Black Power*. Commenting on this point in a dialogue with a former teacher, Cone observed:

> God's stand against oppression is his affirmation that all men have a common humanity in freedom. This means that I cannot be free until all men are free. And if in some distant future I am no longer oppressed because of blackness, then I must take upon myself whatever form of human oppression exists in the society, affirming my identity with the victims. *The identity must be made with the victims not because of sympathy, but because my own humanity is involved in my brother's degradation*[8] [emphasis added].

This is a powerful statement and conviction about the universal dimension of the Gospel and liberation theology by one who was often accused of being an exclusivist! What is most significant is that the statement was made only two years after the appearance of Cone's first book. This was not just an isolated statement. Rather, it is a theme we find throughout Cone's developing theological project. That is, Cone's theology has always been such that the universal dimension of the Gospel of liberation has been present. One has to read his works systematically to see this.

Black theology is a theology of protest, which equates liberation with salvation. It is a theology of the people; of the marginalized and forgotten of history. One wonders whether black theology would have come into existence at all had Christianity, as expressed by Westerners, been authentic. Would there have been a need for black theology had the Gospel taught by white preachers and slaveholders during American slavery been consistent in word and deed with what is required in the Jewish-Christian faith?

When Malcolm X criticized Christianity he was actually criticizing an inauthentic type of the Christian faith that was transmitted to blacks. Christianity was not the religion of *all* people, but of white people. Said Malcolm:

> Christianity is the white man's religion. The Holy Bible in the white man's hands and his interpretations of it have been the greatest single ideological

weapon for enslaving millions of non-white human beings. Every country the white man has conquered with his guns, he has always paved the way, and salved his conscience, by carrying the Bible and interpreting it to call the people "heathens" and "pagans"; then he sends his guns, then his missionaries behind the guns to mop up.[9]

Cone points out that Malcolm began his ministry with many similar scathing attacks on Christianity as practiced both by whites and blacks. The Christianity that was taught to blacks was oppressive rather than liberating. Rather than making their burdens lighter, it made them heavier. "According to Malcolm, whites had no moral conscience that was applicable to their relations with blacks. The morality which whites derived from Christianity was limited to their own kind and never applied to blacks and other Third World people, because whites did not regard them as human beings."[10]

The nineteenth-century black abolitionist, orator and statesman Frederick Douglass distinguished between "slaveholding religion" and "Christianity proper," pointing out that most whites conveyed to blacks the former.[11] W.E.B. DuBois also criticized white religion, concluding that it falls short of what Jesus requires. "A nation's religion is its life, and as such white Christianity is a miserable failure."[12] Elsewhere he wrote against the church of John Pierpont Morgan, admonishing that it was not "the church of Jesus Christ."[13] Black critics of Christianity would not have had cause to criticize a religion that refused to participate in the oppression of blacks, Native Americans, and others. Had white Christians taken seriously the Gospel of liberation, black theology in its present form may not have emerged. However, there undoubtedly would have been a need for black expressions of the Jewish-Christian faith even if racial and other factors had not called black theology into existence.

Black theology emerged because of the continued failure of white religionists and theologians to relate the Gospel to the pain and suffering of African Americans. "It arises from the need of black people to liberate themselves from white oppressors."[14] Black theology identifies with African Americans and their oppression, and considers the Gospel in the light of black suffering. It addresses a different set of questions than traditional theology, and generates different answers. It asks, for example, What do Jesus Christ and the Gospel mean to people with their backs pressed against the wall? What does it mean to say that the Source of all persons is the one God; that all have the image of God etched into their being; that all persons are equal before God and loved equally by God? What does it mean to affirm that there is one supremely loving and good God who is father, mother, brother, and sister to all? What is the concrete existential meaning of such questions when some believers are oppressors and others their victims? Cone began to get at these and similar questions as he sought a different way of thinking about, and doing theology.

The Changing Meaning of
Black Theology in Cone's Work

In his first book Cone said the fundamental task of black theology is that
of analyzing "the black man's condition in the light of God's revelation in
Jesus Christ with the purpose of creating a new understanding of black dignity among black people, and providing the necessary soul in that people, to
destroy white racism."[15] Its purpose "is to *analyze* the nature of the Christian
faith in such a way that black people can say Yes to blackness and No to
whiteness and mean it"[16] (emphasis added). Black theology has the task of
making sense of black experience(s) and all which it implies in a racist nation.[17] A close reading of Cone's works reveals that the kind of analyzing and
theologizing about black experience(s) that was a first step in the early period
of his writing ultimately gives way to a different order of priorities. Around
the middle period of his development, which may be dated from about 1975,
theology (theologizing) becomes not the first, but the second step.

Neither black theology, nor liberation theology in general, was intended
to be an ivory tower or academic theology, although there is great risk of this
happening today. Indeed, some theology posing as liberation theology may
be little more than theology produced at a desk, and without close connection
with the oppressed. It is important to understand that black theology emerged
in the heat of black struggle, not as a result of long years of cool, relaxed,
uninterrupted theological reflection. Black theology arose outside the walls of
the academy. It was, from the very beginning, *a people's theology; a church discipline*, rather than an academic discipline.[18] As such, it can be "true to itself
only when validated in the context of people struggling for the freedom of the
oppressed."[19]

With the publication of *A Black Theology of Liberation*, Cone made explicit
what he had only implied in his first book. He said that the essence or content
of the Gospel and of theology is liberation—liberation from racial, social,
economic, and political oppression. In this book he defines theology as "a *rational study* of the being of God in the world in light of the existential situation
of an oppressed community, relating the forces of liberation to the essence of
the Gospel, which is Jesus Christ"[20] (emphasis added). Theology is not Christian theology unless it emerges out of the community of the oppressed,
thereby identifying itself with the oppressed and their condition.[21]

By characterizing theology as "rational study" in the early period of his
development, Cone was revealing the influence of traditional Western theologians on his thought. He may have had a sense that something precedes
the more intellectual enterprise of rational study, but he was not able, at the
time, to identify it in an explicit and clear way. He did know, however, that
theology meant nothing if it did not say and do something about black suffering. He was also aware that *commitment* was essential to the formula. The

problem was that he had not made a complete *epistemological break* with Western modes of thinking about theology. He was not able explicitly to say that commitment to actions that lead to the liberation of the oppressed comes first (not chronologically, but epistemologically), and that theologizing or rational study comes afterward or "at sundown."

Allan Boesak was critical of Cone's early focus on "rational study" in his attempts to define theology. Boesak, in agreement with Gutiérrez, believed the point of departure of theology lay elsewhere, viz, in "reflection upon action transforming the world."[22] The starting point for theology is the activity of the church and that of human action in the world to eradicate oppression. Of course, it may be that reflection upon the actions of the church in the world at a given moment may reveal that its actions are not geared toward setting the captives free. In this case the church is put on notice that it needs to determine *who* it will side with: the oppressor or the oppressed. In any event, liberation theology begins, not with rational study of the being of God, but with reflection on the church's activity in the world regarding the oppressed. Revealing a penchant for the definition of theology given by Gutiérrez, Boesak writes:

> Theology is not an automatic mental or spiritual process, nor merely a philosophical exercise. "We believe," states the report of a theological workshop in Asia, "that theology is not detached, cool, objective, or neutral. Theology is passionately involved. It begins with the experience of the actual struggles, suffering and joys of particular communities."[23]

Where the black community and the struggle for liberation are concerned, the first act of theology is direct involvement and commitment to the liberation of blacks from all forms of oppression.

Although Cone's definition of theology as "passionate language"[24] seemed to imply what Gutiérrez had in mind when he spoke of "historical praxis," Boesak rightly contends that Cone's early point of departure was fundamentally "rational study," despite later efforts to alter the wording slightly. In his second book, Cone wrote: "Christian theology is never just rational study of the being of God. Rather it is a study of God's liberating activity in the world, his activity on behalf of the oppressed."[25] He was closer, in this regard, to what Boesak had in mind, but from this description the emphasis is still on "rational study." The implication is that theology begins with theorizing, and only later are the theories applied to a concrete situation. This is precisely the way much of Western theology and ethics are done. Theory, presumably, can somehow be forced onto a given situation, rather than the theory itself being informed to a large extent by specific contexts or situations.[26] Liberation theology focuses on theory emerging out of the context itself.

This early tendency of Cone's reveals the strong influence of traditional European-American theology as he was trying to work out his theology. This has always been a real problem for black scholars. Most earned their doctoral degrees in white institutions where very little attention is given to experiences other than those of the dominant white group. Consequently, when black scholars begin to write, they often discover that they have to work extra hard to emancipate themselves from the influence of white scholars who thought nothing of the gifts of African Americans. Cone too had to struggle with this.

It is significant that even in Cone's early writings he did not back himself into a corner as he was endeavoring to work out a satisfactory definition of theology. He gave no final, once-and-for-all definition of anything during the early period. Rather, any definition of theology he proposed was "to be tested by the working out of a theology which can then be judged according to its consistency with a community's view of the ultimate."[27] This also bordered on abstraction, but it was an important admission. Not only was Cone unfamiliar with Gutiérrez's book, *A Theology of Liberation* (which was not translated into English until 1971), but he was not conversant enough with Marxist principles at the time to see in them a tool for socioeconomic analysis. Neither was he familiar with the sociology of knowledge, which later helped him to unmask many hidden assumptions and ideologies in capitalistic society and its traditional theologies. His later study of the works of sociologists of knowledge, e.g., Werner Stark, Peter Berger, and Thomas Luckmann, helped to expand his awareness of the on-going interaction between social and theological factors.

By the time of the appearance of *God of the Oppressed* (1975), the sociology of knowledge had made a significant impact on Cone's thinking. By this time social and historical context had become more important in his understanding of theology than the idea of "rational study." He began to place more emphasis on "the social basis of theology."[28] Cone's continued grappling with the definition of theology is evidence of the seriousness with which he took the critique of Boesak and others. This kind of responsiveness to critics is typical of Cone, though he tends to be more receptive to the criticisms of his black colleagues than to those of white theologians who refuse to take black theology seriously.

In each of his earlier descriptions of the task of black theology Cone made reference to the term *analyze*.[29] He realized during the inchoate stage that any authentic Christian theology must arise from the community of the oppressed. He understood the Gospel of God as "the proclamation of God's liberating activity," and held that the oppressed black community is a participant in this activity. Cone also indicated that the perspective of black theology "begins with man,"[30] i.e., it is anthropocentric. The concern, he said, is "with concrete man, particularly with oppressed man. This is the point of departure of Black Theology, because it believes that oppressed man is the point of departure of Christ."[31] Even during the early stage of his development Cone recognized that there was more to theology than "rational study," although he was not clear in stating just what the nature of this *more* was. This clarity came later, however.

At the present stage of his development Cone appears much closer to Boesak and Gutiérrez in his understanding of theology in general, and liberation theology in particular. Presently, he places more emphasis on theology as critical reflection on a prior socioreligio-cultural and political condition; critical reflection on the church's and the human community's activity in society and the world to make it more humane for all persons. Theologizing is no longer the first step for Cone. Presently he would not disagree with Gutiérrez's description of the task of theology.

> Theological reflection would then necessarily be a criticism of society and the Church insofar as they are called and addressed by the Word of God; it would be a critical theory, worked out in the light of the Word accepted in faith and inspired by a practical purpose—and therefore indissolubly linked to historical praxis.[32]

There must be what Gutiérrez calls "a clear and critical attitude regarding economic and sociocultural issues in the life and reflection of the Christian community."[33] There is need for more than the practice of simply using the Bible and revelation as the point of departure. There must be critical reflection on a prior commitment and relevant actions to completely eradicate massive, systematic forms of oppression. Cone indicated an awareness of this point in 1975 when he described theology as "language about God," and then proceeded to say that "it's more than this, and it is the 'more' that makes theology Christian."[34] This was still somewhat abstract, in that Cone did not state the nature of the "more." However, he was showing signs of being dissatisfied with his earlier description of black theology.

Gutiérrez contends that theology "must start with facts and questions derived from the world and from history,"[35] for it is in the world, in history, in life that we do theology and ethics. We do not authentically engage in these in an abstract metaphysical arena that is separate from life in this world. Theology must critically reflect on the world even as it endeavors to engage in the process of radically transforming the world. Indeed, the true work of theology begins by doing what is necessary to remove all practices that lead to defiling the image of God in persons, but particularly in oppressed, poor persons. Only later does it reflect. Yet there is a real sense in which one acts and reflects simultaneously. What is important for us is that neither Cone nor other liberation theologians ignore the importance of critical reflection in theology. What they hold with disdain is the tendency of some theologians to never get beyond their rational reflections and interpretations of the world, evil, and suffering. For liberationists, theology at its best is about doing whatever it takes to eliminate specific forms of oppression and underlying causes.

Cone makes it quite clear where he stands regarding the point of departure in theology.

> We do not begin our theology with a reflection on divine revelation as if the God of our faith is separate from the suffering of our peoples. We do not believe that revelation is a deposit of fixed doctrines or an objective word of God that is then applied to the human situation. On the contrary, we contend that there is no truth outside or beyond the concrete historical events in which persons are engaged as agents. Truth is found in the histories, cultures, and religions of our peoples. Our focus on social and religio-cultural analyses differentiates our theological enterprise from the progressive and abstract theologies of Europe and North America. It also illuminates the reasons why orthopraxis, in contrast to orthodoxy, has become for many of us the criterion of theology.[36]

This is a long way from Cone's earlier descriptions of the meaning and task of theology. He now contends that theology "is critical reflection upon a prior religio-cultural affirmation and political commitment in solidarity with the oppressed. . . ."[37]

The Methodological Components of Liberation Theology

All theology is contextual or situational. When liberation theologians use the term "context" they do not have in mind the sense of individual or "me-ness" one finds in the liberal Protestant usage. Instead, the focus is on the centrality of social location in theology. Social location is "not particular to the individuals," but is the common experience of all persons of the same group or class.[38]

Theology emerges out of a specific sociopolitical and cultural context. This may be the most differentiating factor about the many types of liberation theology.

> Local historical variations (nature and degree of oppression, composition of oppressed and oppressing groups) naturally produce variations in liberation theology (e.g., the theology of black power, feminist theology). All liberation theology originates among the world's anonymous, whoever may write the books or the declarations articulating it.[39]

The names of the various forms of liberation theology often reflect both the type of oppression from which the group seeks liberation, and the racial-ethnic or gender makeup of the group. For example, blacks in the United States and South Africa have been victims of racial oppression and economic exploitation for the past several hundred years. They therefore subscribe to black theology, which stresses racial analysis (although they are expanding to include class, gender, and other analyses). Women, in virtually every place in the world, are victims of male domination. Consequently, women have developed various forms of feminist theology, placing emphasis on sexual analysis. *Black womanist* theologians emphasize racial, sexual, and class analysis. Latin Americans have been victimized by powerful capitalist interests in the United States and other "developed" nations, and therefore place greater emphasis on class analysis. In addition, *mujerista* theologies in Latin America focus on sexual, racial, and class analysis. Africans outside South Africa, e.g., Ghanaians, tend to stress the importance of the indigenization of the Christian faith, or cultural liberation. Many Asians, on the other hand, adhere to liberation theology, but also emphasize the importance of making a place for their plurality of religions in theological dialogue. Whatever the context, all liberation theologies emerge from the absent of history — from the underside.

The emphasis on context in liberation theology has caused much concern among white theologians. Some, like Schubert Ogden, have insisted that liberation theology is too provincial and narrowly focused. In this connection, Ogden maintains that ". . . each of the theologies of liberation characteristically orients itself to but one form or another of human bondage — political, economic, cultural, racial, or sexual — as though freedom from it were the whole of emancipation."[40] That Ogden wrote this is unfortunate since by that time even James Cone's theology had explicitly expanded to include other forms of analysis and oppression, e.g., classism and sexism.[41]

Concerned that black theology not be susceptible to the criticism that it fails to take the universal dimension of oppression seriously, Cone wrote the following in 1979:

> We Black theologians should not only be prepared to answer what a certain segment of the Black community thinks about the ultimate, but also the question, "What is the truth as applied to humanity?" *I do not believe that we should limit our analysis of the truth to a certain ethnic manifestation of it in the Black community.* This means that our development of a Black Theology must start with the particularity of the Black experience but cannot be limited to it. Therefore, we should create a perspective on Black Theology that invites other oppressed peoples to share with us in the search for the truth that defines us all. *We must not allow Black Theology to reduce itself to an ethnic particularism*[42] [emphasis added].

Cone made a similar point in 1971 during an interview with William Hordern. Elsewhere, but in 1979, Cone wrote of the international character of racism and its linkage with classism, sexism, and imperialism. He insisted that any adequate analysis of racism "must reflect the global perspective of human oppression."[43] By the time Ogden wrote *Faith and Freedom*, there was already sufficient evidence that Cone was intentionally working (as were other liberationists) to expand his perspective on oppression. The seeds of this expanded view of oppression were already present in the early stage of his writing. Therefore, Ogden's criticism was at best misplaced. He, like many white scholars, failed to pay close attention to the level of progress in liberation theology by 1979 — or he and they did not care to be aware. Although in existence only ten years by that time, liberation theology had progressed significantly. Ogden's is the classic case of the white theologian who ventured to criticize liberation theology prior to close reading and scrutiny of literature in the field!

Tissa Balasuriya, a Sri Lankan theologian, raised a concern similar to Ogden's, although for a different reason. Balasuriya contends that though liberation theologies may fail to address the problems of global domination or fail to make the connection between local suffering and oppression with that on a global scale,[44] they are nevertheless "valid and necessary." They generally come into existence because of the failure of earlier theologies which make the claim of being universal, but in the end fail to take local situations of oppression seriously.[45] What Balasuriya calls for is the creative relating of the local contexts of oppression with the global situation. Balasuriya, not unlike Cone, prefers a universal approach that will foster respect for all created persons regardless of race, gender, class, age, or creed.[46] Neither Balasuriya nor Cone believes that the world is ready for this kind of theology. As long as the false universalism of dominant group theologians continues to be perpetuated there is need for on-going emphasis on contextualism in liberation theology.

In addition to the focus on context, liberation theologies share several other methodological traits in common. Cone has acknowledged many of these similarities.[47] I now want to list and discuss six of these. It will be evident that more attention is given some elements than others, but it should be remembered that each of the components is important in itself. To get an adequate sense of what liberation methodology is all about, it will be necessary to consider these elements both individually and interrelatedly. No one of these, viewed in isolation, gives a clear picture of liberation methodology. Also, it is generally acknowledged that Latin American liberation theologians have led the way in explicating the elements of liberation methodology.[48] For this reason the discussion that follows considers the contributions of several Latin American liberation theologians in addition to those of Cone. This is a methodology shared by all liberationists. Near the end of the chapter I shall include some specific contributions of black theology.

Commitment and Involvement: The First Step. All liberation theologians contend that theology (or theologizing) is not the first, but the second act; "it rises only at sundown." Theology begins by reflecting on actions the church or other religious bodies outside the church are already engaged in. "Theology must be able to find in pastoral activity the presence of the Spirit inspiring the action of the Christian community."[49] A commitment to actions and involvement in the total eradication of oppression is the first step. Theology is not just rational study of God, human beings, and the world. Rather, it begins with critical reflection on historical praxis. "It attempts to ponder the faith from the standpoint of this historical praxis and the way that faith is actually lived in a commitment to liberation."[50]

Witvliet has good insight into the significance of commitment in the theology of Gutiérrez.

> So when Gutiérrez speaks of this commitment as the primary element and as theology as [*sic*] the "second step" which follows, this methodological insight is not a speculative principle but an accurate reproduction of the actual course of events. Here, of course, one can also ask the question, as José Miguez Bonino was to do later, whether all theology, even where that is not intended, is not a "second action" which follows a social commitment that is not put into words and explicated.[51]

The liberationist contends that sociopolitical commitment and involvement in the struggle for liberation comes first, and theology develops from it. "Liberation theology reflects on and from within the complex and fruitful relationship between theory and practice."[52]

Cone concurs with this view of theology as the second, rather than the first step.[53] Interestingly, the practice of beginning the theological enterprise with reflection on a prior sociopolitical commitment is not foreign to dominant theologies of the West. Dominant group theologians have often done their reflecting from the standpoint of the values of the status quo. That is, they too have been committed to a prior sociopolitical situation, but it has generally had to do with maintaining the present order. The *subject* of their praxis tends to be the rich and comfortable in society, not the "least of these." Liberation theologians have employed social analysis in order to unmask such tendencies. Many of the dominant ideologies that have led to oppression and exploitation have hidden agendas, assumptions, or commitments. The white man, for example, has historically entered the homelands of nonwhites (including the indigenous peoples of the Americas), ostensibly to preach the Gospel. However, the real commitment was not to the Gospel, but to increasing the wealth and power of the dominant group. Indeed, as Vine Deloria points out, often they arrived with the Bible in one hand and the gun in the other. Only later did the white man reflect upon his actions, and usually for the purpose of justifying them.[54]

The emphasis on commitment to actions to liberate the oppressed is important as the first step, since it means that the primary emphasis is on making the most of persons — of placing human dignity on a much higher plane than rational reflection. It means, too, that persons who suffer as a result of domination and dehumanization do not have to wait until a study has been completed, or until "concerned" individuals have engaged in critical reflection and theorizing about their suffering. Instead, liberation methodology requires that efforts geared toward liberating the oppressed be given first priority. Yet we cannot make as clean and sharp a separation between actions to liberate the oppressed and the act of theorizing or critically reflecting on such actions. In other words, some reflection necessarily takes place during the first step as well. This, I think, is why liberation theologians speak of *action-reflection*. Action and reflection are really two moments in a single, dynamic process.

By making theology the second step, liberation theologians have made what Gutiérrez calls an *epistemological break*. This involves a reordering of priorities, and where we begin in the knowledge process. It means that the fundamental emphasis or starting point in the theological enterprise is not on purely rational discussion and the production of abstract manuscripts that have little to do with the elimination of human misery that results from oppressive societal structures. Rather, the starting point is *solidarity with the oppressed* and commitment to actions geared toward enhancing all persons. The aim here is not to undermine any instance of human suffering (individual or collective), or even to entertain arguments about who or what group suffers most. This kind of nitpicking ultimately leads to what King characterized as a "paralysis of analysis," since critics insist on first determining which group "suffers most" before they are willing to engage in liberating actions. Interestingly, this has never been a problem for the poor and the oppressed. Many whites cannot seem to get beyond this concern, however, and are taken aback when blacks remind them of the long, continuous river of black suffering.

Jon Sobrino sheds some light on this when he writes that "human beings suffer in every part of the world. The suffering on which the theology of liberation focuses is the *widespread suffering* of others"[55] (emphasis added). Liberation theology is concerned less with the suffering of an individual here and there, though no thinker-activist in this tradition would turn her or his back on an individual experiencing some form of pain. Much of traditional theology has been quite effective in dealing with individual suffering. The aim of liberation theology, however, is to *do* something to eliminate massive, systematic pain and suffering first and foremost, followed by critical reflection on the actions taken. It then considers the implications of these actions for even more improved actions. This on-going process of action-reflection-action (which is repeated until liberation emerges) is illustrative of the dynamism that is inherent in this component of liberation methodology.

By making commitment the first step one need not be "saved" (from personal sins) first, in order to recognize injustice and to immediately begin taking actions to remove it. Whether one is a Martin Luther King, Jr., or an "unsaved" guerrilla in the mountains of Central America or the ghettos of the United States fighting for the liberation of the oppressed, the criterion is that one be committed to setting at liberty the least of these. In the case of those who claim to be Christian the burden will always be on them to do whatever it takes to eradicate injustice. Interpreting Juan Luis Segundo on this important point, Robert McAfee Brown writes:

> ... it is a pre-theological conviction, available to anyone, that "the world should not be the way it is." But if one is a Christian, one can never condone the present unjust order, and one must be committed to its victims, the poor. That is the starting point for everything else — not abstract principles but commitment to the poor.[56]

As was pointed out previously regarding black theology, liberation theology is not a theology born in the classroom, nor a result of neatly constructed theological formulas. It is first and foremost a theology of grassroots people, and its point of departure is a firm commitment to doing whatever it takes to protect, preserve, and uplift the image of God in all persons, but especially those forced to the periphery of society. Authentic commitment presses one in the direction of radically transforming, or even destroying sociopolitical and economic structures that trample persons to the ground. The genuinely committed can see the integral relationship between knowing and doing; between knowledge and the radical transformation of society and the world. *To know is to do!*

In this regard one liberationist is quite to the point:

> True knowledge of reality leads us to change that reality. Theological knowledge must share in that transforming impetus. Theological reflection must embolden people to deeper commitment and further action.... It will be "critical reflection on praxis" that not only springs from engagement but leads to newer and deeper engagement. It will be "a theology which does not stop with reflecting on the world, but tries to be part of the process through which the world is transformed."[57]

This is illustrative of the epistemological break with dominant theologies, since liberation theology insists on the need to go beyond merely reflecting on the world to actual involvement in radically changing it. But it is also a break in the sense that it begins from below (from the underside), and with a radical option for the poor and oppressed, as well as commitment to their liberation.

Liberation theologians see plainly that evil exists not only in a few individuals, but in institutional structures created and sustained by them. Therefore, it is not just a matter of dealing with a few evil and sinful individuals. Evil social structures generally cause more harm and pain to greater numbers of persons than do single individuals who choose to do evil. This is an important point, for though institutions need radical transformation, at some point in the process there is need to get to the root of the problem of individuals that causes them to willingly carry out socioeconomic and political policies that degrade persons. Structures must be radically changed, but so must the individuals who maintain them! Although not all liberation theologians have taken this point to heart, Gutiérrez is cognizant of its importance when he writes that *"liberation envisions not only a new society but a new kind of person,* one increasingly free of the bonds preventing us from shaping our own lives"[58] (emphasis added).

In any case, the fact that liberationists believe social structures must be radically transformed implies that such structures may need to be replaced entirely, in order to clear the way for more humane ones. It is one thing to argue for an "ethic of breaking bread" and sharing, but one must first have access to bread to break and share! This suggests a rejection of those approaches that take as normative the idea of the slow process of amelioration in the social struggle. Liberationists want to do away with suffering, injustice, and oppression right now! They do not want to merely ease the pain through an indefinite series of well calculated steps, as is the method of liberal coalition agendas. The desire is to end the suffering today. Liberationists believe, however, that even efforts at reform make some contribution on the way to total liberation and empowerment.

The quality of the commitment to actions for the liberation of the poor and oppressed is everything. Commitment is characterized by *solidarity* with those forced to the margins of society. It "implies identification with oppressed human beings and social classes and solidarity with their interest and struggles."[59] The social and historical praxis of the oppressed is the starting point. Beginning here opens new insights and interpretations of the Scriptures. Liberation theology is created in the context of the liberative process. It does not arise before, or apart from, the day to day struggles of the people. Rather, it emerges in the context of the struggle.[60]

It is not enough for members of the oppressed group, or concerned members of the dominant group, to deliver eloquent oratories against oppression and in favor of all persons to be fully human and to be able to live lives commensurate with such proclamations. Nor is it enough to merely give verbal support to the struggle against all forms of oppression. The quality of one's commitment has less to do with what one says, but a great deal to do with what one does! Liberationists would not disagree with James Baldwin's view that his own survival was dependent, not upon what whites say, but what they actually do. The point is obvious. Talk is cheap! The quality of one's commitment to the struggle for total liberation is fundamentally determined by one's actions to make this an immediate reality. Actions within the context of a specific community of oppression should be calculated to obtain the maximum possible good for *all* members, rather than the greatest number.

The quality of one's commitment, then, may be determined by the nature and extent of one's actions against human oppression. Mere verbal proclamations are inadequate and unacceptable. Verbal claims to commitment are little more than abstractions, if not accompanied by radical actions designed to liberate the oppressed.

Cultural Identity. The second methodological component is the focus on cultural identity. Cone has written that it is necessary to affirm "our cultural resources as well as those found among other oppressed people who have similar experiences of oppression."[61] Convinced that divine suffering is revealed in the suffering of the marginalized of the world, liberationists maintain further that "theology cannot achieve its Christian identity apart from a systematic and critical reflection upon the history and culture of the victims of oppression."[62] They therefore reject any attempt by the dominant group to undermine the history and cultural heritage of blacks, Native Americans, Latinos, Asians, Africans, and others. In addition, the oppressed are urged to free themselves from a too heavy dependence upon European and European American thought.

It is important that members of oppressed groups work deliberately to recapture the memory of their heroes and sheroes and their historical and cultural heritage.

> Human history has been written "by a white hand," from the dominating sectors. . . . The perspective of the "defeated" of history is different. Efforts have been made to wipe from their own minds the memory of their struggles. This is to deprive them of a source of energy, of historical will, of rebellion.[63]

The achievement of total liberation is dependent, in part, upon an oppressed peoples' ability and willingness to regain the memory of the systematically oppressed people of their group.

In the case of African Americans, this means that they must "call the names of their ancestors" and reaffirm their contributions to this nation and the world. Blacks must strive to preserve their heritage and to pass it on to their posterity. This is one reason it is so important that an oppressed people rewrite and preserve their history in light of their own experience, rather than uncritically trusting that historians in dominant groups (both outside and within oppressed groups!) will present an accurate, balanced view of the facts. For example, just as African Americans must not naively trust that white historians will include their experiences, black women must not uncritically assume that black male historians will include their experiences. The nineteenth- and twentieth-century black feminist Anna Julia Cooper pointed to this.[64]

Yet, as the oppressed rewrite their history they should guard against romanticizing it. They should learn to take their history seriously, but without thinking that this alone will insure the freedom they seek from oppressive structures. Oppressed groups should be mindful of the retort of Vine Deloria, Jr., to his own people: "Who really gives a damn if the Oglalas were a great warrior band of the Sioux? That won't help to solve the problems that exist today."[65] Deloria does not mean that this aspect of Sioux history is insignificant and unworthy of remembering. Rather he means that this should be seen in light of where his people find themselves today. It is not remembering simply for the sake of remembering that is important and helpful in the liberation struggle. Remembering is but one aspect (albeit an important one!) in a much broader liberation process.

Since all liberation theologies are contextual, they are first and foremost informed by their respective cultural heritage. It is precisely because of the *situated* character of these theologies that they disparage abstract discussions that have little to do with the experiences that inform them. Writing about the situational character of black theology, Witvliet contends that it "calls first of all for a historical and biographical approach: it has a history which has to be known before analysis and evaluation of separate texts make sense. In other words, knowledge of the context is a first condition for understanding the text itself."[66] Therefore, in order to understand the need for black and other forms of liberation theology, one has to first learn something about the history of a particular oppressed group. Among other things, this knowledge will reveal that the oppression a particular group fights against today has a long history, and did not just come into existence a few years ago (as many younger whites imagine to be the case with the black struggle). By taking cultural identity seriously, liberation theologians can test the validity of the structure of logic as defined by the group they represent. No criterion of truth is valid which does not take culture seriously.

The Role of the Social Sciences. A third methodological consideration is the strong emphasis on the social sciences, including political theory and social philosophy. Cone expresses this point well when he maintains that the most important conversation partners for liberation theologians are not metaphysicians and abstract, reputedly value-neutral philosophers in universities. Liberationists are more interested in conversing with social scientists and political activists who are engaged in the liberation of the marginalized.[67]

In a related sense, Segundo contends that the most important consequences and considerations of theology "can be summed up in one word, which is more or less taboo: politics."[68] He believes it is essential for theologians to introduce the most significant elements of the social sciences into their work.[69] Both Hugo Assmann and José Miguez Bonino are in agreement with Segundo.[70] The critical analysis of the actual sociopolitical and economic situation in society is fundamental for Assmann, who refers to this process as the "sociologization of theology."[71] Of course, such an analysis is designed to determine the root causes of poverty, classism, racism, and other forms of systematic oppression. This kind of analysis helps unmask the institutionalized nature of violence and other forms of oppression. Social science contributes to theology by providing it with a clearer view of history, a critical approach, and tools for critical social analysis. These aid in uncovering hidden assumptions, as well as underlying, basic causes of oppression. They help expose the systemic nature of social oppression, and can assist in determining how evil social systems operate to crush human beings.[72]

Dependence upon the methods of the social sciences, and particularly the sociology of knowledge,[73] is useful because it aids liberationists in unmasking the presuppositions and hidden assumptions in presumed dispassionate, disinterested, and value-neutral theologies. We learn from the sociology of knowledge, for example, that there is no such thing as a totally detached, value-free theology.[74] This should serve as a warning that when we read the Scriptures, for example, we do so through the grid of our own sociocultural context, whether we admit it or not. We read and interpret the Scriptures and everything else from where we are situated in society. In this respect we are all "situated." The rich and the poor, then, will probably not see the same things when they read the Bible. African Americans will not see what European Americans see in the Scriptures. Women of all races and classes will not see what men see. Whatever we do is socially conditioned, "and in creating a theology of liberation we must be aware of the pervasive connection between ideology and theology."[75] Liberation theologians have been willing to admit what many traditional theologians have not: that when we engage in social analysis and the theological enterprise, our values and cultural background are great influences. We are never as neutral and disinterested as we like to think. "The sociology of knowledge makes abundantly clear that we think always out of a definite context of relations and action, out of a given praxis."[76]

Cone also develops this idea of the on-going integral relationship between sociological and theological factors convincingly in *God of the Oppressed*.[77] Though it is often difficult to acknowledge, we all bring value presuppositions and "preunderstandings" to bear upon whatever we do. We hear and see what we do because of where we are situated in society. Writing on Karl Mannheim's sociology of knowledge, conflict sociologist Lewis Coser explains its meaning:

> To Mannheim, the sociological viewpoint "seeks from the very beginning to interpret individual activity in all spheres within the context of group experience." Thinking is never a privileged activity free from the effects of group life; therefore it must be understood and interpreted within its context. No given individual "confronts the world and, in striving for the truth, constructs a worldview out of the data of his experience.... It is much more correct that *knowledge is from the very beginning a co-operative process of group life*, in which everyone unfolds his knowledge within a framework of a common fate, a common activity, and the overcoming of common difficulties"[78] [emphasis added].

We are persons-in-relationship. Therefore, no individual exists in a vacuum. Every person affects and is affected by his or her social environment. Every person makes, and is made by, society. We are what we are because of the group or community which produced us. Our beliefs are molded in the context of our communal environs. Liberation theologians view the sociology of knowledge as a key component of their methodology. It shows us that all theology involves an ongoing interplay between theological and social factors.[79]

Yet a word of caution is in order. Despite the heavy dependence on the social sciences, it is imperative that liberation theologians themselves always approach them critically and with a degree of suspicion, especially if they are dependent upon social science studies made by others. Liberationists must know something about the social scientist's reason for doing what he or she does. Though the social scientist endeavors to provide a clear, objective, unbiased picture of the actual state of a given problem in society, the conclusions that two or more of them arrive at after studying the same problem and using the same data are often at variance with each other. For example, some well known social scientists in the United States have concluded that racism is no longer a significant social problem, claiming that it was essentially solved during the civil rights struggle of the sixties.[80] Others, however, conclude that the evidence conclusively reveals that racism continues to be a very serious problem, but that it is often difficult to detect its presence because of cosmetic changes that occurred during the sixties.[81] The point I am making is that when the liberationist who is not capable of doing her or his own social analysis is confronted with contradictory conclusions drawn by social scientists, there is need for a criterion to help determine which set of results to follow.

A good rule of thumb is to seek either the views of those who are the victims, or the views of social scientists who are known to be in solidarity with them. For example, if social scientists have studied the problem of racism and have drawn contradictory conclusions as to whether it is still a problem, one reasonably sure way to settle the matter is to ask African Americans in all social classes whether they believe racism to be a pervasive problem. The importance of making inquiries at all class levels is that many affluent blacks often have substantial vested interests in the status quo. Their response, therefore, may not be different from that of members of the dominant white group. Blacks who are lower on the socioeconomic totem pole are more likely to talk "straight from the shoulder" about the continued existence of individual and institutional racism.

During the eighties the Reagan administration, following the views of writers like George Gilder, concluded that poverty and hunger were no longer problems in the United States. Other social scientists disagreed. Here again, the liberationist is admonished to go directly to the victims, or to social scientists known to be in solidarity with them. In other words, one should consult those tens of thousands of Americans who stand in soup lines in subzero weather. Ask those who live in slum areas and sleep on the streets in Mississippi, Philadelphia, Indianapolis, Detroit, Cleveland and other major urban centers whether poverty is a problem. Consult the thousands of persons who stand in welfare and unemployment lines who are insulted and humiliated by insensitive claims-takers. In a nutshell, when in doubt, *the victims must cast the deciding vote*. But since the poor and the oppressed tend to be powerless and unorganized it will be necessary for them to organize and insist on casting the deciding vote. Those who pretend not to know whether sexism is really a problem should pay special attention to the voices of women who insist that individual and institutional sexism crushes their humanity. Liberation theologians will have to avoid the mistake of viewing social scientists and their methods with an uncritical eye. They will especially have to invoke the "hermeneutic of suspicion" when social scientists make claims to absolute neutrality.

Some social scientists will be more helpful to liberation theologians than others. More often these will be the social scientists who have a firm, deliberate commitment to human dignity and radical actions that lead to the development and implementation of policies and programs which make it possible for all persons to live fully human lives.[82] Liberation theologians agree with Oliver Cromwell Cox's description of the role of the social scientist:

> Clearly, the social scientist would be *accurate and objective but not neutral*; he should be *passionately partisan in favor of the welfare of the people and against the interests of the few* when they seem to submerge that welfare. In a word, the reason for the existence of the social scientist is that his scientific findings contribute to the betterment of the people's well-being[83] [emphasis added].

Cox, unlike many of his contemporaries, was not pretentious in this regard. The social scientist does have value interests. The message for liberation theologians is that those social scientists who have an option for the oppressed and downtrodden are the ones to listen to when contradictory conclusions are drawn from the data.

Praxis. I introduced this fourth methodological component in the discussion on commitment and involvement. Praxis refers to *action, activity, action-reflection*. It may be described as reflective political action that includes cultural identity. For liberationists the very reason for doing theology arises out of the experience of oppression. Theology is critical reflection upon a prior religiocultural affirmation and political commitment. It involves being in solidarity with the poor and oppressed. The phrase "solidarity with the poor and oppressed" is significant in this type of theology, since one's critical reflection might well be on the prior religious and cultural affirmations of the oppressors. The *subject* of one's critical reflection, then, is crucial. The subject, for liberationists, is the oppressed.

Contrary to what many critics say, praxis does not undermine the importance of reason and critical reflection for action. Criticized by some theologians who made the claim that he does not take reason seriously enough,[84] Cone responded in a way that should silence his critics:

> Black theology must not reject reason, for without it there is no way to assess the validity of one claim over another. Without reason, theology cannot be critical.... As black theologians who reject much of the function of reason in western philosophy

and theology, we must be careful not to allow our rejection of reason per se to be dependent on white people's misuse of it. *Reason is an important tool of theological analysis, and without it the community is left exposed to fanatics and other self-appointed prophets of God.* If what is preached and sung as a part of the black story cannot stand the test of reason and the structure of logic as defined by our history and culture, then black theologians must excise these false expressions from the black community. It is our task to unmark [sic] false prophets and preachers by showing that what they claim contradicts the faith of the people. *Passion therefore does not exclude reason. It controls reason by refusing to entertain ideas that are not related to the struggle of freedom*[85] [emphasis added].

Reason and critical reflection have a place of prominence in liberation theology. The problem for liberationists is not that philosophers and theologians depend so heavily upon critical reflection, for liberationists do also. Instead, the problem is philosophers and theologians tend to begin their activity by reflecting upon a prior commitment to the values of the dominant group, and they seek to justify these values at the expense of those at the margins of society. When traditional philosophers and theologians engage in action they do so from the vantage point of the dominant group. The subject of their praxis is seldom the oppressed. The praxis of liberationists, on the other hand, is from the perspective of the oppressed community. Though the emphasis in praxis is on action rather than ideas, the intent is not to denigrate the importance of ideas. However, because doctrine or ideas reigned for so long at the expense of praxis, liberation theologians found it necessary to make an adjustment. The goal is a balance between "orthodoxy" and "orthopraxis" (between doctrine, and deeds or actions).[86] In order to "modify" the often exclusive emphasis upon ideas, doctrine or orthodoxy, it was necessary to highlight, or strongly emphasize orthopraxis. Gutiérrez maintains that the concept of orthopraxis is unsettling for some. He might also have said that throughout the history of thought, scholars over-emphasized or overstated their own position in order to correct the view of a contemporary or predecessor. This sometimes led to a degree of balance. However, scholars of oppressed groups who engage in the liberation struggle need not initially concern themselves with balance in their position. This was Cone's stance in his first two books—indeed, in all of his books! Because of the massive injustices suffered by blacks for over four hundred years, Cone expresses no interest in trying to balance his perspective. This has been the least of his worries, and is why many white theologians claimed to be turned off by him, and unwilling to engage him in dialogue. (We know now, however, that what many of these theologians wanted was balance in the arguments, not the eradication of oppression!)

Liberation theologians like to quote Karl Marx's eleventh thesis on Feuerbach: "The philosophers have only interpreted the world in various ways; the point is to change it."[87] This may well be the chief paradigm for liberation theologies.[88] Liberation theology confronts oppressive conditions

in the world from the perspective of the oppressed. It is not sufficient just to mentally work through the problem. This is the point of Sobrino's discussion of the differences between Latin American and European theology. The latter effectively works out societal problems and their solutions at the level of thought, but then fails to take the necessary steps actually to solve the problems in society.[89] Though liberation thinkers also engage in rational, logically consistent argument, they generally do so from a concrete situation of oppression, which is not to imply that their reasoning is any less rigorous than that of academic theologians who tend to reason from *a priori* first principles. "Furthermore participation in a concrete historical process — such as the lives of the oppressed — enables one to perceive aspects of the Christian message that theorizing fails to reveal."[90] Liberationists engage in critical reflection for the purpose of changing the world. For them, to know is to do! Doing, then, is   •
the criterion for theology. Too much time is spent explaining the world. The point is to change it.[91]

Yet truth, finally, is to be found neither in merely interpreting the world nor in changing it, but in the on-going dialectical interaction between critical reflection and action. Each is important for the other, and completes the other. Effective actions to eradicate oppression and establish a just social order where no group dominates over any other is ultimately linked to good, solid theory. On the other hand, theory is solidified as it reflects critically upon actions already taken to liberate the oppressed. Aware that some liberationists will question the attention he gives to theory in Christian political ethics, Bonino has given four reasons as to why theory is important in the liberative struggle: it is unavoidable; it can make explicit our assumptions while being critical of actions to be taken; it can bring "unity and coherence to the struggle"; and it can enable us to make our experience available to others, thereby making it possible for them to become participants in the struggle.[92]

Cone also emphasizes the importance of theory (in his courses), "combined with active participation in the black church and community on behalf of the liberation of the poor."[93] In addition, he is critical of both the lack of self-criticism among some black theologians and careless scholarship. This implies a concern for the importance of reason and critical theoretical reflection and its linkage with liberative activities. Theory and praxis can be separated for the sake of analysis and discussion, but in concrete situations they are two moments, dialectically related, in one process.[94]

Praxis is not synonymous with practice, if by practice is meant some kind of action. Praxis points to an on-going tension between action and reflection. Robert McAfee Brown illustrates this process. "When we act, reflect on the action, and then act in a new way on the basis of our reflection (or when we reflect, and then act, and then reflect in a new way on the basis of our action) we are illustrating praxis."[95] What is new in this process is that the point of departure is the praxis of the marginalized of the world. Theology is not done from the topside, but from the bottomside.

The Frame of Reference. The fundamental difference between the methodology of liberation theology and that of traditional theology is its frame of reference and its emphasis on being in solidarity with the oppressed. This is the fifth methodological element. It is crucial for our understanding of liberation methodology. The point of departure differentiates liberation and other theologies. Gutiérrez highlights this when he distinguishes between liberation theology and progressivist theology. The frame of reference of the former is a radical break with other forms of theology since it insists that active commitment to the liberation of the poor and oppressed comes first, and critical reflection follows.

If theology is critical reflection on and from within historical praxis, then the historical or "concrete praxis in question is the liberation praxis of the oppressed." It is important to grasp the significance of this point. The perspective or frame of reference of liberation theology sets it apart from traditional theology. Its frame of reference is such that merely knowing that praxis comes before theology or reflection is insufficient. One must also know *whose* praxis is at stake. That is, one must know the historical subject of that praxis. For the liberationist the historical subject of praxis is the people at the margins of the world, not the privileged and powerful. Were this not the case, theology would soon be little more than a meaningless academic exercise. For liberationists, theology is done from the bottom rung of society. Problems, strategies, and proposed solutions are all viewed through the eyes and situation of the oppressed. This is the distinctive character of the frame of reference of liberation theology.

Doing theology from below is not an easy task, for it means that one has to work diligently to see the problem of pain, suffering and oppression not through the lens of a more privileged class, but through those of the victims. Only thus can one understand the essence of liberation theology. White liberals often miss the point of liberation theology precisely because of their failure to grasp the significance of its frame of reference. When one internalizes the idea that the frame of reference in liberation theology is radically different from that of traditional theology in that it is *a view from below*, it will not be difficult to understand what is meant by "being in solidarity with the poor and oppressed." From the bottomside, being in solidarity means getting down to dirt-level; to the level of the nonperson, the forgotten of history, and viewing the problem of oppression and suffering from that vantage point. As long as well-meaning Christians, for example, are not willing to do that, it will always be possible for them to place their level of commitment at a point beyond which they are not willing to go. That is, they will not be able to see that authentic commitment to the people who are the least means a willingness to give up everything, pick up their cross daily, and follow Jesus and the oppressed! Persons who claim to be adherents to this theology of solidarity and liberation must ask themselves, What am I willing to do, or not do, to set at liberty the captives, who through no fault of their own are crushed to the earth?

To be in solidarity with the poor and the oppressed means to be willing to join with them both in determining the socioeconomic and political causes of their oppression, and to do whatever it takes to eliminate them. It means to share their suffering, not for the sake of winning favor in order to gain salvation beyond the grave, but as a sign of genuine commitment to total liberation.

When we view the situation from the bottomside, we are actually looking at the world in a new way. It has little to do with merely sympathizing with those at the margin of the world. Identification with the oppressed forces us to see how we are in complicity with the forces and powers that disregard the sacredness of persons. When we identify with the poor and the oppressed we become aware that the poor are not poor by choice. They are poor because the rich are rich, and the latter are rich because of their exploitation of the poor. That individual wealthy persons are not aware of any intentional efforts to exploit the poor is not the point. Rather, what is important is that capitalistic systems benefits some, while crushing the masses of people. The problem is not just the bad actions of individuals here and there.

> The evil that leads to such a situation is not the fault of a few individuals or even a lot of individuals (though that can help); *it is the fault of the entire system in which those individuals operate* — a system in which the few benefit in handsome fashion while the many are exploited in ugly fashion. *In this analysis, evil is "systemic," or "structural,"* suggesting that the sickness of our society is much more deep-seated than we had thought, and suggesting the even more drastic thought that a drastic illness may call for drastic surgery[96] [emphasis added].

There are surely evil individuals who are the keepers of oppressive structures. There are also well-intentioned individuals who find themselves caught up in employment situations in evil structures. But because of the potential for the massive destruction of large numbers of people, the deeper concern must be the eradication of systemic evil, rather than the saving of individual souls (though this too is important). It is the system itself that is oppressive and dehumanizing, which is why the mere changing of individuals into "persons of good will" is not likely to lead to liberation. Since "good" people are trapped in an evil system it is necessary to radically transform the system.[97] The reference to *surgery* in the quotation above implies a cutting away in order for real growth and health to occur structurally. An implication of this is that until radical surgery occurs in the socioeconomic order, the masses of people will continue to be victims of economic exploitation and myriad forms of oppression.

When it is understood that the framework is different in liberation theology, it will more easily be seen that being in solidarity with the poor and
oppressed is more costly than many are willing to see from the topside. Being
in solidarity means siding with the oppressed. This means changing sides, for
the truth is that the noncommitted have already adopted the side of their class
or group. They need to change sides. This does not mean that one should
drop everything and go off to join forces with the oppressed in another country. Such an action is not necessarily morally plausible, since such a one
always reserves the right and privilege to leave the battle zones overseas and
return to comfortable status and security in the United States.

Changing sides is really more of a state of mind. One can stay right here
in the United States and be a revolutionary. What the committed person, in
solidarity with the oppressed, can do is find those places — both nationally and
internationally — where this government and the economic structure wreak
havoc on the lives of the masses, and begin working from where they are to
put an effective end to such imperialist activity. One has to undergo a radical
transformation of attitude and outlook, giving up their present commitment
to working to preserve the values and privileges of the status quo, and redirect
that commitment to liberating the downtrodden from forces over which they
have no control.

Being in solidarity with the oppressed is costly and requires cross-bearing.
McAfee Brown tells us just what this will likely require of dominant group
members who are sincere about trying to be Christians.

> It would mean becoming "betrayers of our class," taking strong issue with
> the assumptions, norms, and values of the society that supports us, feeds us,
> and pays us. It would mean breaking with the convictions of many of our
> friends and most of our society. For, as Gustavo [Gutiérrez] himself points
> out, "We cannot be for the poor and oppressed if we are not against all that
> gives rise to the exploitation of human beings." Jurgen Moltmann, no
> "liberation theologian," has grasped what this means: "Whoever wants genu-
> ine communion with the victims must become the enemy of their enemies. . . ."
> To be free from the oppressive prison of one's society means to become a
> "stranger among one's own people."[98]

Ada María Isasi-Díaz observes the tendency of many to waterdown the
meaning and power of the term solidarity.

> The proof of this is how fashionable its usage has become, how easily it rolls
> off the tongues of all sorts of speakers, how unthreatening it is. If the true
> meaning of solidarity were understood and intended, visible radical change
> would be happening in the lives of those who endorse it with their applause.
> Solidarity is *not* a matter of agreeing with, of being supportive of, of liking,
> or of being inspired by, the cause of a group of people.[99]

Doing theology from the bottomside is expensive. Those who claim to
be committed to the oppressed will need to comply with Jesus's instructions

to the rich young ruler that he sell all that he has, give to the poor, take up his cross daily, and follow his Lord (Luke 18:22). Being in solidarity with the least of the sisters and brothers does not mean that one necessarily has to give up a living wage, decent house, car, and other personal possessions. As each of us lives within — and works through — the tension produced by Jesus's instructions to the rich young ruler, it may mean that some will decide to give up these things in the face of massive suffering and pain around them. The point is that we never really escape the burden this tension places on us. Each of us will have to determine how we will respond. In this respect none should expect to be let off the hook easily.

The Hermeneutic of Suspicion. The final methodological element to be considered is the "hermeneutic of suspicion." Synonymous characterizations include *ideological suspicion*, or the *art of suspecting*. This points to the need to see the connection between what is said in dominant circles and what is actually done. One should be suspicious when it becomes evident that what is being done is inconsistent with what is said. James Baldwin suggested this technique when he addressed the World Council of Churches in 1968.

> . . . if it is true that your testimony as Christians has proven invalid; if it is true that my importance in the Christian world was not as a living soul, dear to the sight of God, but as a means of making money, and representing some terrifying divorce between the flesh and the spirit; if that is true (and it would be very difficult to deny the truth of this) then at this moment in the world's history it becomes necessary for me, for my own survival, not to listen to what you say but to watch very carefully what you do, not to read your pronouncements but to go back to the source and to check it for myself.[100]

Baldwin knew what many liberationists assert today, that the very survival of African Americans (and other oppressed groups) has depended much upon their being suspicious of what Christians in the dominant group say. Not what white Christians say, but what they do, is indicative of what they really believe.

Segundo writes that the liberation theologian's "suspicion is that anything and everything involving ideas, including theology, is intimately bound up with the existing social situation in at least an unconscious way."[101] Theological ideas are intertwined with sociological and other factors. There is really no way for people to keep their ideas from being "tainted" by their history and culture. All persons seem to possess assumptions that "we hold so deeply as to be scarcely aware of them," which suggests that the socialization process is so thorough and subtle that there is seldom conscious awareness of assumptions. The indication is that tools are needed to unmask hidden, unconscious assumptions. The social sciences provides such tools.

If all groups could be trusted to admit their assumptions and presuppositions there would be no need to invoke the hermeneutic of suspicion. The truth is that most are not willing to make such admissions. This seems particularly true of the dominant group, perhaps because of its many economic and other advantages in the present arrangement of society.

Bonino writes that "we cannot receive the theological interpretation coming from the rich world without suspecting it and, therefore, asking what kind of praxis it supports, reflects, or legitimizes."[102] Does it support the praxis of the dominant group, or that of the oppressed? From a strictly pragmatic and survival standpoint it behooves the victims of massive and systematic oppression to retain a healthy sense of suspicion regarding the dominant group. There are those (especially among the privileged) who object to this, claiming that such a stance is not theologically sound, and that it militates against dialogue and reconciliation between groups that have been alienated. This may be true, but the desire to survive in order ultimately to obtain liberation dictates the necessity of suspicion. Any group forced to the periphery of society would be well advised to be suspicious of those who are denying them the right to live to the fullest as human beings.

Ideological suspicion refers "to those dangerous, latent interpretations or ideologies that color our basic assumptions more than we care to admit." The oppressed would do well to be suspicious, because the theology of the dominant group is generally adapted to its own interests. The assumptions of the oppressor are often hidden. This task of exposing them is left to the "organic intellectuals" of oppressed groups. The task of unmasking hidden assumptions is done most effectively through critical social analysis.

Any person or group can talk the language of liberation. Many of those who speak language similar to liberation theology do all they can to attenuate its concrete effects.[103] Liberationists are quite aware of this tendency in church and academic circles.

> At present much effort is being made to domesticate liberation theology. People are using its terminology but emptying it of any real meaning. They are also talking about pluralism, which really comes down to non-commitment.[104]

It is not difficult to locate persons in churches and seminaries who talk the language of liberation, but do nothing to eradicate oppression and injustice. At best, what they really want to do is "talk about the issues in a sensible, calm manner." It is easier and safer for them to identify themselves with pluralism and universality, but this is often done in order to avoid having to identify with the oppressed, and commit themselves to eliminating specific forms of oppression. In this way they never have to commit themselves to anything but "the problem in general." They have a penchant for identifying with liberation struggles thousands of miles away, while failing to commit themselves and their resources to liberating the oppressed in their own country. Balasuriya has raised a concern about this too. "They are supportive of the struggles of the oppressed peoples in other countries against capitalism and neocolonialism. But they are less energetic in articulating a theology that would voice a prophetic critique of their own situation."[105]

As for those who question the necessity of the hermeneutic of suspicion as a methodological element, attention should be given the numerous betrayals suffered by blacks and Native Americans in the United States. In the case of African Americans, Rayford Logan wrote a detailed account of the numerous betrayals they endured between 1877 and 1918. He could have continued his study up to the time the book was first published in 1954, since the betrayals continued up to and beyond that period.[106]

It would be naive for blacks to suspend the hermeneutic of suspicion at the present time. Whites must earn the trust of African Americans. Blacks can help in this process by telling whites the truth about themselves and how they really feel about them. Malcolm X emphasized the importance of the naked truth between blacks and whites.[107] In a related sense, it is necessary that blacks stop trusting whites as readily as they do. Many blacks are so naive and gullible in this regard that one wonders whether they realize that their ancestors were enslaved by the people they so uncritically trust. Instead of continuing to forgive whites so easily, the need is to begin thinking about the implications of this cheap forgiveness, and what it means for the black struggle to be free.

The Black Experience and Liberation Methodology

Though an entire book might be devoted to fleshing out Cone's method, the purpose of the present discussion is to indicate what he and black theology in general contribute to liberation methodology. As a form of liberation theology, black theology shares the methodological elements already discussed. However, because all types of liberation theology emerge from a particular sociocultural context, each makes specific methodological contributions applicable to the situation out of which it develops. Since black theology emerges within the socioreligious and cultural context of a people victimized by racial and other forms of oppression forced upon them since the middle of the fifteenth century, we need to ask what does it mean to do theology in light of such a brutal reality? Cone views the black struggle for liberation as the chief issue and question for black theologians. What, then, are some key methodological elements in black theology?

Taking the Lived-Story of Blacks Seriously. First, black theology can be done effectively only if the black story of pain, struggle, and periodic victory is taken seriously. The theological reflections of black theologians must emerge from both participation in, and commitment to, the lived-story of African Americans. The commitment must be to the *whole* story. This means that special efforts must be made to include the heretofore absent voices and experiences of black women, youths, and senior citizens. Black theologians can criticize the black experience only because they have arisen out of it and give it a place of prominence in their work. This is why Cone, for example, can be an effective, even if unpopular, critic of the black church.

Black theologians will always take the "structures of logic" seriously, but only in light of the faith and struggle of African Americans. This is not to imply a general disregard for the history of Western thought and the problems it has sought to address. But it does suggest that black theologians should not allow Western thought to dictate the boundaries within which reflection on the black story should take place. Black faith can only be tested by involvement in, and commitment to, the black struggle. Cone develops this idea further.

> To be sure, as black theologians, we should be interested in the history of western thought, including its more recent concern about language and semantic logic. And we should be interested in assessing the validity of the claims of faith as compared with other human assertions. But our interest in western philosophy, ancient and modern, is not defined by western philosophy itself, but our struggle for freedom.[108]

Cone does not throw out the baby with the bathwater. Blacks are to retain the best in Western thought, though it must be indigenized, if it is to be relevant to black experience. The faith of African Americans cannot be tested by white Western philosophers and their structures of logic, since their systems of reasoning did not emerge from the context of black oppression. Whatever is said about black faith must arise from an attitude of commitment to the black story of struggle and the faith upon which blacks so heavily depend. It is precisely this belief and participation in the black religiocultural heritage that motivates Cone's scathing critique of black church leadership (which is discussed in more detail in Chapter 6).

Passionate Language. Second, the language of black theology is passionate. Cone contends that this passionate language "reflects the rhythm and feelings that arises out of the struggle of freedom."[109] The passionate character of theological language links it with black song, sermon, testimony, and prayer. Anyone who has ever heard Cone lecture knows how important this is for him. He lectures with much fervor and passion. Indeed, how could he or anyone involved in and committed to the black story and struggle for liberation do otherwise? When one listens to Cone's lectures one detects a great sense of urgency, both in what he says, and how it is said. This is because of his recognition of what King characterized as "the fierce urgency of now," regarding the black situation. According to Cone this was evident during the second phase of King's thinking about the American dream. During the post–March on Washington period King said he watched the American dream "turn to a nightmare as I moved through the ghettos of the nation and saw black brothers and sisters perishing on a lonely island of poverty in the midst of a vast ocean of material prosperity. . . ." He watched the dream turn into a nightmare as the war in Vietnam escalated and the war on poverty was shot down on its battlefields.[110]

The state of emergency in the black community is such that no one who is committed to the struggle can afford the luxury of cool, calm, dispassionate discourse on the black situation. So in a real sense, the same passion that goes into black preaching and singing must be evident in the lectures and writings of black theologians.

The Significance of Reason. A third methodological element in black theology is the emphasis it places upon reason. Black theology recognizes reason as a crucial tool for theological analysis. There must be some way to ascertain most reasonable hypotheses when trying to determine the truth of matters that pertain to black experience. Reason is considered the best tool for this purpose, and Cone implies the need to assume the truth or validity of reason. Sources of black theology such as sermon, testimony, song, folk tales, narratives, prayers, black literature, and so on must be able to stand the test of reason and the structure of logic as defined, not by the dominant culture, but by the heritage of blacks. It is possible, after all, to be both passionate *and* reasonable.

The Contextual-Dialectical Method. Cone is convinced that the method of black theology must be derived from, and informed by, the data of black religion. He believes the best method is the "contextual-dialectical" one in which there is an on-going tension and interplay between black theology and the black religiocultural experience. This fourth component is important because it helps clarify how truth is perceived in black theology.

Rejecting the view that persons are capable of arriving at absolute truth, Cone explains what he means by saying that black theology uses the contextual-dialectical method.

> Truth is a happening, a divine event that invades our history, setting slaves free from bondage. This divine truth is not abstract or objective but is contextual and dialectical. To understand its meaning, we must be in the sociopolitical context of the liberation struggle. When theological thinking arises out of an historical context, it is of necessity dialectical, that is, paradoxical.[111]

This dialectical method points to the complexity of experience and how various paradoxical aspects interrelate. Unlike functionalist models which stress the unity or organic nature of society and the need to merely make a reform here and there when some element is out of harmony with the whole, the contextual-dialectical method enables us to see that there is a complex diversity of elements in society, each with special interests, and therefore in tension. The truth about anything, then, will not be found by pointing to a single aspect. Rather, truth often has a paradoxical quality about it. Cone gives the illustration of black theologians who, because of the situation or context of white racism, equated divine revelation with the liberation of blacks. By doing so they did not intend to emphasize the dimension of particularity while denying God's universalism. The paradoxical quality of their equating divine revelation with black liberation was "merely intended to affirm that there is no divine universalism that is not at the same time particular."[112] Rather than view universality and particularity as empty, abstract attributes of God, black theologians concretize them, thereby placing God in the midst of the marginalized. This translates into electing the latter for liberation in order that all persons everywhere may know that all are created for freedom.

Summarizing what he means by the contextual-dialectical method, Cone writes:

> Black Theology's reflections on liberation is derived from the social context of the black struggle of freedom, as found in our prayers, songs, and sermons. In these black expressions are disclosed the truth about our struggle. *Liberation therefore is not an idea but an event that happens in black history*, enabling us to know "We'll soon be free, when de Lord will call us home."[113] [emphasis added].

Latin American liberationists agree with this contextual dialectical method and apply it to their own situation. However, the methodological point of departure is different for black theology and Latin American liberation theology. Cone observes that the Latin Americans begin with Marxism and social analysis and move to Scripture "for secondary support." Black theologians, on the other hand, begin with Scripture and the historical and cultural experience of African Americans, and then move to social analysis for secondary support.[114]

Leonardo Boff, a Latin American liberation theologian, describes the order in which the three moments or mediations occur in the process of liberation. For him the theology of liberation begins with "a radical criticism" of social reality. The *socioanalytic mediation* comes first. Once the structural causes of a situation of oppression are known, one may then proceed to the *hermeneutic mediation*. This mediation considers the interpretive principle of liberation to determine what the Bible requires in the context of oppression. The third moment is action-response, or the *mediation of pastoral action*. These mediations are not separate and disconnected phases, but "constitute moments in a single dialectical movement, which is faith in search of efficacy and lucidity, in solidarity with the oppressed."[115] Boff leaves no room for doubt as to which of the three mediations he believes to be most crucial in the process. "The critical point seems to me to reside mostly in the first moment, that of the socio-analytical interpretation of historico-social reality...."[116] In any event, it is important to remember that Latin American liberation theologians tend to begin with critical social analysis and move to the Bible, while black theologians begin with the Bible and then proceed to social analysis.

Beatriz Melano Couch made a significant contribution to this aspect of Latin American liberation methodology at the Theology in the Americas

Conference in 1975. Agreeing that social analysis is the place to begin, she pointed to limitations, which, when eliminated, would strengthen this method of doing theology.

> ... we in Latin America stress the importance of the starting point, the praxis, and the use of social science to analyze our political, historical situation. In this I am in full agreement with my male colleagues of the Latin American theology of liberation, with one qualitative difference. I stress the need to give importance to the different cultural forms that express oppression, to the ideology that divides people not only according to class, but to race and sex. *Racism and sexism are oppressive ideologies which deserve a specific treatment in the theology of liberation.* [117] [emphasis added].

Critics argue that liberation methodology is confusing at some points, or at best remains in an undeveloped state. Liberationists respond that this way of doing theology is still relatively new. Rough areas remain that need smoothing out, but there has been much progress over the past two decades. Part of the difficulty of producing a coherent method for doing liberation theology lies in the fact that the several types have not been in dialogue very long. In addition, sociocultural, religious, and other differences have contributed to the difficulty of reaching agreement on some points. Cone was mindful of this when he reflected on the EATWOT dialogues and the effect on developing theological method. "Because black and Third World theologians have been doing theology for a short time, and doing it together for an even shorter time," he said, "we do not have a fully developed method for making theology." [118] This is not an admission that liberation methodology is defective, or that liberationists do not generally agree on the key points of methodology, for clearly they do. Rather, Cone merely points out that liberation methodology remains in a developing or processive mode. Indeed, because liberation theologians have sought to both identify and appreciate *difference*, agreement is of secondary importance.

This rather long chapter has sought to examine the meaning and methodology of liberation theology. Gutiérrez gives an excellent summary statement on the nature of liberation theology. It is not a new theme for reflecting, but a new way of doing theology. It critically reflects upon historical praxis, with a view to radically transforming systems of exploitation, as well as the church. The work of liberation theology does not end with critical reflection upon the world. Instead, it endeavors to be part of the process of radical transforming activities that lead to liberation. Writes Gutiérrez:

> It is a theology which is open — in the protest against trampled human dignity, in the struggle against the plunder of the vast majority of people, in liberating love, and in the building of a new, just, and fraternal society — to the gift of the Kingdom of God. [119]

We find in this statement much of what has been discussed in the present chapter.

It was found that though Cone had no problem giving a definition of theology in the early period of his development, some liberation theologians were disturbed by his early attempts at definition. Influenced by the theological systems of European and European American theologians and philosophers, Cone initially defined theology in terms similar to those who influenced his thinking while he was a seminarian and a graduate student. Allan Boesak challenged his early penchant for defining theology as "rational study," and urged a definition that more clearly distinguishes black theology from the traditional theology of which it was so critical. Cone was able to make the appropriate changes in his definition, later agreeing with Gutiérrez and other liberation theologians. Black theology is a theology of liberation. The point of departure is critical reflection on a prior religious and political context and commitment. It seeks to identify with, and understand the oppressive conditions of black people in the light of, and under the judgment of, the Gospel.

Although liberation theologies differ as far as sociocultural and political contexts, they share common methodological traits. Several of these elements have been discussed. They include commitment and involvement as the first step; the necessity of cultural identity and political commitment; the importance of the social sciences and political theory; historical and social praxis; the frame of reference; and the principle of the hermeneutic of suspicion. As a form of liberation theology, black theology shares these methodological traits, but it reflects upon what it means to be black. "Black Theology," Cone contends, "must uncover the structures and forms of the black experience, because the categories of interpretation must arise out of the thought forms of the black experience itself."[120] This chapter has also considered the effect of black experience upon liberation methodology, and how the points of departure of black theology and Latin American liberation theology differ.

We now have ample general background on the origin, meaning, and methodology of the theology that is so closely identified with the name James H. Cone. This prepares us for the discussion of the transitions or shifts in his thinking over the past two decades. No single theologian has done as much as Cone during this period to establish a solid foundation for black theology, and to raise some of the essential questions with which black theologians and ethicists must grapple in the twenty-first century. There are many other questions and issues to be raised and addressed, but Cone's contribution has made it possible to be much further along than might otherwise be the case.

The thesis of the present work is that though there have been both subtle and pronounced transitions in Cone's thought since the appearance of his first book in 1969, many of his present views appeared in rudimentary form at that time. Many of his more mature views are an outgrowth of what he implied during earlier periods of his development. In some instances there is merely an accentuation of earlier views.

There is much more substance in Cone's first two books than many critics have heretofore acknowledged. This, in part, is why I contend, against Witvliet, that *Black Theology and Black Power* (1969), not *God of the Oppressed* (1975), is Cone's most important book.[121] Cone's first text, laced with the power of anger and polemic, effectively laid the foundation for the later discussion of the importance of contextuality and the relationship between social and theological factors in *God of the Oppressed*. In the earlier book Cone asked questions different from those being raised by white scholars. He saw, even then, that where one is situated in society has much to do with the types of questions asked and the kinds of responses given. Also, when reading Cone's first book, one gets a sense as to why there was little dialogue between African Americans and whites. Witvliet's statement that *God of the Oppressed* "is written from the discovery of the contextual determination of all theology,"[122] can therefore be misleading, if he means that this discovery was not made until 1975. It would be more accurate to say that the "discovery" was actually made in Cone's first two books, and that his dialogues with Third World liberation thinkers, his critical assessment of the works of sociologists of knowledge, his further investigations into black religious and cultural sources, and his own maturation as a theologian enabled him to give a more pronounced and systematic treatment of the contextual determination of all theology. To get a clearer sense of the earlier forms of Cone's thought, one has to take seriously his frame of reference and the fact that his perspective is from the underside.

Cone says emphatically that *Black Theology and Black Power* is intended as a word to the oppressor — "a word to Whitey." However, if one reads the book closely and suspends judgment of Cone, it will become clear that his real aim in that text is altogether different. That is, I do not believe that Cone ever wrote "for" white people. Rather, from the appearance of his first book to the publication of *Martin & Malcolm & America* (1991), Cone has always written and done theology "for" black people. This thesis is the guiding idea of the next chapter.

3. For My People

THIS CHAPTER considers one of several themes that has always been present in the writings of James Cone, although it may appear to those who read his works too hurriedly that there was little evidence of it in his earlier works. The theme of this chapter might better be put in the form of a question: For whom does Cone write and do theology? To be sure, Cone states in his first book that the subject matter therein is "a word to the oppressor, a word to Whitey." This phrase is reminiscent of Malcolm X, who said that he decided while in prison that he would devote the rest of his life to "telling the white man about himself."[1] This notwithstanding, I shall argue that this early publication was also — and more importantly — a word to, and for, oppressed black people. In other words, at bottom, Cone has always done or practiced theology for his people. Likewise, Malcolm X always spoke the truth for blacks.

I therefore reject the view of Deane Ferm and others who contend that during the early period of his writing Cone was primarily interested in writing to and for whites, and that his predilection for writing for blacks is evident only in the middle and later stages of his development. Any person who reads the early works of Cone for the first time and draws such a conclusion may not be completely at fault, since Cone himself may have contributed to such misconceptions.

Those who read Cone's works closely will find that there is much continuity in his writings. Even amid all of his emotionally charged words, the early Cone knew — indeed, expressed from the very beginning — whose side he was on and for whom he would really be writing and doing theology. Like Malcolm X he did want to tell whitey a few things. It is difficult to imagine that anyone can read Cone's first two books today, and conclude that he failed to accomplish this part of his goal. The key question is, "Did he do all that he did, primarily *for* the white man?"

It may be argued that since much of Cone's writings were hammered out in the heat and struggle of the black power movement he did not believe that it was either necessary or useful to engage in arguments about his audience, about the need for socioeconomic analysis, or about the need for developing a global perspective. These were all themes that loomed large in later writings. The aim of these earlier writings, however, was not to present a balanced,

objective statement of black-white relations free of emotions and value-pre-
suppositions. In Cone's view the magnitude and longevity of black suffering
and pain were such that it was not possible for him or any black person to
overstate their case, no matter what white and black critics said.[2] Instead,
Cone believed that it was necessary to expose white racism in white theology,
the white church and community, and other structures controlled by whites.[3]
He made no secret of his own rage and anger during that period regarding
contemporary forms of white racism, the brutality and inhumane treatment
directed against blacks since the middle of the fifteenth century, and the silence and permissiveness of white theologians on the race question.[4]

In those days Cone believed that much of theology was too cool, detached, and uninvolved in the concrete flesh and blood issues in society.
There was too little commitment to life and death issues which affected black
people. It was time for the theological community to say something; to get
upset; to have the courage to express moral outrage, and then proceed to do
something about it.[5] Knowing precisely where and with whom he stood,
Cone felt compelled to say something from a theological perspective that
would acknowledge the mistreatment of his parents; their sacrifices, and
those of countless unnamed black ancestors at the hands of white racists who,
in most cases, claimed to be Christians!

Therefore, the question that this chapter raises and addresses is whether
there was ever a time when Cone wrote and did theology primarily for
"whitey." Some will contend that based upon admissions Cone made in his
first book, the issue I raise should be of no concern. However, this conclusion
should not be drawn too hastily. A closer examination of Cone's early works,
as well as later ones in which he reflects upon his early views, seems to support
the thesis of this chapter, viz, that Cone has always written and practiced
black theology for his people.

The title of Cone's book *For My People* (1984) suggests what I have in
mind. In this title he implies his commitment to and love for the black community, church, and heritage. Cone has always loved black people, which
does not mean that he ever hated white people. He has, however, hated what
whites have done, and continue to do, to his people and other people of color.
One senses in the title that he (like Malcolm X before him) is not concerned
about "the white man,"[6] if being concerned means spending time worrying
about what the latter thinks about his work as a theologian. Thirteen years
prior to the writing of *For My People*, Cone expended a lot of time and energy
lecturing "to" whites and issuing angry diatribes, as if he believed that once
they knew how blacks felt about whites' behavior in and out of the church,
they would straighten themselves out and begin taking the Gospel seriously.
This was also the approach of King, who, unlike Malcolm X, believed in the
essential goodness of whites.[7] "King assumed that the moral sensitivity of
whites would not allow them to violate the ideals of democracy and the moral

vision of the Jewish and Christian faiths. He believed they needed only to be showed and challenged to put into practice what they publicly proclaimed."[8] Yet there is also a sense that Malcolm X appropriated this method, although his rationale was different. For example, one of the myths about Malcolm is that he advocated violence against white people. The truth is that Malcolm was a *master of the threat of violence*. Peter Goldman characterizes this stance well. "One cocked one's fist and gambled that cocking it would be enough."[9] Although he claimed not to believe in the moral sense and essential goodness of "the white man," Malcolm may not have been absolute in this stance — whether for philosophical or pragmatic reasons — since he so often appealed to the threat of violence rather than explicitly encouraging violence. Nevertheless, Cone writes that "Malcolm thought the threat of violence was sufficient to scare whites into recognizing blacks as human beings."[10] This should not have been one of Malcolm's limitations, since he questioned whether the white man has an adequately developed moral sense.

Though his scathing critique of white theology and culture was appropriate at the time, and may even have done some small good, it was not long before Cone realized that there was something more important at stake than trying to convince white Christians that their practices contradicted the mandates of the Gospel. It was more important to give his own religious and cultural heritage prominence in his work. There was a state of emergency in the black community, and it was there that his time, energy, and talents were needed.

When one first reads *Black Theology and Black Power*, it is not difficult — although it is inaccurate — to conclude that Cone was primarily addressing white people. It is especially tempting to draw this conclusion when one reads the following statement:

> This is a word to the oppressor, a word to Whitey, not in hope that he will listen (after King's death who can hope?) but in the expectation that my own existence will be clarified. If in this process of speaking for myself, I should happen to touch the souls of black brothers (including black men in white skins), so much the better.[11]

From this quote it seems that Cone was addressing a white audience. But was this really the case? Read the statement again. There are two key phrases that are overshadowed by the opening line. These phrases are: "in the expectation that my own existence will be clarified," and "in this process of speaking for myself." The phrase, "a word to Whitey," is the one that usually impresses first-time readers of *Black Theology and Black Power*. It is as if this phrase leaps from the page, grabs the reader by the throat, and threatens holy hell or death if he or she does not decide right then and there to forget everything but... ! Few readers seem to remember that during this period Cone was at a stage when he was trying to find his own niche, to clarify his own existence. Should it not be understandable that he would speak primarily "for" himself, in hopes of obtaining this clarification? Cone wanted his theological peers to hear him, but this was of secondary importance. He had had enough experiences with whites in Bearden, Arkansas (where he grew up), Evanston, Illinois (where he attended seminary and graduate school), and elsewhere; he knew how they had responded to Malcolm and King; and he knew the long history of black-white relations well enough to know by the publication of that first text in 1969 that because of where whites are situated in American society, it was not likely that they would really be receptive to what he had to say. Yet it is possible that his affirmation that the words of his first book were "to Whitey" was an important part of the dynamic at work that would ultimately help him clarify his existence, and that of his people.

Black Theology and Black Power is characterized by a highly emotional tone. It is permeated with anger and passion. The reader's initial impression may be that the book is directed at racist white people. As indicated earlier, there is some truth in this; one has to be cognizant of what was fundamental to Cone at the time. Although he says that the book "is a word to Whitey," we must question whether it is accurate to say that whites comprised his primary audience in 1969. Was his statement in *A Black Theology of Liberation* (1970) that "this book is written primarily for the black community and not for white people,"[12] a new position for him? Or was this merely a more explicit statement of what, on balance, he basically tried to convey in the first book? Let's consider this for a moment.

In his first book Cone made it clear that he wrote as an angry black man; that he primarily spoke for himself; and that it would give him satisfaction if what he had to say influenced persons — white or black — who were willing to risk everything for the total liberation of the oppressed.[13] He said he would be pleased if those of "the John Brown School," i.e., those who would risk everything, including life and limb (both their own and that of others!) to gain the complete freedom of black people, listened and responded to what he had to say. But it was his own testimony and need to clarify the deeper meaning of his existence and reason for being that seemed more important to him than trying to make a point to white oppressors or to explain to them what they neither wanted to hear nor were willing to accept if they did listen. Surely by this time Cone knew the white mentality well enough to know that at best whites would hear him out, but this alone would not prompt them to take the radical steps necessary to contribute in significant ways to the liberation of blacks from racial oppression and economic exploitation. The implication is that Cone's deeper desire was to write for, and address his own people, a theme that was not stated explicitly until the publication of his second and subsequent books. However, upon closer examination of the first book, one can see that even there he was more interested in speaking to his people. A key problem, however, was that his deep need to vent his anger and fury over the "I don't give a damn about black dignity and freedom" attitude of many whites often overshadowed his deeper intentions. This need is further evidenced by his desire to speak for, to, and with black people about their plight in the United States and what it will take to gain liberation.

When one reads Chapter Four of *Black Theology and Black Power*, which deals with the relationship between the black church and black power, it should become clear that Cone's intention is to say a forceful, prophetic word to the leadership of black churches about their role in the black liberation struggle. Cone's is a harsh critique of the post–Civil War black church, but I am convinced that only one who loves the black church truly, and is aware of what it can become in the struggle for liberation would risk making such a sharp critique. Indeed, Cone has paid dearly for his criticism of the powers that be in the black church. Yet he has refused to let the black church off the hook as long as it is not in the forefront of the liberation struggle.

In three of the books written after the publication of *Black Theology and Black Power*, Cone made explicit reference to his audience. There is not even the slightest indication that he was writing "a word to Whitey." In *A Black Theology of Liberation* he states that he was writing for the black community.[14] He could not be more explicit than that. The book was written for members of the dominant white group only secondarily. "Whites may read it and to some degree render an intellectual analysis of it, but authentic understanding is dependent on the blackness of their existence in the world."[15]

Anticipating the principle of "ontological blackness" that would be introduced later in that text, Cone did not hesitate to say that most whites who read it will completely miss the point. Their understanding, he held, will be hampered by their "whiteness," i.e., their unwillingness to see through eyes other than their own; their attitude about who they are and where everybody else who does not look and act like them must be in relation to them. Cone was not, then, concerned whether whites read the book. Indeed, after the unfavorable reception his first book received from much of the white reading public, he was convinced that most whites who read his second book would not understand its meaning. In light of present day assessments of his theology by misinformed white scholars and students, it seems that Cone's prediction was accurate!

The Cone of this period knew that most whites would have difficulty with *A Black Theology of Liberation*. He had not, by this time, determined the reasons for this, but he knew that it had something to do with the vantage point from which whites see reality, and that from which blacks see and experience it. In other words, social context had something to do with it. At this stage he not only lacked the sociological tools to make sense of this, but he did not have the peace of mind to even consider it in a critical and systematic way. However, Cone was not completely unaware that dynamics similar to this may have been at work.

Insisting that ideas and concepts developed and espoused by white oppressors have little relevance for blacks, Cone made the point in his second
book that most whites who read it would conclude that it falls short of being
"rational." He believed they would exhibit such an attitude because they are
outside the "social matrix"[16] of the black community.

> Not understanding the oppressed condition, the oppressor is in no position
> to understand the methods which the oppressed use in liberation. The logic
> of liberation is always incomprehensible to the slave masters. In the position
> of power, masters never understand what the slaves mean by "dignity." The
> only dignity they know is that of killing the slaves, as if their humanity de-
> pends on the enslavement of others. Black Theology does not intend to de-
> bate with whites who have this perspective.[17]

Cone had not yet thought through the implications of this statement. Indeed,
this would not happen until the publication of *God of the Oppressed* nearly five
years later. But what is significant is that he recognized even in the 1970 publication that one's position in the socioeconomic order determines, or at least
has much to say about, the types of questions likely to be raised as well as the
answers given. Where one stands will have much to say about what is
legitimate and illegitimate, rational and irrational, logical and illogical. What
makes sense to the privileged and powerful may not make much sense to the
underprivileged and powerless. From where white theologians stand it is
difficult for them to understand the message of black theologians. Black theologians are the descendants of a people torn from their homeland like a baby
from its mother's womb, and forced into a form of slavery unparalleled
throughout history as we know it. It is not that the practice of slavery was new
or unknown on the African continent.[18] What was new about the enslavement of the Africans by the white man, however, was its cruelty and utter
disregard for black humanity and dignity. What is important here is that even
in the early stage of his development and at the height of his anger and resentment, Cone was aware that sociocultural factors affect how one perceives and
does theology. He developed this idea thoroughly in the middle period of his
development, although the seed was planted earlier.

Make no mistake about it. In 1969 and 1970 Cone was writing for black
people! He knew that only those whites who are "black persons in white skins,"
or "ontologically black," may hope to understand and appreciate the deeper
meaning of black theology. Whites in this group are so committed to the struggle for black liberation that they will do whatever it takes to make it a reality.
They, unlike "good white liberals," are neither put off nor appalled when blacks
say as Dan Freeman says in *The Spook Who Sat by the Door*: "I'll do any damn
thing to be free. . . . Anything whitey can do to keep me on my ass, I can do
double to be free and when I'm gone there are others to take my place."[19] That
there have been, and are, committed whites in the world, is easily verifiable.
The name of the nineteenth-century abolitionist John Brown comes to mind.

One has to be encouraged by the role of whites like Beyers Naudé in the black struggle against apartheid in South Africa,[20] or by the prophetic voice of an Abraham Heschel or Robert McAfee Brown in the United States.

The second book in which Cone states expressly that he writes for his own people is *My Soul Looks Back* (1982). In this testimonial (not biography) of his spiritual and intellectual strivings he reports the need to write for his people, since he shares with them a similar religious, social, and cultural tradition. "Because I am black *I am writing primarily to the black church community. It is my personal testimony of how I have struggled to keep and to live the faith of the black church*"[21] (emphasis added). Cone grew up in the black community and was reared in the black church. His father, proud and self-determined, refused to compromise his principles, even if this was the only way he could get along with whites in Bearden, Arkansas. His mother, a very religious, spiritually inspired, and God-fearing woman, believed that God would see black people through their trials and hardships. Though shielded somewhat from racist attacks when he was a youngster, Cone did experience racism firsthand in school, and especially when he went North to attend seminary. (No black child ever completely escapes confrontation with racism, as Martin Luther King, Jr., recalled regarding his days as a youngster living in a comfortable middle class environment.)

The third publication in which Cone explicitly asserts that he writes for African Americans is *For My People* (1984). "Although this book is addressed to all persons who are interested in the Christian Gospel and the human struggle for justice," he wrote, "*it is primarily addressed to the black church in particular and the black community in general*"[22] (emphasis added). It is revealing that though Cone expressly indicates his primary audience, he is aware that any person committed to the Gospel message of liberation may find his book valuable. This is reminiscent of his earlier reference in 1970 to the concept of blackness as ontological symbol. This universal dimension in Cone's writing — present even in his first book — gives lie to the criticism that his early theology was exclusivist, and that he only developed a more universal perspective in the middle and later periods of his development. Deane Ferm, a white theologian who is an able interpreter of "third world" theologies, grossly misinterprets Cone on this point.

Commenting on what he believed to be Cone's theological posture in 1975, Ferm accused him of exclusivism, inasmuch as Cone identified black theology with a black God and black people.[23] However, he maintains that two years later Cone was moving more in the direction of an inclusive and universal perspective. He also contends that Cone is "moving to the right and closer to the views of DeOtis Roberts and Major Jones, who see reconciliation as a key factor in liberation."[24] Ferm believes his assessment of Cone is correct, based upon statements Cone made to the Black Theology Project in Atlanta in 1977. Ferm quotes Cone.

> I think that the time has come for black theologians and church people to
> move beyond a mere reaction to white racism in America and begin to ex-
> tend our vision of a new socially constructed humanity in the whole in-
> habited world. We must be concerned with the quality of human life not only
> in the ghettoes of American cities but also in Africa, Asia, and Latin Amer-
> ica. For humanity is whole, and cannot be isolated into racial and national
> groups. Indeed there will be no freedom for anyone until there is freedom
> for all. . . . Liberation knows no color bar. Unlike oppression that is often
> limited to color, the very nature of the Gospel is universalism, that is, a liber-
> ation that embraces the whole of humanity.[25]

Ferm's error in interpreting Cone is typical of otherwise careful white theologians. Many of these scholars have not been able to get beyond what they
perceive as strong rhetoric in Cone's earlier works, although, once again,
Susan Thistlethwaite is a refreshing exception in this regard, and is forging
a different standard.[26] Only by following her example will white theologians
be able to grasp the profound truths in Cone's books. Presently it is nearly
impossible for white theologians, exclusive and narrow in their theology, to
read a radically different theological perspective (especially one coming from
within the ranks of the disinherited) openly and "objectively." In fact, as
pointed out earlier, there is evidence that many white theologians who feel
compelled to criticize black theology are not very familiar with the recent
literature. As for Cone's theology, critics ought at least to do him the honor
of first reading his words! In any event, I want to make two additional comments about Ferm's misinterpretation of Cone.

In the first place, Ferm implies that there was a period when Cone,
unlike Roberts and Jones, did not take reconciliation seriously. During the
seventies Roberts and Jones were among Cone's chief critics on this point. Yet
a close examination of Cone's first book reveals that he has always believed
that reconciliation has a major place in the struggle for liberation. Where he
differs from critics is his insistence that reconciliation comes *after* liberation
and justice have been achieved.

To be sure, a kind of spiritual liberation was achieved through the life,
death, and resurrection of Jesus Christ. Jesus freed human beings so they can
free themselves from all forms of bondage. The resurrection experience of
Jesus may be interpreted, in part, as spiritual reconciliation with God, which
is available to all who believe. Unfortunately, many people do not get beyond
this more spiritual reconciliation in order to see the relationship between this
and the concrete reconciliation that must occur in the social order. Reconciliation in the sociopolitical arena is not possible short of concrete liberation
and justice. In terms of power and sociopolitical positioning in society, une-
quals are irreconcilable.

Nowhere in his theological project does Cone disparage the idea of reconciliation. In his view liberation has always been its necessary precondition. Furthermore, the terms of reconciliation, according to Cone, are not to

be dictated any longer by those with their feet on the necks of black people. Contrary to the practices of many, reconciliation, for Cone, has never been a cheap option. Rather, if it has any value at all, it is costly. Whites are in no position to talk the language of reconciliation to African Americans as long as the conditions of oppression exist. Until the price of reconciliation is paid, Cone has no interest in even discussing the issue with whites and those blacks in agreement with them. In part that price has to do with long overdue reparations to blacks for over two hundred years of slavery and stolen labor, and another hundred and twenty-five years of racial discrimination in areas of basic opportunity such as employment, education, and housing.

Cone was critical of the view of Roberts and Jones that even during the oppression of blacks, it is important to seek reconciliation between the races. For Cone, there can be no reconciliation worth the name as long as there are oppressors and oppressed. Reconciliation can occur only between equals, i.e., only when there is shared power and privilege in a socioeconomic order in which the basic human needs of every person are met. Such a system will allow no person or group to accumulate a surplus of goods before fundamental human needs are met for everybody. Reconciliation can occur only when the supreme dignity of every person is honored. Roberts and Jones, as well as many white critics, e.g., Ferm, failed to grasp this crucial point. Ferm is mistaken when he contends that by 1977 Cone was moving more in the direction of Roberts and Jones that reconciliation is a key factor in the liberation struggle. Cone has never believed reconciliation to be of secondary importance. The point is that he has given it a location different from that of his critics, which in itself does not necessarily mean that it diminishes in importance. Blacks must play the key role in stating the terms of reconciliation. Even the most cursory reading of the chapter "Revolution, Violence, and Reconciliation" in *Black Theology and Black Power* makes this unmistakably clear.

In Chapter 2 I referred to Sobrino's discussion of the differences between European and Latin American theology. Sobrino is convinced that European theologians (and their American counterparts) generally attack concrete problems of life at the level of thought first and foremost. The problem of massive pain and suffering is seldom addressed in concrete ways. It gets thought about, criticized, and analyzed, but not solved! It often gets worked out only in the mind. This is not the way of the liberationist, who believes that the ministry of Jesus Christ is done when the hungry are fed, the sick, the widow and orphan are visited, and the captives are set free. In the face of human misery and injustice the first act ought to be an action-oriented commitment to do whatever it takes to eradicate such a condition.[27] It is not enough to solve or overcome human problems at the level of thought. Conditions that force persons to the level of nonpersons must be overcome at the level of life, which, after all, is the point where persons suffer.

White theologians, seminarians, and pastors know full well that God is reconciling the world and created persons to Godself through Christ. They understand this clearly in their minds. What they have not quite figured out yet is just what this means in relation to their devilish behavior in the world — behavior that keeps the races, genders, and classes apart. They have not, by and large, come to terms with what they ought to be doing about it. They know in their minds what is required of them, but they have not accepted this at a gut level.

The second comment about Ferm's misinterpretation of Cone is that Cone has always taken the universal dimension of the Gospel seriously. In this he was influenced both by his own understanding of the Gospel, and King's emphasis on universalism which "had to precede an acknowledgement of any form of particularism."[28] If one reads Cone's works systematically and carefully, it is difficult to miss the emphasis on the universal dimension in his theology. This aspect is present even in the first two books, despite the claim of critics that these are the most "exclusivist" of his works. I beg to differ with this criticism on at least two grounds.

First, even in *Black Theology and Black Power* Cone indicated that he was aware that blacks were not the only ones who were victims of oppression.[29] It can be argued that the contextual or particularistic dimension (stressed by Malcolm X) was dominative for Cone in the early phase of his development, but it cannot be argued that the universal element (which King made central) was absent.[30] Cone was aware that others besides blacks were victims of oppression, but the times were such that there was (and continues to be) a need for emphasis on black oppression. This is a point that black theologians cannot afford to compromise.

Secondly, in his first two books, Cone introduced a principle that makes it possible for whites to participate in the black struggle for liberation. In the first book he wrote of "black men in white skins,"[31] while expressly introducing the principle of "blackness as an ontological symbol" in the second.[32] In the latter text he stated that the focus on blackness did not mean that only blacks were victims of oppression. It is most unfortunate that Cone did not develop this principle systematically, nor drew out its many implications for the relationship between oppressed and oppressor in the struggle for liberation. Cone ceased using the term "ontological blackness" almost as quickly as he began using it. However, the concept or spirit of the term continues to be pervasive throughout his works. Blackness as ontological symbol connotes, in part, the universal aspect of oppression, a theme that is present in all of Cone's writings. That he has always insisted on the contextual character of all theology is not to be taken as evidence that at some point he undermined the importance of the universal dimension. Cone has tried to keep the particular and the universal in dialectical tension.

The question still before us is whether there has been a radical or pronounced change in Cone's earlier stance regarding his reading and listening audience. I think not. What has happened, it seems, is that over time he simply became much more explicit about the subjects of his deepest concern. The seed was planted in 1969. Cone wrote for black people in the late sixties and the seventies. He writes for black people today. The language of his early books often concealed this concern, causing many to see only the "word to Whitey." An overwhelming concern for his people, however, has always been present in his thought. In this regard we can see the influence of Malcolm X. Yet Malcolm admonished that blacks must forget about making an impression on the white man or trying to change his mind about them. Instead, they must focus on seeing themselves with new eyes and change their own minds about themselves. This essentially came to be Cone's view as well.

Writing for Black People: The Early Period

Upon completion of his graduate studies, Cone made a mistake that few young black scholars have been able to avoid. When he tried his hand at his first scholarly articles on white theologians and the so-called "death-of-God" movement, they were promptly rejected by editors of theological journals.[33] Upon reflection years later, he concluded that not only was his heart not in the writing of those articles, but the subject matter had nothing to do with his own religious or cultural experience. It said nothing of his experience of oppression, what the Gospel says about it, and what he and others who claim to be committed Christians ought to be doing about it. Looking back on this period he wrote:

> How could I continue to allow my intellectual life to be consumed by the theological problems defined by people who had enslaved my grandparents? Since there was nothing in Euro-American theology that spoke directly to slavery, colonization, and poverty, why should I let white theologians tell me what the gospel is?[34]

Cone slowly came to accept the reality that his entire sociocultural context was radically different from that of white theologians. How, then, could he think that his theological perspective would be the same as theirs?[35] Indeed, why would he even want it to be? White theologians simply could not know the trouble, the agony, and the pain that was so prevalent in his hometown of Bearden, Arkansas, and hundreds of black communities throughout the United States. White theologians could not know in a direct sense what it means to have black skin in America. They could read about it and they could be told about it, but they could not know that experience in quite the same way as blacks.

Cone could see that the experience of being black in America necessarily affected his own theology in ways that were totally different and unfamiliar to white theologians. This in itself makes it very tough, though not impossible, for them to adequately understand the black theological project that insists that the primary content of the Gospel is Jesus's proclamation of the liberation of the oppressed.

Through his later study of sociologists of knowledge Cone discovered the truth that all theological language, whether that of whites or blacks, is socially and culturally conditioned and determined. "The social environment," he contended in 1975, "functions as a 'mental grid,' deciding what will be considered as relevant data in a given inquiry."[36] Indeed, even in 1973 Cone was writing about what he then called "the social context of theological language." There was an awareness that African Americans and whites could not participate in effective dialogue precisely because they live in two worlds: that of the oppressed and that of the oppressor. He held that "thinking, or thought, can never be separated from our socio-political existence. If one is a slave, then one's thinking about God will have a different character than if one is a slave master."[37] Cone reasoned that if theological ideas are socially and culturally determined, then no theology (including liberation theology!) is totally neutral, value-free, and disinterested. No theology is totally unaffected by the sociocultural milieu out of which it emerges. One's place in the society will determine, to a large extent, the kinds of questions raised, and the answers sought.

As for the matter of the importance of writing out of the context of one's own experience rather than trying to produce publications that are unrelated to it, Cone was influenced by various black writers he read in preparation for the writing of his first book. James Baldwin was among those he read. Commenting on the importance of writing out of one's own experience, Baldwin wrote:

> One writes out of one thing only — one's own experience. Everything depends on how relentlessly one forces from this experience the last drop, sweet or bitter, it can possibly give. This is the only real concern of the artist, to recreate out of the disorder of life that order which is there.[38]

As a fledgling teenage writer, Baldwin was advised by Countee Cullen, then in his prime, to avoid trying to imitate other writers, and to write out of his own experience. Baldwin took this advice to heart,[39] as Cone did later.

It is difficult enough to write out of the context of one's own experience. It is not surprising that Cone met with frustration and rejection when he attempted to write about matters outside his own context. Unfortunately, this error is still made frequently by young black scholars and black students in predominantly white educational institutions. For example, white faculty members are often insensitive to black religious or cultural experiences. This is frequently the case because they either do not know, or care to know, about black experiences. Therefore, the papers of black students who insist on writing out of their own context are often not well received. In too many instances the grade says more about the instructor's rigidity, insensitivity, and blindness than the student's ability, and the quality and content of the paper. Cone experienced something similar to this while in seminary.[40] It is an experience that other African Americans can attest to as well.

In any case, Cone came to see that there is an inextricable, continuous interaction between theological ideas and the social environment. Theologians reared in different social contexts will not likely share the same theological perspectives, unless those who have been the beneficiaries of an oppressive and dehumanizing political and economic system radically reorder their priorities and thought patterns. What theologians think about God and the world in which they live is affected by where they stand in society.

> Like white theologians, black theologians do theology out of the social matrix of their existence. The dissimilarity between Black Theology and white theology lies at the point of each having different mental grids which account for their different approaches to the gospel. . . . What people think about God, Jesus Christ, and the Church cannot be separated from their own social and political status in a given society.[41]

Cone is not different from other liberation theologians in this regard. It is because of their suspicion that there are hidden assumptions in the traditional theologies of the dominant group that they have been able to see the importance of the social matrix out of which one's theology develops. From beginning to end, ideas are social in origin. This does not mean that the individual plays no part in the development and acceptance of those ideas, for humans are, after all, persons-in-relationship. This means that the individual both makes, and is made by, the community. The point to be stressed here is the intimate, though often unacknowledged relationship between our ideas and our social situation. In this regard the Cone of 1973–1975 probably could not have agreed more with Horace Cayton's contention that "we are all imprisoned within our culture. It is almost impossible to break through the customary ways of perceiving the world about us in order that we may question in a fundamental sense the values held by society."[42]

Cone must necessarily write to and for black people. There was much pent-up, deep-seated resentment, anger, and rage in him as a result of earlier experiences with white racism, such as his deeply disturbing experiences with the blatant racist attacks of some of the seminary officials and professors where he attended seminary. In addition, there is the matter of the inhumane treatment that all blacks have experienced in one way or another as a result of individual and systemic racism and economic exploitation. Cone's sanity and sheer survival were dependent upon his ability to find a way to creatively vent his frustrations and anger. The best mechanism, he concluded, was writing theology for his people; telling their story of suffering and trying to determine what the Gospel says about the condition of human bondage.

When Cone finally discovered that he simply could not write about the experiences of white theologians and theological movements that had nothing to do with his experience of suffering and pain, he began to find his voice. In addition, he found that when one "writes about something that matters to him or her existentially, and in which his or her identity is at stake, then the energy for it comes easily and naturally."[43] Writing, then, is no longer a drudgery or burdensome task that one wishes that someone else would do. Rather, it is therapeutic, and becomes a great joy. When Cone came to the decision that his ". . . intellectual consciousness should be defined and controlled by black history and culture and not by standards set in white seminaries and universities," he experienced a deep inner liberation and conversion that began to manifest itself in his writing in the form of both energy and passion.[44] It was all a matter of accepting who he was and accepting his history and culture; of deciding once and for all for whom he was going to write and do theology. It was a matter of clarifying his own existence and reason for being. Once he settled this for himself he was able to begin doing theology in ways that only James Cone could do it. He was no longer stifled nor worried about how his views would be received by the white theological establishment. His own creativity and imagination were liberated and made their way to the forefront.

It can also be said that Cone had to write out of the context of the black experience because only when he has expressed himself adequately here, will he be truly liberated enough in his own being to engage in and succeed in other tasks. Writing out of his own social and cultural context would itself be liberating. Perhaps in part this was what James Baldwin had in mind when he wrote about his rationale for having spent so much time writing about what it means to be black in America. "I have not written about being a Negro at such length because I expect that to be my only subject, but only because it was the gate I had to unlock before I could hope to write about anything else."[45]

Writing for Black People: The Middle and Later Periods

After the publication of *The Spirituals and the Blues* (1972) and subsequent dialogues and debates with other black theologians and pastors, Cone has tried to write more expressly out of the depths of his own experience and that of black experience generally. Although he has been critical of his religious and cultural heritage, he has also exhibited a strong sense of pride. Having delved deeper into the African and early African American sources of the black religious tradition, Cone has intentionally endeavored to liberate himself from over-dependence on the ideas and concepts of white scholars.

He feels so strongly about this that he has not hesitated to write about his own embarrassment as a result of his earlier "captivation by white concepts."[46] Such dependence was one of the major criticisms raised by several of his black colleagues during the early period. Charles Long, Gayraud Wilmore, and his brother, Cecil Cone, were among these critics.[47] It was a critique that Cone took to heart. He set out immediately to investigate black and African sources, and to incorporate his discoveries into his theology. His investigation helped him see that black story determines both the content and the structure of black theology. This idea is expressed forcefully in *God of the Oppressed*.

Cone has never contended that black theologians should completely divorce themselves from the concepts and categories of white theologians.[48] Yet some black theologians have argued for a complete separation. However, it is difficult to see, realistically, how this would be possible inasmuch as the history of black presence in this country is so intertwined with the history of whites. Blacks cannot avoid that sense of "twoness" that DuBois wrote about at the turn of the century[49]; the sense of being African on the one hand, and American on the other. King wrote about this tension as well.[50] It does not seem that blacks can expect much more than what King advised, viz, to recognize and accept the dilemma of being simultaneously of African descent, and American; make a conscious effort to discover the cultural inheritance of both; and be more intentional about taking their African heritage much more serious than in times past.[51]

For My People, No Matter What!

As implied earlier, it would not be accurate to say that when Cone first started writing he wanted primarily to address the white community, and that he initially had only a secondary interest in the black community and church. He did have some things to say directly to whites during the late sixties and early seventies, but the preponderance of the evidence suggests that his fundamental audience has always been the black community and church. In what way, then, can it be said that the subject of this chapter may be considered a transition in Cone's theological project?

In light of what has been said to this point, the shift or transition under consideration is very subtle indeed — not at all as pronounced as some of the other shifts in Cone's thought. Was Cone's early writing really a "word to Whitey" or not? Both yes and no may be the reply. Yes, because one cannot read Cone's early works and conclude that he did not tell the white man about himself. But no because his words to the white establishment and its keepers primarily served to pave the way to do what he really wanted to do, to speak words of truth to his own people. Black people needed to know that after the assassinations of Malcolm X and King, they still had witnesses to the black story among them. Like Malcolm and King, these had to be persons who did

not fear "the man" and would, like Esther, proclaim that they would go before
the powers, and if they perish, they perish! Like Malcolm and King, they
must vow to never sell out the people.

In a sense, what I have in mind is something like the relationship between revolution and liberation. Liberation is the ultimate goal. Revolution
is a means. Blacks do not really want revolution. They want liberation, but
it seems that the only way they will get it is through revolution. A similar
dynamic is involved in the relationship between Cone's "word to Whitey" in
the inchoate phase and what he really wanted to do. The word to whitey was
not the chief aim. Speaking the truth to his people was the goal. The word
to whitey had a cathartic effect, making it possible for Cone to speak a clearer,
more forceful word to his people.

Although Cone said that *Black Theology and Black Power* was a word to the
oppressor, he also said in that same text that his primary purpose is to address
black people! It becomes unequivocally clear in subsequent texts, however,
that his audience is the black community and church. This shift or focus
becomes much more pronounced in *My Soul Looks Back* and *For My People*. The
same idea was present in the first two books as well. Before proceeding to a
further discussion of why Cone made what appeared to be a shift in who he
wrote and did theology for, it may be helpful to say something about the two
major publications that make no direct reference to audience.

In *The Spirituals and the Blues* (1972) and *God of the Oppressed* Cone reveals
how seriously he took the earlier criticisms of his black theological colleagues.
Further, in both of these publications he expresses gratitude to his "black
brothers and sisters who provided a critique — both positive and negative — of
my earlier attempts to interpret the black religious experience. . . ."[52] By implication this suggests that there is a primary audience, black people. In *God
of the Oppressed*, Cone writes: "Because of the encouragement and critique of
my Black colleagues, I have been motivated to probe more deeply the
resources of the black experience as a primary datum for the development of
a Black Theology."[53] He expresses no concern about what whites think of him
or his theology. Gone are all signs of wanting black theology to be "accepted"
as a "legitimate" or "bonafide" way of doing theology. No longer is there concern about what whites think of the black theological enterprise. What is important is what black folk think about black theology.

By now we should be getting the picture that Cone must speak, not to
or for whites, but to and for African Americans. Cone has written that "liberation theology has been created by people who consciously seek to speak to and
for the victims of the economic and political injustices as represented in
racism, classism, and sexism."[54] Presently Cone is forthright about the role
of liberation theologians generally and black theologians in particular as
spokespersons for and with the black and other oppressed groups in a racist,
sexist, classist, and capitalist society.

In *My Soul Looks Back*, Cone contends that he was never concerned about white approval when he first began writing black theology. However, this may not be the whole story. He often found himself engaged in shouting matches with white theologians during the early period. If there was no need or desire for approval by his white colleagues, why the initial verbal fights with them? Why the feeling of frustration and disappointment when he was excluded from theological gatherings as in the case of the Theology in the Americas Conference in 1975? It is difficult to believe that Cone did not desire — at least initially — the approval of his white colleagues. After all, in the face of odds that whites generally do not have to confront, he successfully completed the requirements for the doctor of philosophy degree. He had earned the right to be a peer or colleague of other theologians. To have responded angrily when he was denied his place was a human reaction that he need not have played down.

Cone said that he "was writing for black people, and only they could stand in judgment of what I was saying."[55] There we have it! Upon reflection nearly thirteen years after the publication of *Black Theology and Black Power*, Cone writes that he was fundamentally concerned with addressing only those people who were in a position to judge his work — black people.

Therefore, although he wrote in his first book that he intended it to be a word to the white oppressor, one cannot dismiss his simultaneous burning desire to speak to, for, and with the black community. After all, he does say rather emphatically in that book that the very purpose of black theology is to "speak to and for black people as they seek to remove the structures of white power which hover over their being, stripping it of its blackness."[56] Since Cone was describing the purpose of black theology in this first book, it becomes clear that his fundamental concern was and remains black people. The goal of black theology "is not . . . to address white people, at least not directly."[57] The validity of black theology is not dependent upon whether whites are able to understand it or whether they accept or reject it.

One gets the sense that by the time of the publication of *My Soul Looks Back* and *For My People*, Cone had developed the position that writing for or to whites would at best be counterproductive. His travels throughout the Third World may have convinced him that any attempt on the part of black theologians to lecture to whites did little more than entertain them. Their social position, i.e., where they stand in society,[58] is so different from that of blacks that it is very difficult (not impossible!) for them to see what African Americans see. Far too many whites have shown that they are not willing to alter their sense of values radically enough to be able to identify with black suffering in any meaningful way. Many who speak the language of liberation in white churches and seminaries, for example, are not willing to make the sacrifices and changes that will contribute significantly to the total liberation of blacks.

Lecturing to whites about their Christian responsibility in the liberation
struggle, and trying to prick their consciences, has not led to positive radical
changes in the socioeconomic condition of blacks. Cone now sees that generally whites are just not serious when it comes to black liberation. Many listen
to his lectures, read his books, and are passionately outraged at white racist
practices, but only momentarily. "Tears yes, action never!" Many of these
people hear Cone's words, but his message of liberation never gets through.

The goal, Cone seems to suggest, is to do whatever it takes to direct
blacks and other oppressed groups to the path which leads to full liberation
in a radically reconstructed society. In yet another sense Cone's position is
similar to that of Malcolm X. He is not even concerned with the white man!
Presently Cone seems to be saying that it is not the proper business of black
theologians to entertain whites. No more name calling and finger pointing!
The primary concern is what the oppressed themselves can and must be willing to do to effect their total liberation. In this respect the struggle for liberation and the radical transformation or remaking of society must be "sub-
versive," not "superversive." That is, change must come from the bottom
rather than the top. The oppressed must play the key role in the liberation
struggle. They need not look for messiahs, another Malcolm X or Martin
Luther King, Jr. Writes Cone:

> As a people we have reached a critical juncture in our history: we must
> decide what kind of future to make for ourselves and how and with whom
> to make it. Will it be a future that is derived from the values of white,
> capitalist America and its European allies, or will it be formed from the
> liberating values of our own history and culture and of other oppressed
> peoples who are struggling for freedom throughout the globe? Will it be a
> future that is tied to the values of white religion, which enslaves the poor,
> or will it be defined by the liberating elements in black religion and the
> religions of the poor in all communities?[59]

Cone's concern is to generate a deeper sense of self-determination in African
Americans and other oppressed groups in this country and throughout the
world. The oppressed must decide the nature of their future, and whether it
will simply be a remake of white capitalist values wherein it will be guaranteed that only a few will prosper, and own and control the means of production and distribution, and where the masses will work hard their entire lives
with few returns. The oppressed must decide whether they will reject the
values of the dominant culture for a set of communal values that puts the
enhancement and well-being of persons and the community first. Will their
option and preference be for oppressed peoples? Will they look to Europe and
America for the solution to their problems, or will they look to Africa, Asia,
and other parts of the Third World? Will their future society be based on the
values of their own ancestors who began fighting for liberation from the moment of their captivity?

Cognizant of the long history of black suffering, pain, and struggle, Cone is also aware of the failure of the civil rights movement to effect structural changes that would have guaranteed a significant alteration in the lives of the people. When he reflects on this situation today he concludes that whites simply cannot be trusted to set at liberty their black sisters and brothers unless forced to do so through coercive measures. The concept of the hermeneutic of suspicion takes on a special meaning for Cone today. In his travels throughout the Third World he discovered that most nonwhites suffering from economic and political exploitation have at least two things in common: they are all people of color, and their oppressors are either North American whites, or Europeans! There may have developed in Cone's mind the image of white people uniting against nonwhites throughout the world. Kenneth Kaunda drew this conclusion about whites when he reflected upon the liberation struggle in Zimbabwe. "Beneath all the bluster and moralizing and cant," he said sadly, "one simple, crude lesson seems to be taught by the recent sordid history of Zimbabwe—whites of the world stick together!"[60]

The idea that whites always seem to be able to unite against nonwhites in the world may have added further to Cone's own suspicion and distrust of whites. Such a position seems to be born out by more recent events. How can the United States in good conscience bomb the Libyans, the people of Iraq, and storm Grenada when it barely raises a protesting voice against white racist murder and enslavement of people of color elsewhere in the world? Some may not see it as such, but others are standing in a different place, and therefore see it as more instances in which white people of the world unite against people of color, but cannot seem to unite against the exploits of each other. Indeed, where is the united voice and action of the Western powerhouses regarding the crimes against women and children in Bosnia?

Another reason Cone must necessarily write and do theology for his people is that he recognizes that the true liberators of the oppressed will—must—come from within the ranks of the oppressed. Those who have been wronged must be the ones to seek redress. This stance is not a novel one in the black socioreligious tradition. It is reminiscent, for example, of Henry Highland Garnet's call for resistance among the slaves in 1843.[61] This was also the stance of the nineteenth-century abolitionist Frederick Douglass, who came to believe, against many white abolitionists, that those who are oppressed must be the ones to sound the death knell to oppression. "Hereditary bondmen, know ye not who would be free, themselves must strike the blow?"[62] Douglass's stance marked a significant break with the well known white abolitionist of that period, William Lloyd Garrison. Douglass recognized, as did many of his black successors in the struggle, that black self-determination is an essential element in the fight for liberation. Though the assistance of committed whites should not be shunned, it is necessary that blacks themselves take the lead in the struggle. Whites have an important part to play, but it can be played out better in their own churches and community, which are bastions of racism.

Historically, oppressors have never voluntarily liberated the oppressed, or done so out of purely moral considerations. The principle to be gleaned from this is that the oppressed should not depend on their oppressors to set them free. Often those within the ranks of the oppressors who have made vows of commitment to the liberation of the oppressed have been willing to go only so far, and seldom have they understood why the oppressed themselves have wanted to be in the forefront of their own struggle. Many white liberals found themselves in this situation in the sixties when, during the second stage of the civil rights movement, blacks began demanding some role changes at the level of leadership. This proved disturbing for good white liberals, as King pointed out in *Where Do We Go from Here?*[63] Malcolm X's response to this issue was similar. "If we are going to work together, the blacks must take the lead in their own fight. In phase one the whites led. We're going into phase two now."[64]

Self-determination and a willingness to do whatever it takes to effect total liberation is the best hope the oppressed have of overcoming bondage. They must use their talents, gifts, and other resources to liberate their community. This is why Cone could give as the title of one of his books, *For My People.* The focus of his writings is on black people and their liberation from racial, socioeconomic, and other forms of oppression. It is they who must make this happen. No longer does Cone try to convince whites in or out of the church of the morality of the fight for liberation, or that the fundamental content of the Gospel is liberation.

Because of the state of emergency in the black community, African Americans can no longer spend time and resources trying to make sense of what whites think of their efforts to liberate themselves. Here Cone would not disagree with the nineteenth-century black nationalist Christian Martin Delany.

> I care but little what white men think of what I say, write or do; my sole desire is to so benefit the colored people; this being done, I am satisfied—the opinion of every white person in the country or the world, to the contrary notwithstanding.[65]

Contemporary black scholars like Manning Marable have taken a similar stance. In *Blackwater* (1981), Marable said unequivocally that "this work is written for black people and speaks to their condition. It is not written or designed for our oppressors."[66] It is crucial that African Americans hear this message. The magnitude of black suffering and pain is such that every ounce of energy, and every available resource in the black community must be devoted to the struggle against the forces of evil that seek to destroy. As long as the feet of oppression rest so heavily and securely on the necks of blacks they cannot afford to devote time and energy to what the oppressor thinks of how they seek to liberate themselves. There is no time to lecture to whites about their inhumane behavior. The message and work of liberation is to be directed toward the victims of oppression. In this regard Cone reflected on the early stage of the development of black theology:

> How could black theology retain its black identity by directing its message primarily to whites? Even during the earliest stage of black theology, its critique of the churches was always directed more to the white church than to the black church. This was probably due to its dependence on the black power movement, which leveled a similar attack on white society, and to the presence of a great number of black pastors and church executives in the white church as its interpreters. . . . We spent entirely too much of our time writing protest documents to whites, who, as we should have known, were not going to disinherit themselves of their privileges in order to relieve the suffering of the black poor. Reaction to white racism consumed too much of the mental energies that should have been directed to black churches in an effort to have them make Jesus' liberating gospel their primary concern.[67]

I have argued in this chapter that James Cone has always written for and to the black community and church. It must be said, however, that in the case of this first theme there is still a transition of sorts that occurred in his approach. The change is much more subtle than transitions to be discussed in subsequent chapters. The argument of this chapter has been that contrary to Cone's explicit statement in his first book that that was a word intended for whitey, the real — though often unacknowledged — intention was to address black people and the black condition of oppression. The first transition, then, is really a movement from an implicit to an explicit and more pronounced emphasis on who Cone's audience was when he began doing and writing theology. His deepest concern has always been for his people. We see this in his first book, *Black Theology and Black Power*, where he urges blacks to awaken from their slumber and regain their historical attitude of self-determination and resistance against oppression.

In the next chapter I shall explore a second transition in the theology of Cone. In this case I will consider whether, at the height of his anger, Cone had an awareness of the importance and necessity of social analysis in the struggle for liberation. Although Cone moved from a posture of angry diatribes to the socioeconomic analysis of racism and other forms of oppression in the black community, can it be said that there was ever a time in his theological development when some form of social analysis was not present? The next chapter seeks an answer to this question.

4. Socioeconomic Analysis in Cone's Theology

A STUDY OF HISTORICAL and contemporary struggles for socioeconomic and political liberation will reveal that during the initial stage the oppressed tend to respond to their condition with much passion, anger, and polemic. This is often the stage characterized by rebellion and protest, neither of which is identical with revolution. Revolution, if it comes at all, comes at a later stage. Often during the early period, the leaders resort to strong invective as a way of inciting the masses. Much emphasis is placed on consciousness raising, as well as putting the dominant group on notice that the oppressed will no longer accept their condition.

The early phase of liberation struggles is not generally a time when the leadership gives much thoughtful consideration to drawing up blueprints for the new society. Neither is it a time when much attention is given to critical social analysis to determine the underlying causes of oppression. It is enough that the leaders and their people experience the pain and suffering caused by racism, for example, firsthand. That the problem may be a power complex that is itself integrally enmeshed with other evil social structures of power is generally not a concern in the early phase either. It is, rather, a time when frustrations are expressed and efforts are made to rally the masses to take their destiny into their own hands. In addition to consciousness raising, it is a time for making the protests of grassroots people known to the powers that be.

During the initial stage of a liberation struggle, then, there may be a great deal of name-calling and finger-pointing. This happened during the period of the sixties and the emergence of contemporary black theology. There was much pent-up anger and nervous energy that needed an outlet before other facets of the liberation struggle, such as the development of a critical social theory and a blueprint for the new society, could be undertaken. The object was to let the powers that be know that the "beaten Christs" of the black community had had enough, and that they wanted the immediate eradication of racism and economic exploitation. The concern was not for the slow amelioration of the socioeconomic conditions of blacks, but for total, immediate change. Generation after generation of blacks had been told that

78

"these things take time." They wanted to be treated like human beings and to be respected as persons both in theory and practice, right now!

One might characterize this first phase of the liberation struggle as the conflictual stage. This is not to say, however, that there was not conflict all along. The problem is that as long as the oppressed are in a passive mode, conflict is inflicted upon them by the powerful and through societal structures. When they begin to raise their voices in protest the conflict continues, but they are now more in control of their destiny. The status quo becomes disrupted; the social equilibrium that protects the privileged and keeps the disinherited in their places becomes unbalanced, and the masses are no longer "behaving as they should"!

The first stage of the liberative process, then, is both an exciting, and challenging time. There are many opportunities for growth on both sides. Members of the dominant group often feel embarrassed; many of them have been heard to say, "They [blacks and others] are trying to force a guilt-trip on me." What dominant group members often do not see at this point is that the counter-conflict generated by the aggressiveness of the oppressed is healthy, and can ultimately lead to better human conditions for all. It means that for the first time in a long while there will necessarily have to be some give-and-take, and that the "forgotten of history" will no longer passively accept unjust, inhumane treatment.

Unfortunately it is often assumed that anger is both dangerous and unhealthy. It is dangerous, we are told, especially if it is uncontrolled. In such cases the angry person or group is accused of being irrational. "Irrational," by the way, is the response to almost anything of which the dominant group disapproves! "Anger is unhealthy," we are told, "in that it throws one off balance mentally, and prolonged cases of such anger may lead to serious breakdowns in bodily health." I think it appropriate to consider the role of anger in the early and later stages of the development of black theology, and whether this was deemed a positive or negative trait.

Anger and Social Analysis in the Early Period

In *For My People*, Cone discusses both the strengths and the weaknesses of the newly developing black theology in the NCBC documents from 1966 to 1970. He reports that, to its credit, black theology saw clearly the relationship between the Christian faith and the black struggle for liberation. Unlike white theology, it identified liberation with salvation.[1] This means that salvation takes on a more inclusive meaning. Not only must souls be liberated, but persons' bodies must be liberated from the suffering and oppression caused by sinful social structures.

Another positive point is that black theology, following the example of Malcolm X, was the first to expose and criticize the existence of individual and institutional racism in the white churches, condemning it as anti–Christian and as a heresy. It observed that the church cannot be Christian and racist simultaneously.[2] The newly emerging theology even challenged conservative tendencies in many black churches, though it was aware of the prophetic strain in the best of the black church tradition, and the fact that the black church is more consistently prophetic than its white counterpart. Unlike Malcolm, however, black theology pointed to both the strengths and limitations of the black church. Malcolm focused only on the negative aspects, which partly explains why large numbers of black Christians did not take him seriously.

There was also encouragement of a heightened sense of ecumenism among black churches. The newly emerging black theology was not concerned with ecumenism in the sense that the World Council of Churches and the National Council of Churches had been, i.e., in the sense of nationwide and worldwide denominational unity. Rather, it saw a tremendous need for black church unity. Black churches needed to break down the denominational and other barriers between them, and unite around the common theme of the liberation of black people. White-led church councils on unity were spending much of their time and resources promoting denominational unity, while many of their practices remained racist. Black theology was opposed to talking about denominational unity that was not linked to liberation and justice issues.

Looking back, Cone saw as one of black theology's greatest weaknesses, a tendency toward anger and emotionalism in its attack on white racism. In his later view, black theology of the early period was highly reactionary and lacked social analysis. Though Cone ultimately conceded that some degree of reaction was appropriate and necessary because of the enormous evil of racism, he later believed that "one's theological vision must be derived from something more than merely a reaction to one's enemy."[3] Yet initially he viewed anger as an acceptable response to the brutality of racism.

Some psychologists have argued that anger is a normal response to threats to one's life. Rollo May, for example, contends that "you ought to feel rage when someone is out to kill you; that's what anger is for biologically — an emotional reaction to someone's destroying your power to be."[4] Social psychologist Kenneth Clark says that it is unnatural for blacks, for example, to love white oppressors. Rather, he believes that anger and resentment are the more natural responses to racial brutality.[5] Regarding the predicament of black South Africans, Alvin Poussaint admonishes that, "Either you have to strike back or accept your own demise."[6] Anger, then, can often be a healthy, natural, human response brought on by an unacceptable action against a person or group. An angry response does not necessarily mean that one is being irrational in the process. Depending on the situation, an angry response may be the only reasonable one to give.

The angry response of black theology to white racism in the sixties and seventies was quite appropriate. But does this necessarily mean that those who were participants in the struggle at this juncture were totally oblivious to the idea that liberation would not come in on the back of anger alone? Was Cone, for instance, so completely consumed by anger and resentment that he believed that a few polemical lectures and theological treatises would alone be sufficient to end racism and other abuses to black people? Can it be said that an angry Cone was completely oblivious to the need for social analysis during the early phase of his development? Is there evidence of an awareness of either the need for this type of analysis of the problems confronting blacks, or evidence that Cone himself actually engaged in social analysis during the early years of his writing?

Indeed, Cone observes, fifteen years after the publication of his first two books, that one of the greatest weaknesses of black theology in the early stage was that it lacked social analysis.[7] Witvliet agrees with this, and says that social analysis was lacking in both the integrationist and nationalist strands of black theology in its inchoate period. He further contends that "the historical connection between racism and capitalism is not noted, far less that between racism and sexism."[8] Witvliet concludes that though the universal dimension was unquestionably present in black theology of that period, there was very little evidence of analysis of power relationships. Therefore, in his view black theology in the first stage was primarily a survival theology rather than a liberation theology.

However, I find it difficult to agree that social analysis was completely lacking in the early phases of black theology. Though it is surely the case that, generally, social analysis was lacking in the first stage, I am not convinced that the same can be said of Cone's contributions. No, there were no systematic attempts at critical social analysis during the early period. On the other hand, there seems to be ample evidence that Cone was both aware of the need for social analysis, and on occasion, actually gave signs of engaging in such. So one of the underlying questions of this chapter is, how shall we understand the idea that Cone moved from anger in the early period to social analysis in the middle and later phases of his development? Does this mean that at some point during the early period Cone spent the bulk of his time writing and issuing angry diatribes to white racists? Does it mean that it was only after his contact with feminist and Third World theologians that he began to see that racism is not the only social issue warranting a theological response? Was it only at this point that he recognized that racism is linked to other forms of oppression and has a historical connection with capitalism? To the latter question especially, Witvliet gives an affirmative response.

It was above all the critical questions of Latin American and feminist theologians which led black theology to leave behind the image of America

> as a closed society, as a white monolithic block, and to have an eye for racism
> as a power complex which is deeply entangled in other systems of domina-
> tion, which manifest themselves not only outside but also within the black
> community, systems which include sexism and the widening gulf between
> the black middle class and the hopeless situation of the black underclass.[9]

Witvliet, right about so much in his argument, leaves something to be desired
on this point, as the discussion in the present chapter will reveal.

In *For My People*, Cone contends that both Malcolm X and King were
more perceptive in recognizing the importance and necessity of social analysis than were black theologians and the clergy of the NCBC.[10] We know from
various references to King and Malcolm in *Black Theology and Black Power* that
Cone was influenced by both men, although more by Malcolm. Cone in fact
acknowledged this during the question-answer period that followed a lecture
he gave at the University of Dayton on March 6, 1986.[11] The significance of
this is that Malcolm was a keen social analyst. For example, he developed a
global perspective of the social question long before many of the "accepted"
leaders of the civil rights movement. Malcolm was able to connect the problem of racism and economic exploitation in the United States and other so-
called "developed" nations with oppression in Third World nations like Africa
and Asia. In addition, he was able to link these to capitalism. Furthermore,
Malcolm could see, several years before King, that nonwhites throughout the
world had a common enemy, namely, the white man.[12] Surely Cone, even
during the early period, was influenced by Malcolm's ability and efforts to unmask the hidden causes of black suffering and pain. In addition, although the
early Cone could not accept King's passion for absolute nonviolence in the
social struggle, he was aware of King's ability to analyze the problems and
to propose solutions. This too undoubtedly had an effect on the young theologian.

In his later writings on Malcolm and King, Cone concluded that both
men arrived at class analysis late in their lives, and neither developed it in
a systematic way. In addition, the concepts of integration and separation of
King and Malcolm, respectively, "as they inherited and developed them, did
not encourage them to view the American political economy as a primary
cause of oppression of blacks." Both the integrationist and separationist
schools believed the political economy in the United States to be fundamentally sound. What was wrong, essentially, was that blacks were excluded from
it! But Martin's and Malcolm's leadership was initially marred by their failure
to recognize the unsoundness of capitalist political economy.[13]

King read Marx while in seminary in 1949 and was clearly moved by his
analysis of capitalism.[14] Malcolm never read Marxist and socialist literature,
although during the last months of his life he dialogued regularly with Third
World socialists and young socialists in the United States. In this way he
gained an appreciation for socialism, but lacked the knowledge to give an

informed interpretation and critique of it.[15] His later speeches include criticisms of capitalism and positive comments on socialism, but he continued to primarily focus on race analysis, "and class analysis was always secondary."[16] This was primarily because so much of Malcolm's energy during the last months of his life was devoted to just trying to stay alive. This prevented him from being able to read socialist literature and to consider it in a comprehensive and critical way. Malcolm was clearly a revolutionary, but Cone rightly contends that he was *not* a Marxist revolutionary. Only gradually did Malcolm and King recognize the contradictions in capitalism, and that it was based on the exploitation of the poor masses by the rich few. According to Cone, King, more than Malcolm, reflected critically and seriously on socialism "when he realized that the black poor (as well as the white poor, a reality that surprised him) were getting poorer and the white rich richer, despite the passage of the much-celebrated Civil Rights Act and President Johnson's War on Poverty."[17] But because of the social climate in the United States and the general disdain for socialism, King was very cautious about his public utterances on democratic socialism. At SCLC staff retreats he often asked that all tape recorders be turned off whenever he wanted to talk candidly about capitalism.[18] Such caution made it as difficult for him to incorporate class analysis into his thinking as it did Malcolm.

Although Cone considered both Malcolm and King to be keen social analysts, both were limited because of their failure to fully incorporate class and gender analysis. This served to limit their race analysis as well. The early Cone was limited in this way too.

Pointing out that he did not deal with Marxism in his earlier texts,[19] Cone proceeds to say that this was due in part to shallow academic exposure to Marxism and to an internalized acceptance of the white middle class version of the American dream.[20] During the early period he actually believed that the achievement of this dream was possible for all Americans! Like Malcolm and King in the early stage of their work, Cone did not consciously view capitalist political economy as fundamentally unsound. However, there may have been some subconscious rumblings in this regard.

Although Marxist analysis is clearly absent in Cone's first three books, can it be argued conclusively that there was no social analysis present? After all, there was the influence of both Malcolm and King, both of whom Cone himself said (upon reflection) were sharper social critics than any of the pastors in the NCBC. Surely Marxism is not the only kind of analysis that will enable one to get to the cause of social problems in capitalistic systems. Why would it not be possible to arrive at a reasonably clear analysis of the problem and its causes without applying Marxist principles? Is it not within the realm of possibility that one can arrive at a conclusion similar to Marx's without necessarily using Marxist principles? Class analysis would simplify the task, but there may be other means. Empirical observation can reveal a connection between racism and economic exploitation, for example, but a tool, e.g., class analysis, is needed to critically analyze the relationship.

So I ask again, can we detect in Cone's early writings an awareness that something more than angry diatribes against traditional European American theology and white racism would be needed in order for black liberation to become a reality? That Cone did not yet know what the "something more" was does not necessarily mean that he was unaware of the need for this "something more" if there was to be any hope of liberation. In fact, a close examination of his first two books will reveal his recognition that some type of critical social analysis was needed. He had no clear guideposts, and he did not have a firm handle on a method. But he did seem to have an awareness of the need for social analysis.

There was much talk about the need for a radically reconstructed society in Cone's early works, but he lacked the critical tools needed to effectively analyze the American socioeconomic system. He knew that a key weapon was missing from his arsenal, but he did not know at the time what it was.

At this point I want to develop the hypothesis that Cone at least knew that something more than anger and emotionalism was needed in his early theological project. I do not want to read more into the early Cone than is actually there. At the same time, and in keeping with the theme of this book, I want to show that there is no sharp separation between the early and later Cone's awareness of the need for social analysis, and indeed that the roots of the later view can be traced to the early period. I think this can be done in a way that will not lead to giving him more credit in this regard than is warranted. Yet it is important to show that amid all of his anger and rage of the first stage we can still find substantial evidence of an appreciation for social analysis, even if he himself was not the refined social analyst of the middle and later stages.

As late as 1979 Cone was not willing to concede that his anger and so-called "intemperate" statements to white theologians during the early period were inappropriate.[21] Indeed, he felt then, and now, that the magnitude of the atrocities of Watts, Detroit, and Chicago elicited that type of response from blacks. The bruising of the egos of a few white male theologians was not of much consequence when one considered the brutality inflicted upon African Americans by racist whites and the structures they control. Cone was not concerned about engaging in cool, detached argument. From the vantage point of several years of hindsight he said that "the reality of Black suffering did not provide the context for such reasoned arguments."[22] From his perspective the response he gave was reasonable, and even if white theologians found it displeasing to engage him in discussion and debate because of what they considered "intemperate" remarks, he wondered whether this was the primary reason for their silence regarding black theology, or whether it was at best a smoke screen.

Statements like those Deane Ferm makes about Cone and Joseph Washington are the types that Cone finds problematic in this regard. Interpreting black theology, Ferm reveals no positive sentiments regarding the theological projects of some black theologians, because he believes they have closed themselves off to dialogue with white theologians. "The militant views of Cone and Washington," he writes, "made it difficult, if not impossible, for nonblack theologians to enter into dialogue with them."[23] Ferm and many other white theologians saw Cone as the villain in matters pertaining to black-white theological dialogue. Dialogue was hampered, according to them, because of Cone's alleged provincial outlook and his militancy. The real concern might have been Cone's unwillingness to allow white theologians to define the ground rules of the dialogue that was to take place. Neither would he allow them to define the theological enterprise for him. Having effectively taken this away from theologians of the dominant group who had been used to calling the shots, one can better understand why Ferm and others could conclude that it is "difficult, if not impossible" for whites to dialogue with Cone.

In any event Cone reasoned, there were black theologians, e.g., Wilmore, Roberts, and Jones, "whose language was more congenial to their theological etiquette."[24] But even these theologians were not taken seriously by many of their white counterparts. Cone concluded that there was some other reasons for their silence and disregard. So he did not hesitate to admonish white theologians to "keep your damn mouth closed, and let us black people get our thing together."[25] Although not the fundamental cause of the alienation between black and white theologians, such language did not contribute to unity either. This had much the same effect as Malcolm's sharp rhetoric regarding "blond haired blue eyed devils" and the oppressive nature of Christianity (as practiced by both whites and blacks).

Cone's basic concern was to identify the Gospel with the suffering, pain, and agony of black people and their fight for complete liberation. He cared little about the response of white theologians during that period. He was more concerned with, and helped by, the critique of black theologians. Besides, the point was not primarily to engage in dialogue with theologians of the dominant group, but to commit oneself to being in solidarity with the poor and oppressed and to take whatever actions necessary to effect their liberation.

Preferring that whites be reticent for a period of time and listen to blacks in order to really hear what was being said, Cone was clearly disturbed and angered by the appearance of two books on black power written by white scholars in 1968 and 1969.[26] He wrote of his disapproval:

> The problem with both books is the white audacity to speak at all, especially about Black Power. Who do they think they are, pontificating about their brutality against us as if they have a relevant word about black humanity? They should know that the long history of white silence on black liberation

renders their ideas irrelevant for both black and white people. Perhaps their
"nice" books might have been a contribution during the eighteenth or nineteenth century, but not today. Too much time has passed and too many
blacks have died because of the likes of this kind of rhetoric.[27]

In the 1986 edition of *A Black Theology of Liberation*, Cone admits that his sometimes "intemperate behavior" may have made it impossible for whites — "whose
intentions were more honorable than my responses suggested" — to engage in
meaningful dialogue with him.[28] In this regard he makes explicit reference
to the texts by Joseph Hough and C. Freeman Sleeper. Though he does not
include in the 1986 edition the earlier criticism he made of these authors,[29]
he does point out that in light of the long history of black suffering and the
silence of white theologians he simply could not always control either his pen
or his tongue. "It was not a time to be polite but rather a time to speak the
truth with love, courage, and care for the masses of blacks,"[30] he said.

The real problem, as Cone saw it, was that whites were silent when they
should have been vocal. The time for them to have expressed their prophetic
fervor was during American slavery, the Jim Crow era, the period when there
were scores of blacks being lynched. The time for them to be prophetic was
not when blacks were already asserting themselves (as in the middle and late
sixties), telling their own stories of pain and suffering; and trying to effect
their liberation. This was the time for whites to be silent and hear the stories
told by blacks. Just as African Americans desired to make their own protests
known; to plead their own cause during the abolition era of the nineteenth
century rather than sit back and passively allow good white people to speak
for them, blacks during the civil rights movement wanted to do the same.

Cone contended that it was too easy during the sixties for whites to
publish books on black power. There was no real cost or sacrifice in this practice for many white scholars, though there were financial and other benefits
for them. Whites need not have waited until black power had become "popular" before they began devoting energy to researching and writing in this area.
Cone viewed such contributions to the struggle as too little too late, and as
a way for white liberals to pat themselves on the back, implying that they had
made their contribution to the black liberation struggle.

At any rate, Cone believed that the decades of the sixties and seventies
were not times for blacks to be unemotional, detached, and polite. These
were times to speak the truth, and to do so with radical love, courage, and
tenderness for oppressed and suffering blacks. Cone's was indeed passionate
language. It was language that not only contributed to the alienation of many
whites (who were already alienated from blacks by choice!), but some blacks
as well. Much like Malcolm X, Cone's concern was not to soothe the consciences of otherwise good white people, but to state the case of the black community as strongly and as forthrightly as possible. Cone had little patience
with white theologians who wanted to discuss whether black theology was

"real" or "authentic." He was angered initially as a result of misrepresentations of black theology. He had no appreciation for characterizations of black
theology like the one given by Andrew Greeley, who described it as a "'Nazi
mentality,' a theology filled with hatred for white people and the assumption
of a moral superiority of black over white."[31] Understandably, Cone had few
kind remarks to make about such caricatures. What is interesting is that these
misrepresentations continue, and there are few signs of abatement!

During the early period of black theology, Cone made it unequivocally
clear that any white person who was even remotely sensitive to black self-
determination would never be so presumptuous as to attempt to speak "for"
black folk. It was inconceivable to him that whites could know how blacks
really feel about them. Those who are really sincere will "keep silent and take
instructions from black people." [32] The goal of black theology, he felt, was to
destroy everything white.[33] By this Cone did not mean what whites generally
interpreted such statements to mean, viz, the literal annihilation of all white
persons just because they have white skin. His real meaning had to do with
the destruction of everything that whiteness had come to stand for or symbolize in the United States and other parts of the world, e.g., the oppression
of nonwhites, economic exploitation of the masses, racism, militarism, neocolonialism, and so on.

Now, once again, is it conceivable that in the early phase of his development Cone could have been aware of the importance of social analysis? Is
there a sharp shift from the anger of that period to the more pronounced
recognition of the need for social analysis during the middle and later periods? Or is it really a matter of a change in focus or level of concentrated attention? It is to these questions I now turn.

6

An Early Awareness of a Need for Social Analysis

I am not convinced that Cone had no awareness of the necessity of social
analysis in the early stage of his theological project. Though he was not dependent upon Marxism during that period, he was surely aware of Marx and
even used the term "praxis," although there is no evidence that he had the
level of appreciation and sophistication that would equal the level developed
in the late seventies.[34] But the point to be stressed here is that Cone was aware
of Marx and believed him to have been a revolutionary who should be looked
at more closely by black Americans. It is also of interest to note that during
this early phase Cone was dependent upon an interpretive work on Marx,
Gajo Petrovic's text, *Marx in the Mid-Twentieth Century.*[35] Even in this period
one can sense that at some point in Cone's development Marx and the idea
of praxis would play a significant role in his theological project. Before proceeding with the discussion of Cone's attitude toward social analysis in the
middle period of his development, I want to consider implications in his first

two books that there was a need both for critically analyzing racism and related social problems, as well as an awareness of the need for actively engaging in actions that will lead to the eradication of oppression. The early Cone was clearly not as critical of capitalism and did not have the proper tool to critique it even if he had been, but there were instances when he wrote of his frustration with the American ethic of individualism and of capitalism itself.

One of the major limitations of the first phase of the development of black theology was its failure to engage in critical social analysis. According to Cone both he and the black clergy radicals of the NCBC proceeded on the naive assumption that nicely worded appeals to the moral sense of white people would move them to do justice and to commit themselves and their resources to the liberation struggle. They believed that racism and racial discrimination would be eliminated as a result of their appeals to the "Christian" consciences of whites. The radical black clergy believed "that if the contradiction between racism and Christianity were clearly pointed out to [whites], they would change and act in a Christian manner."[36] This was equivalent to believing that the solution to the race problem is, at bottom, more information and education. But it was also indicative of the belief in the essential goodness of whites, a view deeply rooted in black history and culture and which was promoted by King.

W.E.B. DuBois was under the influence of such naive thinking when he went to the University of Pennsylvania as an "assistant instructor" (although he lamented the fact that he was not allowed to teach!) in sociology in 1896. It was there that he engaged and completed the massive, classic, sociological study, *The Philadelphia Negro*. Wanting to do what he could to foster better race relations and to aid in the development of increasing understanding of what it means to be black in the United States, DuBois was initially confident that if people only knew the facts about race, i.e., scientific facts, this would be sufficient to lead to better relations between the races. He wrote about this in his *Autobiography*.

> The Negro problem was in my mind a matter of systematic investigation and intelligent understanding. The world was thinking wrong about race, because it did not know. The ultimate evil was stupidity. The cure for it was knowledge based on scientific investigation.[37]

The University of Pennsylvania had offered DuBois a "pitiful stipend," a one year appointment that did not allow him to teach, except "once to pilot a pack of idiots through the Negro slums"; and his name was never even entered in the school catalogue![38] Needless to say he was not offered a regular faculty appointment even after completion of the original assignment. He therefore accepted an appointment at Atlanta University, vowing to continue his scientific study of the difficulties of race and how these are intertwined with economic and political considerations. The program of studies of blacks was to be "primarily scientific—a careful search for Truth conducted as thoroughly, broadly, and honestly as the material resources and mental equipment at command will allow!"[39] But DuBois, like other blacks before and since, learned differently. The use of the word "primarily" in the previous quote may be interpreted to mean that he was no longer convinced that the solution to the race problem lay primarily in "detached" scientific study and more knowledge. Saunders Redding points out that by 1903 DuBois no longer believed that truth or an increase in knowledge alone would "encourage [or] help social reform."[40] He was discovering what Reinhold Niebuhr would write about thirty years later in *Moral Man and Immoral Society* (1932), namely, that more intelligence and knowledge about the nation's social problems are not alone sufficient to solve those problems. Mere appeals to reason and rationality are not likely to lead to the solution of social ills, particularly when exorbitant self-interest is involved, which is frequently the case. Individuals and groups do not engage in acts of human oppression simply because of ignorance. That persons are finally informed of their wrongdoing through social scientific study is no guarantee that they will voluntarily reverse their behavior.

In *For My People*, Cone includes himself each time he points to the failure of early black theologians to include social analysis in the struggle for black liberation. *We* were naive, he wrote, "because our analysis of the problem was too superficial and did not take into consideration the links between racism, capitalism, and imperialism, on the one hand, and theology and the church on the other."[41] Linking theology and racism came very slowly, for *we* "did not have the theological training" to adequately challenge European American theology. They knew that this theology was racist, in other words, but did not have sufficient theological training to articulate this theologically. This deficiency, this early inability to articulate the theological meaning of the relationship between Christianity and the black experience "created a theological ambiguity in the early NCBC documents." Cone maintains that this could have been obviated had "[they] . . . used the tools of the social sciences and . . . given due recognition to the Christian doctrine of sin. . . ."[42] Had they done this, he contended, they might have avoided such heavy dependence upon moral suasion as the means to social change. Their failure to engage in social analysis is the reason they lacked a program that would effect radical change. "It seems that *we* thought that change would occur through rhetoric alone. There is no analysis of the depth of racism or capitalism"[43] (emphasis added). And, if we subscribe to Witvliet's view, there was no analysis of the historical connection between racism, capitalism, and other forms of oppression.

In addition, Cone includes himself in several other places with black radical clergy of the early period who, he says, failed to engage in social analysis and the formulation of programs to eradicate black pain and suffering. In each instance he does not say, *they*, but *we*, failed to do this. Reflecting on that period he wrote of *their* naive response to the white churches' response to James Forman's "Black Manifesto" in 1969 which demanded a mere $500 million in reparations for several hundred years of forced black deprivation and stolen labor.[44] Black religionists were disappointed and angered by what amounted to white indifference, or at best the tendency to thank black Christians for initiating such a challenge, saying as otherwise good white people have often been heard to say, "We always appreciate being challenged to do more in the area of race relations." The general tendency is then to return to business as usual. Black religionists were naive to think that mere appeals to whites about the morality of reparations would prompt them to grant compensation. According to Cone, they seemed to think that if they could only make white religionists feel guilty enough about their mistreatment of blacks, this would lead them to take the necessary steps to liberate them. Cone thinks that Vincent Harding's critique of the NCBC documents of this period was on target.

Harding makes a careful analysis of these documents and then points to what he identified as the unfortunate tendency of the black clergy radicals to try to usher in the total liberation of blacks merely through rhetorical expressions designed to appeal to the moral sense of whites.

> Perhaps most importantly, [the documents] remind us that rhetoric has not often been turned into action, because rhetoric did not become analysis and analysis did not develop program and program did not lead to insistent, careful organizing of our people to effect radical change.[45]

According to Cone some of their mistakes and disappointments could have been avoided had they critically analyzed the existing situation of blacks, and taken history more seriously. There needed to be more conscious effort to develop program strategies that would lead to deep-rooted changes. Failure to analyze their situation and the methods they were using led to embarrassing moments, as in the case of black caucuses in white denominations. The continued existence of these caucuses depended almost solely upon the financial resources of these denominations. It was with these very churches that the black caucuses were doing battle. Understandably, most, if not all of these caucuses failed to accomplish any significant goals. As long as their existence depended almost exclusively upon what Cone characterized as "white" dollars, there is no assurance that they will not be co-opted, or that the funds will continue to be made available if the attack upon the funding source becomes too severe or radical. It was neither logical nor reasonable, Cone concluded, for the oppressed to depend too heavily upon the resources of their oppressors. Of course, if the economic resources came from within the oppressed community itself, Cone surmised that these concerns would be minimized. Once again, we see Malcolm's influence on Cone, who believed no black organization that depended upon "white" dollars for its existence would survive for long. Even if it did survive, it could not be effective in the liberative struggle because the commitment of many white philanthropic organizations to authentic black liberation is too shallow. "Any movement of freedom that is dependent upon the oppressor's support for survival is doomed to failure from the start."[46] So firmly does Cone believe this that in his own outline of a blueprint for the new black community, he is adamant that blacks not seek financial resources from the white church and community. Rather, they are to be totally dependent upon the resources of the black community and church.[47] The initiative to create, and the funding to support, programs that present a radical challenge to racism must come from the black community itself.

In their heated and emotional attacks on white racism, black clergy radicals of the middle sixties gave little thought to social analysis. However, as noted earlier, Cone believes that despite their blindness to class and sex analysis, both King and Malcolm were much more perceptive in this regard in that both were not only committed to the struggle for black liberation, but were good social analysts as well.

> The reason why King was and still is more radical than the clergy of the NCBC and other interpreters of black theology was the integrity of his commitment and the depth of his analysis. Commitment without analysis leads to romanticism and eventually to despair. Analysis without commitment leads to opportunism and eventually to a betrayal of one's people.[48]

In addition, Cone praised both Malcolm and King for having developed a global perspective on social problems and for having made the connection between racism, capitalism, and imperialism (though this became more focused nearer the end of their lives).[49] What Cone does not mention is that Malcolm developed an internationalist perspective several years earlier than King.[50] However, Cone acknowledges that the internationalism of both men "was their most important contribution to the African-American struggle for freedom in the United States." Because of them, "African-Americans have become much more internationally minded, supporting the antiapartheid struggle in South Africa and the struggles of the poor against the rich around the world."[51] Though neither King nor Malcolm was ever a professed socialist there are those who believe they were in fact socialists toward the end of their lives (whether they admitted it or not, and neither did).[52]

The Early Attitude Toward Marxism

Continuing with his criticism of black theology's initial failure to engage in social analysis, Cone writes of the aversion of the black church and community to Marxism. In part this has been due to "the mutual marginality of

Marxists and the black community, as well as the sectarian nature of the former and the reformist attitudes of the latter."[53] Black religionists have generally found it difficult to separate Marxism as an effective tool for socio-economic analysis from its more negative atheistic ideology. However, Cone maintains upon reflection on the period, that the clergy of the NCBC years would have done themselves and the struggle much good had they been able to utilize Marxism as an instrument for analyzing racism and related problems.[54]

What is crucial for our purpose is that Cone maintains that he did not deal with Marxism in his early texts, implying both that he knew too little about Marx at the time (which was true), and that he had no idea how useful Marxism could be in analyzing racism, capitalism, and other power complexes. Cone does not give himself sufficient credit regarding the latter half of the previous statement. Though I know of no explicit reference to Marx or even to an interpretive work on Marx in Cone's first book, there are instances in that text where he seems to speak the language of Marx without actually referring to the name. For example, he writes that "Black Theology believes that the problem of racism will not be solved through talk but through action. Therefore, its task is to carve out a revolutionary theology based on relevant involvement in the world of racism."[55] Here it seems that Cone desired to go beyond mere theory or reflection on racial injustice, to actions to eradicate it. The fact that he insisted on an action orientation in his first text suggests that his declaration that he did not deal with Marxism in his first two books is an overstatement, though it is true he does not deal with Marxism in a systematic and sustained way until later. There seems to have been an awareness that something more than talk and emotional outbursts was needed in the struggle.

By 1970 it was evident that Cone was at least aware of Marx (though only through a commentator). In Chapter Five of *A Black Theology of Liberation*, he quotes from Gajo Petrovic's book, *Marx in the Mid-Twentieth Century*, several times.[56] In addition, as noted previously he uses, but does not incorporate into his work, the term "praxis." Here he apparently was impressed with Norman A. Bailey's essay, "Toward a Praxeological Theory of Conflict," where praxis is referred to as "directed activity."[57] There is also evidence that he was reading selections by Karl Marx during this period.[58]

In light of Cone's admission that he did not deal with Marxism in his earlier texts, what can be said about his half a dozen or so references to Marx in *A Black Theology of Liberation*? I think at least two observations can be made.

First, there is no evidence that Cone had read enough of the primary source material by Marx to be knowledgeable enough to fully incorporate Marxist principles into his work during that period. He had not internalized or assimilated enough of Marx's thought to enable him to make what he later believed to be a necessary critique of capitalism, followed by a proposal for an alternative economic system that would be based on the principles of sharing and equality.[59]

It is telling that Cone made several references to Reinhold Niebuhr's book, *Moral Man and Immoral Society* (1932), in *A Black Theology of Liberation*. The Niebuhr of the early thirties had been considerably influenced by Marx. Niebuhr incorporated in that text many Marxist principles, as well as his own critique of Marx. There is every indication that the Cone of 1970 had a deep admiration for Niebuhr's book. Cone even contended that that text "moves in the direction of blackness."[60] The reference here, of course, is to blackness as an ontological symbol. Cone viewed Niebuhr's book as an "exception" to the "esoteric word game" that white theologians generally play with concepts like revelation and redemption, failing to make them relevant for the concrete world.[61] Cone also referred to passages in *A Black Theology of Liberation* that reveal the strong Marxist influence on Niebuhr during the thirties.[62] Though he did not explicitly call attention to the Marxist influence on Niebuhr, it is interesting that he had so much appreciation for such passages while developing his theological project.

Secondly, the references to Marx in *A Black Theology of Liberation* are instructive in light of the thesis of my book: Cone had *an awareness of Marx in the early phase of his development*. It is therefore possible to say that he was at least courting Marx at that time, but had no way of knowing how or even whether he (or black theology) and Marx would be compatible, especially when he considered the attitude of most black religionists toward Marxism. Cone knew neither the strengths and weaknesses nor the implications of Marxism for the black struggle for liberation. Though he did nothing with Marx in a systematic way at that time, Cone goes too far when he says that he did not deal with Marxism during this period. It is true, however, that the black clergy radicals of the NCBC failed to acknowledge the possibility that Marxism might be able to strengthen their message.

Social Analysis and the NCBC

Earlier it was found that when Cone reflected on the first phase of black theology he was critical of the failure of the black clergy radicals of the NCBC to engage in social analysis and to develop programs that would present a radical challenge to white racism. Cone included himself in this criticism, often saying, "*we* failed." It may have been a noble thing for him to do, but the evidence does not support the view that Cone had no awareness of the need for social analysis. Further, it appears that some social analysis was present in his early writings.

Cone was the only black professor at Adrian College in Michigan when he first read about the NCBC. Isolated in a community with a population of 25,000 with fewer than a hundred blacks, Cone wanted to join the NCBC, but did not know how to make the right contacts.[63] This was around 1967, approximately a year after the group formed. It was not until the publication of his first book that he actually joined. The NCBC had already issued its Statement on Black Power on July 31, 1966. It was a document that was radical in the sense that it supported the emerging phenomenon of black power. It was primarily a reformist document. For example, it was clear that the members of the organization still identified with America and its values and believed the American social system was basically sound, needing only an adjustment here and there. The document referred to "our country" and "our beloved country" as if blacks had reason to be in love with the United States and to support its basic values. It also spoke of giving "our full support to all civil rights leaders as they seek for basically American goals."[64] Although the black clergy radicals appeared to be trying to find the right handles to articulate their views, they were still too enamored by the integrationist approach of King and the method of moral suasion. There was no indication in the document of a willingness to break with the existing socioeconomic and political system entirely.

The point here is that Cone, not yet a member of the NCBC, had nothing whatever to do with this basically integrationist document, which was more rhetoric than analysis. Neither did he have a hand in the drafting of other documents produced by the NCBC, e.g., the statement on Urban Mission in a Time of Crisis (1968),[65] or the National Committee of Black Churchmen's Response to the Black Manifesto (1969).[66] The naïveté of the leadership is apparent in the latter document's offer to "participate in whatever conferences and negotiations may ensue from the demands of our brothers for the reparational relief of the suffering of black people."[67] They seemed to assume that Forman's presentation of the Black Manifesto in Riverside Church would alone be sufficient to cause white churches and philanthropic organizations to make reparations. The document then urged that whites in these agencies "receive these demands with the utmost seriousness." Again the assumption seems to have been that a mere appeal to the conscience or moral sense of whites would lead them to do the right thing regarding the issue of reparations. (It is interesting to note that even in *Moral Man and Immoral Society*, Niebuhr advised blacks to be wary of trusting the moral sense of white men!)

The key here is that Cone was not yet involved in the drafting of NCBC documents, and therefore it is neither accurate nor fair to include himself in the criticism that the black clergy radicals did not take social analysis seriously. As a matter of fact, his own ideas would not be evident in the documents until the writing of the Statement on Black Theology in June 1969. This statement, delivered at the Interdenominational Theological Center in Atlanta, bore "the unmistakable stamp of Cone's perspective and style."[68] Wilmore contends that the drafting of the statement was primarily Cone's responsibility.

By the appearance of the Statement on Black Theology, Cone's first book was in bookstores. Few of the members of the NCBC knew of him prior to the appearance of that book. Although many were pleased with the book, some found his scathing attacks on white Christianity and the black church disturbing. However, Cone's book did for many of the more receptive members of the NCBC what they themselves had not been equipped to do: provide a theological basis for relating black power and the Christian faith. Wilmore wrote of his own response to Cone's book:

> I remember someone giving me a review of the book from the Detroit Free Press in an unguarded moment. I whooped for joy. Here was a mature and scholarly presentation, albeit ebullient with youth, of what we could not find words to say from the first day that Benjamin Payton and I sat down in his office to compose the draft of the Black Power statement. Who was this young professor who articulated the faith of the new breed of Black churchmen as if he had been present at every interminable committee meeting and midnight bull session that had taken place among the members of the NCBC from its inception? It was for me a moment of spiritual exultation and I went out to find the book, which I read through in one sitting.[69]

In Wilmore's view, Cone, more than anyone before the appearance of *Black Theology and Black Power*, set the tone and described the content of black theology. No one cut the umbilical cord (that held the emerging black theology to traditional European American theology) as effectively as did Cone. Whether he knew it or not, Cone had become the "resident theologian" of the NCBC.[70]

When Cone got involved in the NCBC the tone and the mood of the documents being produced underwent considerable change. There was still a tendency to appeal to the method of moral suasion, but a spirit of black pride and self-determination was also present. In addition, there was evidence of restlessness on the part of NCBC members. There was a sense of urgency in their appeals to white churches that was absent in the earlier documents. One could sense that they were running out of patience, as is indicated in the following extraction from the Statement on Black Theology.

> As black theologians address themselves to the issues of the black revolution, it is incumbent upon them to say that the black community will not be turned from its course, but will seek complete fulfillment of the promises of the Gospel. Black people have survived the terror. We now commit ourselves to the risks of affirming the dignity of black personhood. We do this as men and as black Christians. This is the message of Black Theology. In the words of Eldridge Cleaver: "We shall have our manhood. We shall have it or the earth will be levelled by our efforts to gain it."[71]

There is no evidence of critical social analysis in that document. However, the next statement issued by the organization, "A Message to the Churches from Oakland, California" (November 1969), is more radical than anything that preceded it. Since the publication of Cone's first book made him a celebrity and the "resident theologian" for the group, and since he had a major hand in the drafting of the Statement on Black Theology, it is reasonable to assume that he had a major hand in the drafting of the Oakland document as well. In his stimulating analysis and critique of a number of the NCBC documents, Vincent Harding attributes the radical tone of the Oakland statement to the impact of the Black Manifesto that was delivered by James Forman in April of that same year.[72]

It would be a mistake to underestimate the influence of Forman on the Oakland document. Since the Black Manifesto was issued seven months before the appearance of the Oakland statement, the members of the NCBC had witnessed enough in terms of the nonresponsiveness and at best the indifference of the white churches to the demand for reparations, to know that little or nothing would be done in concrete ways. Many of them were angered and disillusioned by the response of the white churches. This in itself may have caused them to lean more in the direction of Forman, and to even state explicitly their refusal to back away from supporting the Manifesto because of its "anti-capitalistic implications."

But Harding leaves out an important factor for consideration here, the recent presence in the NCBC of James Cone, and the impact he was making on black clergy radicals. Also, there is the fact that just as in the case of the Black Theology document, the Oakland statement bore "the unmistakable stamp of Cone's perspective and style." Had Cone not used Malcolm's phrase, "by any means necessary," in his first book, the same phrase that appears in a slightly different form in the Oakland statement? Had he not written of the development of new values, black self-determination, and black unity in his first book?[73] When seen in context it was not just Forman (the nonchurchman) and the ideology of the Manifesto to which the NCBC clergy were reacting. Because of the impact of Cone's book, it is quite possible that the Oakland statement would have had a similar tone whether the Manifesto appeared when it did or not! But the point is that the Manifesto did appear. It therefore seems more reasonable to say that the Oakland document was inspired by the combined influence of its "resident theologian" (Cone) and James Forman (the nonchurchman).

Yet it cannot be denied that the Oakland document, with its welcomed new sense of radicalism, still lacked adequate substance and concrete proposals for programs that would bring down racist structures.[74] Yet Cone is not completely fair when he says that social analysis was totally absent in all NCBC documents. Though social analysis is indeed missing in nearly all of the documents, it can be argued that there is evidence in the Oakland document that strongly implies that the committee — perhaps due to Cone's influence — was at least on the fringes of social analysis.

The Oakland document made explicit reference to the idea of radically altering the existing system and establishing and implementing a new religious, cultural, economic, and political order.[75] There is awareness of oppression in the Third World, which implies an awareness of global suffering and pain[76]; awareness that white Americans as well as Europeans are engaged in oppressing others who do not look and act like them[77]; awareness that the historic black churches also have responsibilities in the liberative process[78]; and a recognition that it may be necessary to resort to means other than moral persuasion and negotiation in order to accomplish their objectives.[79] Such references are evidence of at least seeing the importance of social analysis.

This seems to be a case of being aware that there is a need but not quite knowing how to meet it at the time. This is not unlike the concern that Wilmore expressed after reading Cone's first book. He knew what needed to be said when he and Benjamin Payton endeavored to draft the Black Power statement in 1966. He just did not have the theological tools to connect black power and the Christian faith. That he and Payton were not able to provide the theological foundation that was needed was not necessarily evidence that they had no idea of what was needed. The same may be said of those who drafted the Oakland statement. There was an awareness of the need for social analysis, but the drafters simply did not have the necessary tools at the time. Yet there was evidence of an ensuing courtship.

Evidence of Social Analysis in the First Stage

I have maintained throughout this chapter that there is evidence in Cone's first two books of social analysis. It was not Marxist analysis, but he did have other tools at his disposal. No attempt will be made to present the early Cone as one who was a keen social analyst who intentionally sought to unmask the hidden ideologies in traditional Euro-American theologies and social thought. Cone had not yet matured enough to accomplish this task. My intention is to dispel the notion, fostered by critics (as well as Cone himself!), that there was absolutely no evidence of social analysis in the early literature on black theology. I want to go further than Cornel West, who is only willing to credit Cone's "latest writings" with evidence of social analysis. In my view there was not only evidence of the awareness of the need for critical analysis of racism and the economic system, but there were instances in which some attempts were made to critically analyze these. There was not a complete absence of social analysis during the early stage of Cone's writing. An examination of key passages in Cone's first two books will support this thesis. No attempt will be made to exhaust such passages.

Is There Social Analysis in Black Theology and Black Power?

I have placed a question mark after the title of this section because some will undoubtedly refer quickly to Cone's own assessment of the first phase of black theology and his conclusion that *their* analysis of the problem of black suffering and pain was too shallow and superficial. There was a failure to adequately connect or consider the links between racism, capitalism, and imperialism.[80] Because of this shortcoming Cone concludes that *they* (himself and the black clergy radicals) were naïve. I do not wish to argue against the idea of the superficiality of the analysis of that period, nor the failure to see the connections between racism, capitalism, and imperialism. When one scrutinizes the documents of the NCBC the inevitable conclusion is that there was a high degree of political naïveté among black clergy radicals. The documents also revealed their inability to see the relationship between capitalism and the social problems adversely affecting blacks. What I take issue with is Cone's suggestion that social analysis was absent during the first period, and in his early writings (including his written contributions to the NCBC). Whatever might be said about the level of naïveté and political unrealism of most of the NCBC clergy, it cannot be said to the same degree about the young Cone.

Cone tells us that one reason *they* failed to link theology and racism, for example, was because they did not have sufficient theological training to adequately challenge the traditional theologies.[81] But this was not the case with Cone! He was already the recipient of the Ph.D. degree in systematic theology. The criticism he makes may well have applied to most of the members of the NCBC, but it did not apply to him in quite the same way. Now of course, if Cone's criticism was that no one in the group was trained in social and political theory, Marxist and other forms of social analysis, we may agree with him wholeheartedly. But this is not the criticism he makes. His contention is that the members of the organization were not sufficiently trained theologically. If this is what he really meant, he cannot include himself. Admittedly, during the first period he was still under the influence of the teachings of white theologians. There is strong evidence, however, that even during this period he was working to overcome this limitation. He was trying to liberate himself "from the bondage of white theology," and "any direct dependence upon [his] white theological mentors."[82] This is indicated by his many references to black writers and social scientists in *Black Theology and Black Power*, and the reference to his belief that it takes time for black theologians to separate themselves from the thoughts of white theologians.[83]

Having been trained in predominantly white seminaries and graduate schools, most black theologians find that they have to go to school all over again in order to learn what the black religious and cultural heritage contributes to theology and ministry. This has usually meant setting up a disciplined program of reading and reflecting on historical and contemporary African and African American literature (including histories, slave narratives, auto-biographies, sermons, novels, and other works) *after* the doctorate has been earned! This is another instance of how blacks need to do twice as much as whites in order to perform essentially similar teaching responsibilities. "And then whites have the audacity to ask why Blacks do not do more to help themselves. It's because they are tired from always having to do twice as much as white folks!" as the Rev. William A. Jones so aptly put it. It is to their credit that having struggled through graduate school with their white peers, black theologians are able to find that second and third wind to then turn their attention and energies to learning more about their own history and tradition in order to be able to speak a comprehensible truth to their people.

Cone's problem was not that he did not have theological training. Rather, he had not liberated his mind from the overbearing influence of white theologians he studied in seminary and graduate school. The ensuing dialogues with black colleagues would ultimately push him to do an in-depth study of black and African sources of the black religious and cultural tradition. This would take him a long way toward relieving himself of over-dependence upon white sources.[84]

Cone contended that during the early period he and NCBC clergy seemed to think that mere moral suasion alone would lead to the desired changes in the black struggle for liberation.[85] Indeed, that was precisely the case, but only prior to Cone's involvement with the organization, which would have been before the delivery of the Statement on Black Theology. It has been shown that in the Oakland document there is evidence of an awareness that something more than appeals to the conscience of white Christians and non–Christians would be needed to bring about liberation. Cone also addresses the tendency of black religionists to issue resolutions against racial exploitation and other social problems and to assume that this alone will move the powers that be to mend their evil ways. In an especially revealing passage in his first book, Cone writes:

> But we must warn our black churchmen that there are dangers in making confessions and writing papers. It is so easy to think that a careful, rational articulation of the problem means that the oppressor will concede and cease his work of dehumanization. But the evaluation of the problem is merely the first step in problem-solving. The black church must be willing to proceed with a concentrated attack on the evils of racism. It also must realize that the war is not over because one battle is won. The fight against injustice is never over until all men, regardless of physical characteristics, are recognized and treated as human beings. When that happens, we can be certain that God's Kingdom has come on earth.[86]

Well worded theological documents are not likely to press the dominant group into meaningful, radical actions on behalf of the oppressed.

The phrase "evaluating the problem" appears to have reference to analyzing the problem. So some level of analysis was taking place during the first
stage! It was not deep-rooted analysis capable of unmasking and exposing all
of the hidden assumptions behind traditional theology and politics, but at
least some attempts were being made to do so. Yet Cone recognized that it
was absolutely essential that they move to the next level, that of "a concentrated attack on the evils of racism." Unfortunately (and this happened frequently during the early period), Cone did not give us a clue to the nature
of this concentrated attack. But we have to keep in mind that at this point
in the struggle it was very difficult for him to draw out all the implications
of everything he said. However, because the early Cone, like Malcolm X, was
not opposed to retaliatory violence which aims at liberation — not vengeance —
it may not be going too far to say that the concentrated attack Cone referred
to in the previous quotation was not to be limited to the more "acceptable"
strategies for liberation. Something more than talk would be needed. It must
not be assumed, however, that Cone was in complete accord with Malcolm
X's policy of self-defensive violence. Philosophically he supported Malcolm's
stance that blacks should do whatever is necessary to protect, defend, and
enhance black dignity. But pragmatically he was closer to King's insistence
on nonviolence. Presently he believes self-defensive violence makes African
Americans even more vulnerable to white violence. "Martin rightly insisted
that defensive violence cannot be used by a 10 percent, weaponless minority
as a program of social change."[87] Cone concluded that in this regard King was
much more realistic and profound than Malcolm. "On the issue of violence,
Malcolm's value system was hardly different from that of the whites he
criticized." Cone argued that blacks had to survive if there was to be any
chance of liberation, and their chance of survival is greater through nonviolence than self-defense as an action policy. Both self-defense and "survival"
strategies like nonviolence root deep in black history. Although most African
Americans shared Malcolm's view of self-defensive violence rather than
King's commitment to nonviolence, Cone believes King's was the more
responsible and helpful stance.[88]

Yet Cone was adamant that moral suasion must be supported by "relevant action." In terms of the church's failure to be prophetic and to be an instrument for the liberation of the oppressed, it may mean walking out of
communion services, or withdrawing one's membership from a given denomination, or from all denominations! It may mean that a "more forceful confrontation" is needed.[89] Those who accuse Cone of being concerned only
about the liberation of blacks should consider again the passage where he
argues that injustice will prevail "until all men [he might have said persons!],
regardless of physical characteristics, are recognized and treated as human
beings."

In another significant passage, one which I believe is the most indicative of the presence of social analysis in Cone's first book, he calls for the inter-relatedness of love, justice, and power and is critical of what might be called "microcharity" efforts by otherwise-good white people. Such efforts are often intended to placate blacks and the poor on the one hand, and appease white guilt on the other. Cone contends that blacks should reject handouts and de-mand instead to be treated like persons with infinite dignity and worth.

> It seems that whites forget about the necessary *interrelatedness of love, justice, and power* when they encounter black people. Love becomes emotional and sentimental. This sentimental, condescending love accounts for their desire to "help" by relieving the physical pains of the suffering blacks so they can satisfy their own religious piety and keep the poor powerless. But the new blacks, redeemed in Christ, must refuse their "help" and demand that blacks be confronted as persons. They must say to whites that authentic love is not "help," not giving Christmas baskets but *working for political, social, and economic justice, which always means a redistribution of power*. It is the kind of power which enables the blacks to fight their own battles and thus keep their dignity[90] [emphasis added].

Here it seems that Cone is aware that the nature of the problem confronting blacks has a level of complexity that a sentimental kind of love characterized by microcharity, or good deeds that solve merely the problem of immediate pain, hunger, and so on, simply cannot adequately address. Microcharity or the meeting of immediate needs, is a principle and practice that must be in-cluded in any adequate Christian social ethics, but by itself is inadequate. Cone was aware that another principle needed to be included—a principle that goes beyond (but includes) the meeting of immediate needs to determin-ing the causes of the needs. This may be termed "macrocharity." This princi-ple requires a critical look at the sociopolitical and economic structures in order to determine whether the nature of the system itself is such that prob-lems like poverty, racism, sexism and classism are inevitable concomitants. Clearly, in the early phase of Cone's development, he at least seemed to be aware that justice for African Americans is possible only through a radical redistribution of power. He was aware of the need for critical social analysis, but did not have the tools necessary to effectively engage in such analysis in 1969. This leads to the issue of whether there was progress in this regard by the appearance of his second book.[91]

Is There Social Analysis in A Black Theology of Liberation?

Upon examination of Cone's second book we detect more passages that reveal his awareness of the importance of social analysis, though here again it is not evident that he had the necessary social science tools. One detects, as indicated earlier, an awareness of Karl Marx in the second book that was not present in the first text, but there is no evidence of his familiarity with

Marx's own writings. Rather, he has a vicarious relationship with Marx, basically through secondary works. There also seems to be evidence in *A Black Theology of Liberation* of Cone's ability to analyze the social system in order to determine what it is capable of doing to those who rebel against it.

One rather striking passage that implies Cone's sense of the need for a radically reconstructed socioeconomic order, for example, appears at about the midway mark in his second book. Here one finds Cone expressing concern that black theology avoid the mistake of putting new wine into old wineskins.[92] Cone did not explicitly link this metaphor with the socioeconomic system, but the implication was surely there. Did the reference to new wine and old wineskins merely have to do with religious matters? Cone himself admonished the black theologian to "be especially careful not to put this new wine (the revelation of God as expressed in Black Power) into old wineskins (white folk-religion)."[93] The parenthetical reference to "Black Power" points to the political implication of the "new wine." Surely one can interpret this concern that black theology not run the risk of putting new wine into old wineskins to mean that Cone had a sense of the need for a radically transformed social order. If the structure (the wine bottle) is corrupt, it does not matter how often or how much the contents (the wine) are changed or reformed. Corruption inevitably has the last word in such cases. The contents will degenerate into something less than what it began as if the structure itself is not replaced. It is necessary to change both the contents and the structure, a truth of which the early Cone was aware.

In *For My People*, we find Cone expressing his disappointment that black clergy radicals of the early period failed to give serious attention to the Christian doctrine of sin.[94] Once again his actual wording implies that he too was guilty. But in *A Black Theology of Liberation*, he does a more than adequate job of analyzing the concept of human sin from a black perspective.[95] According to Cone's analysis the oppressed know more about human nature than anyone else because of their encounter with "both the depravity of human behavior from the oppressors and also the healing powers as revealed in the Oppressed One."[96] As victims of long years of suffering and pain, they are not as confident about the goodness of human nature as some, particularly white oppressors. Blacks certainly are not as confident about the goodness of human nature in whites. They know too that sin means more than selfishness.[97] According to Cone's analysis, blacks have "experienced the brutality of human pride."[98] The reference to human pride reminds one of Reinhold Niebuhr's primary description of sin. For Niebuhr, sin is pride in any one or a combination of its several forms, pride of power, of knowledge, and of virtue.[99] What is important is that Cone's reference to "the brutality of human pride" in his analysis would seem to imply a Niebuhrian influence on his early doctrine of human nature, and few religious scholars analyzed the doctrine of human nature as thoroughly as Niebuhr did in the early forties.

It is important to point out that when Cone says that only the oppressed know what human nature is because they have experienced both the "depravity of human behavior from the oppressors," and "the healing powers as revealed in Jesus Christ," he does not mean that only white oppressors are depraved and tend toward human pride. Anyone who has read his critique of the black church in his first book[100] knows that he was just as aware of corruption, human depravity, and sinful pride among blacks. Cone was not suggesting that whites are inherently more depraved and susceptible to the sin of pride than blacks or any other group, for he recognized that the color of one's skin or the nature of one's gender does not make wrong right! A close reading of his first two books reveal, however, that because of racism and the radical imbalance of power and privilege in the United States, whites have more opportunities and resources to engage in depraved behavior toward other groups (which is not to imply that these other groups are somehow better off because they have been deprived of power and privilege!). Because of the nature and longevity of black suffering and pain, it is understandable why Cone was inclined to point only to the depravity of whites. Suffice it to say that Cone gave a reasonable and realistic analysis of the doctrine of human nature, and therefore the criticism he makes of himself and black clergy radicals that they did not consider seriously enough the depth of human sin does not apply to him in quite the same way it does to them.

Before moving on to a consideration of Cone's more mature understanding of the importance of social analysis I want to point to at least two other passages in *A Black Theology of Liberation* that imply either his awareness of the necessity of social analysis, or his actual involvement in it during the first phase. One of these pertains to his concern about whites who are outraged about social problems thousands of miles away, while showing little or no concern for similar problems in their own local community. More specifically, Cone wondered how whites could be so concerned about the devastation and destruction of life in Vietnam when the destruction of the black community in the United States had been in process for several hundred years without significant, sustained outcries and appropriate actions from whites. Cone's effort to analyze this situation is revealing, especially for one who allegedly failed to take social analysis serious in the early phase of his development.

> The destruction of black humanity began long before the Vietnam war and few white people got upset about it. It is therefore appropriate to ask, "Is it because white boys are dying in the war that whites get so upset? Can we expect them to be equally involved in the destruction of their racism when the war is over? In view of their lack of concern for the oppression of black people before and during this ungodly massacre of Vietnam, is it likely that whites will turn their energies toward the oppressed in America?"[101]

Cone concluded that in view of past and present attitudes toward blacks, it was expected that after the war ended whites would once again be free to deal with the race issue "the same way it always deals with any problem: Declare to black people what is required for them to exist, for their presence, and then proceed to destroy everyone who thinks otherwise."[102]

How is it possible, Cone wonders, for whites to have been so concerned about the war in Vietnam, while simultaneously ignoring the miserable condition of blacks — a condition primarily caused by whites! When viewed through the eyes of the oppressed there is nothing logical about this. If there is any logic in it at all it may be that Cone said all that needed to be said about it at the time. "The one way I can understand this logic," he wrote, "is to see it for what it is — the logic of oppressors."[103] Being white, he reasoned, it is understandable that the oppressors would become concerned about humanity when whites were being destroyed. Cone recognized the inconsistency and hypocrisy of the tendency of many white liberals to claim solidarity with the oppressed in other countries, while failing to commit themselves and their resources to the elimination of black suffering and pain in the United States. In this context he quoted Jean Paul Sartre approvingly: "The only way of helping the enslaved out there is to take sides with those who are here." This is the same type of advice that Third World theologians have given to liberal European Americans who have been so outspoken against apartheid in South Africa, while remaining strangely silent regarding racism and capitalistic exploitation in the United States.

In what may be the best example of Cone's use of social analysis during the early period, he gives an excellent analysis of what the social system will do to those who rebel against it. He also unmasks some of the causes of suffering. This appears in his discussion of freedom and suffering. Cone contends that the truly free person always participates in the liberation of those who are oppressed. But when one asserts their freedom in this way, they inevitably encounters the sociopolitical structures of oppression, and the keepers of these structures will view this as intolerable and unacceptable.

> When the rulers first perceive that one is a menace to the society, their initial response is to try to silence the undesirable by cutting off the sources of physical existence and social involvement. This is to remind the rebel who's boss. The oppressors hope that by making it difficult to live, the rebel will come around to seeing the world the way the rulers view it. Coupled with economic oppression is social ostracism. The intention is to demonstrate the perversity of the rebel's involvement by picturing him as the destroyer of the "good." At no time is the rebel given the opportunity to define his way of looking at the world, because the mass media belong to the oppressors who will not permit the seditious presence to extend itself.[104]

If these several types of harassments fail to break the spirit of the rebel, the system may resort to political and "legal" means to force submission and compliance. This is what happened to the top leadership of the Black Panther Party of the sixties.

Liberation, freedom, is not a gift or prize that is given willingly by oppressors. In a political economy that is more concerned with profit-making than making the most of all persons, liberation must be demanded, and ultimately taken, by some type of coercive means. No mere appeal to reason and moral conscience will lead to liberation. Malcolm X contended that never in the history of the United States has the government done the right thing by blacks because of its moral sensitivity or because of its "internal good will."[105] In addition, power does not understand mere verbal appeals for justice, fairness, and liberation. Power understands one thing only — power! Since Cone was influenced by Malcolm, he probably learned this from him as well. "Power," said Malcolm, "recognizes only power," and it will take a step back from nothing "but more power."[106] If the oppressed are to be liberated they will have to learn to communicate with oppressors in ways they can understand. If one expects to be understood one does not speak German to a person who speaks only French, Malcolm admonished. By the same token one does not confront a man who has come to lynch you by proclaiming how much you love him (and all of your other enemies). Chances are he will not understand what you are talking about. You will not have communicated effectively. Your neck dangling at the end of a rope will undoubtedly be the consequence. "Find out what language a person speaks," said Malcolm, "speak their language, and you'll get your point across."[107] Lynchers are more likely to understand retaliatory violence than turn the other cheek tactics. From a pragmatic standpoint the early Cone was closer to Malcolm in this regard. Presently he is sympathetic philosophically, but is pragmatically supportive of King's survivalist nonviolence approach.

There are other passages in chapters Six and Seven of *A Black Theology of Liberation*, which suggest an awareness of the need for analyzing the structures of society.[108] I think, however, that enough has been said for now to support the contention that social analysis was not completely absent from Cone's early writings. I now want to examine Cone's present stance on the importance of social analysis in the theological enterprise.

The Necessity of Socioeconomic Analysis

It has already been established that Cone was influenced in various ways by both King and Malcolm X from the time he first began writing theology, though in many (not all!) ways he was more influenced by Malcolm. He had intentionally moved in the direction of black power even before King's assassination, although it was this latter event, more than any other, which served as the catalyst intensifying the level of energy that enabled him to write *Black Theology and Black Power*.[109] However, Cone never overlooked the fact that King's life and work made a significant impact on him. This is evident from the publication of his first book, and in a very pronounced way in his last

(*Martin & Malcolm & America*). If King and Malcolm were influential for Cone, and if he believed both men to be far ahead of the black clergy radicals of the NCBC regarding the seriousness with which both took social analysis,[110] it seems to follow that when he himself began writing theology there would be evidence of awareness of the necessity of critically analyzing social problems that affected blacks. The evidence suggests that Cone was aware that this was a necessary ingredient in any authentic liberation movement, even if he was not as intentional about including this aspect in his early works.

In the Preface to the 1986 edition of *A Black Theology of Liberation*, Cone contends that though his view of European American theology is basically the same as it was when the book first appeared in 1970, there are four "significant shifts" (I call them *transitions*) in his theology during the sixteen year interval between the appearance of the two editions.[111] One of these transitions considered to be the correction of weaknesses or limitations, according to Cone, related to his failure to give serious attention to an economic and class analysis of oppression.[112] This admission is actually related to his contention that there was an absence of social analysis during the first period of black theology. Though it is difficult to date the more intentional shift to including social analysis in Cone's work, a good guess would be that the transition began to occur during the interim between the publication of *A Black Theology of Liberation* (1970) and *The Spirituals and the Blues* (1972). In the Preface of the latter work Cone acknowledges the critiques of "black brothers and sisters" of his earlier efforts to interpret the black religious and cultural experience.[113] Though that particular book was really a response to the criticism of Cecil Cone, Long, and Wilmore that his theology was really in need of *blackenization*, it is difficult to imagine that Cone was not already thinking more deliberately about the place or role of social analysis in black theology during this period. After all, in the 1972 publication he describes black music as both social and political.

> It is social because it is black and thus articulates the separateness of the black community. It is an artistic rebellion against the humiliating deadness of western culture. Black music is political because in its rejection of white cultural values, it affirms the political "otherness" of black people. Through song, a new political consciousness is continuously created, one antithetical to the laws of white society.[114]

Cone must have been thinking about the necessity and role of social analysis in a more intentional way during this period, for even before the appearance of *God of the Oppressed* (1975), he was trying to make sense of why it was so difficult for black and white theologians to communicate effectively. Why, he wondered, was it so difficult for oppressors to really hear and respond meaningfully to those who were trying to do theology out of the context of their experience of oppression?

By 1973 Cone was already writing about his "conviction that thinking, or thought, can never be separated from our sociopolitical existence. If one is a slave, then one's thinking about God will have a different character than if one is a slave master."[115] In other words, all theological language is conditioned by where one stands in society. He was convinced of the integral relation between social context and theological ideas. Surely during this period Cone was intentionally thinking about the need for social analysis — the need to look for causes and links between social problems; to unmask and expose false ideologies that are hidden in theological and political postures. Surely he was thinking about the impossibility of doing the real work of liberation theology if one does not know the real truth about oppressive sociopolitical and economic structures.

Cone came to believe that social analysis could generate hope for change, and any analysis that did not lead to such hope must be defective.[116] Since theology is the second act, the first step is commitment and solidarity with the poor and oppressed to do whatever it takes to gain their liberation. Social analysis therefore becomes a necessity since the liberators will need to know what the problems are, their nature, and their deepest causes. Only when such analysis takes place will they be able to develop the types of programs and strategies that will lead to a radically transformed social system. Social analysis enables us to know who the poor are and why they are poor. "Social analysis," Cone writes in his mature period, "is a tool that helps us to know why the social, economic, and political orders are composed as they are. It enables us to know who benefits from the present status quo."[117] It also helped him to see that the oppressed must not lock themselves into playing by the oppressor's rules if their aim is total liberation and empowerment. As Audre Lorde put it:

> For *the master's tools will never dismantle the master's house.* They may allow us temporarily to beat him at his own game, but they will never enable us to bring about genuine change.[118]

Cone would learn, through his dialogues with Latin American liberation theologians — from the time of their first real discussion of similarities and dissimilarities between their theologies in 1975 — that in order to do the deeper, more comprehensive analysis necessary for the work of liberation, he had to take class analysis much more seriously. In short order he also learned that class and race analysis are not complete without gender analysis. Classism and sexism are discussed in the next chapter.

On page 2 of his first work Cone wrote, unapologetically, that the book was being written out of a particular attitude — an attitude that would not allow him to approach his subject in a cool, detached way. He was furious over the way blacks were being treated, and he did not care who knew it or who was offended by it. He was writing as "an angry black man, disgusted with the oppression of black people in America and with the scholarly demand to be 'objective' about it." He expressed his disinterest in being detached and dispassionate in his discussion of black suffering and pain. He seemed to be aware that many white scholars, following the tradition of Max Weber, believed it impossible to carry on a rational discussion of an issue if one is emotionally involved. Cone, on the other hand, proceeded in the tradition of Weber's rival, Gustav Schmöller, who believed in the value-laden approach to social science which did not demand a detached, dispassionate approach, partly because it was not possible to approach any study with total value-neutrality.[119] This was also the position of black social psychologist Kenneth Clark, whom Cone quoted several times in his first book.

As late as July 1983, Cone could say before a group of Catholics that he would not endeavor to be "objective" and "fair" in his analysis, inasmuch as "these terms are often used by the powerful in order to control the words and actions of their victims in the struggle for justice."[120] Too much had happened; the blood of too many blacks had been spilled, to talk about approaching the problem of black suffering objectively and dispassionately. Indeed, for Cone, the only way of approaching the discussion of this problem was through as much passion and emotion as he could muster. This is not to say that Cone had no concern for careful scholarship. But this does not have first priority when it comes to speaking the honest-to-God truth about black oppression. What the opponents of this view seem to hold is that the admission of value premises and passion in a study precludes the possibility either of objectivity or of careful analysis of the issues. Through the use of social analysis and sociology of knowledge liberation theologians have shown convincingly that there is no such thing as total detachment and objectivity. "We cannot be 'objective,'" writes Cone, "but must recognize with Imamu Baraka, that 'there is no objective anything'—least of all, theology."[121]

I think the aim of this chapter has been achieved, but in addition to what has already been said as to why the social analysis of the first period of black theology was as shallow as it was, there are at least three other observations that can be made. First, deep-rooted social analysis was simply not a priority for early black theology. This is consistent with the pattern of many liberation struggles in their early stage. Most of the energies of black theologians went into reacting to policies and demands. In addition, it was all that the black clergy radicals of the NCBC could do to formulate the outlines of a new way of perceiving and doing theology. They experienced enough difficulties with this task, let alone having to develop "proper" tools to engage in critical, comprehensive social analysis.

In the second place, there was a tremendous amount of emotion during this period. There was a deep need to "speak one's peace"; to get some things off one's mind; to tell whitey about himself! In a debate with Bayard Rustin in the early sixties Malcolm became furious when accused of allowing emotionalism to enter the debate.

> When a man is hanging on a tree and he cries out, should he cry out unemotionally? When a man is sitting on a hot stove and he tells you how it feels to be there, is he supposed to speak without emotion? This is what you tell black people in this country when they begin to cry out against the injustices that they're suffering. As long as they describe these injustices in a way that makes you believe you have another 100 years to rectify the situation, then you don't call that emotion. But when a man is on a hot stove, he says, "I'm coming up. I'm getting up. Violently or nonviolently doesn't even enter into the picture — I'm coming up, do you understand."[122]

Black clergy radicals also had a need to vent their frustrations. This state of mind and attitude generated a lot of rhetoric. However, if one looks closely, one will discover many useful principles of an emerging theology, especially in the works of Cone.

Although Cone knew that his emotional protests would not lead to radically transformed structures in society, he was convinced that what was being said both needed to be said, and needed to be said the way it was being said. He knew it would take a revolution to effect the kind of liberation he was talking about, and he understood the difference between protest and revolution and believed both have their place in the liberation struggle. Grace and James Boggs illustrate this difference rather well.

> Rebellion is a stage in the development of revolution, but it is not revolution. It is an important stage because it represents the "standing up," the assertion of their humanity on the part of the oppressed. Rebellion informs both the oppressed and everybody else that a situation has become intolerable. They establish a form of communication among the oppressed themselves and at the same time open the eyes and ears of people who have been blind and deaf to the fate of their fellow citizens. Rebellions break the threads that have been holding the system together and throw into question the legitimacy and the supposed permanence of existing institutions. They shake up old values so that relations between individuals and between groups within the society are unlikely ever to be the same again. The inertia of the society has been interrupted. Only by understanding what a rebellion accomplishes can we see its limitations. A rebellion disrupts the society, but it does not provide what is necessary to establish a new social order.[123]

Telling the white man about himself was necessary in the first phase of the struggle. This was the rebellion stage of the emerging black theology. It was not sufficient, however, to bring a radically reconstructed society into existence. Some black religionists may not have been aware of this, but James Cone knew, even during this period, that only a revolution could bring about a radically reconstructed society. Revolutions overturn and destroy corrupt systems to clear the path for systems of justice for all.

Thirdly, black theologians of the first stage — whether more influenced by the integrationist approach of King or the black nationalist-separatist approach of Malcolm X — were themselves committed to the capitalist system and interested in making it within the context of the present economic structure. They thought that capitalist political economy was itself an essentially sound system. Their desire was that blacks, especially the middle class, be included. They wanted their piece of the American pie. Most did not know (nor care to know) enough about Marxist social analysis to critique capitalism and consider replacing it with a more democratic economic system. Cone himself was a capitalist during this period, but he remained open to new possibilities regarding political economy.

To have begun writing theology, as Cone did, with feelings of anger and moral outrage is not inappropriate in itself. In fact, it ought to be encouraged! Most liberation struggles begin in emotional outrage and prophetic protest against oppressive conditions. The point is to have the wherewithal to move beyond this phase to begin engaging in the critical analysis of undesirable oppressive conditions. But the key is that the oppressed themselves must decide how much passion to exhibit or not to exhibit. The dominant group's position is so morally untenable that it cannot tell the oppressed when they have moved far enough beyond the protest stage that they are now in a position to deal with the problem in a "rational" and "acceptable" manner.

We must accept Cone's admission that he lacked sufficient social science tools to adequately analyze the economic structure of the United States and to relate the evils of that system to racism and other forms of oppression. Yet he was both aware of, and at times engaged in, social analysis during the inchoate period of black theology, even though he did not have the tools necessary to critically analyze the economic system. This is why he was initially unable to see the links between racism, capitalism, imperialism, and later, sexism. When he began to take Marxism more seriously in the second stage and to engage in dialogues with Third World theologians, he was able to make the deeper analysis which was absent during the earlier stage. In part it was because of his study of Marxism,[124] sociologists of knowledge, and his dialogues with Third World liberation theologians that his perspective on oppression began to expand. He was also being challenged by women. Whether or not he ever held a limited or narrow view of oppression, i.e., whether he ever believed blacks were the only oppressed people in the United States and that theology had only to do with their plight, is the subject of the next chapter.

5. Developing Perspective on Oppression

THERE ARE SEVERAL important questions to be addressed in this chapter. Has there ever been a time when Cone's theology excluded white people? Was he ever only concerned about the liberation of blacks? Was he aware, in the early stage, of other forms of oppression? How does he handle the problem of particularity and universality in his theology?

When Cone speaks in the early phase of saying *yes to blackness* and *no to whiteness*; of accusing white Christianity and theology of being the anti–Christ, did this mean the total rejection of white people? Did it ever mean that? What does Cone mean when he admonishes whites to hate their whiteness and begin asking how they can become black?[1] Did he mean to convey the idea that no person with white skin is capable of espousing an authentic version of the Christian faith, and that none are ever to be trusted in the liberation process?

Often accused of being an exclusivist and a racist after the publication of his first two books, it is interesting to observe that Cone suggests in at least three places in his first book — in varying degrees of explicitness — that whites can and must be part of the liberation process.[2] For example, he speaks of "black men in white skins" in the first text,[3] implying that there may be whites who are sincere in relating the Gospel to the liberation of the oppressed; and more specifically he refers to blackness as a state of mind, a state of being, or as a way of thinking. In Cone's own words:

> Being black in America has very little to do with skin color. To be black means that your heart, your soul, your mind, and your body are where the dispossessed are. We all know that a racist structure will reject and threaten a black man in white skin as quickly as a black man in black skin. It accepts and rewards whites in black skins nearly as well as whites in white skins. . . . [T]here seems to be enough evidence that though one's skin is black, the heart may be lily white. The real questions are: Where is your identity? Where is your being? Does it lie with the oppressed blacks or with the white oppressors?[4]

This is not to suggest that Cone was oblivious to what it means to have black skin in America. He knew that even the most sincere white skinned person does not suffer quite like blacks; that such whites, by virtue of their white skin, benefit from the system of racism and economic exploitation even though they are against racism and do not practice it. Yet it seems that from the time of the appearance of his first book Cone never intended to exclude whites from participating in the struggle for liberation. When he wrote of destroying whiteness he did not mean the indiscriminate killing of all people with white skin. When he insisted on the death of whiteness,[5] or that the goal of liberation theology is to destroy everything white,[6] he meant that the only way they could participate meaningfully in the liberation process was by rejecting everything that whiteness had come to symbolize in the United States and throughout the world. Whiteness had come to stand for racial, sexual, class, economic, political and other forms of oppression. The destruction of everything white simply means destroying white values that lead to the oppression and dehumanization of the majority of created persons in the world who are not white!

Like DuBois who, by 1903, came to the realization that the nature of black suffering was such that he could not—indeed would not—remain "a calm, cool, and detached scientist," Cone's early writings were laced with rhetoric and passion. Although these were functional, one may not be wrong in thinking that in part they prevented many whites (and some blacks) from understanding Cone's early theological perspectives. The rhetoric and polemic, however, may also have contributed in some way to causing many not to take him seriously, although some used this as an excuse. Cone's language in the early period of his theological development was often so strong that many claimed to be unable or unwilling to hear the truth he wanted to convey. To get to the real Cone, then, it will be helpful to take a clue from Rudolph Bultmann and do some demythologizing. Otherwise, one will need firsthand experience of what it means to be black in the United States.

By the time of the publication of *My Soul Looks Back*, and *For My People*, James Cone's understanding of oppression had deepened considerably. Presently, for example, he has a global perspective on oppression and sees the connection between the various forms of oppression and monopoly capitalism. The issue of racism has been effectively linked with classism, sexism, militarism, and the like. Each of these now has a key place in Cone's analysis of oppression. Though they are interrelated social problems, each is a separate problem in itself, with its own structure, or what Walter G. Muelder has aptly described as "an Individual Totality lockstitched into the ambiguities of contemporary history."[7] No form of oppression is totally reducible to any other. Muelder points to his own earlier tendency to subsume one form of oppression under another.[8] He now sees that racism, despite what some have wanted to believe, is not reducible or subsumable under the class problem. The same may be said of other forms of oppression. However, though no one of these can be reduced to the other, neither is it possible to make an absolute separation between them.

The thesis of this chapter is that although Cone initially thought of racism as the fundamental social problem confronting blacks (and he still holds this view to a large extent today), he recognized that there were other social problems adversely affecting both blacks and other groups. He expressed this awareness in his first book, and during a dialogue with William Hordern in 1971. Cone did not give these other social issues the degree of attention he gave racism in its individual and institutional forms, but in light of early criticisms that he had a too exclusive perspective on oppression,[9] it is important to affirm that he was not as exclusive in his early thinking on oppression as some critics have alleged. There is no evidence that Cone was callous or indifferent to people victimized by other forms of oppression. He seemed to have some awareness of classism, militarism, and the women's struggle for liberation. As for the latter, it cannot be said that he was aware of sexism as an issue for the black church and community during the early period of black theology. He simply had a general awareness of a women's movement during the sixties, but from all indications he believed as did most black males of the period (including Malcolm X and King), that the gender issue was really a problem for the white church and community and that the attempt to solicit black involvement in that movement was intended to weaken or undermine the black struggle.[10] King and Malcolm X were sexists. Likewise, Cone was and continues to be sexist, although a recovering sexist.

Cone both anticipated and sorely wanted to avoid the accusation that black theology only had something to say about the black situation of oppression.[11] The principle through which he tried to ward off this criticism (albeit unsuccessfully) was his controversial concept of "blackness as an ontological symbol." His twofold description of blackness as *physiological* and *ontological*, was intended to point to the particular (physiological) and the universal (ontological) dimensions in his understanding of oppression, theology, and the Gospel. As it turned out, however, he was misunderstood by both white and black theologians, though for different reasons. It should be pointed out, however, that during this period Cone had not yet turned the corner on the issue of sexism. Consequently, his symbol of ontological blackness did not yet explicitly include gender oppression. Indeed, it may be argued that presently it does not explicitly include gay and lesbian oppression. By definition there is no reason why the symbol of ontological blackness should not include these forms of oppression.

A consideration of Cone's description of *blackness* should take us a long way toward understanding that though he saw racism as the fundamental issue for blacks, he never believed this to be the only problem that needed to be addressed, and he did not believe that blacks were the only victims of oppression. Although he intended from the outset to develop a black theology, which, like all theologies, is contextual, it can be shown that in addition to this the universal dimension has always been present in Cone's theological project. Furthermore, he has always taken this as seriously as the dimension of particularity. The more explicit emphasis on the universal dimension in his mature thought has caused Louis-Charles Harvey considerable concern because he thinks that if Cone is not careful he may lose that sense of the particular that is so important in black and other forms of liberation theology. Racial analysis was dominant during the early period of Cone's development, but there is evidence that he had an awareness of forms of oppression affecting other groups, including whites. In order to support this view I shall consider Cone's understanding of blackness; his explicit references to other forms of oppression during the early period; his view of classism and sexism; and the concern raised about his more expanded conception of oppression and the danger that could result.

The Significance of Physiological and Ontological Blackness

Deane Ferm has suggested that Cone initially introduced the distinction between particular and universal, physiological and ontological blackness in *Black Theology and Black Power*.[12] It would be more accurate to say that Cone merely introduced the idea (in that book) that there are two kinds of blackness. The fact is that he did not actually introduce the terms *ontological* and *physiological* blackness until the publication of *A Black Theology of Liberation* about a year later.

In his first book Cone talks about "black men in white skin,"[13] which is an anticipation of the concept of blackness as ontic or ontological symbol, that would appear in the second text. Blackness on this level has nothing to do with color per se. Cone intended to show from the beginning that there is a universal aspect in oppression and liberation; that though the predicament of blacks is unique, other groups suffer from other forms of oppression. Cone did not initially name these. However, he believed the concept of liberation applies to all persons since all are created by the One God and are united by God's will. This implies that persons who are committed to the Gospel imperative of the liberation of the oppressed, but whose skin color is different from that of the oppressed, could still participate meaningfully in the liberation struggle. Cone implied as much in his first book.[14]

As he was trying to grapple with and make sense of the particular and the universal in oppression and liberation, Cone said that being black has little to do with skin color. This prompted a sharp criticism from Gayraud Wilmore, though Cone made this statement only to highlight another important point about the difference between the two levels of blackness. He did not intend to imply what Wilmore apparently thought, viz, that having black skin in the United States has not meant that blacks have been subjected to brutal treatment.

Cone first introduced the two types of blackness with an explicit terminology in *A Black Theology of Liberation*, relegating much of the discussion to a footnote! In this text he shows obvious concern for wanting to ward off the anticipated criticism that black theology is concerned only about the suffering and pain of blacks, and that there is no place in the struggle for well-intentioned whites.

When reading Cone's first book it is not difficult for one to get a sense that he is concerned only to express the anger of black people and to highlight their brutal mistreatment at the hands of whites in and out of the church. He exhibited signs of awareness of the suffering of other groups. His more immediate concern was the predicament of black-skinned people. But by the appearance of the second book there is strong evidence that Cone was at war within himself. It appears that his description of blackness in this book is an uneasy response to critics who contended that his first book had a much too exclusive tone regarding oppression. These critics included black theologians like J. DeOtis Roberts and Major Jones. In his second book he tried to respond to his critics by introducing the concept of blackness as an ontological symbol.

In this regard Cone tried to appropriate Paul Tillich's use of symbol.[15] Tillich held that it is not possible to adequately speak of ultimate things, e.g., God, without the use of symbolic language. Symbols, like signs, point beyond themselves to something else.[16] But, unlike signs (and this distinction is crucial), *symbols participate in the reality for which they stand.* A symbol, unlike a sign, cannot be replaced arbitrarily or on a moment's notice. It will take a revolutionary upheaval of massive proportion to replace it. Tillich uses the example of the American flag to make his point.

> ... the flag participates in the power and dignity of the nation for which it stands. Therefore, it cannot be replaced except after an historic catastrophe that changes the reality of the nation which it symbolizes. An attack on the flag is felt as an attack on the majesty of the group in which it is acknowledged.[17]

The flag as such is specific and particular. But because of its symbolic character it participates in another reality which makes it possible for many persons to share in that reality. To attack the flag, then, would be tantamount to attacking the citizens who acknowledge and identify with it.

Tillich gives several other characterizations of symbol, but I want to mention but one other, since it seems relevant to Cone's use of ontological blackness as a symbol. This characterization has the twofold reference to "opening up dimensions and elements of reality which otherwise would remain unapproachable" and unlocking "dimensions and elements of our soul which correspond to the dimensions and elements of reality."[18] This may be our experience after having sat through a profound play, which "gives us not only a new vision of the human scene, but opens up hidden depths of our own being."[19] This sensitizes us to the point of being able to grasp what the play is actually intended to reveal to us. It is through the symbol of the play or some other work of art that some heretofore unknown or dormant dimension within us is awakened, thereby making us more receptive to reality. It is not that these previously unknown dimensions were completely absent in us. Rather, it may take the symbolism of a play to help get us in touch with these inner dimensions that in turn enable us to open ourselves to concrete realities, e.g., suffering and pain experienced by blacks. Symbols put us in touch with the deeper dimensions of ourselves and help us make the connection with more profound realities. This is what Cone had in mind when he introduced the concept of blackness as ontic symbol. The interpretation that follows goes beyond Cone's treatment, but I think it consistent with the spirit of what he initially proposed in outline.

The symbol of black skin not only represents a particular people with an extensive history of oppression, but it also points to and participates in a deeper reality that includes all created persons. The symbol of blackness is particular or specific in the United States, in that it represents black-skinned persons who have been the victims of racial oppression from the time they were torn from the African continent and forced into slavery in the Americas. But as a symbol, blackness in its more particular form points beyond itself to another reality, the reality of free beings, all of whom have the image of God etched into their being. But even as it points beyond itself to this other reality, the particular is not cancelled out. Rather, it is included in the deeper reality, so that an affront to the particular (i.e., black-skinned persons), is an affront to a more universal reality (i.e., all persons, and the image of God in them, since all are derived from a common Ground or Source). Blackness as symbol, then, becomes a state of mind or being which is applicable to all persons, but it never loses touch with the particular reality — black-skinned persons who suffer racial, economic, sexual, and other forms of exploitation just because they are black.

In a sense, one can say that ontological blackness both transcends and includes what Cone has called physiological blackness. My interpretation of blackness as ontological symbol, then, raises the question of why it was necessary for Cone to introduce both ontic and physiological blackness in the first place. In my view (and I think this is consistent with what Cone had in mind during the early period) the concept of *blackness as ontic symbol is both particular and universal*. That is, it includes both the specific or concrete blackness (i.e., it represents black-skinned persons who actually suffer from oppression), and the idea of blackness as a state of mind or being, which takes into account all forms of oppression as well as makes it possible for all committed persons outside the oppressed community to identify with and participate in the struggle for liberation.

This dual emphasis in blackness as ontic symbol is intended both to make us aware of the particular forms of oppression that black-skinned and other persons suffer, and to put us in touch with a deeper reality in which all persons participate and are thereby connected with one another. Therefore the oppression of any group amounts to the oppression of even the oppressor group. Thought of in this way, ontic blackness makes it possible for well-intentioned people outside the oppressed community to participate in the struggle for liberation. If blackness becomes a state of mind or being for persons outside the community of oppression, it must be possible for them to be participants in the struggle for freedom.

However, as implied previously, the principle of ontic blackness does not, or should not, suggest that everybody experiences suffering or victimization in the same way. Though we may all be on the same ship (and this may even be questionable!), we are not all first-class passengers! Blacks are not second, third, or fourth class passengers by choice. "The basic difference between black oppression and so-called white oppression," Cone contends, "is the fact that the latter is voluntarily chosen and the former is forced upon the black community."[20] Whites become victims of a type of oppression as a result of their decision to oppress blacks, other people of color, and the poor. In this sense blacks are left with few choices which make sense, while whites can choose, for example, between living in the city or the suburb. The "oppression" the white suburbanite feels is not caused by blacks. Though in the metaphysical sense it is true that the oppressor is also the victim of oppression, since to oppress any member of humanity is to oppress one's own humanity, Cone has pointed to some dangers that are inherent in claims that whites are as oppressed as blacks.

> If white intellectuals, religionists, and assorted liberals can convince themselves that the white condition is analogous to the black condition, then there is no reason to respond to the demands of the black community. "After all, we are all oppressed," they say, rationalizing with a single stroke the whole white way of life. By equating their own condition with the condition of the black ghetto they are able to sleep at night, assuring themselves that we are all in the same boat.[21]

Cone made this observation in 1970, but had not by this time explicitly adopted gender analysis. Indeed, this was at best a peripheral issue for him. Today, however, he would not hesitate to say that what he wrote in 1970 about the relation between black and white oppression could also have been said about those who claimed that all women suffer the same oppression, or that all African Americans suffer the same oppression. Indeed, Audre Lorde took white women and black men to task for their racism and sexism, respectively. Against white feminists she argued that not all women, by virtue of being women, suffer the same oppression. Nor did she allow black men the luxury of claiming that all blacks essentially suffer the same oppression.[22] Susan Brooks Thistlethwaite has dealt with this issue in an admirable and helpful way as well.[23] Cone himself readily identified with this position *after* 1976. This tradition of challenging the racism of white feminists and the patriarchy of black men is rooted in the work of nineteenth-century black feminists such as Sojourner Truth and Anna Julia Cooper.

The massively and systematically oppressed have been forced into their condition of oppression and do not seem to have the power to reverse this state of affairs. Black theology makes a distinction between the oppression all humans experience when any human is the victim of dehumanization, and that which groups of people experience as a result of choices others make in the sociopolitical order. In other words, a distinction is made between oppression on the metaphysical and sociopolitical level.

Blackness, as Cone used the term, has both a particular and a universal dimension. It means that blacks are victims of oppression, and this must be taken seriously. It also means that other groups suffer from oppression, and any adequate theology of liberation must necessarily address this because of the universal dimension of the Gospel. Black theology must be concerned not only about the particular suffering and pain of black people, but all people everywhere. In 1970 Cone commented:

> The focus on blackness does not mean that only blacks suffer as victims in a racist society, but that blackness is an ontological symbol and a visible reality which best describes what oppression means in America.[24]

As an ontological symbol blackness refers to all forms of oppression, while blackness as a "visible reality" has to do with the particular forms of oppression suffered by black-skinned persons.

Cone makes his most precise distinction between physiological and ontological blackness in a footnote. There Cone describes blackness as a physiological trait as referring to "particular black-skinned people" who have been victims of racism, and "who have the scars that bear witness to the inhumanity committed against them."[25] It is these people, Cone maintains, who hold the key that will unlock the door to divine revelation. In order for American theology to approach the semblance of being authentically Christian it must come to terms with blacks.

Ontological blackness is described as having to do with "all people who participate in the liberation of men from oppression. This is the universal note in Black Theology. It believes that all men were created for freedom, and that God always sides with the oppressed against the oppressor."[26] Blackness, on this view, stands for freedom and liberation and is "the most adequate symbol for pointing to the dimensions of divine activity in America."[27] To decide the blackness of a given white-skinned theologian, Cone advised only that we consider for whom she or he writes and does theology: "the oppressed or the oppressor?" If a work is written for the former it may be deemed black. If not, it is white, and is to be rejected. It is interesting to note that for one who was accused of being too exclusive, Cone said in his second book that he would not condemn a person merely because he or she "happen to look like white Americans."[28] It was never white skin per se that Cone detested. Rather, he rejected what it stood for or symbolized in the world. He did not detest persons with white skin, for whites too, are created in God's image, a belief that Cone took to heart early in his life. What he rejected was whiteness, which is, among other things, the perverted attitude that persons with white skin are superior to blacks and other people of color. Cone did not reject persons with white skins, but persons whose attitude, mental outlook, and actions always lead to the exploitation of other persons and groups. Cone has never expressed hatred for white-skinned people in his writings or lectures, although he has always been aware that whiteness as a state of mind has generally been expressed by persons with white skins.

Concretely, whiteness, according to Cone, is the symbol of all forms of oppression, and represents everything that is antithetical to the Gospel and the liberation theme. Whiteness is against blackness.[29] So in a sense we can say that any person, regardless of skin color or gender, can be guilty of whiteness! If one is not committed to the liberation of all persons, he or she is probably thinking white. Boesak describes some characteristics of committed whites in the South African context who are ontologically black. There are white Christians, he contends, "who have understood their own guilt in the oppression of blacks in terms of corporate responsibility" and who have not hesitated to repent of their sins and then proceed to be in solidarity with the oppressed blacks in South Africa. Such whites have deliberately taken the black struggle or "the condition of blackness upon themselves." In addition, they have given up all paternalistic actions and attitudes and are intentionally trying "to identify with what blacks are doing to secure their liberation."[30] The only conceivable hope for whites is that they become black!

If one is to grasp the distinction Cone makes between the two types of blackness, it is imperative that he be read with an open mind. It is also necessary to admit to oneself that because of what one has heard or read about Cone there may be a cultural bias against everything he has written. Such a self-admission may be helpful in preparing one's mind to differentiate between the two levels of blackness. Any pretentiousness about openmindedness will lead to frustration, or at best, to confusion and the unwarranted judgment that Cone was, and is, a hater of white-skinned persons; that he believes that only blacks are victims of oppression; and that only whites have played the role of oppressor in history. Nothing could be further from the truth! Cone has always been aware that even the most exploited of the

exploited, namely blacks, have sometimes exploited other blacks, particularly black women. However, in the early period he had no explicit awareness of black male patriarchy.

Cone has always emphasized the suffering and pain of blacks. If one expects to understand his theology adequately, every effort must be made to see that his emphasis on the oppression and struggle of his own people, rather than emphasizing oppression and liberation for all persons in general, is neither unusual nor an unacceptable practice. History seems to support this view. When God led the Israelites out of bondage, for example, the emphasis was upon the liberation of a particular people at a particular time in history. But particularity did not mean exclusivity; it did not mean that God was unaware and unconcerned that there were other oppressed peoples in the world. When the American colonists appealed to England for their freedom and later fought for liberation in the Revolutionary War, their interest was only in their own freedom. They were white people demanding freedom from other white people. Yet they simultaneously suppressed the freedom of black men and women, Native Americans, and white women. They were concerned about the freedom of their own kind, and when they obtained that freedom blacks remained in chains, and they killed the native peoples. Though many of these whites may not have felt that blacks were being oppressed, since many of them believed blacks to be subhuman at best, there were some who were aware that blacks too are persons, victimized by racial injustice and economic exploitation.

When white women fought for suffrage in the nineteenth century they were primarily concerned about the rights of white women.[31] When the "father of American personalism," Borden Parker Bowne (1847-1910), emphatically defended the right of suffrage for women, his primary concern was the rights, not of all women, but of white women! Though it is known that some white women, e.g., Sarah and Angelina Grimke,[32] were concerned about the rights of all persons, regardless of race, gender, or class, most were only interested in obtaining the rights of white women.

The point should be clear by now: Although Cone vowed to do whatever it takes to help liberate his people, he was never so myopic and exclusive in his theology as to suggest that only blacks are victims of oppression. Because the plight of blacks was not being adequately emphasized and represented during the late sixties and the seventies, it was necessary for a radical and prophetic voice like Cone's to emerge. Indeed, for Cone it is the role of the black theologian to speak the truth to the people — to be prophetic. In this connection he wrote the following in *A Black Theology of Liberation*:

> The black theologian must assume the dangerous responsibility of articulating the revolutionary mood of the black community. This means that his speech about God, in the authentic prophetic tradition, will always move on the brink of treason and heresy in an oppressive society.[33]

It must be remembered that Malcolm X and King were no longer on the scene, and even the black clergy radicals of the NCBC were floundering in their attempts to properly articulate the black condition theologically. Cone recognized and accepted the universal dimension of the Gospel. Yet he did not hesitate to stress the note of particularity. When he considered the long history of black suffering he could not allow this concrete particular reality to be subsumed under the rubric of suffering, oppression, or evil in general. Those who speak and write so comfortably about suffering and evil in general are at best erecting smoke screens. Cone began addressing this matter quite early. It is one thing to be committed to humanity in general, and another to connect this with the concrete, existential expressions of particular forms of evil and oppression that a given group may be experiencing.

> ... Black Theology is suspicious of people who appeal to a universal, ideal humanity. The oppressors are ardent lovers of humanity. They can love all men in general, even black people, because intellectually they can put black people in the category called Humanity. With this perspective they can participate in civil rights and help blacks purely on the premise that they are a part of the ideal man. But when it comes to dealing with particular Blacks, statistics transformed into black-encounter, they are at a loss.[34]

So as we can see, Cone took both particularity and universality seriously in the early stage of his development. Some years later he said that the development of black theology must necessarily begin with the particularity of the black religious and cultural experience, but that it must remain open to other contexts and experiences of oppression as well.[35]

It will not be difficult to misunderstand, misinterpret, and become confused over Cone's concept of blackness if one fails to keep in mind the distinction he makes between physiological (particular) and ontological (universal) blackness. When reading the many passages in his early works about black being more favorably disposed than white in the eyes of God, for example, one must constantly be alert to the way Cone is using the term blackness in specific passages. Otherwise one may make the mistake of concluding that Cone has held at one time or another that God looks more favorably upon blacks than upon whites, when what he has really meant is that God rejects whiteness and what it symbolizes in the world, while approving of blackness and its emphasis upon the liberation of blacks and all other exploited groups.

Deane Ferm is a perfect example of the white scholar who read Cone, but misinterpreted his use of the term blackness. Ferm contends that Cone contributed to the so-called "identity crisis" in black theology in the early seventies with his "ambiguous use of the term black both as a reference to the black community and as an ontological symbol not dependent on the color black."[36] The identity crisis had to do with black theologians debating about the true sources of black theology; whether black theology should be exclusive or inclusive, and so on. Several black theologians criticized Cone's theology for not being black enough, in light of his heavy dependence upon white scholars and the too little attention to black and African sources of the black religious experience.[37] They charged that the early Cone had merely "blackenized" an otherwise white theology, i.e., presented a version of white theology that was clothed in black. In any case, Ferm contends that Cone contributed to this identity crisis by using the term black in an "ambiguous" manner. He further maintains that by 1975 there was still noticeable evidence of this "ambiguity" in Cone's writings.

That the double use of the term black has been present in Cone's writings since the appearance of his first book is indisputable. He ceased using the terminology of blackness as an ontological symbol almost immediately after he introduced it in 1970, but the spirit and principle of ontic blackness continues to be present in his writings. Ferm is right in suggesting that the double use of the term black was still present in Cone's writings by 1975, but I would go further and say that this continues to be the case today. This is another reason that it is imperative that those interested in grappling with Cone's theology return to his first two texts and work toward a clear understanding of the two levels of blackness found there.

Ferm's characterization of Cone's use of the term black as "ambiguous" has connotations that are too negative. The term "ambiguous" in this regard is a misnomer. It is not the double use of the term black that is ambiguous, for Cone explains the characteristics of both types rather well. However, since the dual use of the term was intended to take seriously both the particular and universal aspects of the Gospel, as well as oppression and liberation, one can say that Ferm is not wrong to say that Cone's use of blackness as an ontological symbol may have contributed in some way to what Cecil Cone called the *identity crisis* in black theology. While James Cone was endeavoring to do justice to the particular and the universal elements in the Gospel, some black theologians accused him of being too exclusive in his theology to include whites. Others accused him of being too inclusive.[38] Cone's brother belongs to the latter group, while J. DeOtis Roberts and Major Jones belong to the former.

Cecil Cone contended that Roberts had an identity crisis because of his commitment to "an integrating, universal theology." Such a theology, he contended, is not from the black religious experience. Rather it is "a white concern," and therefore the source of his identity crisis.[39] God, not white people, is the point of departure of black theology, according to Cecil Cone.[40] Since James Cone was struggling to make a place for this universal dimension in his theology — though he tried to do so by keeping it in dialectical relationship with the particular dimension — his use of blackness as an ontological symbol would have been a contributing factor to the identity crisis (assuming that his brother's analysis is correct).

In any event, Cecil Cone contended that his brother had a serious identity crisis in the early period of his theology. In addition to what was said about his emphasis on the universal element in the Gospel, the identity crisis centered around the failure to take African and slave sources of the black religious heritage seriously[41]; and a tendency to be more loyal to the advocates of black power principles than to the black religious experience.[42] The starting point of black theology is God, not the political emphasis of black power, Cecil Cone said. Failure to recognize this truth, he says, is where his brother and Joseph Washington and others erred. By making politics the point of departure in their theological projects they failed to see that they were "being more influenced by Euro-American conceptions of freedom than by the religious freedom of the black religious experience."[43]

Consideration of at least two more points will further substantiate my argument that James Cone's early writings were not just concerned about the oppression of blacks. Ferm contends that major black theologians are divorcing themselves from "thinking black."[44] Such an interpretation exposes his misunderstanding of the meaning of the two levels of blackness in Cone's theology, and especially his misunderstanding of ontic blackness. If Ferm understood this he would also understand why black theologians, particularly Cone, would never separate themselves from "thinking black," no matter how much they expand their conception of oppression beyond racism. One who has an adequate understanding of the two kinds of blackness knows that no matter how committed one is to the universal dimension in liberation theology, all theologies are contextual, i.e., are done out of the context of a particular sociocultural and political milieu. As long as racism is a factor in the oppression and exploitation of blacks, black theologians are obligated to think black — both in the physiological and the ontological sense. Thinking black, as Cone understands it, has never meant excluding other oppressed peoples.

Cone's use of the term black can be confusing, especially when laced with strong rhetoric, as is often the case in the early writings. He seldom told the reader how he was using the term black or blackness in a given passage, and this contributed to the possibility of confusion. The reader must not become overwhelmed by the strong polemic and passion so evident in the early period, but rather should engage them and be empowered by them. Otherwise it will be difficult to know the sense in which Cone is using black or blackness. Cone was responding to a state of emergency in the black community, and had every reason to be polemical and passionate. If the reader sees Cone as a "black racist," then every passage that refers to God siding with blacks and being against whites will be interpreted to mean that God cares for blacks and for no other group, and least of all for whites. On the other hand, if one works deliberately to understand the distinction he makes between the two levels of blackness, and if one works hard at reading Cone with an eye on the long history of forced black deprivation and the role of the white church in this process, the passages that refer to the term black will not be as confusing.

It cannot be denied that Cone's double use of the term *black* can be confusing. But if one knows how seriously he takes the universal dimension of the Gospel and the biblical teaching that all persons are equal before God, it should not be difficult to understand that his use of the terms black and blackness is not intended to exclude whites, though it is intended to deny or reject what whiteness represents in the world. For did Cone not say, "the resurrection event means that God's liberating work is not only for the house of Israel but for all who are enslaved by the principalities and powers?"[45] A few representative passages will reveal why readers sometimes turn away in anger and frustration because they believe that Cone is entirely too exclusive in his theology and is not universal enough to include whites.

One of the most glaring of such passages appears in *A Black Theology of Liberation*. Cone has written: "The goal of Black Theology is the destruction of everything white so that black people can be liberated from alien gods."[46] The tone of the passage implies a strong distaste for persons with white skins. Some readers may conclude that Cone and other adherents of black theology hate whites as a matter of course, and are seeking to eliminate them from the face of the earth. My sense, however, is that this passage is not only laced with strong rhetoric, but the phrase, "the destruction of everything white," does not mean the annihilation of white-skinned persons. Rather, the reference is to the destruction of the white way of doing things, such as the practice of oppressing people of color throughout the world, or of destroying the environment. The passage also has to do with the need for blacks to liberate their own minds from whiteness, which in this instance means freeing themselves of complacent and apathetic attitudes and developing a sense of black self-determination and black pride.

Another troublesome passage is the following: "Either God is for black people in their fight for liberation and against white oppressors, or he is not. He cannot be both for us and our white oppressors at the same time."[47] Here one may conclude that God is for blacks and against whites. Cone is much too good a theologian to suggest something like this. God has no favored race, gender, or class of people. God is no respecter of persons, but loves oppressed and oppressor. But in the case of oppression God has a "strategic concentration" on the oppressed. God has an option for the weak and the downtrodden — for the least of these. This is not to say that God loves these more than those who have beaten them to the ground. God's "aggressive love" always goes out to all created persons. God loves *all* persons, but God does not love all persons in quite the same way. In addition, God most assuredly is against all forms of human oppression.

The more casual reader of Cone might really be thrown by the words "what we need is the destruction of whiteness, which is the source of human misery in the world."[48] Again, it should be kept in mind that Cone is speaking symbolically, not in a literal sense. Whiteness is an attitude; a way of thinking, acting, and living in the world. Presumably even black-skinned persons can be guilty of whiteness. Black politicians or capitalists, for instance, who misuse less fortunate blacks are blacks who are thinking and acting white.

It would have been a great service had Cone developed the two types of blackness and his use of the term white(ness) further. In part, this failure may be due to debates with other black theologians in the Society for the Study of Black Religion, where it was strongly advised that he drop the term ontological blackness. Yet, as John C. Bennett indicates in his critique, Cone's failure to provide a more detailed and explicit explanation could have been intentional. In this context Bennett writes:

> I think that he must intentionally preserve this ambiguity because he wants all white people, in the first instance at least, to feel the lash of his rhetoric against whiteness as such. And he wants to keep the emphasis on those who are literally black because they are the largest oppressed community in the United States.[49]

As can be seen Bennett, like Ferm, believes there is an element of "ambiguity" in Cone's use of the term black. Though I think the term ambiguity implies too much regarding Cone's use of black, the greater part of Bennett's interpretation has weight. He obviously cannot be classified as a "casual reader" of Cone. There is a sense in which Cone wanted to use the term black in such a way that whites would not be able to get off the hook too easily regarding their social responsibility to oppressed blacks in this country. He wanted to reveal his awareness of other forms of oppression. At the same time he wanted to use the term black in a way that whites would feel a sense of conviction, as well as hypocrisy if they chose to continue ignoring their Christian social responsibility to blacks by devoting their sole attention to other forms of oppression, especially in other parts of the world. So, as we can see, Cone was aware of forms of oppression besides the racist treatment and economic exploitation against blacks. A brief consideration of evidence of this early awareness particularly in light of critics who said his conception of oppression was too narrow and too exclusive should prove both interesting and helpful.

Awareness of Other Forms of Oppression: The Early Period

J. DeOtis Roberts and Paul Holmer are two theologians—one black and the other white—who accused the early Cone of being too exclusive to include whites. Roberts was committed to the integrationist model. Therefore, one gets a sense as to why he was not able to see beyond Cone's rhetoric to realize that though he informed his readers in his early writings that blacks were his primary concern, he was from the beginning cognizant both of the existence of social problems other than racism, and of the need for theology to address them. He implied such an awareness in his second book:

> . . . the resurrection of Christ means that all oppressed peoples become his people. Herein lies the universal note implied in the gospel message of Jesus. The resurrection event means that God's liberating work is not only for the house of Israel but for all who are enslaved by principalities and powers. The resurrection conveys hope in God.[50]

For Cone the resurrection event was always evidence that God intends to liberate not one select group from oppression, but all groups. The phrase, "for all who are enslaved by principalities and powers," suggests that God's liberating work is not just for the house of Israel; not just for blacks; not just for any one group to the exclusion of other marginalized groups. God's liberating work is for all oppressed groups.

The primary social issue for Cone during the early period was white racism in all of its manifestations. He indicated, however, his awareness that there were social problems affecting other groups. Aware in 1970 that from a numerical standpoint there were more poor whites in America than poor blacks, Cone refused to debate this issue with white liberals, "since it is not the purpose of Black Theology to minimize the suffering of others, including white people."[51] Although racism was for Cone the fundamental social issue, he never contended that blacks were the only persons who suffered from exploitation. He was in fact quite explicit about this, contending that "there are, to be sure, many people who suffer, and they are not all black."[52]

The generic use of the term *man* in some of his early statements may imply an awareness of other forms of oppression besides racism. "Black Theology merely tries to discern the activity of the Holy One as he effects his purpose in the liberation of man from the forces of oppression." The use of "man" here may not merely refer to blacks, but to any group in the human family that is victimized by some form of oppression. Of course, several years would pass before Cone came to the realization that authentic commitment to the struggle for liberation means that all male theologians must take patriarchy seriously in every community, as well as women's stories of abuse and pain as a result of male violence. Before this, however, Cone was blinded by his tendency to subsume gender and class issues under the rubric of race (as white socialists tended to subsume race and other social ills under class).

Cone must have been disturbed by the tendency of whites who wanted to know which group suffers the most. He pointed out that not all blacks may always suffer more than some whites.[53] His chief contention during the early period, however, was that blacks, more than any other group, had the boundaries of their being defined by whites, and that this contributed significantly to their peculiar kind of oppressed condition.

Reflecting on the early period of his writing thirteen years later, Cone wrote about his perspective on oppression when he first began writing and doing theology.

> While *I never assumed that blacks in the United States were the only victims of oppression*, I did think that the most obvious and severe oppression stemmed from the racial attitude of whites. *The problems of classism and sexism, though present vaguely in my mind*, did not appear to warrant the same attention as racism[54] [emphasis added].

Cone also maintained (in the early period) that he "was aware of the women's movement, but considered it at best secondary to the Black struggle and at worst simply a White attempt to usurp the revolutionary significance of the Black liberation struggle."[55] So once again, Cone, though years later, indicates that the seeds of one of his more mature perspectives were actually planted in his earliest writings. He has always known that any type of liberation theology worth the name must be concerned about the liberation of all oppressed people and not just one's own group. However, a particular form of liberation theology rightly focuses on the liberation of those most closely identified with it.

I have found no evidence that supports those critics who contend that Cone's theological project has been so narrow that it is limited to a single kind of oppression. It seems a natural occurrence that a member of an oppressed group would be primarily concerned about that group's liberation. Such a tendency does not necessarily mean that there is a total unawareness and lack of concern for other oppressed peoples. Though justifiably angry because of racial oppression, Cone has never shown a desire to oppress whites as they oppress blacks.

The most serious limitation or contradiction in this regard, however, is historic and contemporary black male sexism and the tendency of black men to dominate, abuse, and oppress black women. Black feminists have wondered why black men project this rage onto black women rather than the forces that cause the rage. White racist oppression of black men is not acceptable as a justification for black male oppression of black women.

In 1892 Anna Julia Cooper lamented the fact that black men spoke clearly on most issues, including race. But "when they strike the woman question they drop back into sixteenth century logic."[56] More contemporary black feminists saw the need for consciousness raising among black men if there is to be hope of authentic dialogue and genuine unity between black men and women.

> But the Black male consciousness must be raised to the realization that sexism and woman-hating are critically dysfunctional to his liberation as a Black man because they arise out of the same constellation that engenders racism and homophobia. Until that consciousness is developed, Black men will view sexism and the destruction of Black women as tangential to Black liberation rather than as central to that struggle.[57]

If, as this chapter proposes, Cone was never as exclusive in his thinking about oppression as some critics say; if he has always had at least a degree of awareness of types of oppression other than white racism, when and why did he begin to give more explicit, intentional consideration to other specific forms of oppression like classism and sexism? Is such attention consistent with his theological project? It is appropriate to address the class and gender issues because of the significant place each now has in Cone's theology. It will be seen, however, that the gender question poses a greater challenge to black male theologians and nontheologians than does the class question at the present time. This may be because in many circles black liberation is still too tied to the idea of the uplift of black manhood, which, in itself, should not preclude the recognition of sexism as a major problem in the black community.

Black Theology and Classism

Cone was aware of the class question at the beginning of his writing career, but he felt that this issue was secondary to that of white racism. Contrary to his claim that there was no awareness of Marxism in his early theological-political consciousness,[58] there was some awareness, as I showed in Chapter 4. Therefore, his claim in 1982 that his "introduction to Marx came with my encounter with Third World theologians, especially Latin American liberation theologians"[59] is misleading. However, it may be that his dialogue with Latin American liberation theologians (which he says began in an informal way at a symposium sponsored by the World Council of Churches in Geneva in 1973), served to accentuate the significance of class analysis for him. As noted in Chapter 4, Cone's first awareness of Marx and the class question appeared in embryonic form in his early writings. However, in the beginning his tendency was to ignore the class question in favor of racial analysis. In addition, he was highly suspicious of white socialists in both North and Latin America. As for the Latin Americans, Cone simply had not travelled in Latin American countries, and therefore did not have sufficient contact with them. In addition, he was aware that some Latin Americans claimed that there was no race problem on their continent, and therefore they perceived the fundamental issue to be classism. Cone knew, however, that there were more blacks in South America than in North America, and he wondered how it could be claimed that racism was not a problem when there were no blacks among the circle of Latin American liberation theologians. In addition, he was suspicious of white North American theologians and socialists because they welcomed Latin American liberation theologians but refused to recognize African American liberation theologians. They seemed to be able to conjure up a sense of radicalism about everything except the elimination of white racism, an issue they tried to ignore.

Though the initial meeting between African American liberation theologians and Latin American liberation theologians at the World Council of Churches symposium in Geneva in 1973 was not intended as a forum for these two groups per se, what was shared between them left a deep impression on both sides. Cone did not soon forget Paulo Freire's comment that he (Cone) "is a Third World man because he was born in the world of dependence — of exploitation — within the First World." In addition he had spoken of Cone as his friend.[60] The comments by Hugo Assmann went even further (though they were prevented from continuing the dialogue to determine similarities and dissimilarities in their respective experiences of oppression). In addition to picking up the theme of Third World people in the United States, i.e., poor and oppressed people,[61] Assmann pointed out that it was more important for Latin Americans to dialogue with African American theologians than with white theologians from Europe and North America. In this regard he commented:

> My biggest mistake in the first days of the symposium was that I was speaking to the participants and not to my friends who represent Black Theology.... I would like to say to *my friends in Black Theology*: I don't know how this dialogue with you can be improved, but it is more important than European theology for us Latin Americans. *I don't want to destroy the connection with you*[62] [emphasis added].

Assmann made a minor capitulation from his earlier stance. According to Cone their initial attempts at dialogue were strained because Assmann felt so strongly about class analysis and was so critical of its absence in Cone's theological project. Cone, on the other hand, was emotionally charged and highly critical of Assmann because of the absence of racial analysis in his project.[63] Yet Cone was still able to make the explicit reference to Assmann as "a good friend" at the Theology in the Americas Conference in Detroit in 1975.[64] At any rate, Cone said that Freire's and Assmann's referral to African Americans as Third World people indicated that "an openness was created from the Latin American side."[65] This was reciprocated by black theologians.

What is most interesting is that in his remarks at the Geneva symposium, Cone was talking the language of a sociologist of knowledge, which indicates that he was in the process of researching and thinking through his fourth book, *God of the Oppressed*. It is in this book that the idea of an on-going interplay between ideas and social context was systematically developed. In the context of his brief remarks in Geneva, Cone indicated that as long as we live in a world of oppressors and oppressed, it will be impossible to communicate on a level that really matters in terms of liberation and creating a social order where no group will dominate over any other merely because "they have different realities to which the symbols and the language refer."[66] All language, theological and otherwise, has a social context. The social context and location of the oppressed and the oppressor make communication difficult, if not impossible. The oppressed generally do not see either the problem or its solution(s) in quite the same way as the oppressor. Robert McAfee Brown reminds us that where one stands in society has much to do with what he or she sees or does not see!

Two years passed before the Latin Americans and blacks had another dialogue. The occasion was the Theology in the Americas (T.I.A.) Conference in 1975. To the dismay of black theologians the Conference was planned by whites as primarily an occasion for Latin American and white North American theologians to get together.[67] This angered black theologians, and by conference time tensions were high. The Latin Americans and blacks insisted on the primacy of class and race analysis, respectively. It was reported that the Latin Americans "were too antagonistic toward any other contradiction (i.e., race and sex)."[68]

There was much anger exhibited on both sides at the Detroit conference. However, Cone believes they left with a much better understanding of each other and a promise to conduct a continuing dialogue. Looking back on that meeting nearly ten years later Cone wrote:

> It was at that time that it became clear to me that either black theology would incorporate class analysis into its perspective or it would become a justification of middle-class interests at the expense of the black poor. Although claiming to speak for the poor, we actually speak for ourselves.[69]

In this connection Cone recalled E. Franklin Frazier's controversial book, *Black Bourgeoisie* (1957). Frazier pointed out that, given the opportunity, members of the black middle class will exploit the black poor for profit as quickly and decisively as would whites.

After the Detroit conference Cone saw more clearly than ever that the problem of racism is even further exacerbated by socioeconomic exploitation, and that members of a racially oppressed group might very well oppress less privileged members of the race. Manning Marable has shown that this tendency does in fact exist in the black community, and has for a long time.[70] It was probably during this period that Cone began to seriously question the efficacy of capitalism for blacks, other people of color, and the poor. He was now convinced "that economic analysis is not only an option but a necessity." However, today he is dismayed that so few black theologians have taken classism in the black community seriously.[71]

> How can we provide a genuine check against the self-interest of black theologians and preachers who merely use the language of liberation and the gospel in order to justify their professional advancement? Unless black theologians and preachers face the class issue, the integrity of our commitment to justice for the poor will remain suspect to other freedom fighters and to the poor we claim to represent.[72]

By 1977 Cone was openly expressing the influence of Latin American liberation theology and the importance of class analysis for the liberation struggle.

In his keynote address at the first meeting of the Black Theology Project in Atlanta in 1977, Cone indicated the need for a global perspective which takes seriously the struggles for liberation all over the world. He was adamant about the need for dialogue, but declared that he would not "listen to anybody who refuses to take racism seriously, especially when they themselves have not been victims of it."[73] But he realized that he too must willingly listen to and learn from others and their particular oppression. As for Marxism he vowed not to accept it lock, stock, and barrel, since the Marxist worldview is atheistic, which contradicts the experience of most blacks. Neither would he accept forms of Marxism that reduce all problems to class analysis while ignoring racism as a valid point of departure. He was aware that there are racist Marxists as well as racist capitalists, and black theology must resist both. He also knew that there are classist whites and classist blacks, and that this too must be resisted. However, Cone refused to reject Marxism as a tool for social analysis, since it could help to unmask hidden ideologies and assumptions that are underlying causes of oppression in capitalist societies.

If black theologians reported the influence of Latin American liberation theology and the significance of class analysis for black theology, what of the influence of black theology and racial analysis on the Latin Americans? Cone recalls that the most significant dialogues between blacks and Latin Americans occurred in 1979 in Matanzas, Cuba, at a conference that focused on the theme "Evangelization and Politics." Here the Latin Americans faced (for the first time) the question of racism headon.[74] Their joint statement at the close of the conference reflected just how far they had progressed since that first encounter with blacks in Geneva six years earlier.[75]

It is significant that by 1975 Cone was well on his way to developing a more explicitly global theology that would take seriously all forms of oppression. He had not by this time completely included class and sex analysis, but he was being transformed. Gutiérrez, on the other hand, seemed to have already arrived at that point. At the 1975 T.I.A. Conference in Detroit, Gutiérrez, arriving several days late, and helping to lessen the tension between blacks and the Latin Americans, said:

> Our question is rather how can we say to the poor, to the exploited classes, to the marginated races, to the despised cultures, to all the minorities, to the nonpersons — how can we say that God is love and say that all of us are, and ought to be in history, sisters and brothers.[76]

Here one sees Gutiérrez's concern for class, race, and gender oppression. During this same period, however, Cone was undergoing consciousness raising by conducting dialogues with women in the Third World and the United States, and within a year would be so convinced of the moral credibility of some of the feminist issues being raised that he would take a public stance against sexism, especially in the black church and community.[77]

Black Theology and Sexism: The Great Challenge

In *Martin & Malcolm & America*, Cone says that King was a liberation theologian long before the term came into vogue.[78] Although contemporary liberation theology is essentially a Christian phenomenon, there is no fundamental reason why it would be inappropriate to at least cast Malcolm X in the company of the forerunners of black liberation theology as well.

Refusing to elevate Malcolm and King to sainthood, Cone portrays both as *human beings* who were men of integrity and courage, and committed to ongoing disciplined study. They were "reluctant leaders" in solidarity with the black masses, who fostered an internationalist perspective on oppression, and gave their lives for the liberation and empowerment of their people.[79]

Both Malcolm and King greatly influenced Cone, who even appropriated their limitations into his early theological project! As human beings they were bound to have shortcomings. Cone identified two chief flaws in each man: sexism and classism. (Neither was a classist, however. Their limitation in this regard was their failure to incorporate class analysis into their thought until the last years of their lives.) By far "the most glaring and detrimental" shortcoming was their blindness to sexism.[80] Both men uncritically allowed their attitudes and practices regarding women to be "shaped by their acceptance of patriarchal values as the norm for the family and society. Not unlike the pattern of white religious bodies, the black church and the Nation of Islam provided religious justification for the subordination of women."[81] Their uncritical acceptance of black male privilege blinded them to the connection between racism and sexism. Malcolm and King were sexists, and their sexism hampered their efforts to achieve total liberation for their people.

King did not acknowledge the contributions of black women like Jo Ann Robinson, Mary Fair Burks, Dorothy Cotton, Septima Clark, and Ella Baker in organizations with which he was affiliated. Nor, interestingly, did he ever refer to the work of Fannie Lou Hamer in Mississippi.[82] Malcolm did meet Hamer, and heard her speak. Cone contends that this helped him "to realize that intelligence and commitment to freedom are not limited to the male gender."[83] King's failure to acknowledge the contributions of black women in the civil rights struggle did not endear him to some black women who otherwise supported his work. Pauli Murray, an Episcopal priestess, was one of these:

> I had not been a passionate admirer of Dr. King himself because I felt he had not recognized the role of women in the civil rights movement (Rosa Parks was not even invited to join Dr. King's party when he went abroad to receive the Nobel Peace Prize), but I was passionately devoted to his cause.[84]

Although both men believed woman's place was in the home, Malcolm was more vocal and explicit in his views about women. No matter what the basis of his misogynistic tendencies, for most of his twelve years in the Nation of Islam he browbeat black women and blamed them for the predicament of black men. Nowhere is this more evident than in the series of speeches he gave on black women in 1956 at the Philadelphia Temple. Malcolm clearly described black women as tools of the devil, a characterization rooted in medieval thought.

> "How do you think this black man got in this state?" he asked his audience. "By our women tricking him and tempting him, and the devil taught her to do this." "The trickiest in existence is the black woman and the white man." "If you go to court with your wife, she will always win over you because the devil can use her to break down more of our black brothers. . . . It is this evil black woman in North America who does not want to do right and holds the man back from saving himself."[85]

The focus during this period was on black male assertiveness. Bothered by other aspects of the controversial Moynihan Report on the black family in 1965, black men agreed with Moynihan's assumption that they were more oppressed than black women and that it was time for the black man to take the leadership position in the black family. Black women were in a terribly awkward position, since they wanted neither to say or do anything to divide the black community on this issue, nor to associate with racist white feminists.

Both Malcolm's and King's views on women were changing during the last years of their lives. Neither lived long enough for us to do more than speculate about how they might have further changed had they lived through the women's movement of the sixties and seventies and the emergence of womanist thought. According to Cone any changes in the two men were minor in comparison with the contributions of Frederick Douglass and W.E.B. DuBois regarding women's rights.

By the time of the publication of *God of the Oppressed*, Cone was making overtures that implied a desire to turn the corner on the issue of sexism. Though exclusive language (e.g., use of the masculine pronoun) was still present,[86] there were also instances in which he used inclusive language.[87] Again, Cone had not completely turned the corner, but there was indication of an awareness that the use of generic and exclusive language is a convenient way of keeping other groups and their experiences invisible or at the margins. Also in *God of the Oppressed* he makes a very explicit statement about the equality of the sexes. "*There is no place for male dominance of females.* There can only be equality, an equality of power defined in the context of struggle"[88] (emphasis added). This should not be taken to mean that Cone had by this time been completely transformed. He had not. He was more conscious of the issue of sexism by 1975, but was not able to fully incorporate sexual analysis into his emerging theological project. This would not happen for another year.

It was not yet apparent in 1975 that Cone recognized sexism as a serious problem in the black church and community. He has acknowledged that his education on the women's liberation movement began at Union Theological Seminary where he teaches. Union had a significant percentage of women students who had enough courage and tenacity to put forth their own agenda, which Cone was compelled to listen to:

> The power and influence of white women at Union made it very difficult for anyone to ignore the legitimate claims of feminism. As a member of the Union community, serving in the role of a teacher, I could not say that women's liberation was merely a white problem and not of any concern for blacks, if I expected to be an effective teacher of all students, regardless of color and sex. If I expected white students and professors to listen to the legitimate demands of black theology, then must not I, as a black man, listen to the legitimate demands of feminist theology, even if it is being written exclusively by white women?[89]

Cone's broadening perspective apparently began as a result of issues raised by white and black women students. Yet it is significant that by 1975 one could see signs that the general issue of sexism was not as peripheral as it was during the early period. It is also important that something was happening in Cone's life during this period of the middle seventies that was raising his consciousness and sensitivity to the gender issue. His early commitment to the universal dimension of the Gospel and his own experiences of pain are contributing factors in this expanding perspective on oppression.

This increased awareness was due to dialogues not only with white feminist students, however, but with black women students as well. It was also during this period that Cone began to wonder whether "Black women, as women, have a distinctive contribution to make in our definition of black religion that is as significant as we claim our Black experience is in the context of North American Christianity."[90] He confessed that in the early phase of his efforts to develop a black theology "the distinctive contribution of Black women was not a part of my theological consciousness."[91] It was not that he was unaware of the existence of the women's liberation movement, and that it claimed the attention of some black women. He simply believed, like most black men (then and now), that it was basically a white movement, designed to co-opt black women, thereby undermining and weakening the black struggle against racism. It was not until he began to listen to and converse with "Black and other Third World women," that he discovered that there was more to the feminist movement than the interests of white women,[92] many of whom are themselves racists. Both Angela Y. Davis[93] and bell hooks[94] do an excellent job of explicating and documenting this view from slavery to more recent times. For example, both point to the racism of such well known nineteenth-century feminists as Elizabeth Cady Stanton and Susan B. Anthony. Both women were initially supportive of blacks' struggle for political rights as long as it was linked with their own. However, when Frederick

Douglass began focusing on suffrage for black men, Stanton and Anthony began displaying their racism. They argued against the franchise for black men on the ground that white women had superior intelligence and culture. Anna Julia Cooper argued vehemently and eloquently against this white feminist stance. Cooper asked: "Is not woman's cause broader and deeper, and grander, than a blue stocking debate or an aristocratic pink tea?"[95] Woman's cause, she argued, is linked with every oppressed group.

Audre Lorde also reproved white feminists for their failure to acknowledge the differences between their own oppression and that of black women. Time and again she reminded them that it is a myth that all women suffer the same oppression. The oppression of women is no respecter of sexual preference, racial-ethnic, class, or age boundaries, "but that does not mean it is identical within those differences."[96] The refusal of many white feminists to recognize "differences of race between women and the implications of those differences" is the most serious barrier to an effective bonding of white and black women.

Increasingly, Cone could see that black men often became defensive and belligerent when charges of black sexism were made either by black women or by sensitized black men. He discovered that though black women seminarians at Union remained silent on the gender issue for a long time, their silence was not to be interpreted to mean that sexism was absent in the black church and community. It simply meant that they did not want to be a divisive factor in the black struggle against racism.[97] But their silence was broken when it became apparent that black men were refusing to even consider the possibility that sexism might be a problem for the black church and community. More and more the issue of sexism was raised at conferences on women in the ministry. Charging that their black brothers were often insensitive to their experience of pain (often from physical assault!) and exclusion, and often refused to hear their stories of pain, black women contended that when black men did give the appearance of listening they often pointed out that sexism is subordinate to the "more important race question" which adversely affects all blacks. Often black men viewed the concerns of their black sisters as a joke. Cone himself was guilty of this for a period of time.

> Because black men knew that women were deeply committed to the racial struggle, they did not even take seriously black women's concern for sexual oppression. They merely laughed, treating the hurt and pain of our sisters as a joke.[98]

Black women came increasingly to see that the reality of the racism which dehumanizes all blacks did not make blacks immune to the tendency to ignore and misname differences in their community.[99]

When Cone first recognized the gravity of sexism in the black church and community he was almost dumbfounded and uncertain as to what he should be saying and doing. His silence ended when he was invited by black women students at Garrett-Evangelical Seminary in 1976 to address them on the theme, "New Roles in the Ministry: A Theological Appraisal." This speech was undoubtedly "the first attempt of a Black male theologian to address this issue [sexism] directly."[100]

Cone was the first black male theologian to endure the burden of representing men at conferences called by black women students.[101] When Cone finally took a public stance against sexism he often had to stand alone, as he had done on other occasions. By 1976 he knew precisely where he must stand if he was to be consistent both with the Gospel and with the chief tenets of the theology he was helping to develop. Sexism is also a black issue, however much black men in particular (and some black women!)[102] contend otherwise. All blacks genuinely committed to the struggle for liberation must face the question of sexism in the black church and community squarely and honestly. Mere concern about the liberation of all blacks from racial exploitation will leave more than half the race still victimized by the sexual oppression of white and black males. In this case white women are better off than black women, for generally they are only oppressed by white males, since black males have no formidable power to oppress them by systematically excluding them from opportunities such as education, meaningful and gainful employment, the housing market, and similar life-chances.

The very survival of the black community and church is dependent upon the willingness of African Americans to face up to the issue of black sexism. Cone emphasized this in the address delivered before black women students at Garrett.

> The time has come for us to deal honestly with our differences, our hurts, and our pains. We cannot pretend any longer that all is well and that the problem of male-female relations is limited to the White community. It is in the Black community as well; and it is time we face up to the need to speak openly and frankly about what is right and wrong in our community in relation to Black men and women.[103]

Not long after he read that paper, he and black women and men students at Union Theological Seminary came together for the first time to discuss the same theme. Jacquelyn Grant, then a graduate student under his guidance, recommended that he present the same lecture to that group.[104]

Grant became a leading advocate of a black feminist theological critique of what she perceived as a major contradiction in black theology, viz, the invisibility of black women and their experiences and a blindness to black male patriarchy in both the black church and community. In a seminal article written while still a graduate student, Grant challenged the sexism of black male liberation theologians, the racism and sexism of white male theologians in the United States and Latin America, and the racism and classism of white feminists.[105] She challenged liberation theologians to see and hear black and other Third World women.[106]

Grant charged that black men uncritically accepted and appropriated white patriarchal views and practices. She said that black men needed to seriously consider the question, "How can a White society characterized by Black enslavement, colonialism, and imperialism provide the normative conception of women for Black society?" Black theology, according to Grant, would never be authentic liberation theology until it comes to terms with sexism, and the interconnection between racism, sexism, and other forms of oppression. Grant argued against those black men and women who still insisted that the black woman's chief problem is related to her race rather than her sex.

Looking back on the Garrett address nearly ten years later, Cone concluded that it was rather tame.

> When I now read that October 1976 paper, I am embarrassed by how mildly and carefully I approached the theme of women's equality in the church. It was anything but radical, somewhat analogous to a southern white liberal reflecting on racism. But black male seminarians, almost without exception, were greatly disturbed by my paper. If my paper can be compared to that of a southern white liberal, the reactions of many black male seminarians were similar to those of most reactionary southern white racists. They quoted the Bible to justify that women should not be ordained, and some even insisted that they should not even be in the pulpit.[107]

What is important is that sexism is no longer a peripheral issue as it was in the early period of Cone's development. He came to urge openly that black men not take the question of sexism as a joke. The consequences of the black male's failure to take sexism seriously are too great, and it is certainly not worth gambling with the life and health of the black church and community to accept complacency about the failure.

The number of black men who are becoming sensitized to the gender issue may be growing, but often when they do accept the claim that sexism is a problem in the black community they view it as a relatively recent phenomenon. This simply is not the case.[108] It can be shown, for example, that sexism has existed in the black community and church at least since the nineteenth century (and possibly much earlier). A look at the lives of Jarena Lee (1783–?), Sojourner Truth (1797–1883), and Francis Ellen Watkins Harper (1825–1911) will support this view.[109] Autobiographical accounts of two other black women preachers of the nineteenth century, Zilpha Elaw (1790–?) and Julia A.J. Foote (1823–1900), give further proof in that each tell of sexist behavior of churchmen opposed to women preachers.[110]

Black feminists have never given just one response to sexism. They have agreed, however, that it is a problem of the first magnitude. There have been at least two responses historically, though the sixties gave birth to a third. The first response, represented in the thought of Frederick Douglass and Francis

Ellen Watkins Harper, was an insistence that black men and women fight for the rights of all blacks, but if forced to make a choice, they should choose to fight for the race, since sex is "the lesser problem."[111] This position was represented in the thought of Virginia Collins in the sixties. A second response is that blacks must always fight for the rights of men and women, and never, under any circumstances, be forced to choose between one or the other. This was the view of Sojourner Truth[112] and Anna Julia Cooper.[113] This view is popular among many contemporary black feminists such as Grant, bell hooks and Baker-Fletcher.[114] Cone supports this view, which is the direction in which many more black men must move.[115] A third response, not found in the nineteenth century, is represented in the writing of Michelle Wallace, who believes that black women must be for themselves first and foremost: they must organize among themselves to fight their own battle for liberation before endeavoring to unite with black men (and white women). Wallace symbolizes the anger produced in many black women of the sixties as a result of mistreatment by black men in civil rights organizations.[116]

As is characteristic of the more mature Cone, having identified the problem and criticized the culprits, he then proposes strategies calculated to lead to the effective eradication of black sexism. What is needed in the black community and church, he maintains, is a systematic policy of affirmative action. This should be applied to all positions, inside and outside the church. It should particularly apply to the position of pastor. "The goal should be to have at least as many black women in positions of responsibility in churches and in community organizations as will reflect their percentage of the overall population."[117] This would mean a substantial increase in the presence of black women in the churches and secular organizations, where they outnumber black men in church membership and many other organizations. It is especially noteworthy that Cone has become so sensitive to the gender issue that he made an explicit apology for his use of sexist language in his earlier writings.[118]

I think the thesis has been established that though the issue of sexism did not have a prominent place in Cone's early theology, it was at least on the periphery of his awareness. An early commitment to the universalism inherent in the Gospel, accompanied by an open mind and willingness to be self-critical as well as to change; his travels throughout the Third World; and his dialogues with white, black, and other Third World women, helped to raise his level of consciousness regarding sexism to the point that he now sees that until this issue is effectively addressed in the black community racism will not be solved either.

Sexual analysis and efforts to eliminate sexism now have a prominent place in Cone's theological project. This should not be interpreted to mean that he is concerned only about the liberation of black women and other women of color. Since Cone's primary concern is his people, it follows that his emphasis would be on the elimination of black sexism. Because of the significance of this issue for the black church and community I shall return to it in Part Three.

An Expanding View of Oppression

Some black male theologians have applauded Cone's forthrightness in relating black theology to other forms of oppression, e.g., sexism.[119] Others, while not rejecting this movement toward a more expanded conception of oppression, have not hesitated to raise a flag of caution.[120] One such critic is a former student of Cone's.

Louis-Charles Harvey helps us in our thinking about Cone's heightened sense of awareness regarding other forms of oppression and its relation to black suffering and pain. In his essay, "Black Theology and the Expanding Concept of Oppression," Harvey expresses his concern that several key first-generation black theologians, especially Cone and Wilmore, have moved from a fundamental focus on black oppression to a more universal focus on human oppression. Harvey contends that this shift is a result of both the dialogues and critical reflection between black theologians and Third World theologians, particularly Latin Americans (since the late sixties), and a declining sense of unity in the black community. He contends that the inchoate stage of black theology was characterized by an exclusive focus on racial oppression as the starting point of black theologians. Though black theologians differed at points in their interpretation of the black religious experience and whether the emphasis should be on liberation or reconciliation, or whether the newly developing theology was black enough, "one factor became strikingly clear: their almost exclusive dependence upon the particularity of a racial definition of oppression as the starting point for black theology."[121] The nature of the black situation in the United States and the prominence of racism in every major American institution makes this kind of approach necessary. According to Harvey, blacks had a need "to develop an indigenous, experientially based theology."[122] The dialogue between black and Third World theologians has led to "the expansion of the term oppression."

For Harvey, this "shift" from a particular focus on racial oppression to the more universal emphasis on human oppression "should be applauded cautiously."[123] He fears that such an expansion may hinder the further development of a distinct black theology by posing a significant threat to its reason for being. He does not want to see black theology assimilated into a more general, all-encompassing liberation theology, such as the "third world theology" that Cone seems to be developing.

There are several things that need to be said about Harvey's insightful essay. First, in keeping with the thesis of my book, the transition (or shift as Harvey calls it) in Cone's thinking from a primary focus on racial oppression to a more expanded, universal perspective on human oppression is really a matter of degree of emphasis. That is, Cone was never as exclusive in his thinking about oppression as many critics claimed. The concept of human oppression and the need for black theology to address all forms of oppression was present in Cone's thinking even in his first two books. Apart from his reference in each of these texts to his awareness that blacks were not the only victims of oppression, his introduction of the principle of blackness as an ontological symbol was intended to point to the universal dimension in his theology and his understanding of oppression.

Even during the early period Cone acknowledged that there are multiple forms of oppression. That he focused on racial oppression does not necessarily mean, as Harvey and others mistakenly assume, that he was only concerned about the plight of blacks. The universal element has always been present, and it is only a logical progression for Cone to have focused more attention on other forms of oppression as he matured and began to talk with Third World people in this and other countries. What Harvey should consider is that in terms of the expanded conception of oppression there is no clear-cut radical break between this and the earlier emphasis on black or racial oppression. Critics who accused Cone of an early exclusive emphasis on racial oppression were reacting to the vehement rhetoric that was so characteristic of his early writings. They therefore failed to see and understand the essential James Cone.

In the second place, Harvey worries that this expanded sense of human oppression may cause black theology to lose its reason for being. He thinks that the nature of black suffering is such that black theologians must continue to focus their energies in this direction if there is to be even minimal hope of black liberation. By broadening their concern to include other forms of oppression there is too much risk of spreading themselves so thin that they ultimately end up being effective nowhere. This, he believes, is precisely what happened in the case of the 1968 Poor People's Campaign that King was planning to lead prior to his assassination. [124] If black theologians do not concentrate their attention on the black struggle for liberation, that struggle may suffer the same demise.

Here I would urge Harvey to remember that a particular and a universal aspect are present in both the Gospel and black theology. If we take the Gospel motif of the liberation of the oppressed seriously, we must come to see that Jesus Christ was not just concerned about the liberation of a single group of persons. He was concerned about the liberation of all groups that are victims of systemic oppression in the world. All persons are created in God's image; all persons derive from a common Ground or Source, so that when any single person or group is beaten to the earth and humiliated, *all* are victimized in the deeper, metaphysical or theological sense. Indeed, whenever persons are violated, the Creator is violated. Any person or group in whom the image of

God is decimated due to the selfish ambitions and lust for power and privilege by others deserves the liberative efforts of all persons who take the Gospel seriously.

Yet Harvey's concern that black theology not lose its reason for being should be affirmed. Black Theology must not be replaced with a more general concept of universal liberation, or notions of liberation in general. The universal dimension of liberation theology is very important, but the element of particularity is also crucial, since all theologies emerge out of a particular sociocultural context. At no point should this be undermined or ignored.

I am encouraged by Cone's contention (after the appearance of Harvey's essay) that even with the greater awareness of other forms of oppression he is still "too much of a race person to allow white Marxists to lure me from the importance of African-American history and culture in the doing of theology and politics."[125] This should be reassuring to Harvey, who implied in his essay that black theologians may substitute class for race analysis some day. Indeed, some may, but Cone is not likely to be one of them. His commitment to and love for his people seem to be unshakable. His openness to other forms of oppression has not diminished his concern for the black situation, which remains the primary focus of his theological project. He wrote of this in 1982.

> While I still think that racism is and must remain the chief focus of my theological and political endeavors, I no longer regard it as the only problem or even the primary contradiction in the world today. Racism is one among many problems, though perhaps the most visible, existing along with sexism, classism, and imperialism. The complexity of the world is such that elevating one of these problems to the first priority does not serve to eliminate any of them. It is to be expected that persons who are the victims of any injustice make their entry into the struggle for freedom at the point where it hurts them the most. But the focus should not be allowed to blind them to other manifestations of injustice as well as their interrelation with each other.[126]

One's awareness that there is a plurality of oppressions and that they are linked and aggravated by monopolistic capitalism in the United States and abroad does not necessarily rule out the possibility that one may identify more fundamentally with a particular form of oppression because it affects her or him most. Although a particular type of oppression may take priority as a point of departure, if one is an authentic liberationist one must be committed to the deliverance of all oppressed peoples. African Americans have historically believed that there is one God who is the God of everybody and who loves everybody. God, as creator, sustainer, and continuer of life, is Love. Love, then, created human beings for Love, to love. Therefore, as long as any person or group is disinherited, none can claim total liberation, for we are all tied to a single Source and destiny. Every oppressed group must have a sense of how the form of oppression it suffers from is linked with other oppressions. In this way it is possible to retain the emphasis on the specific form of oppression that one suffers from most immediately, while remaining cognizant of other types of oppression that impinge upon it. There is, then, a need to be mindful of both particular and universal oppression. This is why I shall call for a *Two-Thirds World Theology-in-Black* as one of the new directions for black theology. It seems to me that this type of liberation theology holds the universal and the particular in creative tension where oppression and efforts toward liberation are concerned. I discuss this idea in Chapter 7.

We can be reasonably certain that Cone will not lose his sense of particularity, no matter how global is his perspective. As long as racism continues to exist in individual attitudes, behavior, and institutional or systemic forms he will continue being "a race man." He states as much in *For My People*, but even before this he discussed his position on the particularity-universality theme with Latin American and North American theologians in 1975. Responding to Assmann, who inquired as to whether blacks and others were placing too much emphasis upon their particular context of oppression, and whether there was not a need for all oppressed groups to unite in a common fight against all oppressors, Cone related a perspective that is consistent with what he has written in more recent publications.

> I think it would be possible, Hugo, for us to actually do what you are commanding and calling for if the members of this conference were primarily people whom I regarded as in the struggle of oppression, that is, if I could readily see that the majority of people here came out of actual concrete struggles, people that I wouldn't have to be as suspicious about. Then I would probably concede a little bit of my own particularity in order to hear what others are talking about. But most of the North American participants here are people I suspect.... [I]n this setting, in Detroit, U.S.A., I see people I've been fighting against. Here I don't talk about liberation; I've got to talk about black.[127]

What Cone is suggesting here is that as long as the behavior of whites is inconsistent with commitment to liberating blacks from all forms of racial and economic oppression, it will be necessary for blacks to emphasize racial oppression in their theological-political project. Sensitive to other forms of oppression, and their linkage to capitalism, Cone retains his sense of particularity regarding the race question. No sensitive white or black person should expect anything less. Rejecting the earlier, narrow, black-white dichotomy when dealing with the problem of oppression, and pointing to the trend of a "widening perspective on human oppression" that takes account of class, cultural and other analyses, Wilmore then proceeds to pose a warning to those who would have blacks give up their emphasis on race analysis.

> But there should be no misunderstanding here. Black theologians are still concerned with racist oppression. Despite the insistence of the Latinos that

> they exaggerate race and color and give too little attention to the class factor, blacks continue to argue that as far as the North American experience is involved, the contradictions within American Christianity are closely related to and aggravated by their historic connection with color prejudice.[128]

As can be seen Wilmore, like Cone, continues to be a race person. Mindful of the need to take other cultures and forms of oppression seriously, there is a basic refusal to undermine the importance of the race question, as long as racism exists.

A final word about Harvey and the concern he raises. In a written response to my query he gave helpful clarification of his position.

> I was only trying to sound a warning. It seems to me that Cone and other black theologians are now focusing more on specific black issues and persons (King, Malcolm X) than on concerns for universalism. Where universalism arises, it is around the notion of oppressed people rather than oppressors.

Cone does continue to be concerned about issues pertaining to universalism, but Harvey is correct in pointing out that when this comes up Cone's focus is on the oppressed, not the oppressor.[129] He is not as concerned about how members of the dominant group can participate in the liberation struggle of the oppressed. To be sure, committed members of the oppressor group do have a role(s), but that is not the real concern of black theologians, and certainly not for Cone. Cone's primary concern is for his people and other Third World people to find ways of bonding in order to effect their liberation. The magnitude of suffering and pain in black and other oppressed communities; the stubbornness of egoistic impulses and the entrenched power and privilege of the dominant white group necessitates devoting all time, talents, energy, and other resources to the liberation of the oppressed.

This is an important point, for many whites tend to designate blacks who have this attitude as antiwhite, antisemitic, antiwoman, and so on, not realizing that they themselves are rather particularistic and provincial when it comes to their own group! Previously it was noted that Cone has described himself as fundamentally a "race man." Such a designation has nothing to do with being "anti-" something else, except antioppression! It is merely one of at least three leadership models in the context of the black community. William A. Jones has given a description of this type of leader.

> The "race man" is the rare creature in the black leadership class. Though not a racist, he is the embodiment of racial pride and has absolute distaste for the system. His primary devotion is to his brothers and sisters in tribulation. He begs no favors from the establishment, but demands justice for his people. While the up-people regard him as militant, revolutionary, and a troublemaker, his own people see him as a spokesman for and champion of their cause.[130]

Blacks in the category of race person recognize who they are; are aware and proud of their religious and cultural heritage; know without question that they live in a racist society with an exploitative political economy; and that if total liberation is to come it must be initiated by blacks who are do-or-die sick and tired of being treated like nonpersons in an ostensibly free and democratic society. Race persons realize that in the minds of too many otherwise good white people, as well as some blacks, too little is viewed as being enough where black interests and human dignity are concerned. Like Malcolm X, and the King of the post–Chicago campaign (of 1966), the race person knows the antics of good white liberals well. Liberals have "extremely heavy consciences and almost nonexistent courage." The race person has no patience with liberals who still think they know more about how blacks should be working to liberate themselves than do blacks. LeRoi Jones (who soon became Imamu Amiri Baraka) wrote of this in 1961.

> Again, I get the feeling that somehow liberals think that they are peculiarly qualified to tell American Negroes and the other oppressed peoples of the world how to wage their struggles. No one wants to hear it. They've heard enough of those benevolent fate tales before. As Nat Cole once said, "Your story's mighty touching, but it sounds like a lie."[131]

In the context of the black community, then, the race person is one who is filled with black pride, self-esteem, and love for his or her people. There is no expectation among such persons that those who presently benefit from the system of exploitation will ever commit themselves to the immediate and total liberation of black people. These are the types of things Cone has in mind when he describes himself as a race person. He does not, by doing this, intentionally demean other groups or imply that racism is the only important social issue.

Whites, particularly those who are committed, do have a role to play in the liberation struggle, but to a large extent their role must be determined by the oppressed. To be sure, blackness as an ontological symbol opens the way for committed whites to participate in the struggle, but the nature and magnitude of black suffering must dictate the nature of their involvement. Conciliatory speeches before black audiences will not do. Rather, committed whites can contribute best by taking every opportunity to be as prophetic as they can be regarding racial, sexual, and class oppression in their own homes, churches, and other institutions. Blacks do not need to hear their prophetic sermons and speeches on racism. White racists who live in their homes and attend their churches need to hear these.

Malcolm X told of how he was once approached by a white young woman student who wanted to know how she could help in the struggle.[132] His response was that there was nothing that she could do. But upon reflection some time later he capitulated. He conceded that he had made a mistake.

He knew that white youths tended to be much more committed than their parents.[133] In his *Autobiography* he gave his final prescription for white involvement in the struggle.

> Where the really sincere white people have got to do their "proving" of themselves is not among the black victims, but on the battle lines of where America's racism really is—and that's in their own home communities; America's racism is among their own fellow whites. That's where the sincere whites who really mean to accomplish something have got to work.[134]

It is not friendship that African Americans need from otherwise good white people. What is needed first and foremost is liberation from white dominance, and the power and resources to be fully human. What is most desired is a socioeconomic system based on the love commandment and the principles of justice and sharing.

Throughout this book I have made references to Cone's criticism of the black church. This almost seems a contradiction since he has a deep love for this institution. I shall argue in the next chapter that it is precisely Cone's love for the black church that leads to his criticism of it. In addition, there have been some subtle as well as pronounced changes regarding his view of the black church and its leadership that needs to be pointed out. It is to these and related matters that I now turn.

6. Cone and the Black Church

THERE WERE NOT a few black religionists who were appalled at Cone's having introduced black theology in 1969. Some were disturbed generally with the idea of "black theology," often claiming with their white counterparts that "there is no such thing as black theology." Most, however, were concerned about specific aspects of this theology. For instance, many had difficulty with Cone's treatment of the violence and reconciliation themes. J. DeOtis Roberts insisted that Cone not only gave the idea of reconciliation too little prominence in his books, but that he did not take it seriously enough. Others were bothered by Cone's identification of black theology with Christianity. Still others did not like his insistence that God is for black people and against white people. And, of course, there were those, e.g., members of the NCBC, who agreed with the general thesis in his first book, but had specific concerns about his heavy dependence upon the works of European and European American theologians. There was also concern that Cone initially seemed to have a shallow knowledge of contributions of the black religious and historical perspective. As shown in Chapter 2 above, and elsewhere, Cone addressed these criticisms in later writings.

Black theology at its best does not aspire to become an academic discipline (though the reality is that it is dangerously close to being just that!). It is, rather, a church discipline.[1] Black theology did not emerge in the seminary or the university. Nor was its appearance the result of intellectual discussions in professional societies. Rather, it emerged in the heat of sociopolitical struggle during the turbulent decade of the sixties. It emerged as courageous black pastors and lay persons struggled in the context of the NCBC and black caucuses to make sense of the meaning of the church in the face of continued racial injustice, systematic brutal violation of black personhood, and economic and other forms of oppression. With the attractions that the emergence of black power had for black youths in church and community, it did not take long for black clergy and lay leaders to see that the black church must take the events of the day seriously and respond accordingly. Black theology was a theology of the streets, a people's theology, and in this sense was viewed as an "earthy" (down to earth) kind of theology. It came into existence as a result of committed and concerned black church persons who worked to relate the Gospel to the concrete issues of the black struggle for freedom.

From the time of the appearance of his first book, Cone has given serious attention to the black church from a theological-historical and contemporary perspective.[2] His primary concern has been to think critically and theologically about the nature and mission of the black church in the face of massive black suffering. Though initially Cone's concern was the role of the black church in liberating blacks from racial injustice, he later broadened his theological analysis to address the church's lack of response to sexism, its missionary policies regarding Third World nations, its attitude toward a capitalistic system that causes pain and suffering to the majority of the people in the world, and other concerns.

To say that Cone's early critique of the black church was scathing is an understatement to many (of the few) black pastors who were familiar with his work. It was this aspect of Cone's theology that was probably most troublesome for black clergy. They could tolerate his criticisms of the white church and many of the themes he introduced and developed in his first two books, but his criticisms of the black church and its leadership was considered sacrilegious. As an internal critic Cone's rhetoric alienated him from many black clergy, much like Malcolm X's external criticism. But unlike Malcolm, Cone did not hesitate to praise the black church and its leadership when historically or contemporaneously they engaged in a liberating ministry. Malcolm's critique was so harsh and so devoid of awareness of the positive contributions of the black church that few black Christians either paid attention to or took seriously his criticisms of their faith.

It is not difficult to imagine what many black pastors thought about Cone's critique of the black church and the way they did their ministry. Many of them undoubtedly thought that Cone committed the unpardonable sin by openly criticizing the black church and its leadership. At this very moment there are black pastors, bishops, and others in the black church community (many who have never read a single work by Cone!) who become as hostile and enraged at the mention of Cone's name as many white students and seminary professors. Before anything else can be said beyond the mention of his name, they are quick to point out that "Cone is not the sole authority on the black religious experience." Inadequately informed black religionists have often been heard to say things like, "Few of these so-called black theologians are in a position to be too critical of the black church and black preachers, since they don't even attend church on a regular basis!" as if the only or chief criterion for being a disciple of Jesus Christ is attending a church every Sunday.

Although it is not possible to address the matter of Cone's view of the black church without some reference to his critique of the white church from slavery to the present,[3] my primary concern has little to do with this aspect of his theological project. In keeping with the general theme of this book, the main purpose is to determine what Cone's initial view of the black church was and whether his interpretation of its role during antebellum and postbellum slavery is consistent with the findings of key scholars in the field of black church history. For the early Cone the black church during the time of slavery was one that was committed to the liberation of black people. However, upon "emancipation" and the advent of the reconstruction years (1867–1877) and up to the Civil Rights campaign of the sixties, there was presumably a great falling away from this more radical strand of black religion. The black church after the Civil War, according to Cone, was as conservative about socio-political matters pertaining to blacks as the white church has always been. Was Cone's assessment accurate? Has his view shifted or changed in some way?

The Antebellum Black Church

Since its inception the black church has been considered the most significant institution in the black community. Some scholars have gone as far as to identify the black church with the black community, and to suggest that neither can be identified apart from the other.[4] The black church was born in protest against racism in the white church. In his early writings Cone espoused the view that after Emancipation the black church was "guilty of prostituting the name of God's church," much like the white church.[5] Yet he has always been proud to point out that originally the black church came into existence "because [blacks] knew that political involvement in societal liberation of black people was equivalent with the gospel. . . ."[6]

The early Cone was under the influence of E. Franklin Frazier's thesis that the process of slavery led to the destruction of all traces of the African religious and cultural heritage within a generation after being forced into American slavery. Frazier maintained that the process of socialization was so brutal and dehumanizing that Africanisms could not have been retained. During the early period of his writing Cone held that the very existence of the black church during slavery "symbolizes a people who were completely stripped of their African heritage as they were enslaved by the 'Christian' white man. The white master forbade the slave from any remembrance of his homeland." Cone was apparently not aware of the opposing view of W.E.B. DuBois and Melville Herskovits.[7]

However, this view changes as a result of his dialogue with colleagues in the Society for the Study of Black Religion. This change is prominent in *The Spirituals and the Blues*, *God of the Oppressed*, and subsequent writings. Wilmore's classic study of black religion had not been published by the time Cone's first three books appeared, but at least by 1972 it was evident that Cone agreed with Wilmore's contention that it is not possible for any group to force its religion upon another.

> But it is a matter of serious debate whether a specific religion belonging to
> a specific people can be transmitted in toto to another people — even in the
> same geographical location — without certain substantive changes due to
> ethnicity, custom, social structure, and many other factors. Especially is this
> true when one people is free and another is enslaved.[8]

Africanisms persisted both during and after slavery. Wilmore points to the
significance of "the creative residuum of the African religions" for antebellum
black Christianity.[9] He contends further that the convoluted form of Christianity that was passed on to blacks during slavery "could not have provided
the slaves with the resources they needed for the kind of resistance they expressed." Rather, according to Wilmore, something more was needed.

> It had to be enriched with the volatile ingredients of the African religious
> parts and, most important of all, with the human yearning for freedom that
> found a channel for expression in the early black churches of the South.[10]

The type of Christianity that Frederick Douglass characterized as "slave-
holding religion,"[11] was a religion of the white status quo. It sought to justify
the enslavement of blacks, rather than resist it and work toward its elimination. Reflecting on the period of American slavery, Manning Marable writes:
"White Christianity as a popular philosophy is not to change the world, but
to alter the prejudices and emotions of those who dwell within the world to
tolerate their real conditions."[12] The strong, persistent desire blacks had for
freedom, and their on-going commitment to the tradition of "blackwater" or
"black radicalism" did not develop as a result of the truncated, adulterated
form of Christianity taught them. Rather, the spirit of the longing for freedom was a result of their remembrance of their homeland, their traditional
African religions, and what they interpreted as the essence of the truth of the
Christian Scriptures. Though most slaves could neither read nor write they
knew that the God of the Christian faith was their liberator, and did not intend for them to be enslaved.

Contrary to what many whites thought, blacks did not accept as Gospel
truth all that they were taught by white religionists. Blacks recognized the in-
consistencies between what whites taught and what they did. Especially was
this true of free blacks like David Walker, who wrote of white Christian
slavers who taught that God ordained blacks and their posterity to a life of
enslavement:

> . . . they were so happy to keep in ignorance and degradation, and to receive
> the homage and the labour of the slaves, they forget that God rules in the
> armies of heaven and among the inhabitants of the earth, having his ears
> continually open to the cries, tears and groans of his oppressed people: and
> being a just and holy Being will at one day appear fully in the behalf of the
> oppressed; for although the destruction of the oppressors God may not effect
> by the oppressed, yet the Lord our God will bring other destructions upon
> them . . . .[13]

Blacks knew that there was something un–Christian about the way whites issued the sacraments to them and then subjected them to the cruel brutalities of slavery. A fugitive slave from Charleston, South Carolina, William Humbert, illustrated this.

> I have seen a minister hand the sacrament to the deacons to give to slaves, and, before the slaves had time to get home, living a great distance from the church, have seen one of the same deacons, acting as patrol, flog one of the brother members within two hours of his administering the sacrament to him, because he met the slave ... without a passport, beyond the time allowed him to go home. ... I looked on the conduct of the deacon with a feeling of revenge. I thought that a man who would administer the sacrament to a brother church member and flog him before he got home, ought not to live.[14]

Although Cone surely knew the tradition of resistance among early black Christians and their awareness of the contradiction between white Christian teachings and white Christian actions, his early writings reveal little evidence of the connection with African religions and other aspects of African cultural heritage. In addition, there is no evidence in his early works of the fact that much of this spirit of resistance may have been a carryover from African religions and the slaves' remembrance of freedom in Africa.

A close reading of Cone's early critique of the black church leaves one with the impression that for him the antebellum black church was similar to what may be called the prophetic church, a church concerned with the socio-political liberation of blacks. In the slave states, the black church was "the home base for revolution,"[15] while free independent black churches in the North often served as links in the underground railroad.[16] Much like the black freedom fighters of the sixties, blacks of the pre–Civil War period often used the church as a platform from which to voice their desire for liberation.

As noted earlier, black Christians in the antebellum period were not fooled into accepting everything the white man taught from the Scriptures, especially the teaching that their enslavement was ordained by God, or that God was concerned about their soul but not the body that houses it. As Cone developed this view in his early writings he displayed a conservative interpretation of the "negro spirituals." He suggested that "most of the Spirituals are otherworldly and compensating in character...."[17] This, he believed, was because of blacks' sense of powerlessness and the absence of hope. Their tendency was to place their hope beyond this world. According to Cone, slaves generally sang of heaven because of their feeling that liberation on earth was hopeless.

Cone cautioned, however, that one cannot say that all of the spirituals had an otherworldly character.[18] But one gets a sense from his early writings that he believed that spirituals with a this-worldly protest character were few and far between. He did point to a few of these that indicated blacks' displeasure with their plight during slavery and their burning desire to be free.[19] Cone acknowledged this trait in a few spirituals in his early work. However, he later made an in-depth study of the spirituals and the blues, and wrote of their theological, sociopolitical, and historical significance for black liberation. Cone pointed to only a few protest spirituals in *Black Theology and Black Power*, leaving the reader with the impression that the greater majority of the spirituals had an otherworldly outlook and had no more than compensatory value. Yet his more mature writings take the opposite view.

In any event, according to Cone's early stance the pre–Civil War black church was one committed to the liberation of blacks from slavery. Apart from his references to the otherworldly, compensatory character of "most of the Spirituals," Cone said little about the conservative element in black religion of that period. Consistent with the thesis of his first book, he said that prior to the Civil War the black church — in the form of certain leaders in independent black churches — tended to equate Christianity and the freedom struggle of blacks in this world. For many black Christians there was an integral relationship between Christianity and earthly justice.[20] There was no radical separation between spiritual and physical salvation. What Henry Mitchell and Nicholas Cooper-Lewter call "core beliefs" in the community of soul,[21] e.g., freedom and equality, Cone designated as "the central theme of the black church" during the antebellum era. In addition, he made the claim that having been born in protest the black church was fundamentally distinguished by its commitment to resistance and actions in the quest for black freedom.[22] It was very clear about its mission, which was cooperating with God in the fight against social injustice. There was no tendency to sit back and do nothing while expecting God to do for oppressed blacks what they could do for themselves.

It is possible that there would be no black church today had blacks during slavery accepted wholeheartedly the white interpretations of the Scriptures and the meaning of the Christian faith. That they did not accept those interpretations is evidenced both by the appearance of the "invisible institution," and the rebellions and protests by black Christians like David Walker, Nat Turner, Henry Highland Garnet, Maria Stewart, and Sojourner Truth. Another indicator was the Richard Allen and Absalom Jones incident at St. George's Methodist Episcopal Church in Philadelphia in 1787. While on their knees at the altar of the Lord, Allen, Jones and other black parishioners were told to leave that area of the church. They left, never to return. It is likely that a good number of them were black women, who have always far outnumbered black men in membership in the black church.

Cone's early study of the black church of the antebellum period led him to conclude that it was in the "blackwater"[23] or "black radicalism"[24] tradition. It was in the tradition of the long continuous river of black struggle for freedom and liberation.[25] Cone indicated his awareness that there were black preachers, Christians, and others who seemed to accept their condition because of their fear of whites,[26] but he was adamant that this notwithstanding, early black churches generally did not accept interpretations of the Christian faith that were not connected to black liberation. Though some black Christians looked to the future, it was precisely this vision of the future that made it impossible for them to equate Christianity and slavery. Some did appear to accept their plight, but most blacks had as great a concern and desire for freedom in this world as in the next.

> The slave's religious principles were colored by his own longings for freedom and based on half-understood sermons in white churches on passages from the Old Testament describing the struggles of the Jews, beautiful pictures of a future life, enchantment and fear, and condemnation of sin. The heaviest emphasis in the slave's religion was on change in their earthly situation and divine retribution for the cruelty of their masters.[27]

John Blassingame suggests that there was indeed "a small minority" of black preachers and others who, because of their literal reading of the Scriptures and their too willing acceptance of white interpretations, actually had a conservative view and therefore counseled slaves on how to avoid the lash. Yet "the heaviest emphasis" in the religion of the slaves was the radical element of protest and resistance to evil in this world. Even slaves who outwardly appeared to accept white interpretations of the Scriptures probably rejected them.

As noted previously, it was Marable who introduced the term "blackwater" to describe the radical, activist strand of black religious faith. Marable makes a real contribution in terms of helping us to understand that tradition, especially in light of the tendency of many early white historians to characterize the black faith as predominantly conservative and otherworldly. Even the late E. Franklin Frazier basically described the antebellum black church in this way.[28] The early Cone was not in agreement with Frazier on this point.

Not unmindful of the clearcut conservative elements within black faith, Marable contends that blackwater is really the other side of black faith, and one cannot fully understand black religion if one does not see that there is a dialectical relationship between these two dimensions. Blackwater is "a partial reaction to the otherworldliness of the black ministry."[29] It is the opposite of the accommodationist strand in the black religious tradition.[30] Those who take blackwater seriously are likely to be race persons. Blackwater is diametrically opposed to accepting black oppression.

There have always been blacks and other oppressed people who have felt that they were not the victims of oppression, believing instead that their plight was ordained by God. The spirit of blackwater rejects this tendency, although it is "a painful break from the consciousness of the master, in favor of creativity and collective emancipation."[31] Blackwater is a challenge to all forms of patience with black oppression.

Cone, Marable, and other black scholars have shown convincingly that the tradition of blackwater can be historically grounded in the black religious tradition. One wonders, however, whether there is reason to believe that the tradition is still alive. Wilmore thinks there is a remnant of blacks who continue to relate black religion to radicalism. "It is my opinion that some persons are still searching for historical foundations within the heritage of black religion to undergird the continuing struggle for justice and liberation."[32] He is certain that there continues to be an "inseparable connection" between black religion and sociopolitical struggles for black liberation. Furthermore, the radical strand with its emphasis on actions that will lead to liberation, "is the defining characteristic of black Christianity and black religion in the United States...."[33]

Wilmore contends that this radical thrust has been present from the time of the preacher-led slave revolts, through the appearance of the radical black clergy and lay persons of the NCBC of the sixties. This perspective is different from Cone's, since he actually held during the early period of his writing that the radical element was lost after the Civil War, and only recaptured (somewhat) in the work of King during the civil rights movement. Cone, unlike Wilmore, Marable, and Albert Raboteau, believed there was a radical break in the blackwater tradition between the period of Emancipation and the beginning of the civil rights movement. But this interpretation underwent a change after his research and study of the history of the black religious tradition. This moved Cone much closer to Wilmore. But for now, suffice it to say that the early Cone believed that "for the pre–Civil War black preacher, Christianity was inextricably related to social justice in this world."[34] He also believed that the black church was the only church in America "which remained recognizably Christian."[35] Its commitment to human freedom in word and deed was consistent with what it means to be a disciple of Jesus Christ. The black church of the antebellum period, unlike the white church, was not born in heresy. The postbellum black church on the other hand, was another matter.

The Post–Civil War Black Church

Cone argued that the black church of the postbellum period strayed from its prophetic heritage. Though once a mechanism for protest and agitation against racial oppression, the black church now accepted things as they were. The liberation of blacks was no longer a priority. The black church now busied itself with seeking the acceptance of whites; with raising money to build churches; with instructing black Christians on how to avoid trouble with whites. Cone noted that at best there were a few "rare instances" in which

the postbellum black churches were more Christian than their white counterparts. However, it was a long time between the end of the Civil War and the
period when black churches again began to show evidence of the influence of
blackwater. According to Cone, the first exceptions appeared during the early
part of the civil rights movement. He believed that it was only during the
early stage of that movement that the black church gave signs of recapturing
the spirit of black radicalism.[36] Cone viewed the work of King as one of these
rare exceptions.

Cone has defined the Church as that body of people whose existence was
called forth by the life, death, and resurrection of Jesus Christ, in order that
they may bear witness to his Lordship by joining with Him in the struggle
against all forces of evil that have led to the subjugation of people of color,
women, and other traditionally excluded peoples. The church is defined not
in terms of theological affirmations, confessions, and personal morality, but
in terms of its social and political commitment to set at liberty those who are
oppressed.[37] The early Cone contended that after the Civil War the black
churches "became perversions of the Gospel of Christ and places for accommodating the oppressed plight of black people."[38] They were at best sanc-
tuaries of "retreat from the dehumanizing forces of white power." Here blacks
could feel safe and protected from the oppressive conditions in white society.
The black church was gradually developing into a place of temporary escape.[39]

During the period of Reconstruction, blacks, especially those who were
free before the Emancipation Proclamation, were able to participate in government through elections and political appointments to a degree that was previously unknown. There may have been a feeling among many blacks that
things were getting better, and that it was not necessary to continue the radical tradition of protest. In addition, after the Civil War many may have been
tiring from the struggle. When the Compromise of 1877 made it possible for
the white Southern leadership to handle race relations without the worry of
federal intervention, the bubble of Reconstruction effectively burst. Even
during Reconstruction the foundation and structures were being laid for new
Jim Crow laws. Those notorious cousins of Pulaski, Tennessee, "Ku," "Klux,"
and "Klan" also emerged during the early part of Reconstruction. The Klan
was effective in terrorizing blacks in rural and other areas.[40] Such tactics must
have had adverse effects on any sense of optimism that recently "freed" blacks
initially exhibited. This may help explain the tendency toward conservatism
and the desire to view the black church as a safe haven from white brutality.
The Klan was thoroughly effective as far as instilling a sense of fear in
blacks.[41] Both during and after Reconstruction the federal government failed
to provide the economic and other resources that would have led to the pro-
tection of blacks from the terrorist activities of the Klan. It must have been
difficult for blacks to know who among the white population was not a member

of the Klan, since it was known that so-called respectable members of the white church and community were often found to be members. Is it any wonder that the radical element in the black church seemed to decline?

Since it was difficult for blacks to know which whites could be trusted, radicalism, understandably, could have made their situation even more tenuous than it was. During slavery they had a better chance of knowing who the enemy was and who could be trusted (though even during this period it was not always easy to know). The law of the land made it possible for them to be enslaved by whites. In this respect they knew where they stood. But during and after Reconstruction, blacks were confronted with a different situation. Now they did not always know where they stood, for the law was no longer consonant with the behavior of the lawmakers. The Emancipation Proclamation officially ended slavery, but blacks were still forced to live lives of peonage. Cone pointed out that under such circumstances "all the strength and will power is sapped from the would-be rebel. The structures of evil are camouflaged, the energy is elusive, and the victim is trained to accept the values of the oppressor."[42] Socialized to believe that their oppression was due to ignorance and inferiority, many blacks were deceived into believing that things would be better for them if only they could become like whites! Cone implies that in part it was the role of the schools of the Freedman's Bureau, the Booker T. Washingtons, and the black churches to teach blacks how to be like their white oppressors.[43] If only they could learn to be like whites they could be accepted, or so they seemed to think.

Cone's conclusion about what happened to the black church and its leaders during this period and the failure to recapture its prophetic fervor has angered and distressed many black pastors and lay leaders. Cone spared no one in his early characterization of the postbellum black church.

> The black church thus lost its zeal for freedom in the midst of the new structures of white power. The rise of segregation and discrimination in the post-Civil War period softened its drive for equality. The black minister remained the spokesman for the black people, but, "faced by insurmountable obstacles he succumbed to the cajolery and bribery of the white power structure and became its foil." The passion for freedom was replaced with innocuous homilies against drinking, dancing, and smoking; and injustices in the present were minimized in favor of a Kingdom beyond this world. Black churches adopted, for the most part, the theology of the white missionaries and taught blacks to forget the present and look to the future.[44]

Finding that after the Reconstruction years the nation had returned to the business of segregation and discrimination, many blacks, according to this view, became frustrated and despondent. Black preachers began to admonish that blacks abide by the laws and moral codes of white society, and some even implied that violations of these would block one's entrance into the Kingdom of God! Some black preachers concluded that violations of the laws of white society was immoral and that the violator was susceptible to disciplinary action by the church and possible expulsion, depending on the nature of the case. Some contended that suffering in this world was a necessary prerequisite for entering heaven. The implication, of course, is that good Christians do not worry about injustice and suffering in this world. "Undue concern about white injustice was thus a sign of a loss of faith, a failure to realize that patience and long-suffering were more pertinent to final judgment than zeal for present justice."[45] Endurance and patience became chief virtues.

Cone did not have many positive and encouraging things to say about the post–Civil War black preacher, characterizing him as the worst kind of "Uncle Tom" who was the transmitter of white values and distorted truths.

> He was the liaison man between the white power structure and the oppressed blacks, serving the dual function of assuring whites that all is well in the black community, dampening the spirit of freedom among his people. More than any other one person in the black community, the black minister perpetuated the white system of black dehumanization.[46]

Before proceeding further, more should be said about Cone's early interpretation of the postbellum black church and the black minister.

In the first place, it is interesting that Cone's early interpretation follows closely that given by Joseph Washington in the controversial text *Black Religion: The Negro and Christianity in the United States*. It was this text that angered so many of the radical clergy and laity of the NCBC, although many whites applauded it. Cone himself disagreed with many of the major theses in the text when it first appeared.

Yet one wonders why Cone seemed to accept, almost uncritically, Washington's interpretation of the black preacher. Washington wrote of the dysfunctional nature of black religion, and of the increasing dissatisfaction with black preachers since the second decade of the twentieth century.[47] Cone's early assessment of the black church takes this perspective seriously. In addition, it may be that he resonated so easily with this view because of his own negative experiences with black bishops of his denomination (African Methodist Episcopal Church). Cone recounts this bitter experience in *My Soul Looks Back*.[48]

In the second place, Cone's sharp distinction between the antebellum and postbellum black church is not accurate. Cone was convinced that after the Civil War the black church too often identified "white words with the Word of God," and believed that if blacks listened and obeyed they would make it to the promised land (Heaven). The black church and its leadership lost its sense of creativity and commitment to the Gospel mandate of liberation.[49] Cone was initially convinced that apart from the leadership of Martin Luther King, Jr., the black church of the postbellum period was functioning outside the prophetic tradition of the pre–Civil War period. Too many black churches of the sixties were involved in the civil rights movement only in a half-hearted way.

No black Christian was as acutely critical of the black church than King. Only Malcolm X, an external critic, was more critical.[50] King's criticism generally centered on the black church's "one-sided, anti-intellectual focus on the heaven theme to the exclusion of problems on earth, and its class snobbery."[51] Black preachers often denigrated education and spent too much time trying to perfect the art of whooping and entertaining, rather than studying so that their sermons would have substance. Much of their time was spent talking about Heaven beyond the grave, rather than focusing on the ideal of a new Heaven on earth. King also lamented the tendency of black churches to become classist as the members attained middle class status. In addition, King voiced his concern that too many black churches had made available various resources, such as money or church facilities, while withholding commitment to the point of actually participating in the protest marches and other actions to break down the barriers to racial justice. In *Where Do We Go from Here*, King wrote that "there are still too many Negro churches, that are so absorbed in a future good 'over yonder' that they condition their members to adjust to the present evils 'over here.'"[52] King was adamant that blacks could not simply pray, shout, and sing and expect God to do the work of concrete liberation.

> *God isn't going to do all of it by himself.* The church that overlooks this is a dangerously irrelevant church.... *We are gravely misled if we think the struggle will be won only by prayer.* God who gave us minds for thinking and bodies for working would defeat his own purpose if he permitted us to obtain through prayer what may come through work and intelligence[53] [emphasis added].

He also wrote of his concern that other areas of the black community, e.g., black newspapers, had strayed from their historic role as protest organs calling for justice and social change.

In Cone's view, the only hope for the black church of the civil rights period was for it wholeheartedly to repent of its sins and join the true mission of the church, which is participation in the black revolution.[54] Black churches must recapture their pre–Civil War heritage; "they must relinquish their stake in the status quo and the values in white society by identifying exclusively with Black Power. Black Power is the only hope of the black church in America."[55]

For Cone the black church lost its soul and the respect of most black youths and radicals in the sixties. It was more concerned about maintaining its institutional structures and fund-raising activities for the purpose of constructing elaborate church buildings, often right in the heart of economically depressed black neighborhoods. Black churches spent (and spend!) too much time celebrating their pastor's anniversary and too little working to find ways to eradicate the mistreatment and unnecessary deaths of black men, women, and children. Even King could say:

> I'm sick and tired of seeing Negro preachers riding around in big cars and living in big houses and not concerned about the problems of the people who made it possible for them to get these things.[56]

Cone suggested that the black church in its constituent community was black in name only, and was little more than a parasite in the community.

> The black church, though spatially located in the community of the oppressed, has not responded to the needs of its people. It has, rather, drained the community, seeking to be more and more like the white church. Its ministers have condemned the helpless and have mimicked the values of whites. For this reason most Black Power people bypass the churches as irrelevant to their objectives.[57]

Was the interpretation of the black church that appeared in Cone's early writings accurate? Was the black church primarily a prophetic church during slavery, but more of an accommodationist or conservative church after slavery and during the early sixties? Did Cone make too sharp a distinction between the black church of the one era and that of the other?

Cone's early interpretation is faulty only because of his radical separation of the two traditions of the black faith. For the sake of discussion and analysis it may be helpful to abstract the protest strand from the accommodationist, but in actual experience — past and present — it can be shown convincingly that the two strands developed *pari passu*. One cannot adequately grasp the significance of the meaning of black faith if these two undercurrents are not acknowledged and understood in themselves, and then as an integral whole. Cone's primary error was that he did not pay enough attention to the fact that in no era of the history of black people in this country can one say that the black church was merely prophetic (radical), or that it was simply conservative. It has always been both of these, despite periods in which one of these factors was dominant or more pronounced than the other.

To date Gayraud Wilmore has done the most systematic work on the relationship between the two undercurrents that run throughout the development of black religion in this country, though, to be sure, he emphasizes the radical strand. He does so partly to give lie to those views of the historic and contemporary black church as a conservative institution that is no more than an opiate. But Wilmore, unlike the early Cone, contends that this double focus of the black faith has existed in every period of its development.

> One of the continuing paradoxes of the black church as the custodian of a great portion of black culture and religion is that it is at once the most reactionary and the most radical of black institutions; the most inclined with the mythology and values of white America; and yet the most proud, the most independent and indigenous collectivity in the black community. In order

to appreciate black religion and the black church—indeed, in order to understand black radicalism anywhere in the world—one must delve into the nature and meaning of this paradox of the religious experience of Africans—both on the African continent and in the diaspora.[58]

All critics of the black church would do well to understand this paradoxical relationship between the more conservative and radical elements if they intend to understand black pride and power, black nationalism, pan–Africanism, and other currents of black belief. These had their roots in the paradox of black religious experience. The black church has never been just radical or just conservative. In sociological terms it is like saying that church (conservative) and sect (radical/prophetic) tendencies have always existed side by side in black religion. Wilmore expresses this admirably in his text, but he insists that the essence or "defining characteristic" of black religion is its radical strand. It is this aspect which makes black religion so radically different from white religion in terms of their approaches to sociopolitical liberation and radical social change.[59]

In light of Wilmore's argument, Cone's interpretation was not as accurate as it could have been. He was wrong to suggest that the black church was prophetic in one era and conservative in another. In every era of black Christianity there has been at least a remnant that has remained dedicated to identifying the Gospel with the black struggle for liberation. Cone makes too great a distinction between the two undercurrents in the early period of his writing. What needs to be determined in a given period is which of the dimensions predominates. Marable has written that "blackwater has largely triumphed, for the time being, over the more conservative accommodationist elements of Christianity," and that black preachers are in the forefront of those who reject the conservative element.[60] This seems, however, to be a questionable conclusion since there is not sufficient empirical evidence to support it. In any case, we can say, against the early Cone, that there has always been, and continues to be a "dual search for the Spirit and for temporal civil and human rights" among black Christians.[61]

A Changing Perspective on the Black Church

In his more recent writings Cone provides many clues regarding his present perspective on the black church and its leadership. In his intellectual and spiritual testimony recounted in *My Soul Looks Back*, he assures us of his continuous critique of the black church.[62] We are also informed that though he was severely critical of the black church in his first book, he has been less severe in his criticism in subsequent publications. This, he claims, is not because the church has progressed to such a degree as to obviate his prophetic critique. Rather, it is because he believed whites would both misinterpret the meaning of his critique and use it in ways that he would not approve.[63] One can see the radical difference, for example, between the tone and extent of his critique in his first and second books. In the former he devoted an entire chapter to criticizing the black church, while in the second text he devotes less than one page of mild critique.[64]

Although his written critiques of the black church were not as severe after 1969, Cone continues to apply the principle of self-criticism to the black church and community. As long as the church's ministry is not effectively geared toward the mandate of liberation it cannot be immune to criticism. Cone writes that "to cover-up and to minimize the sins of the church is to guarantee its destruction as a community of faith, committed to the liberation of the oppressed."[65] It would be hypocritical to point out the sins and weaknesses of the white church and not be critical of the conditions in the black church. Because Cone is so strongly influenced by Malcolm X it is reasonable to say that his severest criticisms are reserved for closed-door sessions with his people. There are some things that blacks must keep between themselves.

Even a cursory reading of *My Soul Looks Back*, *For My People*, and *Speaking the Truth* will reveal Cone's on-going critique of the black church. Though in the early period he was nearly as angry with the black church as with the white church,[66] his anger continues, though his public expressions have been tempered. We discover through systematic reading of Cone's works that there are more than a dozen changes in his view of the black church. Just as with the other transitions in his thinking, some of the changes are subtle and some pronounced. In almost every case, the seeds of each change were present in Cone's early writings.

From the early period of Cone's theology through the present, one detects at least thirteen criticisms of the black church and its leadership. Some of these are criticisms that were raised either implicitly or explicitly in his early theological writings. What this suggests is that by 1982 and beyond, the black church had not, in Cone's view, progressed very far in some areas. I shall address each of these criticisms.

The first criticism: Having pointed out in his first book that black pastors and other church leaders spend too much time with organizational matters, with fund-raising, for instance, for the purpose of building lavish church buildings in the heart of the black community,[67] Cone lifts this up as a major criticism in his more advanced stage of development as well.[68] The priorities of black pastors have not yet been reordered. The primary commitment is not to participating with Jesus Christ to effect the liberation and empowerment of blacks and other oppressed peoples, but to gain status among their clergy peers, to wear expensive clothing and jewelry, to gain the attention and *acceptance* of the white establishment. Pastors spend too much time on their own individual churches and denomination. Most of these activities have little to do with prophetic ministry. Too many black pastors still think that the black church exists only for itself, while the attitude ought to be that it exists for Him who died on the cross and was resurrected.

The second criticism: By devoting so much time, energy, and resources to routine organizational concerns, black church members and pastors — knowingly or not — tend to uncritically accept the religious and cultural beliefs and practices of their white counterparts, according to Cone. An alarming number still believe there is only one right way to worship, to perform the liturgy, and the like, and that is the way it is done in the white church, which presumably sets the standard in all areas of worship for the Church Universal.

In addition, too many black Christians still know more about major white religious personalities and founders of white demoninations than contributions of blacks. Having referred to this in 1969, Cone again mentions it in later writings. Black Christians have been guilty in this regard partly because they have not taken up the study of their social, religious, and cultural heritage. Nor have they paid much attention to African traditional religions that have bearing on black religion in the United States. In many ways black religion is what it is today because of African retentions that black ancestors intermixed with the best of the Christianity taught by white slave masters. Those who are not informed by and connected with their historical roots often tend to "assume the identity of the group that conquers them."[69] Cone wonders why such large numbers of black churches still display portraits of the white Christ; why so much of their church school literature reflects the culture of white America; and why there is continued use of literature for black youth that overwhelmingly portray pictures of white youth.

The third criticism: Cone believes the black church is not making enough significant progress in developing its own theology in its creeds, resolutions, and liturgy. This criticism is also a carryover from the early period. There continues to be a too easy acceptance of the theological affirmations of whites. There is still the sense that only the theology espoused by whites is authentic and that blacks cannot do theology without resorting to their theological principles. Blacks still find it easier to accept Martin Luther's dissent from the Catholic Church as a theological issue. However, it continues to be difficult for them to understand that the action of Richard Allen, Absalom Jones, and others in 1787, which led to the founding of the A.M.E. Church, was no less theological.[70] This separation was not merely a result of social factors. There were theological issues involved as well. For example, white mistreatment of blacks in the church had strong theological overtones, particularly regarding their doctrine of God. How could the One God, who has created us all, and in whom we all live and move and have our being, have intended for some to be slaves and others to be slaveholders?

In addition, the tendency to disregard or disparage the theological enterprise, and the failure to consider the theological implications of the black

struggle in the United States has also had adverse effects on theological education among black clergy and laity. There continues to be an exorbitant number of black clergy who are not theologically trained.[71] Cone understands that
there are complex and multiple reasons for this, but he also knows that in too
many cases black clergy denigrate the significance of theological education
from the pulpit. This has the effect of dissuading many younger, would-be
pastors from seeking formal training. In addition, the black church does not
adequately support black theological schools. "As they see it, their task is to
preach the gospel without critically asking, What is the gospel and how is it
related to black life?" This tends to diminish the level and extent of self-
criticism in the black church, which in turn leads to insensitivity to issues like
sexism and classism, and how they impinge upon one's concept of ministry.
This insensitivity and lack of knowledge frequently leads to responses that are
as conservative as those given by white churches.

The fourth criticism: In the early period, and through the present, Cone
has raised a concern about the absence of accountability in the church. The
tradition in many black churches and denominations is that the pastor or
bishop has carte blanche in their day-to-day work. They often wield a tremendous amount of unchecked power, even when that power is misused — as it
is when used for anything other than ministering effectively with disinherited
parishioners. To be sure, there are other needs in the black community for
which this power should be utilized, but it should always be used to set at
liberty the captives. Cone continues to espouse the view that the accountability of black pastors and other church leaders to Jesus Christ as defined by the
struggle of the people for justice is indispensable for the future life of the black
church.[72] One gets a sense from considering his early and later works that this
criticism is primarily applicable to the more prominent, well-to-do pastors,
bishops, and church executives. Clearly, few African Americans have the
level of relative autonomy and freedom to speak and do the truth as black
pastors.

The fifth criticism: The early Cone also expressed a concern for the lack
of a sense of ecumenism in the black churches. He is much more explicit
about this criticism in later writings. He has not been as concerned about the
black church's failure to share wholeheartedly the ecumenical vision of predominantly white national and international organizations like the National
Council of Churches, the Consultation on Church Union, or the World Council of Churches. Some black churches have an involvement with these organizations, but Cone's greater concern has been the failure of the development
of an ecumenical vision within the black religious community. He suspects
that with all the emphasis that the aforementioned organizations place on
local, national, and international denominational unity, even if that were
achieved there would continue to be blatant and subtle forms of racism inside
and outside the white church. White churches involved in these organizations

seem to desire church unity, but only if it can be had without addressing and solving the evils of racism, sexism, and economic exploitation. Cone writes of this concern in an essay entitled "Black Ecumenism and the Liberation Struggle":

> The absence of any serious commitment of white Christians to eliminate racism in their churches and in the society accounts for the lack of serious dialogue on the part of black independent churches in the ecumenical deliberations of the Consultation on Church Union, the National Council of Churches, and the World Council of Churches in Geneva. We blacks do not believe that church unity with white people is meaningful unless it arises out of a demonstrated commitment to implement justice in the society.[73]

Because it has been nearly three hundred and fifty years, and white churches have not yet shown evidence of sustained, relevant actions to eradicate racism; because there is so much that needs to be done in the black church and community, Cone has persistently turned his attention to black ecumenism and getting blacks to see the importance of a unified black church working toward the liberation of black people. This is consistent with his view that African Americans should do what they do for black people, and that black unity is crucial if liberation is to come. This latter principle is straight out of the thinking of Malcolm X, who asserted that there can be no black-white unity until there is significant black unity, both in the United States and other parts of the world.[74]

Pointing to "the ecumenical significance of black theology," Cone contends that it is not merely limited to exposing the hypocrisies of white theology and the white church. Rather, it has import for the black church because it challenges it to work steadily and creatively toward the actual achievement of the freedom it sings about and that some of its pastors preach about. It challenges the black church not to be like its white counterpart in the handling of black suffering and pain. Having developed an ecumenical vision through the institutional structure of the NCBC during the sixties, Cone believes there is a need for the black church to recapture this. For Cone, Willie White[75] characterized the kind of ecumenism he has in mind regarding the black churches. White expressed this in his definition of the black church.

> The black church is defined by the very ideas which demand a new ecumenism among black Christians . . . not by any or all of the traditionally accepted creeds but by the creed of liberation: the creed that one man does not have the right to oppress another, be the other black or white, baptized by immersion or by sprinkling, fashionably attired or running naked in the jungle. It is defined by the creed that the dehumanization of one man by another is in total contradiction to the way of Christ and must be opposed. And it is this creed that makes possible the . . . black church community.[76]

Any sense of ecumenism among black churches should be defined or measured by a commitment to liberation. Cone's concern, of course, is that too few black churches took this seriously in the sixties and so many fail to do so today. Implying that White's definition of the black church and its commitment to liberation is one that was characteristic of the historic black church, Cone, as if to use this as a measuring rod, asks whether "black churches, as institutions, still regard black people's struggle for political liberation as the theological foundation of their *raison d'être*?" He is certain that few black churches can give an affirmative response.

As a new element in this criticism of the absence of black ecumenism, Cone admonishes that it is no longer sufficient to appeal to historic black religious heroes and *sheroes*[77] as if that alone makes the black church of today relevant. It is necessary to concretize the meaning of those personalities for today, and black churches are not presently committed to a ministry of liberation. Cone concludes that historically black denominations and black churches in white denominations "are not good models of black ecumenism," and that "few of them have made an institutional commitment to organize church life and work for the creation of freedom."[78]

Another significant element added to his criticism of the black church is the failure to take the gender issue seriously. Cone now contends that black ecumenism must include our "struggle to give equal status to women in the church and the society."[79] If it fails to do so it has no right to call itself Christian. God created all persons in God's image, and in Christ there is no male nor female. All persons — male and female — are equals before God, and as people who claim to be Christians it is necessary to work diligently and deliberately to apply this principle in concrete situations. Separation between black men and women continues, Cone believes, because of the selfish interest of black men and the fact that they have more power inside the church.[80]

The sixth criticism: In *Black Theology and Black Power*, Cone reproved the black church and its ministers for having "condemned the helpless,"[81] the poor and the impoverished. As noted previously, both Malcolm X and King were also critical of the black church in this regard. Years later, Cone wrote of the indifference of the black church to the poor and the weak.[82] The black church continues to fall short when it comes to affirming "a oneness based on a practical solidarity with the poor." Since no black person is crushed primarily because of membership in a particular denomination, profession, or class, but because he or she is black, black ecumenism must be broad enough to include all blacks, e.g., the poor and impoverished, women, children and youths, the physically and sexually different, and others, both in this country and other areas of the world with large numbers of Third World people.

The seventh criticism: A criticism of the black church that did not appear in Cone's early writings (possibly because he had not yet travelled in Third World countries) is its failure to develop and implement an adequate philosophy of missions with Third World nations. Though black churches have been sending missionaries to Africa and other nations (except Asia) for many years, their philosophy and practice of missions is little different from that of white churches. The tendency, Cone says, is to go to those countries with an air of arrogance and the attitude that "our way is the best way." In this regard the black church is as backward as the white church. It has shown little respect and sensitivity to the religious or cultural practices of those nations, and has failed to take seriously the discussions about indigenous leadership, especially in Africa. Too often the black church has given no sign of being concerned about the Africans' struggles for liberation and their desire to develop their own leadership in the churches. Neither do African American churches take sufficiently seriously the African traditional religions. Writing of the missionary practices of the A.M.E. and A.M.E. Zion Churches, Cone contends that "the fact that the African mission is controlled by the interests of North American black church people is a disgrace to the legacy of Henry McNeal Turner, not to mention the gospel of Jesus Christ."[83] He is not unmindful, however, that some black churches have done commendable missionary work. In this regard he points specifically to A.M.E. Bishop H.H. Brookins's support of the liberation fighters in Zimbabwe. Cone's concern is that there should be much more of this rather than a few isolated exceptions.

The eighth criticism: Another more recent criticism of the black church, and related to the previous one, is its relative lack of a global perspective, or a failure to see the connections between local or national problems and problems in the Third World. The black church needs to see the relationship between racism, sexism, classism, and capitalism throughout the world. Blacks cannot be free until all oppressed people are free. "Liberation," Cone contends, "knows no color line; the very nature of the gospel is universalism, i.e., a liberation that embraces the whole of humanity."[84] This global, universal perspective does not mean that blacks should either be subordinate or no longer be concerned about the specific struggles of blacks. "We must create a global vision of human liberation and include in it the distinctive contribution of the black experience."[85] The emphasis on the liberation of blacks must not be diminished because of our global perspective. As pointed out in chapters 4 and 5 above, both Malcolm X and King contributed greatly to sensitizing the black community to the need for an internationalist perspective on oppression. Today, however, much work remains to be done.

The ninth criticism: This criticism was pointed to by Cone during the height of his rage in the late sixties and early seventies. During this period he expressed his discontent with capitalism and individualism.[86] He had only a cursory knowledge of Marxism during that period, and would not discover the worth of Marxism as a tool for critical social analysis until just before the mid-seventies. In any event, the later Cone has been very critical of the black church's easy acceptance of capitalism, and its failure to see that in such a system the poor will always be with us. The goal of blacks ought not to be that of getting an equal share of the American capitalist pie, especially since the plight of the masses in such a system will not undergo any significant positive change. The goal ought to be the creation of social and economic structures that are not oppressive but which take seriously the supreme reverence for all persons. Until the black church begins to be critical of capitalism and its dehumanizing effects both in this country and the Third World, Christians from those countries will continue to think of the black church as little more than the white church blackenized!

The tenth criticism: The black churches have paid little attention to the role of social analysis, so essential in helping to realize its dream about a new earth. As indicated in the discussion on the movement from anger to social analysis in Chapter 4 above, the need for social analysis was implied in Cone's early writings. He is not critical of the black church's dream of a new day. Rather, the message he wishes to convey is that dreaming alone is not sufficient to bring the desired liberation.

> We must come down from the mountain top and experience the hurts and pain of the people in the valley. Our dreams need to be socially analyzed, for without scientific analysis they will vanish into the night. Furthermore, social analysis will test the nature of our commitment to the dreams that we preach and sing about. . . . Real substantial change in societal structures requires scientific analysis.[87]

Merely dreaming, preaching, singing, and praying about liberation will do little to actualize it in this world. Important as these activities are, they must be coupled with sociopolitical analysis and activities to make the new earth a reality.

The eleventh criticism: When black churches and black pastors have appealed to the historic radical tradition of the black church in an attempt to convince black youths of the relevance of these, those youths have often inquired as to whether the contemporary black churches actually includes this tradition in their everyday ministries. The sixties was a period when waves of black youths fled from what they viewed as an irrelevant institution. This is one of the reasons radical black clergy of the NCBC began to take the black power movement seriously.

Having referred to this concern of black youths in earlier writings,[88] Cone has continued to express his dismay that the black church still fails to base its ministry on the liberation mandate of the Gospel. This may be one reason that so many black youths, including those of a generation ago (who are now adults), continue to turn away from the church. Many still wonder about the absence of radicalism in most black churches. "Young blacks contend that the black churches of today, with few exceptions, are not involved in liberation but primarily concerned about how much money they can raise for a new church building or the preacher's anniversary."[89] To define its ministry in a way that takes black suffering and the struggle for liberation seriously may not in itself cause large numbers of black youth to rush back to the church, but defining the ministry that way is probably one of the essential ingredients. Besides, the point is not to devise ways to recruit youth into the church, but to consciously develop a ministry that effectively liberates the captives of all age groups.

The twelfth criticism: For a long time it was considered "off limits" to criticize the black church and black pastors. In part, this was encouraged by black pastors and other church leaders who like to remind church members and others that God said: "Touch not my anointed one!" Never mind that the so-called "anointed one" is constantly engaged in devilish behavior and does nothing to set the captives free, or misappropriates church funds! The plea is always the same, "Touch not!" Those who hold such a view maintain that one can criticize any and everything and everybody in the black community, except the black church and black preachers. That this should be so has been an on-going criticism of Cone's. In part the lack of self-criticism in the black church for many years can be attributed to the lack of encouragement for theological education, and there were therefore few persons around to discover and challenge the limitations of the black church.

The tendency in the black church has been to emphasize preaching and not even to include critical theology. Internal self-criticism is crucial to the health and vibrancy of the black church. Cone contends that "seldom has the black church created the context for prophetic criticism to arise from within,"[90] although some of this happened during the life of the NCBC. In addition, true prophets are distinguished from false ones by their willingness to subject themselves to criticism, as did Malcolm X and King. "Only false prophets shun criticism, because they do not want their real motives revealed."[91]

The thirteenth criticism: Cone often pointed out that the black church was too much like the white church. Initially he wrote that the two were alike (after the Civil War) in that neither was authentically committed to a ministry based on Jesus's mandate to set at liberty the poor and the oppressed. But even in later writings Cone contends that the black church is too much like its white counterpart in attitude toward sexism, capitalism, and missions in the Third World. Recognizing that in part the black church has internalized the views and values of the white church because it lost its sense of connection with its past history, Cone has always indicated that though neither church "is a fit instrument of revolution,"[92] the black church has been more prophetic than the white church, and at least has had periods when it was radically involved in the world. The white–American church has no history of obedience; and without it, it is unlikely that it will ever know what radical obedience to Christ means. Since it is identified with the structures of power, it will always be possible for it to hedge and qualify its obedience to Christ. Also, being white in soul and mind, the white church must make a "special" effort in order to identify with the suffering of the oppressed, an effort which is almost inevitably distorted into plantation charity.[93] Since the white church generally seeks the easy, least costly way out in addressing its racism, it is not likely that it will soon be an instrument for genuine liberation.

With its heritage of radical sociopolitical involvement, the black church needs merely to recapture the significance of this heritage and concretize it today. If it would do this there is a real possibility that it may not only save itself, but the white church as well. In any case, it is insane for the black church to continue being so much like the white church in light of the historic and contemporary relationship between them.

Cone has retained a critical view of the black church since the appearance of his first book. Several of the criticisms noted above appeared in germinal form in the early stage of his development, becoming much more focused and pronounced during the middle and later stages. Others, e.g., the absence of black ecumenism, the failure to acknowledge sexism as a major problem, an unacceptable philosophy of missions, a lack of a global perspective, and an easy acceptance of capitalism, are all new criticisms that arose during the middle and late seventies.

Although Cone continues to insist on the need for internal self-criticism within the black church and community, and although he continues to be disturbed by the failure of the black church to liberate itself from thinking and acting like its white counterpart, he has always believed that on balance the black church has been truer to the mission of the Church of Jesus Christ than the white church. Yet, because of his commitment to writing and doing theology for his people, it is not as important how the black church looks in comparison to the white church. What is more important is how the black church is perceived by black people. What is crucial, finally, is whether the black church will take its tradition of blackwater or black radicalism seriously enough to make the sociopolitical liberation of blacks, other people of color, and *all* women the central principle of its ministry, recognizing that its only hope is the realization that it must join forces with Jesus Christ in the battle against all forms of oppression and for complete liberation.

Black churches must return to their liberating heritage. They need to reorder their priorities.

> The concern of the black church should be not in gaining more members for itself but only in liberating the victims wherever they are found. But in order to do that, the black church must divest itself of its preoccupation with itself and become identified exclusively with the interest of Jesus Christ, who is always found among the poor, liberating them from bondage.[94]

It is important to point out that as critical as Cone has been of the black church, he has never desired that black theologians and ethicists make their criticisms as if they themselves are outside the church and therefore are excluded from those criticisms. They are part of the black community. Black theology was born and nurtured in the black community, and consequently any theologizing about the black church and its leadership must take place within that context.[95]

This is not the language of a man who hates or disrespects the black church. Cone includes himself, just as every black theologian must, in the criticisms against the black church. Cone's criticism of the black church is at the same time a criticism of himself inasmuch as he is part of that church. This points to the fact that just because one is critical of something does not necessarily mean a dislike or hatred for whatever is being criticized. On the contrary, it may be argued that we dislike a thing most when we fail to be critical of it when the evidence warrants constructive criticism, which alone can lead to growth.

Cone's Love for the Black Church

No one who has ever heard Cone lecture, talked with him in private, or read his works closely can fail to detect the deep love he has for the black church. Though he made no explicit references to this in his first two books, there were many signs that indicated his love both for the black church and his people. In later writings he was aware that some must be unmindful of his true feelings about the black church in light of his earlier scathing critiques, which spared no aspect that seemed to be out of harmony with the mandate of liberation. In *My Soul Looks Back*, he wrote that "the severity of my criticisms of the black church and my initial endorsement of the politics of Black Power often camouflaged the fact that I was born in a Christian home and nurtured to adulthood in the black church."[96] The black church has always had a prominent place in his life, and he thought highly of the spiritual and practical examples set by his parents.

Cone has variously exhibited deep appreciation for and deep disappointment in the black church. He loves it because of what it has done and is doing for countless thousands of blacks as well as himself. He loves it because of its heritage of struggle for liberation. Yet Cone has been, and continues to be, disappointed because of its relapses into conservatism and concern for spiritual and theological things divorced from political and economic considerations, i.e., those earthy things that are necessary to sustain life and make it possible for persons to live fully human lives. He has great distaste for the church's tendency to be too preoccupied with the spiritual side of its ministry to the exclusion of sociopolitical matters.

Cone does have a great love affair with the black church. One observes that in his early criticisms he went right into his criticisms without any preface or apology regarding his true feelings about the black church, an approach which undoubtedly led many to the (false) conclusion that he cared little for the church. But this began to change, at least by the publication of *God of the Oppressed*. This new approach continued through the seventies and to the present. He now speaks explicitly of his love for the black church and his desire not to put it down or make fun of it. Rather, he makes the claim in several of his later writings that it is precisely his love for the black church that prompts his prophetic criticism when it appears to be out of harmony with the mandate of liberation. One illustration of this is the following:

> Everything I am as well as what I know that I ought to be was shaped in the context of the black church. Indeed, it is because I love the church that I am required, as one of its theologians and preachers, to ask: "When do the black church's actions deny its faith? What are the activities in our churches that should not only be rejected as unchristian but also exposed as demonic? What are the evils in our church and community that we should commit ourselves to destroy?"[97]

Nowhere in Cone's early writings does one find such prefatory remarks before criticizing the black church. Elsewhere he has written that "it is because of my love and concern for the church that I, as one of its theologians, must subject it to severe criticism when it fails to be in society what it confesses in worship."[98] Such statements refute the oft-heard criticism of many black pastors that Cone has neither love nor respect for the church.

There was a period in the late sixties and early seventies when Cone was more actively involved with the Black Methodists for Church Renewal (BMCR), the NCBC, and other "relevant" black caucuses than with a particular local church. The rationale behind this was that these organizations had a sociopolitical bent aimed at liberation. Contrary to what critics thought, this had little to do with hatred of the black church. Cone felt alienated from the conservative black churches of this period, especially his own denomination. Black pastors have often criticized black theologians, claiming that they do not attend church on a regular basis and therefore are not in a position to be too critical of it. Cone has not been one who feels that the most fundamental thing about people's faith is that they attend worship services just for the sake of being able to say that they go to church on a regular basis. Regular church attendance is not the sole criterion for entering the Kingdom. Although James Baldwin came to believe that "the church is the worst place to learn about Christianity," since Christians themselves have given up on Christianity,[99] Cone not only understands the importance of being grounded in a local black congregation, but part of the requirement of some of his courses at Union Theological Seminary is that his students base themselves in a black church. His desire has been to be involved in religious structures (though not necessarily those in church buildings) that are committed to taking concrete steps in the direction of black liberation. This was his position during the inchoate period.

> I was searching for an empirical embodiment of what I experienced in the depth of my being and attempted to write in articles and books. The absence of an institutional embodiment made me wonder whether there was a referent to my ideas. . . . [The] NCBC, BMCR, and other black caucuses were at least partial representatives of my theological definition of the church.[100]

Cone realized what many fail to, that one's mere presence in a local church building every Sunday does not in itself constitute membership in the church! The church is wherever we find a body of people committed to joining in the fight with Jesus Christ and the disinherited against the forces of oppression.

Though it can be said that Cone never relinquished his critical stance regarding the black church, it is very evident that he was troubled about the possibility of whites misinterpreting his criticism and the possibility that they might view the black church as being as evil and demonic as the white church. In order to lessen this possibility he sometimes toned down his criticisms. What often happened, however, is that his critique continued to be sharp after the appearance of his first book, but he interjects prefatory statements like "My questions are not intended as a theological put-down of the black church..."[101] as a means of being true to the prophetic tradition of the church, while making it clear that he respects and loves the black church and believes himself to be an integral part of it.

It is not difficult to make a strong case for Cone's deep "love for the black church" and his "commitment to its faith."[102] Many thinkers have written of the need to criticize that which one loves truly. King said that there can be no deep disappointment about a thing where there is no deep love. "In deep disappointment," he wrote, "I have wept over the laxity of the church. But be assured that my tears have been tears of love."[103] King was disappointed over the way the church had been "blemished and scarred" as a result of "social neglect and fear of being nonconformists." Baldwin has written that he was critical of the United States only because he had a deep love for it.[104] Cone himself wrote in his first book that he was "critical of white America because this is my country; and what is mine must not be spared my emotional and intellectual scrutiny."[105] Few ministers have been as critical of the ministry as Reinhold Niebuhr. "I make no apology for being critical of what I love," Niebuhr wrote. "No one wants a love which is based upon illusions, and there is no reason why we should not love a profession and yet be critical of it."[106] In his biography of the father of "systematic methodological Personalism," Francis J. McConnell wrote of Borden P. Bowne's sharp criticisms of Methodism, even as he strove to be one of its most loyal members.[107]

It would be difficult indeed to disprove Cone's love and respect for the black church. No one who has suffered the kinds of disappointments he has because of the church's failure to implement and live out the true meaning of its radical heritage would continue identifying with such an institution. Neither, I suspect, would one continue to defend that institution's heritage, nor work so hard at challenging it to take the liberative motif of Jesus's ministry seriously. No one who does not have a deep love for such an institution would continue to suffer verbal slings and arrows as a result of sometimes having to stand alone while challenging it to rid itself of sexism, classism, or the acceptance of capitalism.

It is fair to say that James Cone has never criticized what may be described as "the Church proper." That is, like Frederick Douglass, he has not criticized authentic Christianity, or that form of Christianity that takes seriously the ethic of liberation. Douglass, it may be recalled, rejected all forms of "slave-holding religion," or the religion of white slave masters which taught that God ordained that blacks be the servants of whites and that they always remain in subservient roles.[108] In addition, Douglass rejected the religion of those blacks who believed that God intended for them to bear the cross of slavery passively. He wrote of this in one of his autobiographies:

> I have met, at the South, many good, religious colored people who were under the delusion that God required them to submit to slavery and to wear their chains with meekness and humility. I could entertain no such nonsense as this, and I quite lost my patience when I found a colored man weak enough to believe such stuff.[109]

It was not Christianity in its proper or more authentic sense that Douglass rejected. He simply could not accept the teaching that God ordained one group of people to be master and lord over another, and that those under subjection were to passively accept their plight. Likewise, Cone rejected any religion that was not clearly against all forms of human enslavement. Perhaps Malcolm X summed up the sentiment of both men best.

> I believe in a religion that believes in freedom. Any time I have to accept a religion that won't let me fight a battle for my people, I say to hell with that religion.[110]

By the same token, the type of Christianity of which Cone has been so critical neither is for black liberation, nor allows blacks and other victims to fight for their freedom. For Cone, such a religion is at best idolatrous and the absolute antithesis of authentic Christianity. The prophetic tradition of the Jewish-Christian and black faith requires that the church commit and orchestrate all of its resources in such a way to take up the cause of the least of the sisters and brothers who are crushed to the earth by evil social and economic structures. Whatever else authentic Christianity is about, it is most assuredly committed to doing whatever it takes to set at liberty the captives.

That James Cone loves the black church is indisputable. All evidence suggests that he will continue to be critical of it as long as the point of departure of its ministry is something other than liberation. Cone challenges the black church to recapture its tradition of blackwater, or black radicalism.

What remains now is to consider some new directions for black theology. What are some considerations it absolutely must take seriously if it is to be a more relevant and viable theology for African Americans and other traditionally oppressed groups? The final chapter addresses this question.

7. Black Theology: Toward the Year 2000

IN 1961 JUNE BINGHAM wrote a biography of Reinhold Niebuhr.[1] She skillfully presented a picture of a pastor–social ethicist[2] who never hesitated to change his point of view when doing so was warranted by the evidence and changing circumstances. In this and other respects Bingham found in Niebuhr a very courageous person committed to the Christian ministry. Although my book is neither a biography nor a systematic treatment of Cone's theology, I think I have shown that we have in James H. Cone a man who is committed to the ministry of Jesus Christ and who, like Niebuhr, has exhibited the *courage to change*. It has not always been easy for him to adjust his thinking because it has sometimes meant standing alone, even among his black colleagues. Yet my study reveals a theologian (and Cone does understand himself to be a theologian) of much courage, and one who has devoted his scholarly life to contributing to the liberation of black and other oppressed people from socioeconomic, political, racial, sexual, class and other forms of dehumanization that make them appear as nonpersons.

Many who have read Cone's works have misunderstood him. This is so for a number of reasons, not least of which is the tendency to read him with a strong bias for European and European American theology. Most whites who read Cone's works are so situated in society that it is very difficult (although not impossible) for them to really hear and understand his message. Not used to the kind of assertiveness so characteristic of Cone, a black man, many whites are turned off before they have read very far. Most (and this is the case with too many blacks as well) literally have to struggle through his first book, and very few read his subsequent works. This in itself is a major cause for the high degree of ignorance that so many in and out of the scholarly world possess regarding the works of Cone.

Having read and disagreed with everything Cone wrote in his first book, many critics deem themselves "experts" on Cone's theology and proceed to evaluate his entire theological project on the basis of that 1969 text! Another group of critics includes large numbers of persons who have never read a single book or article by Cone. This group's understanding and interpretation of Cone is based on statements of those who, themselves, do not understand

and appreciate his work. For example, there are many white (and some black) seminarians who know about Cone only through inadequately informed white professors. The latter tend to be uninformed only because of their attitude toward experiences different from their own, and their unwillingness to read with "sighted eyes and feeling hearts" and reflect on black theological litera- ture. In addition, they seldom include representative works of black theology for *required* reading and class discussion. To be sure, the incorporation of such nontraditional literature may pose a real challenge to white theologians and their students. But what of black theologians who, for many years, taught the Eurocentric traditions in theology, ethics, biblical studies, church history, and so on? Why should there not be a reversal, with white theologians teach- ing black-oriented, Latino, Native American and other traditions? This would be a challenge for white theologians, but not an insurmountable one.

Black theology, under the leadership of Cone and other first generation black theologians, has come a long way since the years of the NCBC. Rightly contending that black theology did not really begin "with the theopolitical writings of black churchmen in the 1960s," but in fact prior to that period, some black religious scholars have characterized the period of the sixties and seventies as Black Theology I.[3] In this phase we primarily find the writings of Cone, DeOtis Roberts, Major Jones, Albert Cleage, Gayraud Wilmore, Joseph Washington, and others. Pointing to the need for the work done during this period and the belief that many of the books produced by first generation scholars have "become standard curricular fare in many uni- versities and most seminaries,"[4] other black religious scholars indicate their concern that there are those who believe "the early material on black the- ology is both the first and last word in the matter."[5] This of course is a legitimate concern. Contemporary black theology is not a completed or fin- ished discipline.

Calvin Bruce, William R. Jones, and several white theologians pro- duced a volume entitled *Black Theology II*, in which they include eleven essays that point to directions they believe black theology should be taking now that it has advanced beyond the first stage. What really saves this text is the fact that the editors indicate in the opening pages that the proposed redirection of black theology in coming decades is "a cautious statement."[6] Though there are at least a couple of essays which seem to have as their sole aim the denigra- tion of James Cone,[7] most of the selections make constructive criticisms and suggest areas of improvement that black theologians absolutely must take seriously if the discipline of black theology is to remain a viable option. In this regard Bruce's essay, "Black Evangelical Christianity and Black Theology," is helpful in pointing out that during the first phase black theologians paid too little attention to a large number of black Christians who had deeper needs for spiritual liberation and bible study than provided for in the em- phasis on sociopolitical liberation. It was not that they rejected the idea or the need for liberation from mundane things. Rather, they needed something more — something in addition to sociopolitical liberation.[8]

Though Bruce is mistaken in his view that black theology in its first phase was primarily concerned about "establishing the long-awaited Black nation" or some political utopia, he is on target when he points to those blacks who have a strong desire for personal salvation, and to the need for black theology to address this concern. This group believed that with all of its emphasis on racial and economic liberation, black theology had little or no liberating value for them. Bruce contends that this desire for a deeper spiritual relationship with God that is so important to many black Christians must be addressed by black theologians in the next phase. Such desires are, according to him, as legitimate and as much a part of the black religious and cultural heritage as the need for other forms of liberation. He also presses for more authentic dialogue between all black religious persons and the eradication of class barriers. In addition, Bruce admonishes that the concerns of students and youths be taken seriously, "as well as fellow colleagues, laity as well as clergy, the 'disinherited' poor as well as the dispirited rich, and the moderately educated as well as the highly educated."[9] Few things are more important than finding creative and imaginative ways of communicating effectively with *all* segments of the black community. Inasmuch as *all* blacks are victims of racial and economic exploitation, all blacks must be taken seriously and be included in the liberative process — a process which must address whatever needs (spiritual, socioeconomic, and otherwise), exist.

Another of the essays in *Black Theology II* that attempts the positive redirection of black theology is Jones's "The Case for Black Humanism." Jones desires to place this notion beside the black church or black religion, and seeks its constituency among the large number of unchurched blacks, or what he refers to as a "secular 'congregation.'"[10] For him, it is a grave mistake for black theologians to speak and write as if the only hope of black liberation is the black church.[11] Jones's critique and suggestions that black theologians not merely depend upon a sometimes uncertain and unwilling black church to set at liberty the captives is both provocative and necessary. In addition, it has significant tactical implications for the liberation struggle. Recognizing the tremendous potential power and liberative ability of the black church, Jones is right to insist that black theology consider the potential power and possibilities inherent in other sectors of the black community. After all, the struggle for liberation should include not only the liberation of those in the black community who have formal church ties, but *all* black people.

To be sure, then, Jones's critique is a formidable challenge for black theology, and it is imperative that it be met. Jones, a philosopher, has posed other challenges to black theology, particularly pertaining to the traditional black perspective on God and human suffering. No black theologian of the first generation (Cone included!) has given an adequate response to Jones's view of God as a white racist as put forth in his controversial text *Is God a White Racist?*[12] Here Jones questions the idea of black theologians (Joseph Washington, James Cone, Albert Cleage, Major Jones, and J. DeOtis Roberts) that God is the liberator of the oppressed. He calls for the empirical evidence for such a claim. In my view, we black theologians are merely fooling ourselves if we think we can continue writing black theology and speaking a relevant word to the masses of black people if we do not make a conscious effort to meet the challenges of Jones regarding God, black suffering, and the liberation of black folk. This partly suggests the need for black theology in the next stage to consider more seriously the relevance of metaphysics and epistemology. Since much of the literature on black theology from its inception has built into it at least an implied metaphysics it seems that enough time has lapsed so that some black theologians can feel reasonably comfortable in uncovering these metaphysical assumptions and try to make sense of the implications of these for an "adequate" doctrine of God, black suffering, and liberation. I shall consider this topic more fully momentarily.

It is difficult to conclude this work on James Cone, partly because he is still in process, or in transition. But it is also difficult because I have grown more aware with the writing of this book that there is so much more to learn from his work. In any event, my consolation is that mine will not be the last book on Cone. Instead, it is hoped that other black religious scholars (and others who are black enough!) will continue to grapple with his theological system, as we endeavor to push black theology into the twenty-first century.

Some may argue that my book is not as critical as they would have liked. It was noted in the Introduction that Cone himself has always urged younger black theologians to be critical, especially when dealing with his thought. Although primarily intended as an appreciation of Cone, and his contribution, I have been critical where I believed it necessary. My book is only a prolegomenon to more critical and constructive works on Cone, and to bringing black theology and metaphysics together in a more intentional way.

For now, however, it will be helpful to point to some proposed transitions, or changes of focus for black theology, while not losing sight of the best that has gone before. I shall not deal with these in a particular order of importance. Neither shall I attempt to develop any of them fully. This will be the task of later works. It is important, however, to recognize that each proposal is significant in its own right, and when viewed collectively I think we begin to get a picture of a more vibrant, liberating theology of liberation, and one that we can be sure that African Americans in *every* segment of the black community will find that they are able to identify with because it intentionally identifies with them, rather than imply concern only for certain sectors of the community.

Although I think these proposals are important for the work of all black theologians, the greatest efforts to work these into black theological projects should come from second, third and subsequent generations of black theologians and ethicists. Cone and his generation effectively laid much of the foundation for black theology. It is now up to their disciples to work with the following (as well as other) proposals as they endeavor to push black theology into and beyond the year 2000. This means, among other things, that black theologians will have to produce more books on the subject, publication difficulties notwithstanding. They will have to *make* ways for their manuscripts to be brought before the public eye. If the message of black theology is to be gotten to the masses of blacks in and outside the churches, it may even be necessary to pool resources to develop our own publication houses, with the lion's share of the expense burden initially resting with black scholars (in all fields!) who have successfully tapped into the lecture circuit and are thereby able to receive large lecture fees and book royalties. This, of course, will mean the production of manuscripts that will be informative, and written in a way that all blacks can read and comprehend the message. If black theology is to be relevant in and beyond the year 2000; if it is to be a genuine theology of the people; if it is to be a theology that more deliberately focuses on the love of God and what that means for both the oppressed and oppressors, it will have to incorporate at least the following proposals. Although I believe each of these requires individual attention in separate books, I want to suggest in outline what is required.

Black Theology and the Folk

Black theologians will have to immediately begin assessing the impact (or lack of impact) black theology has on *the folk* or *the masses of black people*. Black theology has too long been a theology for academically trained religionists. It is not easy to make such an admission, but in light of the constant need for internal self-criticism we black theologians and ethicists must admit that most texts written on black theology have primarily appealed to the theologically trained who are basically interested in the teaching arm of the church. Renita Weems's and Theodore Walker, Jr.'s books, *Just a Sister Away* (1988) and *Empower the People: Social Ethics for the African American Church* (1991), respectively, are refreshing exceptions.[13] Otherwise, black pastors, lay persons, youths, and non–church going blacks seldom show evidence of familiarity with the names of black theologians or their writings.

In their study of 2,150 rural and urban black members of the clergy, C. Eric Lincoln and Lawrence Mamiya have been able to confirm what black theologians have long suspected.[14] As early as 1974 J. DeOtis Roberts lamented: "We have not reached our most influential black churchmen with black theology and neither have we moved the black masses who are dutiful churchgoers."[15] In *Black Theology in Dialogue* (1987), Roberts reiterates the need for black theology to reach out to black churches and ministry. "After

some twenty years of the development of black theology, black denominations, pastors, and congregations are not greatly moved by the insights of
black theology or black theologians. A way needs to be found to change
this."[16]

This has been a major concern, and not merely one that has come to the
attention of black theologians. Pointing to Peter Paris's work, *Black Leaders in
Conflict* (1978), Deane Ferm writes that "there is little evidence that a parochial
black theology has had much impact even on the black churches."[17] Letty
Russell, a white feminist theologian, and a contributor to the volume *Black
Theology II*, has also pointed to the failure of black theology to consistently be
". . . in contact with either the mass of the black church people or those alienated from the church."[18] Russell appears to be in agreement with William R.
Jones. In addition to her criticisms she points to several useful "insights" of
black theology.[19]

Calvin Bruce also points to black theology's failure to reach the folk. He
indicates that proponents of *Black Theology I* often had a tendency toward
academic interests that catered to white religionists as opposed to doing their
work "for the enlightenment of the black lower classes, particularly the disinherited sectarians. . . ."[20] Bruce found this especially frustrating, and is adamant about the need for black theologians to cease this practice.

I noted previously that the study by Lincoln and Mamiya has confirmed
what some black theologians and other black religionists have suspected.
Robert Hood commented on these findings in a lecture given at Christian
Theological Seminary, in Indianapolis, in 1987. He stated that by and large
the black church constituency has little knowledge of black theology and its
chief proponents. Ministers 40 years of age and older are basically out of
touch with black theology, but this seems to be the age category that has fewer
theologically trained pastors. Black pastors under 40 tend to be more aware
of black theology and its chief leaders and sometimes try to incorporate its
principles into their ministry. These younger ministers tend to possess more
theological training.

Since the black preacher has an entrée to large numbers of blacks, she
or he will play an important role in getting the message of black theology to
the pews and the grassroots. This implies at least a couple of things. First,
it is necessary to work harder, smarter, and more creatively to make it possible for black pastors and aspirants to pastoral and other areas of ministry to
obtain either formal or practical theological training. But second, and equally
important, we will need to devise ways to insure that they will be taught black
theology, black church history, and other subjects directly related to the black
religious experience. Though this happens in the black seminaries and at least
one white seminary, Union Theological Seminary in New York City, it is not
difficult to see the problem we are faced with here. Unfortunately, African
Americans who attend white seminaries are seldom taught black theology or

black church history, so any African American who does not learn about these on his or her own will not be able to take the message of black theology to the black church and community. She or he will be able to do so only if special individual efforts are made to learn this in addition to the required theological program.

Black theologians, social ethicists, and Christian education scholars will have to take the lead in helping to devise programs and other means to insure that black pastors and lay persons receiving theological training — formal and informal — are systematically exposed to the literature of black theology and the black religious experience. Although this is a subject for another book, I would point out here that one such program that made a significant contribution in this regard was the Midwest Christian Training Center in Indianapolis, Indiana, during the mid–eighties. This black clergy and laity leadership development program was intended to be a model for the development of similar projects in other states. A continuing-education project, its primary focus was on providing "how-to" workshops for black clergy and laity. Each workshop was led by a well known black pastor, lay person, or religious scholar on designated weekends at a host of local black churches. The project had an interdenominational focus and sought an equal number of female and male guest presenters. The project was funded by the Lilly Endowment and managed under the aegis of Light of the World Christian Church where T. Garrott Benjamin, Jr., is senior pastor.

Black theologians and black pastors need to find ways of getting the message of liberation and empowerment to the indigenous or organic leadership among grassroots folk, as well as opening themselves to receiving the message of liberation from the folk. To be sure, religious and secular grassroots folk often do black theology daily, though they have not often been aware that this is what they have been doing. But deliberate and sustained efforts should be made both to establish lines of communication and to work together toward the liberation of all in the black community. Pastors and black theologians will have to leave their offices and studies and mix with the folk on a regular basis. As one of my students so aptly puts it: "This will change the content and direction of black liberation theology."[21]

The Conference on Research and the Black Church, cosponsored by the Interdenominational Theological Center (ITC) in Atlanta and the Lilly Endowment in February 1988, was also a good start in the direction of bridging the chasm between black theology and the black church. The participants included black religious scholars, pastors, judicatories, bishops, lay persons, and seminarians. Although the emphasis was on how to get the black church and the academy, black pastors and laypersons, and black religious (and other) scholars together to work in common cause for black liberation, the Conference actually addressed the matter of church and academy reaching and appealing to the entire black community. More recently (October 17–19,

1989, May 22–24, 1991, and June 3–5, 1992) the Conference focused on the plight of the excessive number of black men in correctional facilities. Of the numerous things learned during those conferences one of the most telling is that inmates familiar with black theology have vehemently criticized the silence of black theologians regarding their oppression and the plight of their families. The most stinging critique of black theology was by Rudolph Outlaw who, as a prisoner in Sing Sing, had been introduced to black theology through a program in conjunction with New York Theological Seminary in 1982. In his paper, "A Prisoner's View of Black Theology," Outlaw cited the absence of any reference to the plight of black prisoners and that of their families in the works of Cone, Wilmore, and Cornel West.[22] He also referred to "the apparent inability of many Black theologians and church professionals to identify with our liberation struggle," and to "a decisive gap between their expressed principles and their behavior."[23] He cited James Forbes as the lone "notable exception." Outlaw was clearly disappointed about this apparent contradiction or blindness and what appears to be elitism within black theological circles. Black prisoners (male and female), who constitute more than 50 percent of the prison population in the United States, have been virtually invisible in black theology.

> Whereas we, as poor people, speak about struggle from the context of our lived experiences, Black theologians have not defined our struggle as integral to the struggle of the community we are members of, a fact that vitiates Black theology because its strength lies in its social analysis of the Black community's struggle for liberation and its vision of God's liberating activity on behalf of the poor and oppressed. By ignoring the plight of Black prisoners and thus separating it from the Black community, Black theologians are not encountering the truth of the Black experience that they say enables them to do theology in the first place.[24]

Former inmates who attended and addressed the conferees shared Outlaw's sentiment. It is to the credit of the Conference leaders that the decision was made to focus on aspects of the theme of black men in prison at subsequent conferences.

We cannot continue to say that black theology is *for* black people, as long as the masses of blacks neither know anything of its message nor of what they themselves contribute to it. In addition, black theologians must begin responding to the fact that massive numbers of the folk are being made to disappear early in prisons and cemeteries.

The Truth About Sexism

The issue of sexism in the black church and community was discussed in Chapter 5. My position is that we are still at a point that African American women (of all classes!) must decide what to say about this issue and when.

They do not need black men (or anyone else) to articulate for them. They are capable of speaking for themselves and telling their own stories,[25] as countless numbers of black women have shown throughout our history. So it is not my intention to speak for African American women. Mine is a much more modest aim in this brief discussion: to suggest one black liberation ethicist's perception of the role of African American men as black women continue determining for themselves "when and where [they] enter."

When he wrote of why he eulogized Malcolm X, Ossie Davis said: "Malcolm knew that every white man in America profits directly or indirectly from his position vis-à-vis Negores, profits from racism even though he does not practice it or believe in it."[26] African American men must apply this same principle to ourselves. Everyone of us profits in some way from our position vis-à-vis black women, profits from sexism, whether or not we practice it or believe in it.

It will be painful for most of us to make such a confession, for we realize that in the wider society we do not have the power and resources to control most of the institutions in this country which systematically oppress massive numbers of people. Yet the truth is that within the context of the black community itself we do benefit on the basis of our maleness in ways that our sisters do not. For example, because of traditional views on women in ministry and the hesitation that many black churches still have to ordain women as pastors, prospective male pastors face less competition. This is a clearcut benefit. Such examples can be multiplied both within and outside the church context.

I think we have to be willing to do as Garth Baker-Fletcher has proposed, namely, to confess that we are at best "recovering sexists," just as the most liberal, tolerant white person is at best a recovering racist. That is to say, as long as we continue to benefit from structures both in the black community and the wider society that trample on African American women, we are sexists. Minimally, in order to earn even the privilege of referring to ourselves as "recovering" sexists we will have to openly confess that we benefit from patriarchy, but that we now dedicate our talents, resources, and energy to dismantling sexist and all other structures that dehumanize and depersonalize, and commit ourselves to building person-enhancing structures that serve all persons and give preference to none.

It seems to me that the black church and its theologians must set the example in this regard. Karen Baker-Fletcher, a rising star in the womanist theological tradition, suggests that a good place to begin is for the black church to "accept Black women as equal partners with Black men in ministry."[27] That the black church sees the need to reach out to black men does not necessarily mean the exclusion of efforts to reach out to black women. Baker-Fletcher writes: "It is important to institute some gender-specific programs but this should not dictate who stands in the pulpit on Sunday morning. God calls entire people, male and female, to ministry. God's salvation is for the entire community."[28] The issue here is not one of finger-pointing and accusing individual African American males of being sexists. The focus is on our participation in sexist structures and the fact that we bene-fit from them whether or not as individuals we believe in or practice sexism.

As we move toward the year 2000 it is crucial that African American men come to terms with the truth about our sexism. We know well how inter-meshed is this issue with racism and the way the structures of this society brutalize the entire black community. Even many black women have not been willing to admit that they are being brutalized by us because they too are so aware of how we all suffer from white racism and economic exploita-tion. Black men know that much of our own abusive behavior toward black women is a result of our own sense of powerlessness, low self-esteem, and our inability to strike at the real cause of our oppression. Yet we must come to the recognition — today! — that our oppression and victimization does not justify woman-hating and abusive behavior toward black women (including rape) and our children. Tragically, this type of behavior "often becomes a standard within our communities, one by which manliness can be mea-sured."[29] Black men will have to come to terms with the fact that it is not only black women and our children who are diminished by our abuse, but we are as well. This in turn unnecessarily complicates and hinders the possibility of our bonding together in the struggle for liberation. The abuse must cease to-day! Indeed, Audre Lorde reminds us that abuse is no longer acceptable to African American women, neither "in the name of solidarity, nor of Black liberation. Any dialogue between Black women and Black men must begin there, no matter where it ends."[30]

As recovering sexists it is we and we alone who have the agency to decide whether we will be selective liberators or liberators of and with the entire black community, and ultimately, with the entire human family. That we ourselves are victims of oppression does not preclude the personal agency or freedom to decide whether we will be liberators or oppressors. If we do not get a handle on this there is no legitimate role or place for us in black theology in and beyond the year 2000.

Speaking the Truth to Black Youth

The number one cause of the deaths of black youths today is homicide! This is the case in nearly every major urban center in the United States. In-deed, I am a witness of this tragedy in Indianapolis. Seldom does a day pass without a report of violence inflicted upon members of the black community by black male youths. Often they themselves are the victims, but no par-ticular class, gender, or age group is spared.

Andrew Hacker has referred to this tragic phenomenon as "self-inflicted genocide."

While in one sense these are "free" acts, performed of personal volition, when they become so widespread, they must also be seen as expressing a despair that suffuses much of their race. *These are young men who do not know whether they will live another year, and many have given up caring.* If they are prepared to waste the lives of others, they will hardly be surprised if their turn comes next. *No other American race is wounding itself so fatally.* Nor can it be said that black Americans chose this path for themselves[31] [emphasis added].

Although Hacker rightly accuses white America of having made "being black so disconsolate an estate," an accusation that permits us to see the long arm of racism and economic exploitation as causes of this tragic depopulating of the black community, he implies, but does not develop, another important underlying cause — a cause that cannot be cleanly separated from the others. This has to do with a fast growing spirit of *nihilism* and lost sense of personal-relational values in the African American community, beginning with the highest possible sense of the value of one's own self-worth. Audre Lorde refers to this growing spirit of nihilism when she reflects on the importance of the older members of the community passing on to the younger generation information, values, and the know-how to make do. She observed that there is a "generation gap" that makes it necessary to reinvent the wheel, which means less time spent on trying to achieve liberation.[32]

This problem was brought home to me in graphic and painful ways through theological reflection papers written by two women students in my course on the church and the urban poor. These women (one black and the other white) are roommates who live in a "bridge house" owned by a local white church in the Indianapolis black community. The women work with black youths as part of their field education assignment. Week after week they would reflect on the deaths or violent acts committed against the relatives of the youths they work with. Both women grappled with the question, Where is God and the voice and presence of the Church? The African American woman struggled (and struggles) with the silence of black theologians on this issue. This woman has literally cried in my office and in the hallways of the seminary as a result of the self-inflicted genocide among our youths and their invisibility in black theology. I was not surprised when she chose as her term paper topic, "Nihilism in the Black Community." She dealt with what she perceived as a rapidly decreasing sense of self-worth and dignity and the feeling that there is nothing for which to live among black youths. She concluded (rightly) that these are chief contributing factors to black-on-black violence and death.[33]

In Chapter 1 I pointed out that whether in the makeshift slave detention centers on the shores of the Atlantic, during the Middle Passage, or in the Colonies, black ancestors often committed suicide as a means of rebelling against enslavement and denial of their humanity. Often they gulped down large doses of sand while waiting to be packed into the slave ships. In this sense Karen Baker-Fletcher is right when, having examined novels by J. California Cooper and Toni Morrison, she concludes that nihilism has a long history among African Americans. But whereas historically blacks killed themselves because of their high estimate of the worth of themselves and their deep yearning for freedom, it has today taken on an ominous tone. Today "the nihilism that afflicts Black Americans . . . is insidious, because it is coupled with the disillusionment regarding true freedom and opportunity in the midst of 'freedom' and 'opportunity.'"[34]

I have read newspaper accounts of black youths who have even prepaid their funerals! The black community is fast being depopulated of its youth. Yet they too have been fairly invisible in black theology. Black liberation theologians and ethicists can take us a long way in helping us reestablish a sense of life-enhancing values, and why it is important to teach our youths what Nannie H. Burroughs called the "internals and eternals" rather than focusing on achieving the traditional American dream.

If black theology is to retain its reason for being, it will be necessary to find ways to address the needs of black youths throughout the black community. In an earlier stage black theology not only failed to reach black youths who were consistent churchgoers, but it failed to discover ways of reaching non–church going black youths (and especially those who are most deprived of the bare material essentials of life). Black theology needs to take a long hard look at what is happening to black inner city and rural youths throughout this country. The existence of numerous youth gangs that are involved in brutal acts of violence in schools, black neighborhoods, and in some cases even the church!, is no accident. Neither should so much of the blame be placed on our youths. They are, in a real sense, the victims of structural racism and a political economy that is more concerned about profit margin than about making the most of black and other youths. Most of the brutish acts instigated by black youths are historically linked to the inhumane practice of slavery and continued acts of racial discrimination and economic exploitation. Black youths have no real sense of who they are, or where they came from. Neither do they have any sense of what would be possible for them if this were a society based on the principles of justice and genuine sharing.

Public school systems will not provide what is required for the complete reversal of the state of affairs that presently exists among our youths. This statement is not meant to denigrate the commitment and efforts of those individual public school teachers and administrators who daily strain their potential and resources to try to make a meaningful difference in the lives of youths. It is to say, however, that the nature of the educational system and other supporting systems at this time is such that what is required to completely reverse things in the direction of a truly educated student body simply cannot happen within the context of the present structure. Black theologians, in conjunction with other black scholars and leaders, have key roles to play in producing the necessary solutions to the problems of black youths. We can learn much from the work and workshops of a layman, Jawanza Kunjufu. Kunjufu, primarily concerned about what he sees as a systematic conspiracy to destroy black boys, insists that many have nearly been ruined by the time they reach the fourth grade.[35] He has shown a strong propensity for helping parents, teachers, church leaders, and others to devise ways to help upgrade self-esteem and black pride in black youths. Though his project leaves some things to be desired he clearly has made a good start in the right direction.

Black theologians and ethicists will have to find ways of saying more creatively and forcefully what it means to worship every Sunday, to have mid-week bible study, to spend thousands of dollars renovating already lavish church buildings, and so on, when so many of our youths are absent from church; when so many of them roam the streets all night long, often because they have nowhere to go. We need to be more intentional about getting with church and nonchurch leaders and activists in an effort to find the right solutions, and to implement them *by any means necessary*. One thing that will surely take us a long way in this regard is a better educated group of youths in the church itself, for these are the peers of large numbers of black youths who are outside the church, and are more likely to be able to reach them when our best efforts fail. This means, of course, that Christian education programs will have to be radically deconstructed and reconstructed. The new programs' emphasis should be on the total liberation of black youths. Less attention should be given to recreation, games, and memorization of bible verses. More emphasis should be placed on teaching the Gospel of liberation, its meaning and implications for youth and the church. This in turn requires the leadership of persons who have learned black church history and the principles of black theology well enough to draw out impications for Christian education and youth development. This, of course, means that there must be a radical change in attitudes (from the pastor on down), toward the place and role of Christian education in the church. In addition, it should be remembered that the aim should not be that of increasing youth attendance and membership in churches, though efforts to work with youths to eliminate their pain may well have this effect. The point, after all, is to liberate black and other youths from oppression and suffering.

Not only do black theologians need to help devise ways of meeting the needs of all black youths, but they should devote more efforts to determining, *in conjunction with them*, how best to include them in the struggle for liberation. Youths tend to be more energetic and less fearful than their guardians. They will tend to have more staying power, courage, and determination. Youths, unlike many adults, are not likely to be quitters.[36] Who can forget the role of youth organizations such as the Student Nonviolent Coordinating Committee (SNCC) during the civil rights movement? We can learn much regarding the matter of endurance, courage, and honesty from the participation of black youths in the struggle against apartheid in South Africa. No black youth should be denied an opportunity to participate in the struggle for liberation. It is crucial that black theologians, like their Latin American sisters and brothers at the Puebla Conference in 1979, *make a conscious, deliberate preferential option for black youths in particular*, but all youths in general, for these *are* our children! As James Baldwin so nicely put it: "The children are always ours, every single one of them, all over the globe. . . ."[37]

Doing It for Our People

In addition, if black theology is to be relevant in the coming decades it will be necessary to press the need for black ecumenism and the principle of doing what we do for our people. Now, immediately this will cause many whites and some blacks to be outraged. There has been a strong integrationist strand in the black community and church at least since the seventeenth century, and it has often overshadowed nationalist and other strands. Yet there continues to be no indication that African Americans will ever be fully integrated into American society. Indeed, there is a growing sentiment among some black intellectuals and many more at the grassroots level that it is not to our advantage to be integrated into the present system. This is certainly the view of Cone, Marable, James and Grace Boggs, Malcolm X, King (especially after 1966), and many others. James Baldwin warns against the desire of wanting to be integrated into a burning house or disintegrating social system.[38] Too much black talent has literally been wasted in efforts to work toward the integration of blacks into the American system, though there has never been a time when large numbers of white church and other leaders have indicated a desire for this to occur. If anything the tendency has been to work against such efforts. Having been disillusioned as a result of her own efforts toward integration, and finally reaching the conclusion that there did not seem to be enough room in American society for most blacks to live fully human lives, Jean Smith wrote:

> It's not that we have to do it by ourselves. Rather it is that we have to reorient our efforts and to train ourselves, black people, to build for us. Our immediate objective must be the strengthening of the black community instead of the apparently unattainable goal of diffusion of all black people into the main stream of American life. *We have to become strong so that we can depend on one another to meet our needs and so that we'll be able to deal with white people as we choose to, not as we are obliged to*[39] [emphasis added].

Smith, like so many African Americans before and during her time, finally came to the realization that no matter how hard she tried, integration was not forthcoming. As alluded to earlier, growing numbers of blacks are not excited about being on a train where neither the conductor nor the passengers know the destination.[40]

The nature of the black experience in America is such that there is little reason for blacks to trust, unconditionally, even the most well-meaning white person unless he or she has a long history of having earned black trust along with being an avid liberationist committed to doing whatever it takes to liberate blacks. Historically whites have not understood why African Americans are so hesitant to trust them when they have done one or two good deeds "for" black people. They fail to understand why — in the face of several hundred years of systematic brutal acts committed against blacks — they do not trust individual whites who treat them humanely only on occasion.

Writing as Linda Brent in her 1861 publication, *Incidents in the Life of a Slave Girl*, Harriet Brent Jacobs tells of her escape from slavery. The captain of the ship she was hidden on was disappointed to find, upon successfully delivering her out of the hands of bondage, that she did not trust him.

> He saw that I was suspicious, and he said he was sorry, now that he had brought us to the end of our voyage, to find I had so little confidence in him. Ah, if he had ever been a slave he would have known how difficult it was to trust a white man.[41]

Blacks have known for a long time that the nature and longevity of their suffering requires more than one or two good deeds by white people before it can be said that they have earned the trust of black folk. There continues to be otherwise good white people who think that because they grant one or two token opportunities, blacks should, with hat in hand!, jump for joy. Some of these people have even had the audacity to appear disappointed and hurt when African Americans have responded otherwise to their meager gestures.

In the posthumously published essay "Showdown for Nonviolence," King warned that time is winding up.[42] This prophecy leaves many blacks feeling a great sense of urgency. It is because of this feeling that the hour is late, that blacks must devote their time, talents, resources, and energy to the liberation of their own people. There is no tomorrow for our salvation. We have only today! Black theologians will have to find ways to drive home the point that African Americans must stop looking to the white man and look to themselves. This can be done best by working to develop unity among ourselves. More of the literature on black theology will need to reflect this emphasis. June Jordan is right when she says that "we are the ones we've been waiting for." Blacks are all that they have, and therefore must work to achieve their own liberation.

There will be those coalitionist whites and integrationist blacks who will be sorely disturbed by this. Appeasing such persons cannot be a priority. The first order of business is the creation of black unity for the continued struggle toward total liberation. Both Malcolm X and King recognized the necessity of blacks' creating situations that will allow them to get their thing together. Malcolm spoke of the need for blacks to put whites out of their meetings so they can "talk shop" among themselves, and take care of the business of black folk. Whites, he believed, could better perform their liberative functions in their own communities and churches where racists live, work, and worship. Similarly, King spoke of what may be called a *way-station ethic* ten days before he was assassinated. This was to be a temporary or interim ethic to be deployed by blacks until they could create enough unity that would ultimately lead to an effective power base. Rejecting the black nationalist ideal of absolute separatism, while acknowledging his appreciation for blacks' need to organize among themselves, King went on to say:

> What is necessary now is to see integration in political terms where there is sharing of power. *When we see integration in political terms, then we recognize that there are times when we must see segregation as a temporary way-station to a truly integrated society.* There are many Negroes who feel this; they do not see segregation as the ultimate goal. They do not see separation as the ultimate goal. They see it as a temporary way-station to put them into a bargaining position to get to that ultimate goal, which is a truly integrated society where there is shared power.
>
> I must honestly say that there are points at which I share this view. *There are points at which I see the necessity for temporary segregation in order to get to the integrated society.* . . . [T]here are some situations where separation may serve as a temporary way-station to the ultimate goal which we seek, which I think is the only answer in the final analysis to the problem of a truly integrated society[43] [emphasis added].

If black theology is to serve its purpose it will be necessary for its proponents to be more intentional about the call for black ecumenism and doing what we do *for our people*, no matter how repugnant it may sound to some. We know that the ultimate goal is the liberation of *all* of God's people, but black unity is a necessary precondition. Any future, viable black theology must be deliberate about devising ways to actualize black unity in every sector of the black community. We must not make the mistake of waiting until others agree to take steps to do for us what we alone must do. Rather, there is much to be learned from David Grant's statement in 1975 regarding the centrality of Native American initiatives if liberation is to come. "We have already learned that waiting for someone else to take positive action on Indian issues is a lesson in frustration. If things are to change in line with our expectations, then the answers must ultimately come from ourselves."[44] The message to blacks is that we have no one but ourselves and our God to look to for liberation.

We must not content ourselves with passively waiting for God. Even King admonished that God is not going to do it all for us.[45] Similarly, Malcolm X became frustrated with Elijah Muhammad's wait-on-Allah posture regarding the socioeconomic liberation of African Americans. Said Malcolm:

> Elijah believes that God is going to come and straighten things out. I believe that too. But whereas Elijah is willing to sit and wait, *I'm not willing to sit and wait on God to come.* If he doesn't come soon, it will be too late.[46]

Malcolm did not mean (nor do I!) that God is sometimes not with us. He was speaking figuratively. His emphasis is that we must be proactive in the struggle to break the chains of oppression and not depend on anything or anybody outside ourselves. Nannie H. Burroughs made the point in 1933. "There are no deliverers. They're all dead. We must arise and go over Jordan. We can take the promised land."[47]

The Development of "Race Persons," or Doing Our First Works Over

A related matter that black theologians will have to be more intentional about stressing and incorporating into their theological projects is the need for more race persons, both among the leadership class and throughout the black community. During the sixties there appeared a heightened sense of black pride and cultural identity. This spirit has all but disappeared in many sectors of the black community.

As disconcerting as it may be to some, James Cone was right to stress in *For My People*, that no matter how supportive he is of other liberation struggles, he remains fundamentally a race person. This principle needs to have a central place in black theology. It is not possible for an oppressed, forgotten people to successfully wage war against oppression if they have no sense of pride and connection with ancestors who were themselves fighters for liberation. This, I think, is what Maulana Ron Karenga meant when he said that blacks must free themselves culturally before they can expect to succeed politically.[48] James Baldwin is adamant about the need for blacks to do their first works over again; to intentionally go back to their roots to find out where we have come from and who we are as a means of gauging our future. The journey backward may be time-consuming and painful, but it is one we must make. Writes Baldwin: "To do your first works over means to reexamine everything. Go back to where you started, or as far back as you can, examine all of it, travel your road again and tell the truth about it. Sing or shout or testify or keep it to yourself: but know whence you came."[49]

Whites generally tend to get defensive when blacks talk about the the importance of being race persons; of recapturing their sense of black pride and cultural achievement; and getting themselves together in order to do for their people. Many whites often conclude from such statements that blacks are antiwhite, anti–Jew, antiwoman, and anti- a host of other things. The truth is that the idea of race person has nothing to do with being anti- some other group. Indeed, it has little to do with other groups and everything to do with African Americans. It simply focuses attention on black pride, on resistance to anything and anybody that seeks to oppress blacks, and on doing whatever it takes to organize and unify blacks to work for their total freedom. The true race person has little patience with those who argue against such a perspective. For once again they are aware that unless one has been the victim of systematic and prolonged attempts to destroy the culture and pride of a people, it is not very likely that he or she will understand the expressed need to focus on one's race, culture, and history. In part it will be the task of black theology to keep reinforcing the need for blacks to remember their long history of oppression, and the need to tell that story on every occasion, no matter how "sick and tired" some whites are of hearing it! Like black ancestors who vowed to keep alive the memory of pain and suffering in this world even when they cross over the Jordan, we too must remember and tell the story in season and out!

> When I get to heaven, gwine be at ease, Me and my God gonna do as we please.
>   Gonna chatter with the Father, argue with the Son, Tell um 'bout the world I just come from.[50]

Just as black ancestors sang of going to Heaven and telling God about their trials and tribulations on earth, their posterity must be admonished to do the same during their life on earth. This will be a way not only of expressing blacks' dissatisfaction with racism and other forms of oppression, but of keeping alive the spirit of resistance and black pride. For, as suggested previously, much hinges on the ability and willingness of African Americans to recapture that deep sense of pride or black consciousness. Sam Greenlee's character Freeman, in *The Spook Who Sat by the Door*, had the right idea.

> We got to get our own! But before we can, we got to get that black nigger pride working for us.... [I]f we can find it and use it, if we can get that black pride going for us, then nothing is going to stop us until we're free — nothing and nobody. They'll have to kill us or free us....[51]

The honest ones among us will readily acknowledge that blacks do not stand a chance until we get that pride working for us again. When this happens there will again be blacks around who will do *anything* to obtain liberation. Malcolm X knew, and we need to learn, that nothing less than this will usher in freedom. You'll get it, Malcolm said, when you let the oppressor know in no uncertain terms that you'll do anything to get it.[52] Over thirty years earlier Nannie Burroughs said that blacks "must serve notice on the world" that they are "ready to die for justice. To struggle and battle and overcome and absolutely defeat every force designed against us is the only way to achieve."[53] It is not likely that racial diplomats will readily or comfortably subscribe to such a view. It is not for them. It is for race persons.

The Relations Between Blacks and Native Americans

This and the proposal in the next section are crucial for black theologians as we approach the year 2000. No groups of people in the United States are as close and as far apart as African Americans and Native Americans. On the western frontier in the eighteenth and nineteenth centuries they fought the encroaching Europeans separately and together. The road to black slaves' freedom often led to an Indian camp. The Europeans skillfully played blacks and Indians against each other. "They kept the pot of animosity boiling. Whites turned Indians into slavemasters and slaveowners, and Africans into 'Indian-fighters.' Light-skinned Africans were pitted against dark-skinned, free against enslaved, Black Indians against 'pure' Africans or 'pure' Indians."[54] Both blacks and Indians were considered the enemy of the white man, and often they had to unite to defend their homes and villages. The Europeans sought to exploit them both. Yet even during the nineteenth century, "a Black-Indian friendship limped on despite onslaughts from white social policies destructive to both peoples."[55]

Blacks and Native Americans have much in common historically. Both are victims of numerous white betrayals; both were forced from their home-lands; both had their labor stolen from them; both have been victims of massive attempts by the dominant white group to destroy their religious and cultural heritage, though each group has reasserted itself against such efforts; early historical accounts of the roles of each group in the development of this nation were written and grossly distorted by white hands. Blacks are the only group of people who did not freely choose to come to this part of the world. Native Americans, on the other hand, had the whole country literally stolen from them. They and blacks are the oldest so-called minority groups in this country. Both groups historically have had strong communal and family values. Both have a deep respect for the spirit. My present sense is that there is much more that the two share in common, both historically and contemporaneously.

Although there has been some dialogue between black and Native American theologians, there is a need to make more conscious, direct efforts to both determine and appreciate similarities, differences, and potential areas of bonding in their struggles for liberation. Black theologians must consciously strive to develop ways to dialogue with our Red sisters and brothers, to whom this country really belongs. What can we learn from each other and how can we aid each other's struggle? What can we learn about our connections through cooperative efforts? The purpose here would be not merely to work toward dialogue and meaningful ways of working with the intelligentsia in either community, but with all sectors of each community. If aggressively pursued I think there are rich possibilities in such efforts. Ways must be found to get together in mutually acceptable ways that will serve notice to the powers that be that a socioeconomic affront to either group is an affront to the other, as well as to other people of color, and that joint actions will be taken against such offenses.

The Relations Between Blacks and Latinos

For many years it was generally accepted that when reference was made to "minority group," one basically had blacks in mind, since we were the largest and most visible people of color in this country. Blacks did not often fight to see to it that Native Americans were included with them, an error that will hopefully be rectified when the two groups find ways to work together in common cause. In any event, it is important that attention be given a radical change in demographics.

Presently it is estimated that the Latino, or Hispanic population in the United States is about 75 percent of the black population. Some have put the figure at 17 million Latinos, with another 5 to 7 million or so who may have some kind of alien status, and therefore have not been included in the total count.[56] There are several subgroups of Latinos, but the three chief groups are of Mexican, Puerto Rican and Cuban origin. As the fastest growing people of color in the United States, projections indicate that within ten years the Latino population will exceed that of blacks.

What is of fundamental importance here is that like blacks and Native Americans, blacks and Latinos have much in common and many points at which to proceed with meaningful dialogue and the development of ways to work together against the forces of oppression. Though there are certain factions within each of these communities whose sense of panic in the quest for mere survival militates against, or at least frustrates, creative efforts to join together in common cause, Theodore Cross is right (as far as he goes) when he observes that "the forces driving blacks and Hispanics toward political union are much stronger than those keeping them apart."[57] Cross only refers to sociopolitical forces. However, there are also some religious, or ethical forces involved. It is the business of black and Latino theologians to determine what these are, and to indicate their implications for liberation.

Black and Latino religionists and others who are committed first and foremost to the liberation of the captives will need to work intentionally to determine similarities and differences between their struggles. We know, for example, that both groups have more than one heritage. Blacks have an African and American heritage, and often have experienced an identity crisis, being uncertain at times as to whether they are more African or more American. Unfortunately many have often placed more emphasis on the American side of their dual heritage. They daily deal with the tension that DuBois characterized as "a sense of twoness." Latinos, on the other hand, have not only a Spanish (European) and often an Indian heritage, but often also an African. They are often, in the words of Leo D. Nieto, "meztizos, the product of both Indian and European stock and cultural tradition."[58] Those Latinos who admit the truth of this are, like blacks, often confronted with a kind of "cultural ambivalence." Like blacks and Native Americans, Latinos have had

to be intentional about affirming their own sense of religious and cultural particularity, while striving not to uncritically accept the ways of European
Americans as their own.

Andrés G. Guerrero discusses differences and similarities between blacks,
Chicanos, and Native Americans in *A Chicano Theology* (1987). He has a particularly interesting discussion of the different ways the three groups are
perceived and treated by European Americans. For example, Guerrero contends that although African Americans are at least recognized, seen, and
therefore dealt with by them, Chicanos and Native Americans are not. It is
as if they are invisible.[59] Guerrero says that the issue of racism is a crucial
one for his people, since lighter complexioned Chicanos have access to more
opportunities than darker ones.

The matter of identity has been complicated for Latinos because not only
must they contend with their Spanish and, often, Indian heritage (the one
representing the oppressor, the other the oppressed); not only are they, like
blacks, not certain as to which side of that heritage to place the most emphasis
(though too often the emphasis is placed on the European aspect), but they
are often faced with the dilemma of being neither completely white nor completely black, but brown, and therefore not wanted by either of the other two
groups.[60] Second and third generation Latinos also have to contend with their
American heritage. Yet both blacks and Latinos have had to struggle to re-
assess their understanding of the meaning of the theme of the new Heaven
and the new earth in the context of the present socioeconomic system. Many
members of both groups have uncritically accepted the capitalist political
economy. Fortunately there are factions in both groups that are now wonder-
ing what it means to advocate survival in a political economy primarily based
on the profit motive. Might there not be more humane and democratic models
of economic systems with the primary concern of providing all that is essential
for persons to live fully human lives?

In addition, a contingent within both groups has begun facing the problem of sexism and patriarchy in their communities. Some Chicanos say they
have "inherited certain patterns and values [they] refer to as 'machismo.'"[61]
This refers to the practice of the marginalization of and discrimination
against women. The further claim is made that "if the matter of equality between the sexes is not dealt with and resolved, their true liberation cannot be
achieved by Chicanos. If all of us are not free, then none of us is free."[62] These
are not unlike views held by some (though too few!) black theologians and
other blacks. Although much work needs to be done in both camps in terms
of resolving the issue of sexism, small factions within both have at least made
a start and a commitment to continue their efforts.

There is much that divides blacks and Latinos — e.g., the basic struggle
for survival as seen in the intense and sometimes brutal competition against
each other for the meager employment, educational, housing, public assistance

benefits, and the like that the dominant white ruling class controls and tends to dispense in such a way as to continually pit the two groups against each other.[63] Both are forced to compete for what amounts to economic crumbs in a racist-capitalist state, and generally for the same crumbs![64] As the "two largest and most disadvantaged groups in the United States,"[65] sheer survival demands that blacks and Latinos move immediately to form religious and political alliances so that the impotence of neither is assured as a result of present antagonisms and divisions. No longer should either group allow white power-holders to negotiate with them in the absence of the other.[66]

Although Cross concludes that the forging of effective political alliances between blacks and Latinos are not likely to happen in the near future, he is convinced that the sociopolitical forces that demand such union between them are stronger than the forces that keep them apart.

> Both blacks and Hispanics endure very high rates of unemployment and poverty; both experience intense discrimination in the job, credit, and housing markets. Both groups tend to be disenfranchised by racially gerrymandered election districts, both are forced to put up with inferior public education, and both suffer from very high rates of disease, crime, drug addiction, and infant mortality. Blacks and Hispanics have a sturdy common interest in welfare reform, protected employment, maintaining a high level of public education, and criminal justice reform. Neither group is in a position to accomplish its political objectives without the support and assistance of the other.[67]

It is not merely political analysts and theorists who have come to the conclusion that if blacks and Latinos do not work intentionally to forge alliances the hoped for socioeconomic and political liberation is not likely to come. Nieto points to the need for Chicanos and other oppressed groups to bond:

> ... we must seek coalitions with other oppressed groups in the United States, expressing in so doing our solidarity with each other as well as with similar groups throughout the world. This would include people of other races, nationalities and colors, including white people.[68]

Black theologians have made similar recommendations, although there is little evidence that these have been heeded.

Two-Thirds World Theology-in-Black

If black theology is to be a viable, liberating theology for African Americans in and beyond the year 2000, it will be necessary for proponents to recapture its reason for being, no matter how global an outlook on oppression they develop. In Chapter 5 I discussed the concern of at least one black theologian regarding Cone's expanded view of oppression. Louis-Charles Harvey has expressed the caution that black theologians not allow their perspective on oppression to expand so much that the particularity of black oppression is relegated to a subordinate position. I tried to show that this is not a matter for concern if we remember that Cone has always taken both the particular and the universal dimensions of the Gospel seriously, which means that he must be concerned about all forms of oppression wherever they exist. Furthermore, Cone himself is adamant about being a race person who will always be committed to black liberation.

That Cone writes more and more of developing "a third world theology we can all be proud of" is not a real cause for alarm, particularly if he does not mean to lump all liberation theologies into one barrel. In fact, to view Cone as a "third world theologian" may be problematic, but not in Harvey's sense. Instead, it is a problem in the sense that "third world" is a European construct applied to Latin American, African, and Asian countries being victimized by systematic racial, economic, and class oppression. "Third world" is a term applied to the oppressed by the oppressor. The term as used by many white North American theologians really implies sameness, while ignoring the differences between the various liberation theologies. Engel and Thistlethwaite raise this concern. Following Shiva Naipaul they write that the term "exhibits imperialism, for it is a term of bloodless universality that robs individuals and societies of their particularity."[69] So it is important that whatever term is adopted retain the specific difference between the types. But it is also important that it suggest the similarities. For this reason and the fact that people of color comprise the majority of the world's population, it would be well to bury the term and adopt something like *"Two-Thirds World"* or an equivalent. It seems more reasonable, then, to characterize Cone as a Two-Thirds World theologian, both because people of color have majoritarian status in the world, and because they have been forced to the periphery of the social, economic and political order. Stokely Carmichael had this in mind in 1967 when he spoke of the "third world conditions" affecting black and brown peoples in the Americas. Addressing Latin American revolutionaries in Cuba he said:

> We greet you as comrades because it becomes increasingly clear to us each day that we share with you a common struggle; we have a common enemy. Our enemy is white Western imperialist society. Our struggle is to overthrow this system which feeds itself and expands itself through the economic and cultural exploitation of nonwhite, non–Western peoples — the Third World. . . . *The American city is, in essence, populated by people of the Third World*, while the white middle class flee the cities to the suburbs[70] [emphasis added].

At any rate, it would be more accurate today to characterize Cone as a Two-Thirds World theologian,[71] since he was born in a world of dependence and systemic exploitation within a nation that has been a chief player in the conditions that adversely affect him and his people.[72]

Perhaps the chief criterion that qualifies Cone to be a Two-Thirds World theologian is his attitude and commitment to the liberation of the oppressed everywhere. J. Russell Chandran has written of this criterion:

> In order to be a Third World theologian one must have an orientation to do theological reflection on the gospel of Jesus Christ as it comes alive in the totality of the struggle of an oppressed people to be fully human.[73]

Since Cone meets the criterion of Two-Thirds World theologian, this needs to be affirmed.

Yet the caution raised by Harvey is legitimate. Black theology of the future must necessarily retain both its particular and universal focus on oppression. Both of these elements receive adequate emphasis in what I want to call a *Two-Thirds World Theology-in-Black* (or Red, Brown, or Yellow).[74] Here there is a necessary, ongoing dialectical tension between particular and universal. Neither pole is completely understandable when viewed in isolation from the other. In its next phase of development black theology will have to move more intentionally in this direction. African Americans, Native Americans, and Latinos need to know that they are not alone in the struggle for liberation; that they have sisters and brothers in other geographical locations who are not only fighting for their own liberation, but who are committed to doing what they can to help liberate them as well. In addition, a *Two-Thirds World Theology-in-Black* would keep dialogue center stage, though admittedly, the primary emphasis (for an agreed upon period of time) must be on dialogue among black, brown, red, and yellow peoples of the world.

No oppressed group doing liberation theology today would reject the idea of a global perspective on oppression. Yet none would agree to subordinating the specific concrete concerns of their group. Both Latinos[75] and Native Americans[76] have expressed this concern. Harvey is in good company when he raises a similar concern about black theology and its relation to a more global or expanded perspective on oppression and the importance of retaining the more particular focus on the African American experience of oppression.

Black Theology and Metaphysics

Finally, if black theology is to remain alive and relevant, it will have to do what first generation black theologians so diligently avoided. It will have to take a long, hard, critical look at metaphysics, beginning with an examination of its own implicit metaphysical assumptions. Black theologians will have to lift the moratorium on metaphysics. Although white theologians have been critical of black theology for its failure to engage metaphysics, it has not been a criticism that most black theologians have taken seriously, since many believed it to be a smoke screen to divert attention away from an action oriented theology. Blacks and other liberation theologians have suspected the motives of most white theologians. Furthermore, from a methodological standpoint black theologians are committed to the idea of the epistemological break, and suspected therefore that white theologians were seeking a reversal of this, or a return to doing theology the way it had generally been done by white Western scholars.

It was inevitable that black theologians would have to take metaphysics more seriously than most have to date. Presently however, this is a matter for internal critique. That is, black and other Two-Thirds World theologians are the ones to initially make this critique. Indeed, some have already begun the process. For example, Theodore Walker, Jr., Henry J. Young, Archie Smith, Jr., and others are presently contributing to the dialogue between black theology and process philosophy.[77]

The purpose of taking metaphysics more seriously is not to make black theology more acceptable to the theological academic powers. It is, rather, to help black theology — even as black theology helps metaphysics! — to solve the problems that have caused it difficulty both past and present. For example, black theologians have yet to effectively meet the critique of William R. Jones, who challenged their idea that God is liberating blacks from oppression. The reason black theologians have not been able to respond adequately to Jones is because they have been operating on an assumed or implied metaphysics, and have been unwilling to identify its implications for black suffering, pain, and liberation. Similarly, black theologians have failed to take a critical look at their doctrine of God and evil. However, Major Jones tries to address this issue in *The Color of God* (1987). His aim is to propose an authentic Afro-Americanized God-concept, free of all "alien connotations"; to liberate the Afro-American God-concept from foreign elements that have entered from white religion. Taking a clue from James Baldwin, Jones wants a much wider conception of God, and one that is more consistent with African American experience, struggles, and overcomings.[78] In this Jones was surely on the right track, but he did not consistently follow it.

Jones considers and rejects more than half a dozen theodicies, and concludes with Western classical theism that God possesses absolute power. Black theology, he contends, essentially adheres to the classical view that God is omnipotent and therefore possesses absolute power. Black theology presumably frees this more classical view of alien connotations. However, Jones nowhere indicates the metaphysical difficulties of theistic absolutism; of how one squares or reconciles the idea of an all-powerful, omnibenevolent deity with the existence of so much evil that is beyond human choice. There is no serious grappling with metaphysics in Jones's book, nor with what it means for black theology and the struggle for liberation. Jones ultimately fails to liberate his God-concept of "alien connotations." Metaphysics will take black theologians a long way toward developing a God-concept that is consistent

with the evidence and the facts of the black struggle to become totally empowered and liberated.

Cone's God-concept is also fraught with "alien connotations" which are
primarily derived from uncritical adherence to the classical omnipotent-
omnibenevolent God-concept. In *God of the Oppressed* he rejects theodicies
based either on the denial of God's perfect goodness or of God's unlimited
power.[79] These are the views of William R. Jones and Edgar S. Brightman
(1884–1953), respectively. Cone uncritically appeals to black religious tradition. He concludes that black theology "cannot accept either logical alternative for solving [the problem of black suffering]. It is a violation of black
faith to weaken either divine love or divine power. In this respect Black
Theology finds itself in company with all of the classic theologies of the Christian tradition."[80]

Brightman was the foremost Boston Personalist from the 1920s until his
death. It was he who proposed the radical and unorthodox theory that God
is finite-infinite (one of the theories Major Jones addresses in his book). That
is, God's power is limited by an uncreated, coeternal, internal aspect of the
divine nature called *the nonrational Given*. Yet God remains the most powerful
being in the universe and is perfect love and goodness. What Brightman
essentially did was redefine omnipotence in order to take account of the
strong evidence of shared power in the universe and the inability to reconcile
divine absolute power with the existence of nonmoral evil.

William R. Jones is an African American humanist philosopher who
presented a bold challenge to the liberator God of black theologians in his
book *Is God a White Racist?* Unfortunately, Cone does not engage the views
of either Brightman or Jones, although he does try to respond to Jones in an
endnote.[81] The response, however, is not helpful. Jones sees, as did Brightman, what Cone and black theologians have not wanted to deal with headon.
If black theology is serious about making sense of God and God's relationship
to the world it will have to be willing to subject the classical idea of God to
radical critique in light of the evidence of the continued systematic oppression
of African Americans and other people of color. This effectively means a
reconsideration of the divine attributes of omnipotence and omnibenevolence, for any reasonable "solution" to the problem of evil turns on how one
understands these. Since most theists believe that God must be perfectly good
and loving in order to be worthy of worship, they are not willing to sacrifice
this attribute. What is left, then, is the matter of divine omnipotence and how
one understands it.

Around 1990 Cone made another attempt at discussion of the divine attributes. He reveals sympathy for the view that it is difficult to reconcile
"human suffering and divine participation in history." He points to Richard
Rubenstein's and Albert Camus's frustration with this, claiming with the latter that "if God is omnipotent and permits human suffering, then God is a

murderer." Traditional Christian theology, he claims, has not taken this issue seriously. Although it acknowledges that much suffering is inconsistent with the idea of divine omnibenevolence, there is still a tendency to quote Paul approvingly: "We know that everything works for good with those who love him, who are called according to his purpose" (Romans 8:28). This implies that God somehow approves of suffering, and Cone rightly contends against this view. "Despite the emphasis on future redemption in present suffering, black theology cannot accept any view of God that even *indirectly* places divine approval on human suffering. . . . God cannot be the God of blacks *and* will their suffering."[82]

Yet the same criticism can be made of black theology, since it adheres to the idea that God possesses absolute power. In addition, it contends that God, the liberator, is perfect love. Black theology does not adequately address the question of how a perfectly powerful and loving God can allow nonmoral evil, for example. For if God is perfectly powerful God can surely put an end to this evil, and if God is perfect love and goodness God desires to do so. That such a God has not eradicated nonmoral evil must raise more suspicion among black theologians than it has to date. We clearly need a new way of talking about God's power. Black theology is trapped and embrangled in inescapable contradictions as long as it uncritically adheres to the classical view of an all-powerful God.

Karen Baker-Fletcher's notion of "*a most powerful, liberating God*" is suggestive, for it is conceivable that God can be the most powerful being in the universe without being all-powerful in the traditional sense. What Baker-Fletcher implies is that God has sufficient power to accomplish God's purpose in the world. Indeed, the greatness of God may lie here, i.e., in the idea that God possesses *unsurpassable*, but not *all*, power; that God willingly shares power with creation. This means that created persons have power (to choose within limits), and that nature and the animal kingdom have power. What such a conception tends to do is place more of the responsibility for solving the world's problems, of liberating the oppressed, for instance, upon humans as they learn to work cooperatively together and with the "most powerful, liberating God."

Cone rightly sees that a good God would not will suffering and pain. What he does not see as clearly is that to say that God can use pain and suffering in working out the divine plan for the world is not the same as saying that God wills, is the cause of, or desires that suffering and evil exist. For God is, on his view, omnibenevolent. His concern about God willing or not willing human suffering is not the point since he has concluded that God is good. The real point at issue is divine omnipotence. Having acknowledged that "if God is omnipotent and permits human suffering, then God is a murderer," he neither addresses the problem of human freedom nor the relationship between absolute power and divine goodness. He himself (like Major Jones) does not tell us how he reconciles divine omnipotence with black suffering. Instead, he appeals immediately to black religious tradition, claiming that the faith of the black Christian has always been in a God who possesses absolute power.[83]

When Cone does define omnipotence he does so in a way that does not help us understand the relationship between divine power and love. "Omnipotence does not refer to God's absolute power to accomplish what God wants," he writes. "And John Macquarrie says, omnipotence is 'the power to let something stand out from nothing and to be.' Translating this idea into the black experience, God's omnipotence is the power to let blacks stand out from whiteness and to be."[84] This does not advance us toward a reasonable solution, and it escapes me as to how this might happen unless black theology takes metaphysics seriously. To do so means a willingness not only to critically examine all of the relevant evidence, but to follow it where it seems to lead. If black theology wishes to appeal to religious faith at the point of tough theological issues such as the theodicy question, this should be stated explicitly as part of its method. But even here there are metaphysical implications that needs to be considered.

Another way that black theology may find metaphysics helpful is in regard to the problem of the particular and the universal, a problem that Cone initially tried to resolve by introducing the principles of physiological and ontological blackness. This problem might move closer to resolution if efforts are made to work through either an existing or newly devised system of metaphysics. Cone himself makes many assertions in his works that have profound metaphysical implications. These in turn have significant implications for the struggle for black liberation. The chief of these is the doctrine of the omnipotent liberator.

This will likely be the most difficult of the proposals for black liberation theologians to accept, but accept it we must! One thing that should help this process will be endeavoring to consider some metaphysical system, e.g., personalism, through the lens of black theology, the black religious and cultural experience, and other categories and experiences that are specific to black existence. Indeed, black theology itself is essentially personalistic in that it insists on the fundamental and absolute dignity of all persons as such, and the systematically and massively oppressed persons in particular. It insists on the centrality of the oppressed poor person. It also fosters the view of a personal God who is the liberator of the oppressed. In addition, both black theology and personalism stress the relational or social nature of reality and life. Cone himself has pointed to the need for black theologians to be creative in their use of works by white scholars. So the point is not to force personalistic metaphysics in its present form onto the African American situation as if to suggest that there are iron and rigid rules to which African Americans must adhere. Whatever metaphysical system is adopted must be seen and studied in the social and cultural context of blacks. The black experience of systemic oppression means that personalism will have to take on a more militant form.

It may also ease this process if black theologians work to develop a view of metaphysics that discourages one from feeling that it is a strictly abstract undertaking. According to personalism, metaphysics at its best is not something done with one's head in the clouds or some other place that has no relationship with what is going on in the world right now. The metaphysical enterprise seeks to avoid the kind of abstractions that many purely academic types have wallowed in for so long. One personalist metaphysician has clearly indicated the traditional tendency in metaphysics to emphasize abstraction unnecessarily:

> Abstraction permits scholarly citizens to avoid social responsibility by concentrating on isolated problems which involve no thought of what ought concretely to be, even as they try to formulate precise laws about what is and must be. This very popular antimetaphysical abstraction combines intellectual integrity in its own field with almost complete social escape, precisely because it has liberated itself from metaphysical orientation. *We must scrutinize this scholarly tendency toward abstraction*. . . [85] [emphasis added].

If black theologians can come to see that metaphysics at its best strives for concreteness and is fundamentally about life, it will be less difficult to give it a key place in black theological projects. The type of metaphysics that would be relevant to black theology will require what a colleague suggested not long ago, viz, that the metaphysician *"always keep one foot in the gutters of life where the vast majority of God's people live."* By so doing she or he will not lose sight of the reason for doing theology. The chief reason for taking metaphysics more seriously, finally, is that of making the most of all of God's people and working to actualize God's vision for the world.

Surely statements black theologians make about God, the world, and persons have important implications for what they think about matters such as human liberation. Ways must be found to *put metaphysics to work for liberation* — for the least of humanity. The problem is not metaphysics itself, but the way it has traditionally been used. The purpose of metaphysics, like anything else, should be the enhancement of all persons.

It will not be necessary for all black theologians to devote time to metaphysics, but it is crucial that some do so. The key is to remember why and for whom we are engaging in such studies. Black theologians are called to do what they do for the least of us — for the liberation of the socially, culturally, and economically disenfranchised. Engaging in metaphysical and epistemological inquiry for any other reason will make us something other than liberation theologians. Commitment to and solidarity with the poor and the oppressed require that black theologians travel any road — even the road to metaphysics — if there is a possibility that the fruits thereof may contribute significantly to liberation and empowerment. Black theologians must be committed to Truth and be willing to follow it wherever it leads.

In conclusion, none of the proposals I have made are inconsistent with the basic outline of Cone's theological project. The foundation he has laid makes it possible to propose these new directions for black theology, or what I have designated as a *Two-Thirds World Theology-in-Black*. As a theologian who has exhibited courage to change and to adjust his views in the face of new evidence and relevant experiences, those who have taken Cone's work seriously and who wish to find their own place in the dialogue on black theology (and in the struggle for liberation) must also find and take possession of the courage to change — for the least of us.

NOTES

Introduction

1. Carlyle Fielding Stewart, III, published *God, Being and Liberation: A Comparative Analysis of the Theologies and Ethics of James H. Cone and Howard Thurman* in 1989. Stewart's is an impressive study, and the most thorough analysis of Cone's method, theology, and ethics yet to appear. A major limitation of the book is that it is essentially a rewrite of his doctoral dissertation. As such he includes numerous technical terms which tends to lessen its appeal to college students and the average lay reader.

2. See the select bibliography of writings by and about Cone.

3. An abbreviated version of this essay was printed in C. Eric Lincoln, ed., *Is Anybody Listening to Black America?* (New York: Seabury, 1968), pp. 3-9.

4. James H. Cone, *My Soul Looks Back* (New York: Seabury, 1982), p. 47.

5. *Ibid.*, p. 51.

6. Cone, *Black Theology and Black Power* (New York: Seabury, 1969), p. 2; *My Soul Looks Back*, pp. 44-45, 47, 50.

7. *Black Theology and Power*, p. 3.

8. *My Soul Looks Back*, pp. 47, 50.

9. W. J. Weatherby, *James Baldwin: Artist on Fire* (New York: Donald Fine, 1989), p. 120.

10. Gayraud Wilmore, Foreword to Theo Witvliet, *The Way of the Black Messiah* (Oak Park, Ill.: Meyer-Stone, 1987), p. xiii.

Chapter 1

1. See J. DeOtis Roberts, *Roots of a Black Future* (Philadelphia: Westminster, 1980), p. 12.

2. Gayraud Wilmore, *Black Religion and Black Radicalism* (Maryknoll, N.Y.: Orbis, 1983), p. 216.

3. Carlyle Fielding Stewart, III, "The Method of Correlation in the Theology and James H. Cone," *The Journal of Religious Thought*, Fall-Winter, 1983-84, p. 27.

4. Rufus Burrow, Jr., "Book Review of James H. Cone, *For My People*," *Encounter*, Spring, 1985, p. 187.

5. See Gwinyai H. Muzorewa, *The Origin and Development of African Theology* (Maryknoll, N.Y.: Orbis, 1985). In this text on the origins and sources of African theology, Muzorewa, a former student of Cone's, is quite explicit about the influence of Cone on his theological development. He writes: "Cone gave me what the United States as such could not; the pride and confidence that black people can join hands together, both at work and leisure. In his humility, Professor Cone has skillfully imparted to me the sense of a theological author" (pp. xiii–xiv). In addition, the influence of Cone appears throughout the book. Even the author's use of inclusive language may

204   Notes — Chapter 1

be attributed to Cone's influence. This latter point is significant because Muzorewa is an African theologian. Many African theologians have not yet made the issue of sexism a major part of their theological project, though there is movement in this direction among some. It will be interesting to see what impact Muzorewa is able to make in this regard on the African continent.

Another of Cone's students, Josiah Young, has written a text on black theology in which he too praises his teacher and mentor. See *Black and African Theologies: Siblings or Distant Cousins?* (Maryknoll, N.Y.: Orbis, 1986), p. x.

6. Theo Witvliet, *The Way of the Black Messiah* (Oak Park, Ill.: Meyer-Stone, 1987), p. 4.

7. Alfred N. Whitehead, *Process and Reality*, ed. by David R. Griffin and Donald Sherburne (New York: Free Press, 1978), p. 39.

8. *The Way of the Black Messiah*, p. 125.

9. In 1991 Cone published a book on King and Malcolm in which he deals with the strengths and weaknesses of both, while insisting that in order to adequately understand and appreciate either, each must be balanced with the other. He has stated publicly a number of times that he rarely mentions King without mentioning Malcolm. See *Martin & Malcolm & America* (Maryknoll, N.Y.: Orbis, 1991).

10. See *Martin & Malcolm & America*, p. xv and Chapters 7–9.

11. Joseph Washington, *Black Religion: The Negro and Christianity in the United States* (Boston: Beacon Press, 1964).

12. Cone, "Black Theology: Its Origin, Method, and Relation to Third World Theologies," in William K. Tabb, ed., *Churches in Struggle* (New York: Monthly Review Press, 1986), pp. 32–35; Gayraud Wilmore, Address given at the Black Theology Project, February 5–8, 1986, on the Development of Black Theology; Cone, *For My People* (Maryknoll, N.Y.: Orbis, 1984), pp. 24–28. In fairness it should be pointed out that in his second book, *A Black Theology of Liberation* (New York: Lippincott, 1970), Cone does point out that neither black power nor black theology is new. "Black Power is not new. It began when the first black man decided that he had had enough of white domination. It began when black mothers decided to kill their babies rather than have them grow up to be slaves. . . . ¶Like Black Power, Black Theology is not new either. It came into being when black churchmen realized that killing slave masters was doing the work of God. It began when black churchmen refused to accept the racist white church as consistent with the gospel of God" (pp. 58, 59). For Cone the appearance of black denominations was "a visible manifestation of Black Theology." "The participation of the black churches in the black liberation struggle from the eighteenth to the twentieth century is a tribute to the endurance of Black Theology" (*ibid.*, p. 59). Yet, even in this instance, Cone did not take the origin of black theology back quite far enough.

13. See Gayraud Wilmore and James H. Cone, eds., *Black Theology* (Marykroll, N.Y.: Orbis, 1979), pp. 23–28.

14. Cone, "Black Theology: Its Origin, Method, and Relation to Third World Theologies," p. 35.

15. Cone, *The Spirituals and the Blues* (New York: Seabury, 1972), p. 24. Referring to "a theological and cultural earthquake of major proportions" with the publication of Cone's first book in 1969, Wilmore proceeds to comment on the relationship between the emergence of contemporary black theology and its more historical roots. "Perhaps it would be most accurate to say that it [the emergence of black theology in the late sixties] was the most recent tremor, an after-shock of an eruption that began many years ago in the dark bowels of the slave quarters" (see his Foreword to Theo Witvliet, *The Way of the Black Messiah* [Oak Park, Ill.: Meyer-Stone, 1987], p. v.). But

in my view even this recognition of the historical roots of black theology does not go back far enough. We must return to those struggles in the interior of West Africa in the middle of the sixteenth century. This is where we find the rudiments of black theology.

16. Eric Foner, ed., *America's Black Past* (New York: Harper, 1970), pp. 28, 54.

17. Vincent Harding, *There Is a River* (New York: Vintage, 1983), p. 3.

18. Foner, pp. 29–30.

19. Benjamin Brawley, *A Social History of the American Negro* [1921] (New York: Macmillan, 1970), p. 18.

20. Harding, p. 3.

21. As reported by Olaudah Equiano (1745–1797) in *The Interesting Narrative of the Life of Olaudah Equiano, or Gustavus Vassa the African* (1789), cited in David D. Anderson, et al., eds., *The Black Experience* (East Lansing: Michigan State University Press, 1969). In an interesting passage Equiano tells of conversations he had on the slave ship with some other captives from his own nation. Not at all clear about why he and the others had been forced on board the ship, he sought to find out. "I inquired of these what was to be done with us? They gave me to understand, we were to be carried to these white people's country to work for them. I then was a little revived, and thought, if it were no worse than working, my situation was not so desperate; but still I feared I should be put to death, *the white people looked and acted, as I thought, in so savage a manner; for I had never seen among any people such instances of brutal cruelty; and this not only shown towards us blacks, but also to some of the whites themselves.* One white man in particular I saw, when we were permitted to be on deck, flogged so unmercifully with a large rope near the foremast, that he died in consequence of it; and they tossed him over the side as they would have done a brute. This made me fear these people the more; and I expected nothing less than to be treated in the same manner" (p. 4; emphasis added).

22. John W. Blassingame, *The Slave Community*, rev. ed. (New York: Oxford University Press, 1979; orig. ed. 1972), p. 10.

23. Cited in David D. Anderson, et al., eds., *The Black Experience* (East Lansing: Michigan State University Press, 1969), p. 6.

24. *Ibid.*

25. Harding, p. 3.

26. Sterling Stuckey, "Through the Prism of Folklore: The Black Ethos in Slavery," in Foner, ed., *America's Black Past*, p. 104.

27. Herbert Aptheker, *Essays in the History of the American Negro* (New York: International Pub., 1945), p. 11.

28. Foner, p. 28.

29. Kenneth Goode, *From Africa to the United States and Then...* (Glenview, Ill.: Scott, Foreman, 1969), pp. 18–19. See also the firsthand account of Olaudah Equiano in Anderson, et al., eds., *The Black Experience*, p. 3.

30. Cited in Basil Davidson, *The African Slave Trade: Precolonial History 1450–1850* (Boston: Atlantic, Little Brown, 1961), p. xvi.

31. Brawley, p. 19.

32. Foner, p. 30.

33. Blassingame, p. 7.

34. Lerone Bennett, Jr., *Before the Mayflower* (Baltimore: Penguin Books, 1968), p. 30. Blassingame reports that approximately ten million Africans were brought to the Americas between the 1700s and the 1850s (*The Slave Community*, p. 5).

35. Harding, p. 9.

36. *Ibid.*, p. 14.

37. *Ibid.*, pp. 12, 13, 17.

38. *Ibid.*, p. 5.

39. Mary Berry and John Blassingame, *Long Memory: The Black Experience in America* (New York: Oxford University Press, 1982), p. 10.

40. Brawley, pp. 39–40.

41. Wilmore, *Black Religion and Black Radicalism*, p. 17.

42. Harding, p. 19. In a similar vein W.E.B. DuBois has written of Black Ancestors who "have suffered a common disaster and have one long memory" (DuBois, *Dusk of Dawn* [New York: Schocken Books, 1968], p. 117). This also implies the idea of a long history of continuous struggle.

43. Berry and Blassingame, p. xx.

44. Witvliet, *A Place in the Sun: An Introduction to Liberation Theology in the Third World* (Maryknoll, N.Y.: Orbis, 1985). He does, however, point to the historical prophetic tendencies in the black church tradition (p. 68). In his more recent text, which critically examines black theology in the United States, Witvliet devotes an impressive amount of space to the historical context of the origin of black theology. See *The Way of the Black Messiah*, Part Two.

45. Henry J. Young, *Major Black Religious Leaders: 1755–1940* (Nashville: Abingdon, 1977); *Major Black Religious Leaders Since 1940* (1979). These are two excellent volumes, limited only by the author's failure to include black women religious leaders.

46. Cited in *Major Black Religious Leaders: 1755–1940*, p. 14.

47. Young, p. 15.

48. Wilmore, p. xiii.

49. *Ibid.*

50. *Ibid.*, p. 31.

51. Blassingame, *The Slave Community*, p. 133.

52. Young, p. 13.

53. See Cone, *For My People*, pp. 6–10; Wilmore's general introduction in Wilmore and Cone, eds., *Black Theology*, pp. 4–11. In addition, Wilmore outlined three stages of the development of black theology at the Black Theology Project in 1986.

54. Cone, *For My People*, p. 19.

55. See Paul R. Garber, "King Was a Black Theologian," *The Journal of Religious Thought*, Volume 31, Number 2, Fall-Winter 1974–75.

56. *Martin & Malcolm & America*, pp. 122–123, 131–132.

57. *Ibid.*, pp. 295–296.

58. Cone, *My Soul Looks Back*, p. 41.

59. *Ibid.*, p. 39.

60. *Martin & Malcolm & America*, p. 167.

61. *Ibid.*, p. 168.

62. *Ibid.*, pp. 168–169.

63. *Ibid.*, p. 290.

64. George Breitman, ed., *Malcolm X Speaks* (New York: Grove Press, 1965), p. 40.

65. Malcolm X, *Malcolm X Talks to Young People* (New York: Pathfinder Press, 1991), p. 25.

66. Cone, *Black Theology and Black Power*, p. 3.

67. Cone, *A Black Theology of Liberation* (1970), p. 194.

68. Cited in Cone, "From Geneva to São Paulo: A Dialogue Between Black Theology and Latin American Liberation Theology," in Sergio Torres and John Eagleson, eds., *The Challenge of Basic Christian Communities* (Maryknoll, N.Y.: Orbis, 1982), p. 268.

69. Cone, *God of the Oppressed* (New York: Seabury, 1975), p. 214.

70. Boesak, "Coming in out of the Wilderness," in Sergio Torres and Virginia Fabella, eds., *The Emergent Gospel* (Maryknoll, N.Y.: Orbis, 1978), p. 77.

71. Foner, p. xiii.

72. Anne Wortham, *The Other Side of Racism* (Columbus: Ohio State University Press, 1981), p. 336. Similarly, James Bladwin shows the tendency of even the most sensitive white liberals to counsel blacks to forget about past injustices inflicted upon them. In Baldwin's play, *Blues for Mister Charlie* (New York: Dell, 1972), the white liberal newspaper editor, Parnell James, counsels the black preacher, Meridian, whose son was murdered by a white man: "We must forget about all — all the past injustice. We have to start from scratch, or do our best to start from scratch. It isn't vengeance we're after. Is it?" (p. 61).

73. Gutiérrez, "Freedom and Salvation a Political Problem," in Gustavo Gutiérrez and Richard Shaull, *Liberation and Change* (Atlanta: John Knox Press, 1977), p. 75.

74. *Ibid.*, p. 92.

75. *Ibid.*

76. Cited in Witvliet, *The Way of the Black Messiah*, p. 302, n76.

77. Malcolm X, "Statement of Basic Aims and Objectives of the Organization of Afro-American Unity," reproduced in George Breitman, *The Last Year of Malcolm X* (New York: Pathfinder Press, 1984), p. 111.

Chapter 2

1. Robert McAfee Brown, *Theology in a New Key* (Philadelphia: Westminster Press, 1978), p. 122.

2. Albert C. Winn, "The Reformed Tradition and Liberation Theology," Ronald H. Stone, ed., *Reformed Faith and Politics* (Washington, D.C.: University Press of America, 1983), p. 78.

3. See Susan Brooks Thistlethwaite, *Sex, Race, and God* (New York: Crossroad, 1989) and Thistlethwaite and Mary Potter Engel, eds., *Lift Every Voice: Constructing Christian Theologies from the Underside* (New York: Harper & Row, 1990).

4. Cone, *For My People*, p. 19. The article in question appeared in the November 15, 1968, issue of *Time* magazine.

5. Grant Shockely, "Ultimatum and Hope," *The Christian Century*, February 12, 1969.

6. *For My People*, p. 19.

7. Wilmore and Cone, eds., *Black Theology*, p. 101.

8. Cone and William Hordern, "Dialogue on Black Theology," *The Christian Century*, Volume 88, September 15, 1971, p. 1085. This is a matter that Cone has always taken seriously in his theological project. Commenting further on this point in a letter written to me on November 5, 1985, Cone said: "Even in my deepest rage of the late 1960s, I never believed that only blacks could teach or write black theology. The reason is found in the gospel that embraces all. If black theology is only about blacks and not a search to interpret the gospel for all, then it is not Christian."

9. Malcolm X, *The Autobiography of Malcolm X* as told to Alex Haley [1965] (New York: Ballantine Books, 1992), p. 263.

10. *Martin & Malcolm & America*, p. 166.

11. Frederick Douglass, *Narrative of the Life of Frederick Douglass* [1845], (New York: Signet, 1968) pp. 120–124.

12. W.E.B. DuBois, *Darkwater* [1920] (New York: Shocken, 1972), p. 36.

13. Cited in Manning Marable, *How Capitalism Underdeveloped Black America* (Boston: South End Press, 1983), p. 199.

14. Cone, *A Black Theology of Liberation* (1970), p. 23.

15. Cone, *Black Theology and Black Power*, p. 117.

16. *Ibid.*

17. *A Black Theology of Liberation*, p. 56.

18. Cone, "Reflections from the Perspective of U.S. Blacks: Black Theology and Third World Theology," p. 238.

19. Cone, *My Soul Looks Back*, p. 77.

20. *A Black Theology of Liberation*, p. 17.

21. *Ibid.*, pp. 17–18.

22. Allan Boesak, *Farewell to Innocence* (Maryknoll, N.Y.: Orbis, 1976), p. 12.

23. *Ibid.*

24. *A Black Theology of Liberation*, pp. 45–49.

25. *Ibid.*, p. 20.

26. See Theo Witvliet's illuminating comment on Cone's early description of theology. See *The Way of the Black Messiah*, pp. 271–272, *n*66.

27. *A Black Theology of Liberation*, p. 18.

28. Cone, *God of the Oppressed*, p. 7.

29. *A Black Theology of Liberation*, pp. 21, 23.

30. *Ibid.*, p. 47.

31. *Ibid.*

32. Gustavo Gutiérrez, *A Theology of Liberation* (Maryknoll, N.Y.: Orbis, 1973), p. 11.

33. *Ibid.*

34. *God of the Oppressed*, p. 8.

35. Gutiérrez, *A Theology of Liberation*, p. 12.

36. Cone, "Black Theology: Its Origin, Methodology, and Relationship to Third World Theologies," in Virginia Fabella and Sergio Torres, eds., *Doing Theology in a Divided World* (Maryknoll, N.Y.: Orbis, 1985), p. 99.

37. *Ibid.* In another place Cone has written: "Black Theology is reflection that arises from participation in the black story. The black theologian performs the secondary but vital function of subjecting the story to a critical scrutiny" (Cone, "The Content and Method of Black Theology," *The Journal of Religious Thought*, Fall-Winter, 1975, p. 98).

38. See *Lift Every Voice*, p. 5.

39. Gutiérrez, "Two Theological Perspectives: Liberation Theology and Progressivist Theology," in Sergio Torres and Virginia Fabella, eds., *The Emergent Gospel*, p. 250. Gayraud Wilmore has also written of this, rejecting all notions of a universal theology. "We do not know of any school of Christian theology that is universal. The claim of some white theologians that what they call theology is the universal understanding of the faith for modern people is not only ridiculous, but an arrogant falsification of the nature of all theological reflection. Since 1975, black theologians are less tempted to fall into this way of thinking about their work than formerly" (Wilmore, "The New Context of Black Theology in the United States," in Gerald H. Anderson and Thomas F. Stransky, eds., *Mission Trends No. 4* [New York: Paulist Press, 1979], p. 118).

40. Schubert Ogden, *Faith & Freedom: Toward a Theology of Liberation* (Nashville: Abingdon, 1979), p. 38.

41. Significantly, Robert McAfee Brown, among the most sensitive, aware, and "liberated" white male theologians, knew of this change. Brown writes: "The conference

on black theology, held in August 1977 in Atlanta, made clear that economic analysis was beginning to be taken more seriously by black theologians..." (Brown, *Theology in a New Key*, p. 120).

42. Cone, "An Interpretation of the Debate Among Black Theologians," in Wilmore and Cone, eds., *Black Theology*, pp. 619–620.

43. See Cone's Introduction to Part VI of Wilmore and Cone, eds., *Black Theology*, p. 459.

44. Tissa Balasuriya, *Planetary Theology* (Maryknoll, N.Y.: Orbis, 1984), p. 14.

45. *Ibid.*, p. 13.

46. *Ibid.*, p. 14. Cone, very close to Balasuriya on this point, writes: "The universal dimensions of the gospel message requires that we struggle not only for ourselves but for all. *For there can be no freedom for any one of us until all of us are free. Any theology that falls short of this universal vision is not Christian* and thus cannot be identified with the man Jesus who died on the cross and was resurrected so that everyone might be liberated into God's Kingdom" (emphasis added; see his essay, "Black Theology and Third World Theologies," *The Chicago Theological Seminary Register*, Volume 73, Number 1, Winter 1983, p. 11.)

47. Cone, "Reflections from the Perspective of U.S. Blacks: Black Theology and Third World Theology," pp. 238–241.

48. L. John Topel, *The Way to Peace* (Maryknoll, N.Y.: Orbis, 1979), p. 151.

49. Gutiérrez, *A Theology of Liberation*, p. 11.

50. Gutiérrez, "Liberation Praxis and Christian Faith," in Rosino Gibellini, ed., *Frontiers of Theology in Latin America* (Maryknoll, N.Y.: Orbis, 1979), p. 22.

51. Witvliet, *A Place in the Sun*, p. 127.

52. Gutiérrez, "Two Theological Perspectives, p. 247.

53. Cone, "Black Theology: Its Origin, Methodology, and Relationship to Third World Theologies," p. 98.

54. See Vine Deloria, Jr., *Custer Died for Your Sins* (New York: Avon Books, 1969), Chapter Five; *God Is Red* (New York: Grosset & Dunlap, 1973).

55. Jon Sobrino, *The True Church and the Poor* (Maryknoll, N.Y.: Orbis, 1984), p. 28.

56. Robert McAfee Brown, *Gustavo Gutiérrez* (Atlanta: John Knox Press, 1980), pp. 29–30.

57. *Ibid.*, pp. 46–47.

58. Gutiérrez, "Two Theological Perspectives...," p. 241. The late L. Harold DeWolf, a theistic personalist, espoused a similar view: "Even where good institutional structures are established, if they are operated by men and women who are mainly concerned with personal advantage, new tyrannies, exploitations, and other evils will quickly displace the old. This is the history of innumerable political reforms in municipalities and nations alike. A new world requires new persons" (see DeWolf, "Public and Private Dimensions of Ethical Responsibility," in Paul Deats, Jr., ed., *Toward a Discipline of Social Ethics* [Boston: Boston University Press, 1972], p. 279). Evil in its concrete forms is not likely to be cured by social reconstruction or manipulation alone, although this is a necessity in itself. At some point in the process efforts will have to be made to produce radically transformed individuals who manage societal structures. This also means there is a need for a transformation of thinking about power and power relations at both the interpersonal and corporate levels.

59. Gutiérrez, "Liberation Praxis and Christian Faith," p. 24.

60. *My Soul Looks Back*, p. 78.

61. Cone, "Black Theology and Third World Theologies," p. 5.

62. *My Soul Looks Back*, p. 106.

63. Gutiérrez, "Freedom and Salvation: A Political Problem," in *Liberation and Change*, p. 92.

64. Anna Julia Cooper, *A Voice from the South* (Xenia, Ohio: Aldine Printing House, 1892).

65. *Custer Died for Your Sins*, p. 269.

66. Witvliet, *The Way of the Black Messiah*, p. 104.

67. Cone, "Black Theology: Its Origin...," pp. 100–101.

68. Juan Luis Segundo, *Liberation of Theology* (Maryknoll, N.Y.: Orbis, 1976), p. 66.

69. *Ibid.*

70. José Miguez Bonino, *Doing Theology in a Revolutionary Situation* (Philadelphia: Fortress Press, 1975), p. 90.

71. Deane Ferm, *Third World Liberation Theologies: An Introductory Survey* (Maryknoll, N.Y.: Orbis, 1986), p. 32.

72. Vidales, "Methodological Issues in Liberation Theology," Gibellini, ed., *Frontiers in Latin American Theology*, pp. 41–42.

73. Bonino, p. 90.

74. *Ibid.*, p. 80.

75. Gutiérrez, "Two Theological Perspectives," p. 241.

76. Bonino, p. 90.

77. *God of the Opressed*, Ch. 3. Cone develops this theme throughout the book.

78. Lewis Coser, *Masters of Sociological Thought* (New York: Harcourt Brace Jovanovich, 1971), p. 429.

79. Although I will not go into detail here I want to point out that liberation theologians are not the only ones to emphasize the significance of the methodology of the social sciences. In his emerging personalistic social ethics, Walter G. Muelder describes social ethics as an interdisciplinary field that takes the methods of the social sciences seriously from beginning to end. In light of my belief that there are important congruencies between personalism and liberation theology (especially black theology), Muelder's emphasis is significant, since both stress the importance of the social sciences.

80. Some African American intellectuals also support this conclusion. See William J. Wilson, *The Declining Significance of Race* (Chicago: University of Chicago Press, 1978), and Shelby Steele, *The Content of Our Character* (New York: Harper Perennial, 1990).

81. See Joe Feagin, *Racial and Ethnic Relations* [1978] (Englewood Cliffs, N.J.: Prentice Hall, 1984).

82. Vidales, "Methodological Issues in Liberation Theology," p. 42.

83. Oliver Cromwell Cox, *Caste, Class & Race* (New York: Monthly Review Press, 1959), p. xvi.

84. J. DeOtis Roberts, *Black Theology Today* (New York: Mellen Press, 1983), p. 42.

85. Cone, "The Content and Method of Black Theology," pp. 99–100.

86. Gutiérrez, *A Theology of Liberation*, p. 10.

87. Robert C. Tucker, ed., *The Marx-Engels Reader* (New York: W.W. Norton, 1972), p. 109.

88. Sobrino, p. 15.

89. *Ibid.*, p. 18.

90. Gutiérrez, "Two Theological Perspectives," p. 244.

91. Bonino, p. 81.

92. Bonino, *Toward a Christian Political Ethics* (Philadelphia: Fortress Press, 1983), p. 9. See also pp. 43, 109.

93. *My Soul Looks Back*, p. 77. There is no question about the seriousness with which Cone takes reason. "Black Theology," he writes, "must not reject reason, for without it there is no way to assess the validity of one claim over another" ("The Content and Method of Black Theology," p. 99).

94. Vidales, P. 38.

95. Brown, *Gustavo Gutiérrez*, p. 34. Brown characterizes theology as "a kind of second reflection, so to speak, examining what has already been going on, but now examining it from a theological perspective (in Gustavo's phrase 'in the light of the Word of God...')," *Ibid.*, pp. 43–44.

96. *Ibid.*, p. 69.

97. Winn, "The Reformed Tradition and Liberation Theology," p. 79.

98. *Gustavo Gutiérrez*, p. 71.

99. Ada María Isasi-Díaz, "Solidarity: Love of Neighbor in the 1980s," Thistlethwaite and Engel, eds., *Lift Every Voice*, p. 32.

100. James Baldwin, "White Racism or World Community," Baldwin, *The Price of the Ticket* (New York: St. Martin's/Marek, 1985), pp. 436–437. Presently there is talk among some white theologians about the need for a "hermeneutic of trust," as opposed to a hermeneutic of suspicion. The argument seems to be that "there is already too much suspicion," and that this is the cause of much of the tension between African Americans and whites, for example. "Progress," it is said, "can only be based upon trust." My gut response to this is that white males who have willingly and uncritically received the material benefits of their status as white males without thought and actions to eradicate the effects of this on African Americans, Native Americans, Latinos, women, and children are in no position to even suggest that those outside their group adhere to a hermeneutic of trust. Such a hermeneutic is needed, but it is white men who need to develop it. This should not merely be a trust for other white men, as a way to further solidify their economic and other advantages against the masses of people. Were the masses to relinquish their suspicion in favor of a hermeneutic of trust they would supply the final nails for the sealing of their own coffins! The trust of the masses must be earned by those who so thoroughly benefit from the system of exploitation. Such trust should not be expected until the actions of white men prove beyond doubt that they are in complete solidarity and identification with the poor and the oppressed and that all they do is for the purpose of total liberation and socioeconomic empowerment; that all they do is for the creation of a worldhouse that is more in harmony with God's vision for the whole world.

101. Segundo, *The Liberation of Theology*, p. 8.

102. *Doing Theology in a Revolutionary Situation*, p. 91.

103. Segundo, p. 4.

104. Gutiérrez, "Liberation Praxis and Christian Faith," p. 33, n12.

105. Balasuriya, *Planetary Theology*, p. 11.

106. Rayford Logan, *The Betrayal of the Negro* (New York: Collier, 1965). As for betrayals of Native Americans, Dee Brown has done an admirable job of detailing these in *Bury My Heart at Wounded Knee* (New York: Holt, Rinehart & Winston, 1970). The Sioux Indian, Vine Deloria, Jr., has written much about the betrayals of his ancestors and their posterity by the white man. See Deloria, *Behind the Trail of Broken Treaties* (Austin: University of Texas Press, 1985); Deloria and Clifford Lytle, *American Indians, American Justice* (Austin: University of Texas Press, 1983); Deloria and Lytle, *The Nations Within: The Past and Future of American Indian Sovereignty* (New York: Pantheon Books, 1984).

107. *The Autobiography of Malcolm X*, p. 298.

108. Cone, "The Content and Method of Black Theology," p. 99.

109. *Ibid.*
110. *Martin & Malcolm & America*, pp. 221-243.
111. *Ibid.*, p. 100.
112. *Ibid.*, pp. 100-101.
113. *Ibid.*, p. 103.
114. See Cone's Introduction to Part VI in Wilmore and Cone, eds., *Black Theology*, p. 455.
115. Leonardo Boff and Clodovis Boff, *Salvation and Liberation* (Maryknoll, N.Y.: Orbis, 1984), p. 12. For a discussion of the three mediations see pp. 5-12, 49-56.
116. *Ibid.*, p. 13.
117. See Beatriz Melano Couch's statement in Torres and Eagleson, ed., *Theology in the Americas* (Maryknoll, N.Y.: Orbis, 1976), p. 375.
118. *For My People*, p. 153.
119. Gutiérrez, *A Theology of Liberation*, p. 15.
120. *God of the Oppressed*, p. 18.
121. Witvliet, *A Place in the Sun*, p. 71. See also his text, *The Way of the Black Messiah*, p. 225.
122. *The Way of the Black Messiah*, p. 224.

Chapter 3

1. *The Autobiography of Malcolm X*, p. 201.
2. *My Soul Looks Back*, p. 47.
3. *Ibid.*, p. 51.
4. *Black Theology and Black Power*, p. 2; *My Soul Looks Back*, pp. 44-45, 47, 50.
5. *Black Theology and Black Power*, p. 3.
6. Malcolm X, "The Black Revolution," in Imam Benjamin Karim, ed., *The End of White World Supremacy: Four Speeches by Malcolm X* (New York: Arcade Publishing, 1971), p. 79.
7. *Martin & Malcolm & America*, p. 166.
8. *Ibid.*, p. 67.
9. Peter Goldman, *The Death and Life of Malcolm X* (New York: Harper & Row, 1973), p. 227.
10. *Martin & Malcolm & America*, p. 266.
11. *Black Theology and Black Power*, p. 3.
12. *A Black Theology of Liberation*, p. 12.
13. *Black Theology and Black Power*, p. 28.
14. *A Black Theology of Liberation*, p. 12.
15. *Ibid.*
16. This term was not yet in Cone's vocabulary, but the meaning was present.
17. *A Black Theology of Liberation*, pp. 33-34.
18. Foner, ed., *America's Black Past*. p. 28.
19. Sam Greenlee, *The Spook Who Sat by the Door* (New York: Bantam, 1970), p. 244.
20. More needs to be said about the concept of "blackness as ontological symbol" and how whites genuinely committed to black liberation may best participate in the black struggle. I shall examine this issue in Chapter 5.
21. *My Soul Looks Back*, p. 15.
22. *For My People*, p. 2.
23. Deane Ferm, *Contemporary American Theologies: A Critical Survey* (New York: Seabury, 1981), p. 54.

24. *Ibid.*

25. Cited *ibid.* The complete text of Cone's speech is entitled, "Black Theology and the Black Church: Where Do We Go from Here," in Wilmore and Cone, eds., *Black Theology*, pp. 350–358.

26. See Susan Brooks Thistlethwaite, *Sex, Race, & God: Christian Feminism in Black and White* (New York: Crossroads, 1989), and Thistlethwaite and Mary Potter Engel, eds., *Lift Every Voice.*

27. Sobrino, *The True Church and the Poor*, p. 16.

28. *Martin & Malcolm & America*, p. 76.

29. *Black Theology and Black Power*, p. 141.

30. See *Martin & Malcolm & America* for a thorough discussion of the role of particularism and universalism in the thought of Malcolm and King (chapters 3 and 4).

31. *Ibid.*, p. 3.

32. *A Black Theology of Liberation*, p. 27.

33. *My Soul Looks Back*, p. 39.

34. *Ibid.*, p. 43.

35. *God of the Oppressed*, p. 3.

36. *Ibid.*, p. 52.

37. See Cone's remarks at the Symposium of the World Council of Churches in Geneva in 1973, reproduced in Wilmore and Cone, eds., *Black Theology*, p. 514.

38. James Baldwin, *Notes of a Native Son* [1955] (New York: Bantam Books, 1964, pp. 4–5.

39. Weatherby, *James Baldwin: Artist on Fire*, p. 19.

40. *My Soul Looks Back*, Ch. 1.

41. *God of the Oppressed*, p. 45.

42. Horace Cayton, "Ideological Forces in the Work of Negro Writers," Herbert Hill, ed., *Anger and Beyond* (New York: Harper, 1966), p. 37.

43. *My Soul Looks Back*, p. 51.

44. *Ibid.*, p. 47.

45. *Notes of a Native Son*, p. 5.

46. *My Soul Looks Back*, p. 77.

47. Cone responds to this criticism in several places. See Cone, "An Interpretation of the Debate Among Black Theologians," in Wilmore and Cone, eds., *Black Theology*. pp. 615–620; *My Soul Looks Back*, pp. 59–61; and *God of the Oppressed*, pp. 271–272. In part the latter text was intended as a response to African American critics on this point. Cone has said that their criticisms helped him a great deal. *The Spirituals and the Blues* was his first attempt to delve into African American sources. Although the criticism of Long, Wilmore, and Cecil Cone hurt him, he thought he could best show his appreciation by researching black spirituals, folklore, sermons, slave narratives and autobiographies, etc.

48. White scholars often give the appearance of being disturbed and perplexed by references to "white concepts" and "black concepts." They are quick to say, "There is no such thing as a white or a black concept. There are just concepts, period!" This is also what they say about "black theology" and "white theology." "There is just theology," they say. In their minds I think they have worked this out reasonably well and really believe what they say. But when it comes to acting this out concretely, their concepts and theology come out rather stale, and white. What this seems to come down to is that theirs are just concepts and just theology that white folks put forth like they are really the only concepts and theology!

49. W.E.B. DuBois, *The Souls of Black Folk* [1903] (Greenwich, Conn.: Fawcett Books, 1969), p. 17.

50. Martin Luther King, Jr., *Where Do We Go from Here: Chaos or Community?* (Boston: Beacon Press, 1967), pp. 102–134.

51. *Ibid.*, pp. 122–125.

52. *The Spirituals and the Blues*, p. v.

53. *God of the Oppressed*, p. vii.

54. Cone, "Christian Faith and Political Praxis," p. 54.

55. *My Soul Looks Back*, p. 45.

56. *Black Theology and Black Power*, p. 118.

57. *Ibid.*

58. Robert McAfee Brown, *Creative Dislocation* (Nashville: Abingdon, 1980), pp. 107, 108.

59. *For My People*, p. 2. Gutiérrez expresses a similar view in *A Theology of Liberation*.

60. Kenneth Kaunda, *The Riddle of Violence* (New York: Harper, 1980), p. 74.

61. Henry Highland Garnet, "Call to Rebellion, 1843," Floyd Barbour, ed., *The Black Power Revolt* (Boston: Extending Horizons Books, 1968), pp. 34–41.

62. Frederick Douglass, *Life and Times of Frederick Douglass* [1892] (New York: Collier Books, 1961), p. 144. In Philip Foner's excellent biography, *Frederick Douglass* (New York: Citadel Press, 1969), the author chronicles the events that led to Douglass's break with Garrison's absolute pacifism and dependence upon moral suasion as the only means to black liberation. In part he was influenced in this break by his dialogues with John Brown, who had no confidence in moral suasion. Although Douglass still held to the necessity of moral suasion and peaceful means to liberation wherever possible, he was finally convinced that it was naive to insist that the ultimate destruction of slavery would come about through peaceful means only. By 1860, only months after John Brown and the survivors of the Harper's Ferry incident had been executed in 1859, he was convinced that the eradication of slavery through peaceful means was hopeless, although he himself never advocated violence. Foner writes of Douglass's position. "'I have little hope of the freedom of the slave by peaceful means,' he wrote on June 29, 1860. 'A long course of peaceful slaveholding has placed the slaveholders beyond the reach of moral and humane considerations. They have neither ears nor hearts for the appeals of justice and humanity. While the slave will tamely submit his neck to the yoke, his back to the lash, and his ankle to the fetter and chain, the Bible will be quoted, and learning invoked to justify slavery. The only penetrable point of a tyrant is the fear of death'" (p. 139). For a more detailed account of Douglass's split with Garrison, see pp. 136–154.

63. *Where Do We Go from Here*, pp. 93–94.

64. George Breitman, ed., *Malcolm X Speaks* (New York: Grove Press, 1965), p. 207.

65. Cited in Victor Ullman, Martin R. Delany: *The Beginnings of Black Nationalism* (Boston: Beacon Press, 1971), p. ix.

66. Marable, *Blackwater* (Dayton, Ohio: Black Praxis Press, 1981), p. 9.

67. *For My People*, pp. 112–113.

Chapter 4

1. *For My People*, p. 80.

2. *Ibid.*, p. 81.

3. *Ibid.*, p. 87.

4. Rollo May, *Power and Innocence* (New York: W.W. Norton, 1972), p. 72.

5. Stephen B. Oates, *Let the Trumpet Sound: The Life of Martin Luther King, Jr.* (New York: New American Library, 1982), p. 252.

6. Cited in June Jordan, *On Call* (Boston: South End Press, 1985), p. 17.

7. *For My People*, pp. 88–92.

8. Witvliet, *The Way of the Black Messiah*, p. 233. Cornel West raises a similar concern in his essay "Black Theology and Marxist Thought," Wilmore and Cone, eds., *Black Theology*, p. 556.

9. *The Way of the Black Messiah*, p. 235.

10. *For My People*, pp. 9, 96.

11. See also *A Black Theology of Liberation* (Maryknoll, N.Y.: Orbis, 1986 ed.), p. xvi.

12. See Archie Epps, ed., *The Speeches of Malcolm X at Harvard* (New York: William Morrow, 1968), p. 173.

13. *Martin & Malcolm & America*, p. 280.

14. *Ibid.*, p. 285.

15. *Ibid.*, p. 284.

16. *Ibid.*

17. *Ibid.*, p. 286.

18. *Ibid.*

19. *For My People*, p. 94.

20. *Ibid.*

21. See Cone's Introduction in Wilmore and Cone, eds., *Black Theology*, p. 137.

22. *Ibid.*

23. Ferm, *Contemporary American Theologies*, p. 46.

24. Wilmore and Cone, eds., *Black Theology*, p. 137.

25. *A Black Theology of Liberation* (1970), p. 194.

26. Joseph Hough, *Black Power and White Protestants* (New York: Oxford University Press, 1968); C. Freeman Sleeper, *Black Power and Christian Responsibility* (Nashville: Abingdon Press, 1969).

27. *A Black Theology of Liberation* (1970), p. 195.

28. *A Black Theology of Liberation* (1986), pp. xvi–xvii.

29. It is interesting that Cone excludes this criticism from the 1986 edition. I wonder if this is a capitulation of some sort. Has there been a softening or mellowing on his part? Or is this his way of saying that he is just not concerned about the white man?

30. *A Black Theology of Liberation* (1986), p. xii.

31. Cited *ibid.*, pp. xiv–xv.

32. *A Black Theology of Liberation* (1970), p. 119.

33. *Ibid.*, p. 118.

34. *Ibid.*, pp. 162, 163.

35. Cone makes at least four references to this work. See *A Black Theology of Liberation* (1970), pp. 159, 160, 162, 163. He also refers to Marx's claim that religion is the opiate of the people (p. 224).

36. *For My People*, p. 88.

37. DuBois, *The Autobiography of W. E. B. DuBois* [1968] (New York: International Publications, 1973), p. 197.

38. *Ibid.*

39. Cited by Saunders Redding in the Introduction to DuBois, *The Souls of Black Folk* [1903] (Greenwich, Conn.: Fawcett, 1968), p. viii.

40. *Ibid.*

41. *For My People*, p. 88.

42. *Ibid.*
43. *Ibid.*
44. The text of this document is printed in Wilmore and Cone, eds., *Black Theology*, pp. 80–89.
45. Cited in *For My People*, p. 91.
46. *For My People*, p. 91.
47. *Ibid.*, Chapter X.
48. *Ibid.*, p. 96.
49. See King, "A Time to Break Silence," James Washington, ed., *A Testament of Hope* (New York: Harper, 1986), pp. 231–244. Cone praised both King and Malcolm as internationalists. See *Martin & Malcolm & America*, pp. 311–314.
50. See Epps, pp. 171–174.
51. *Martin & Malcolm & America*, p. 314.
52. Though a questionable thesis, David Garrow implies that King was a Marxist near the end of his life. Garrow writes of this in *The FBI and Martin Luther King, Jr.* (New York: Penguin Books, 1983): "The FBI's still 'Top Secret' quotation of King saying 'I am a Marxist' probably would be discounted by most observers as something King could never have said. Actually, however, such a statement would not have been surprising, for King made mention of his distaste for the American economic order to many friends, even in the 1950s. In a divinity school term paper in 1950–51 King spoke of 'my present anti-capitalistic feelings,' and he reiterated this theme in several sermons in 1956 and 1957, if not earlier. . . . In private, . . . however, he made it clear to close friends that economically speaking he considered himself what he termed a Marxist, largely because he believed with increasing strength that American society needed a radical redistribution of wealth and economic power to achieve even a rough form of social justice. ¶ . . . By 1967 King was telling the SCLC staff, 'We must recognize that we can't solve our problem now until there is a radical redistribution of economic and political power,' and by early 1968 he had taken the final step to the admission that issues of economic class were more crucial and troublesome, and less susceptible to change, than issues of race. 'America,' he remarked to one interviewer, 'is deeply racist and its democracy is flawed both economically and socially.' He added that 'the black revolution is much more than a struggle for the rights of Negroes. it is forcing America to face all its interrelated flaws — racism, poverty, militarism, and materialism. It is exposing evils that are rooted deeply in the whole structure of our society. It reveals systemic rather than superficial flaws and suggests that radical reconstruction of society itself is the real issue to be faced'" (pp. 213, 214).

Garrow labels the King of the post–Chicago era (after 1966) a revolutionary. However, neither this designation nor King's earlier references to the need for a radical redistribution of wealth should be taken to mean that he was in fact a Marxist. One can make a radical critique of capitalist structures without accepting Marxism lock, stock and barrel, as black liberation theologians like James Cone have shown. King could see the need for using Marxism as a tool for social analysis, but this did not make him a Marxist. Indeed, his commitment to both the black Christian faith and personalism, as well as his own empirical observation of the plight of his people, led him to the view of the necessity of a radical redistribution of wealth in this country. By the post–Chicago era King was doing what Malcolm X had already embarked on a few years earlier: recognizing the connections between racism and classism. I think it undeniable that there is evidence that King was moving in the direction of a kind of democratic socialism, though he never professed to being a socialist. The type of vision espoused by socialism is quite compatible with the biblical and personalist emphasis on sharing and respect for persons. To be sure, King's analysis of the American economic system was becoming very acute during the waning months of his life, but this alone is no indication that he was the Marxist that Garrow makes him out to be. Not all revolutionaries are Marxists!

53. *For My People*, p. 92.

54. Cone does an admirable job of discussing the relationship between Marxism and black Christians in *For My People* (Chapter IX), and *My Soul Looks Back* (pp. 123–138). He also shows how each perceives the other. Cone, of course, was not the only black scholar to recognize ways in which Marxist principles of social analysis and the black church could be supportive of each other. Cornel West also examines this in his book *Prophesy Deliverance: An Afro-American Revolutionary Christianity* (Philadelphia: Westminster, 1982). His essay "Black Theology and Marxist Thought" is also an important contribution in this regard (see Wilmore and Cone, eds., *Black Theology*, pp. 552–566). In addition, Manning Marable deals with this issue in his essay "The Ambiguous Politics of the Black Church." He approvingly quotes Harry Golden's rationale as to why communism failed to attract Southern blacks during the civil rights movement: "First, 'they do not depend on nor incorporate Jesus and the Gospels.' Second, 'the great mass of American Negroes do not reject the existing social order, they seek only to share fully in its bourgeois blessing'" (cited in Marable, *How Capitalism Underdeveloped Black America*, p. 206). This latter is consonant with Cone's view in *For My People* that during the mid to late sixties Cone and many of the black clergy radicals of the NCBC were, like most middle class blacks, capitalists who wanted their piece of the American pie, and were not necessarily concerned about radically transforming the economic system in order that there would be more positive results for the masses of blacks. (Practically I am not certain that this is not still the case today, though many of the leading black theologians have verbalized their belief in the significance of class analysis and a form of democratic socialism.) Marable's commentary on the failure of most civil rights leaders — many of whom were either pastors or affiliated in other ways with the black church — to take Marxist analysis seriously is quite appropriate, and one that the mature James Cone would agree with. "The unwillingness to unite with Marxists and militant social democrats who expressed a sincere commitment to destroy racial segregation eliminated any possibility that the Civil Rights Movement would transcend its theoretical parochialism and develop a legitimate agenda to reconstruct the political economy of the United States" (*How Capitalism Underdeveloped Black America*, p. 207).

55. *Black Theology and Black Power*, pp. 135–136.

56. *A Black Theology of Liberation*, pp. 159, 160, 162, 163.

57. *Ibid.*, p. 162, n13.

58. Here Cone cites Karl marx, "Theses on Feuerbach," in Lewis S. Feuer, ed., *Marx and Engels: Basic Writings on Politics and Philosophy* (New York: Doubleday, 1959). See *ibid.*, p. 163, n16.

59. By "equality" I do not mean what is commonly meant in American society — parity and equal opportunity for blacks and other traditionally excluded groups. Equality in the present system means little more than having an equal chance to become oppressors. What I have in mind is similar to Marable's view of the implementation of a system wherein all persons have equal access to the political and economic apparatus and no group is controlled or dominated by another. "Equality within the mode of production means an equal share of decision making power from the shop floor of a factory to the upper echelons of the managerial elite. Equality, defined as the principle of human fairness, must take the place of equal opportunity, which is defined as an equal chance to become our own oppressors" (see Marable, *From the Grassroots* [Boston: South End Press, 1980], pp. 225, 219–227).

60. *A Black Theology of Liberation*, p. 28*n*.
61. *Ibid.*, p. 90.
62. *Ibid.*, pp. 177, 230.
63. *My Soul Looks Back*, p. 44.
64. Wilmore and Cone, eds., *Black Theology*, pp. 23–28.
65. *Ibid.*, pp. 62–64.
66. *Ibid.*, pp. 90–92.
67. *Iibid.*, p. 91.
68. *Ibid.*, p. 77; Wilmore is the author of these words.
69. *Ibid.*, pp. 77–78.
70. *Ibid.*, p. 78.
71. "Statement by the National Committee of Black Churchmen," June 13, 1969, in Wilmore and Cone, p. 102.
72. Harding, "No Turning Back?" *Renewal*, Oct.-Nov., 1970, p. 11.
73. *Black Theology and Black Power*, Chapter 5.
74. Harding, "No Turning Back?" pp. 11, 12.
75. Wilmore and Cone, p. 103.
76. *Ibid.*
77. *Ibid.*, p. 104.
78. *Ibid.*, p. 105.
79. *Ibid.*, p. 106.
80. *For My People*, p. 88.
81. *Ibid.*
82. Cone, "The Gospel and the Liberation of the Poor," *Christian Century*, February 18, 1981, p. 164.
83. *A Black Theology of Liberation*, p. 117.
84. Interestingly, Cone was aware of the deficiency by the time of the publication of *A Black Theology of Liberation*. In this context he wrote: "Since black theologians are trained in white seminaries and white thinkers make decisions about the structure and scope of theology, it is not possible for black religionists to separate themselves immediately from white thought" (p. 117). With the support and helpful criticism of his black colleagues he began to get handles on how to overcome this deficiency in his theological project. This experience has not been unique to Cone. In a sense it would be counterproductive to return to the seminaries and universities for further training to rid oneself of this problem, inasmuch as these institutions are still controlled by the dominant white group and the emphasis is still on teaching the white experience. Even while teaching at Adrian College, Cone entertained thoughts of returning to Chicago to earn a Ph.D. in literature. He talked this over with Nathan Scott, Jr., a black scholar teaching literature and theology at the University of Chicago, but aborted this when riots broke out in Detroit in the summer of 1967 that led to the killing of 43 blacks. He was furious over this, and decided that there was no time to return to graduate school for a second Ph.D. degree. "I had to say something now about God and black peoples' struggle for freedom" (see *My Soul Looks Back*, p. 43).
85. *For My People*, p. 88.
86. *Black Theology and Black Power*, p. 111.
87. *Martin & Malcolm & America*, p. 266.
88. *Ibid.*, p. 269.
89. *Ibid.*; here Cone's reference is to responses to unprophetic, uninvolved black churches.
90. *Ibid.*, pp. 54–55.
91. The reader who wishes to consider other passages in *Black Theology and Black*

Power that seem to have some relevance regarding Cone's awareness of the need for social analysis and the necessity of going beyond making appeals to the consciences of whites may want to examine the following pages: 33, 47, 49–50, 53, 56, 58, 59, 94, 113, 142. In no case is there evidence that Cone expressly refers to social analysis or that he is engaged in the kind of analysis that presently characterizes his work. On page 115 Cone rejects the idea of renewal, indicating that the concept implied the existence of "a core of healthy, truthful substance under all the dirt and rust." It appears that implicit in this rejection was an awareness that there was a need for fundamental systemic change. Also, his criticism of the black church's "response to racism at the level of sheer survival at the price of freedom and dignity" seems to suggest the need for deep structural changes in the social system. In any case, my contention is that every reference to the need for structural change, radical approaches to the problem, taking risks, fighting for the poor, etc., implies an awareness of the need for social analysis. The problem, of course, is that during this first period of his writing Cone not only did not have sufficient tools of the social sciences to make the thorough, radical analysis needed, but he was so enraged because of the several hundred years of brutality committed against blacks, as well as the brutalities and murders of the sixties, that he would not have had the peace of mind to do the type of analysis needed anyway. Indeed, the treatise he did produce was just what was needed at the time. In addition, it should be noted that few if any black theologians gave as sharp an analysis of racism, white liberals and white guilt, the implications of integration for blacks, and the relation of black power, as Cone gave in Chapter One of his first book. Though he does not see the links between racism, sexism, classism, and imperialism, no one can argue that there is an absence of critical analysis in this chapter, even if it is superficial.

92. *A Black Theology of Liberation*, p. 117.

93. *Ibid.*

94. *For My People*, p. 88.

95. *A Black Theology of Liberation*, pp. 186–194.

96. *Ibid.*

97. This is the definition given by social gospellers of an earlier era. See Walter Rauschenbusch, *A Theology for the Social Gospel* (New York: Macmillan, 1917), pp. 47–50.

98. *A Black Theology of Liberation*, p. 159.

99. Reinhold Niebuhr, *The Nature and Destiny of Man* [1941] (New York: Scribner's, 1964), I:186–203. In his treatment of the biblical definition of sin, Niebuhr follows closely the Augustinian strain of theology. When one "seeks to raise his contingent existence to unconditioned significance," he or she succumbs to pride (*ibid.*, p. 186). Niebuhr was aware, however, of the lack of unanimity among religious thinkers that pride is the basic form of sin (*ibid.*).

100. *Black Theology and Black Power*, Chapter 4. See also *A Black Theology of Liberation*, pp. 236–237.

101. *A Black Theology of Liberation*, p. 174.

102. *Ibid.*

103. *Ibid.*, p. 175.

104. *Ibid.*, pp. 176–177.

105. Breitman, ed., *Malcolm X Speaks*, p. 142.

106. *Ibid.*, p. 150.

107. Epps, p. 172.

108. For additional passages that suggest the presence of social analysis or an awareness of its importance see *A Black Theology of Liberation*, pp. 158, 161, 166, 170, 173, 181, 229, 230, 237, 241, 244, 245, 247, 258.

109. *My Soul Looks Back*, p. 46.

110. *For My People*, p. 96. Though Cone does not refer to Malcolm X in this citation, an examination of Malcolm's speeches and interviews reveals the high priority he gave to socioeconomic analysis.

111. *A Black Theology of Liberation* (1986), p. xvii.

112. *Ibid.*, p. xix.

113. *The Spirituals and the Blues*, p. v.

114. *Ibid.*, p. 6.

115. Wilmore and Cone, p. 514.

116. Cone, "Christian Faith and Political Praxis," p. 62.

117. "Reflections from the Perspective of U.S. Blacks: Black Theology and Third World Theology," pp. 240–241.

118. Audre Lorde, *Sister Outsider* (Freedom, Calif.: Crossing Press, 1984), p. 112.

119. For a discussion of the controversy that led to these two perspectives on the approach to the social sciences, see Ralf Dahrendorf, "Values and Social Science," Dahrendorf, *Essays in the Theory of Society* (Stanford, Calif." Stanford University Press, 1968), Chapter 1.

120. Cone, "A Theological Challenge to the American Catholic Church," in *Speaking the Truth*, p. 50.

121. Cone, "The Dialectic of Theology and Life or Speaking the Truth," *Union Seminary Quarterly Review*, Volume 29, No. 2, 1974, p. 75.

122. Cited in Peter Goldman, "Malcolm X: Witness for the Prosecution," John Hope Franklin and August Meier, eds., *Black Leaders of the Twentieth Century* (Urbana, Ill.: University of Illinois Press, 1982), p. 315.

123. Cited in bell hooks, *Feminist Theory* (Boston: South End Press, 1984), pp. 159–160.

124. Cone does not hesitate to credit Cornel West for contributions to his interpretation of Marxism. He points out, however, that his actual introduction to the importance of Marxism came during his travels throughout the Third World and his dialogues with liberation theologians there. See *For My People*, pp. 255–256.

Chapter 5

1. *A Black Theology of Liberation*, p. 12.

2. *Black Theology and Black Power*, pp. 3, 117, 151.

3. *Ibid.*, p. 3.

4. *Ibid.*, pp. 151, 152.

5. *God of the Oppressed*, p. 242.

6. *A Black Theology of Liberation*, p. 118.

7. Walter G. Muelder, "Communitarian Dimensions of the Moral Laws," Paul Deats, Jr. and Carol Robb, eds., *The Boston Personalist Tradition* (Macon, Ga.: Mercer University Press, 1986), p. 250.

8. *Ibid.*, pp. 249–250.

9. See J. DeOtis Roberts, *Liberation and Reconciliation* (Philadelphia: Westminster Press, 1971), and Paul Holmer, "About Black Theology," Wilmore and Cone, eds., *Black Theology*, pp. 183–192.

10. *Martin & Malcolm & America*, p. 274.

11. As late as 1981 a white theologian could say that it was time for black theology to "come to terms with a wider liberation theology. An increasingly vocal element among black theologians no longer find it satisfactory to restrict themselves to

'thinking black.' . . . The time has come for black theologians to make common cause with thinkers of whatever race, sex, color, or nationality who seek for liberation from human servitude of all kinds and who seek to serve the God who abhors all forms of oppression" (Deane Ferm, *Contemporary American Theologies*, p. 58). This is the kind of criticism that was made of Cone during the early phase of his development. One can almost understand this during that period. However, it is difficult to understand such a criticism twelve years after the appearance of his first book! Of course, it is the contention of the present work that if Cone's early works are read closely and taken seriously one will see evidence of a willingness to "make common cause" with any group struggling for liberation, though to be sure, Cone's primary concern in those days was the liberation of black people. It seems to me that even with his more expanded view of oppression, Cone's first love and concern is for his own people. His was fundamentally a race analysis during this period. He was blinded to class and sex analysis. But particularly in the case of Cone, had Ferm read him more closely he would know that by 1975 there were strong signs of clarification of Cone's universal conception of oppression. Indeed, during his dialogue with William Hordern in 1971, Cone explicitly made statements about his commitment and the requirement of the Gospel that *all* be liberated from oppression. Because *all* persons share a common humanity, and because God is against *all* forms of oppression, he argued, no individual or group is free until all are free. By 1977 it was clear that his (and some other black theologians') conception of oppression had expanded considerably, and this came about in part because of dialogues with Third World theologians and white and black women. In his lecture "Black Theology and the Black Church: Where Do We Go from Here," Cone made it clear that "liberation knows no color bar" and that there is a strong emphasis on universalism in the gospel (see Wilmore and Cone, eds., *Black Theology*, pp. 350–359, for the full test). Cone challenged black religionists to "move beyond a mere reaction to white racism in America and begin to extend our vision of a new socially constructed humanity for the whole inhabited world." He was pushing them in the direction of concern for the oppressed in all parts of the world. But this broader conception of oppression does not mean that he and other black theologians will divorce themselves from "thinking black." Indeed, if they take black theology seriously, and there is every reason to believe that they do, they must continue to "think black." Ferm and many other white theologians need to look more closely at the literature of black theology before making their critiques.

12. Ferm, *Contemporary American Theologies*, p. 54.
13. *Black Theology and Black Power*, pp. 3, 151.
14. *Ibid.*, pp. 151–152.
15. Paul Tillich, *Dynamics of Faith* (New York: Harper, 1957), Chapter III. Cone refers specifically to Tillich's use of symbol in *A Black Theology of Liberation* (1970), p. 27.
16. *Ibid.*, p. 41.
17. *Ibid.*, p. 42.
18. *Ibid.*
19. *Ibid.*, pp. 42–43.
20. *A Black Theology of Liberation*, p. 185.
21. *Ibid.*, p. 184.
22. Audre Lorde, *Sister Outsider* (Freedom, Calif.: Crossing Press, 1984), pp. 63–64, 67–70.
23. Susan Brooks Thistlethwaite, *Sex, Race, and God: Christian Feminism in Black and White* (New York: Crossroads, 1989).
24. *A Black Theology of Liberation*, p. 27.
25. *Ibid.*, p. 32n.

26. *Ibid.*

27. *Ibid.*, p. 29.

28. *Ibid.*, p. 28*n.*

29. *Ibid.*, p. 108.

30. Boesak, *Black and Reformed* (New York: Orbis, 1984), p. 22.

31. See Angela Y. Davis, *Women, Race & Class* (New York: Vintage, 1981), chapters 3–7.

32. *Ibid.*, pp. 40–45.

33. *A Black Theology of Liberation*, p. 109.

34. *Ibid.*, pp. 156–157.

35. Cone, "An Interpretation of the Debate Among Black Theologians," Wilmore and Cone, eds., *Black Theology*, p. 620.

36. *Contemporary American Theologies*, p. 54.

37. See Cone, "An Interpretation of the Debate Among Black Theologians," pp. 615–620.

38. *Ibid.*, p. 617.

39. Cecil Cone, "The Identity Crisis in Black Theology: An Investigation of the Tensions Created by Efforts to Provide a Theological Interpretation of Black Religion in the Works of Joseph Washington, James Cone, and J. DeOtis Roberts," Ph.D. dissertation, Emory University, 1974, p. 190.

40. *Ibid.*, p. 191.

41. *Ibid.*, ppl. 60, 192.

42. *Ibid.*, p. 96.

43. *Ibid.*, p. 190.

44. *Contemporary American Theologies*, p. 54.

45. *A Black Theology of Liberation*, p. 21.

46. *Ibid.*, p. 118.

47. *Ibid.*, p. 27.

48. *Ibid.*, p. 193.

49. John C. Bennett, *The Radical Imperative* (Philadelphia: Westminster, 1975), p. 126. Bennett has given an impressive analysis of Cone's use of the term black (see pp. 125–127). Glen Bucher's analysis of Cone's use of the term in his early theology is the most detailed and helpful account of which I am aware. In his article, "Liberation in the Church: Black and White," Bucher convincingly argues that there are six meanings of blackness in Cone's early writings (*Union Seminary Quarterly Review*, Winter, 1974, pp. 95–97).

50. *A Black Theology of Liberation*, p. 21.

51. *Ibid.*, p. 26.

52. *Ibid.*

53. *Black Theology and Black Power*, p. 141.

54. *My Soul Looks Back*, pp. 114–115.

55. Wilmore and Cone, eds., *Black Theology*, p. 363.

56. Anna Julia Cooper, *A Voice from the South* (Xenia, Ohio: Aldine Printing House, 1892), p. 75.

57. *Sister Outsider*, p. 64.

58. *My Soul Looks Back*, p. 123.

59. *Ibid.*

60. Wilmore and Cone, eds., *Black Theology*, p. 511.

61. *Ibid.*, p. 514. It is interesting to note that Assmann equates the poor and the oppressed, wherever they exist in the world, with *Third World people*. Indeed, "poor" and "oppressed" are synonymous with "Third World," and Assmann does not hesitate

to say that these are their true friends. What is really significant, I think, is that James Cone approves of this, and has spoken quite appreciatively of this characterization. In any essay entitled "Black Theology: Its Origin, Methodology, and Relationship to Third World Theologies," Cone writes about Third World theology as if he himself is moving in the direction of a more global or ecumenical theology. As indicated in the text of the present chapter this has caused at least one black theologian some concern. Writing approvingly about this Third World theology, Cone observes that black and Third World theologians, through their dialogues in EATWOT, "have been attempting to develop together a new way of doing theology" (see Fabella and Torres, eds., *Doing Theology in a Divided World*, p. 100). See also Cone's essay, "Reflections from the Perspective of U.S. Blacks: Black Theology and Third World Theology," in Fabella and Torres, eds., *Irruption of the Third World*, p. 239. Cone writes of being "engaged in the exciting task of creating a Third World theology of liberation that we can all support" ("Black Theology: Its Origin, Methodology, and Relationship to Third World Theologies," p. 98). He also refers to "we Third World theologians," which seems to place him in the camp of Third World theologians ("Reflections from the Perspective of U.S. Blacks...," p. 240). Even by 1979 Cone was writing of "the Third World context" in such a way as to imply that black theology and Third World theology are one and the same (Wilmore and Cone, ed., *Black Theology*, p. 364). He also wrote of "Blacks and other Third World women" during that period. The term "other" would seem to suggest that there was for him no distinction to be made between black women and the women of Third World nations.

62. Wilmore and Cone, pp. 512, 513.

63. *For My People*, p. 94.

64. Torres and Eagleson, eds., *Theology in the Americas*, p. 354.

65. Cone, "From Geneva to São Paulo," Torres and Eagleson, eds., *The Challenge of Basic Christian Communities* (Maryknoll, N.Y.: Orbis, 1982), p. 267.

66. Wilmore and Cone, p. 515.

67. *Ibid.*, p. 451.

68. *Ibid.*

69. *For My People*, pp. 94–95.

70. See Marable, *How Capitalism Underdeveloped Black America* (Boston: South End Press, 1983).

71. *For My People*, p. 95. In *My Soul Looks Back*, Cone gives a very helpful discussion of the historical relationship between Marxism and the black church, indicating how each has perceived the other and how each may be strengthened by the other (pp. 123–138).

72. *For My People*, p. 95.

73. Cone, "Black Theology and the Black Church: Where Do We Go from Here," Wilmore and Cone, p. 358.

74. Wilmore and Cone, p. 453.

75. See Wilmore and Cone, pp. 543–551. Cone also refers to this reciprocation between blacks and Latin Americans in his essay, "From Geneva to São Paulo...," p. 276.

76. See his statement in Torres and Eagleson, eds., *Theology in the Americas*, p. 312.

77. See Wilmore and Cone, pp. 364–366.

78. *Martin & Malcolm & America*, pp. 295–296.

79. *Ibid.*, chapters 11 and 12.

80. *Ibid.*, p. 273.

81. *Ibid.*, p. 274.

82. *Ibid.*, pp. 277–278.
83. *Ibid.*, p. 279.
84. Pauli Murray, *Song in a Weary Throat* (New York: Harper & Row, 1987), p. 377.
85. Cited in *Martin & Malcolm & America*, p. 275.
86. *God of the Oppressed*, pp. 8, 10.
87. *Ibid.*, p. vi.
88. *Ibid.*, p. 214.
89. *My Soul Looks Back*, p. 117.
90. See Introduction to Part Five in Wilmore and Cone, p. 363.
91. *Ibid.*
92. *Ibid.*, pp. 363, 364. It is significant that Cone uses the phrase "Black and other Third World Women," for by this period it seems that he increasingly speaks of black and Third World theologies as if they are synonymous. This tendency has been apparent since he began travelling throughout the Third World, participating in EATWOT dialogues and other conferences. More recently he seems to speak of "Third World Theology" more than "Black Theology." Preston Williams, another first generation black theologian, has written that Cone "has attempted to subsume his black theology under the Third World liberation theologies and their American counterparts, which incorporate Marxist social analysis" (see Williams, "Afro-American Religious Ethics," James F. Childress and John Macquarrie, eds., *The Westminster Dictionary of Christian Ethics* [Philadelphia: Westminster Press, 1986], p. 13). It is important to remember, however, that though Cone speaks and writes more of a Third World theology, the issues before the black church and community remain as his primary, though not only, concern.
93. Angela Y. Davis, *Women, Race & Class* [1981] (New York: Vintage, 1983), Chapter 4.
94. bell hooks, *Ain't I a Woman?* (Boston: South End Press, 1981), Chapter 4.
95. Cooper, *A Voice from the South*, p. 123.
96. *Sister Outsider*, p. 70; see also p. 67.
97. *My Soul Looks Back*, pp. 117–118.
98. *For My People*, p. 131.
99. *Sister Outsider*, p. 119.
100. Wilmore and Cone, p. 366.
101. *Ibid.*, p. 7. Josiah Young makes a similar point in his book *Black and African Theologies* (New York: Orbis, 1986). Here he rightly contends that Cone "more than any other black male theologian has substantially taken the black feminist critique to heart" (p. 60).
102. *Sister Outsider*, pp. 119–120.
103. Cone, "New Roles in the Ministry: A Theological Appraisal," Wilmore and Cone, p. 397.
104. *For My People*, p. 134.
105. Jacquelyn Grant, "Black Theology and the Black Woman," Wilmore and Cone, eds., *Black Theology*, p. 418.
106. *Ibid.*, p. 419. For Grant the designation "Third World" has less to do with geographical location than socioeconomic oppression. Black men and women are therefore Third World people as well. Grant clarified this in a footnote: "I agree with the Fifth Commission that 'the Third World is not a geographical entity, but rather the world of oppressed peoples in their struggle for liberation.' In this sense, Black women are included in the term 'Third World.' However, in order to accent the peculiar identity, problems, and needs of Black women in the First World or the Third

World contexts, I choose to make the distinction between Black and other Third World women."

107. *For My People*, pp. 134–135.

108. Rufus Burrow, Jr., "Sexism in the Black Community and Church," *The Journal of the Interdenominational Theological Center*, Volume 13, Number 2, Spring, 1986.

109. *Ibid.*

110. See William L. Andrews, ed., *Sisters of the Spirit* (Bloomington: Indiana University Press, 1986), pp. 104, 105, 147, 208, 209. Andrews presents selections from the autobiographies of three black women preachers of the nineteenth century. The Rev. Jarena Lee wrote of Richard Allen's reluctance to recognize women preachers (p. 36). Julia Foote, the first woman to be ordained as a deacon in the A.M.E. Zion Church and the second woman ordained as an elder, wrote of her initial opposition to women preachers (p. 201). This is significant, since it is a classic illustration of what can happen to the oppressed when they are under the influence of the thinking of the oppressed group, i.e., when they are enslaved by the values and perceptions of the dominant group. In such cases some within the ranks of the oppressed will uncritically accept their position in life as the way things were always meant to be. This is why the principle of the hermeneutic of suspicion is so crucial in the methodology of liberation theologians. The oppressed must constantly examine their own ideas and ideologies and try to unmask any hidden assumptions. They must always be self-critical and ask why they believe as they do. Zilpha Elaw is the other black woman whose autobiography is reproduced in the Andrews anthology.

111. Yet I think Angela Davis's assessment of Douglass's position is accurate. Although concerned about the rights of both blacks and women, he could see that the predicament and suffering of blacks as a race was such that if a choice must be made it was more expedient that blacks be granted the vote. Douglass never supported the idea of black male superiority over women, but he was clearly advocating suffrage for black men at this point. Writes Davis: "When he argued that woman suffrage was momentarily less urgent than the extension of the ballot to Black men, he was definitely not defending Black male superiority. Although Douglass was by no means entirely free of the influence of male-supremacist ideology and while the polemical formulations of his argument often leave something to be desired, the essence of his theory that Black suffrage was a strategic priority was not in the least anti-woman" (*Women, Race & Class*, pp. 77–78).

112. Sojourner Truth, like Frederick Douglass, came to be very critical of the deep seated racism in women's organizations led by white women. This led to mitigation of her earlier position against Douglass (see Davis, p. 83). Also, Gerder Lerner, a white historian, erroneously makes the claim that Sojourner Truth was the lone black woman of her day to intentionally link race and sex. "Sojourner Truth stands alone among black women in the nineteenth century in staunchly combining defense of her race with feminism" (Lerner, ed., *The Female Experience: An American Documentary* [Indianapolis: Bobbs-Merrill, 1977], p. 487). This is a glaringly conspicuous error in light of the fact that Lerner edited a documentary history on black women in 1972 in which she includes an excerpt from Anna Julia Cooper's book, *A Voice from the South* (1892), which reveals Cooper's passion about race and sex. (See Lerner, ed., *Black Women in White America: A Documentary History* [1972] [New York: Vintage, 1973], pp. 572–574.) Sojourner Truth may well have been the leading black woman to speak on race and sex before predominantly white audiences in the nineteenth century, but it is inaccurate to say that hers was the lone black woman's voice.

113. *A Voice from the South*, pp. 120–121. See also the selection from her book in

Bert James Loewenberg and Ruth Bogin, eds., *Black Women in Nineteenth-Century American Life* (University Park: Pensylvania State University Press, 1976), pp. 330–331.

114. Both bell hooks and Karen Baker-Fletcher have been influenced by the work and inspiration of Anna Julia Cooper. Baker-Fletcher wrote her doctoral dissertation on Cooper, "A Singing Something: The Literature of Anna Julia Cooper as a Resource for a Theological Anthropology of Voice." Harvard University, Ph.D. dissertation, 1992. She continues to research and write on Cooper.

115. Anna Julia Cooper, an outstanding black feminist of the nineteenth century, fostered a view of the total liberation of *all* persons regardless of gender, class, and race that anticipated the work of present day black womanist theologians, e.g., Jacquelyn Grant, Katie Cannon, Kelly Brown, Cheryl Gilkes, Delores Williams, and Karen Baker-Fletcher. In addition, Cooper often wrote and spoke of the inherent sacredness and worth of persons as such, and her belief that each is imbued with the image of God (see Cooper, *A Voice from the South* [Xenia, Ohio: Aldine Printing House, 1892], pp. 124–125). Although she did not refer to herself as such, she was very much a personalist. I discuss this philosophy in chapter 7.

116. Burrow. I have also indicated eight things that can be done to start us on the way to effectively eliminating sexism. One contemporary black feminist who has contributed much toward working out feminist theory rejects the idea of separatism between black women and black men, as the former work to eliminate sexist practices. bell hooks acknowledges the existence of male feminists, and encourages bonding between them and women. Such men should be more vocal, however, in public settings (particularly within male audiences), speaking out against sexism in all forms. She writes: "Separatist ideology encourages us to believe that women alone can make feminist revolution — we cannot. Since men are the primary agents maintaining and supporting sexism and sexist oppression, they can only be successfully eradicated if men are compelled to assume responsibility for transforming their consciousness and the consciousness of society as a whole. . . . In particular, men struggle in the area of exposing, confronting, opposing, and transforming the sexism of their male peers. When men show a willingness to assume equal responsibility in feminist struggle, performing whatever tasks are necessary, women should affirm their revolutionary work by acknowledging them as comrades in struggle" (see hooks, *Feminist Theory: From Margin to Center* [Boston: South End Press, 1984], p. 81).

117. *For My People*, p. 138.

118. *Ibid.*, p. 97.

119. James Evans, Jr., "Black Theology and Black Feminism," *Journal of Religious Thought*, Volume 38, Number 1, Spring, 1981, pp. 43–53.

120. Louis-Charles Harvey, "Black Theology and the Expanding Conception of Oppression," *Journal of Religious Thought*, Volume 38, Number 2, Fall-Winter, 1981–82, pp. 5–15.

121. *Ibid.*, p. 5.

122. *Ibid.*

123. *Ibid.*

124. Harvey, pp. 13–14.

125. *For My People*, p. 162.

126. *My Soul Looks Back*, p. 115.

127. Recorded in Torres and Eagleson, eds., *Theology in the Americas*, p. 354.

128. Wilmore, "The New Context of Black Theology in the United States," Gerald Anderson and Thomas Stransky, eds., *Mission Trends No. 4* (New York: Paulist Press, 1979), p. 116.

129. For example, few theologians are more committed to ecumenism than James Cone. Yet he is not concerned about the ecumenical movement of the wcc, ncc, cocu, etc., which is primarily sponsored by Europeans and European-Americans. He has little patience with their call for denominational unity while failing to address the race question in significant and substantive ways. Instead, he has called for an ecumenical movement within the black church; that the black church organize its resources for the total liberation of the black community. Cone contends that black Christians should be committed to developing a greater sense of unity among their own people. What the white sponsored church organizations are proposing is viewed as having little or nothing to do with issues that most affect African Americans. Cone contends that the ncbc was established in order "to transcend the denominational barriers that separated black churches" (*For My People*, p. 85).

130. William A. Jones, Jr., *God in the Ghetto* (Elgin, Ill.: Progressive Baptist Publishing House, 1979), p. 93. Here Jones follows the typology of black leadership developed by Daniel Thompson in *The Negro Leadership Class*. He concludes with Thompson that of the three types of black leaders, the "Uncle Tom," the "racial diplomat," and the "race man," only the latter can adequately deal with a racist society and world. The Uncle Tom or hat-carrying, head-bowing, yes-saying, begging black, is a type of a past generation of blacks, but is not completely extinct. The racial diplomat, more educated and better situated in terms of status, is viewed as an outgrowth of the former, and may generally be found at "interracial" gatherings. The racial diplomat generally favors compromise and reform rather than radical, immediate change. He or she typically serves as liaison between the white establishment and the black community. Unfortunately, too often there is a tendency by racial diplomats to give whites the impression that things are better in the black community than they really are, especially among the masses. "The racial diplomat can always be expected to mediate difference between the natives and the rulers, but always in a way that guarantees an outcome amenable to the rulers" (*God in the Ghetto*, p. 92). What is needed in the black leadership class is more of those in the category of "race man."

131. "Letter to Jules Feiffer," LeRoi Jones, *Home: Social Essays* (New York: William Morrow, 1966), p. 66.

132. *The Autobiography of Malcolm X*, p. 411.

133. George Breitman, ed., *Malcolm X Speaks* (New York: Grove Press, 1965), pp. 220–221.

134. *The Autobiography of Malcolm X*, p. 412. In a similar vein he said: "Whites who are sincere don't accomplish anything by joining Negro organizations and making them integrated. Whites who are sincere should organize among themselves and figure out some strategy to break down prejudice that exists in white communities. This is where they can function more effectively, in the white community itself..." (*Malcolm X Speaks*, p. 221).

Chapter 6

1. *My Soul Looks Back*, p. 77. In *For My People*, Cone makes an important statement in this connection. "It is very important to point out that when black theology first emerged it had no existence apart from the black church. Indeed, it was simply the black church criticizing itself in order to become a more effective participant in the black liberation struggle" (p. 102).

2. *My Soul Looks Back*, p. 88. Here Cone indicates that his critique of the black church has been an ongoing one.

3. *Black Theology and Black Power*, Chapter III.

4. *For My People*, p. 99.

5. *A Black Theology of Liberation*, p. 236.

6. *Ibid.*

7. *Black Theology and Black Power*, p. 91. Here Cone writes: "The white master forbade the slave from any remembrance of his homeland. The mobility created by the slave trade, the destruction of the family, and the prohibition of African languages served to destroy the social cohesion of the African slaves." This was essentially the view of E. Franklin Frazier. Cone makes no reference to the opposing view of DuBois or Melville Herskovits. (See DuBois, *The Negro* [1915] [New York: Oxford University Press, 1970], Chapter XI, and Melville Herskovits, *The Myth of the Negro Past* [1941] [Boston: Beacon Press, 1958].)

8. Wilmore, *Black Religion and Black Radicalism*, rev. ed. (Maryknoll, N.Y.: Orbis, 1983), p. 4; see also p. 26.

9. *Ibid.*, p. 26.

10. *Ibid.*, p. 27.

11. Frederick Douglass, *Narrative of the Life of Frederick Douglass* [1845], (New York: Signet, 1968), p. 120.

12. Marable, *Blackwater* (Dayton, Ohio: Black Praxis Press, 1981), p. 35.

13. Cited *ibid.*, p. 37.

14. Cited in Albert Raboteau, *Slave Religion* (New York: Oxford University Press, 1980), p. 293.

15. *Black Theology and Black Power*, p. 92.

16. *Ibid.*

17. *Ibid.*, p. 93.

18. *Ibid.*

19. *Ibid.*, pp. 93–94.

20. *Ibid.*, p. 103.

21. Henry Mitchell and Nicholas Cooper-Lewter, *Soul Theology* (New York: Harper, 1986).

22. *Ibid.*, p. 95.

23. *Blackwater*, Chapter 3.

24. *Black Religion and Black Radicalism*, chapters 1–3 *passim*.

25. Harding, *There Is a River*, chapters 1–3 *passim*.

26. *Black Theology and Black Power*, p. 100.

27. Blassingame, *The Slave Community*, p. 133.

28. E. Franklin Frazier, *The Negro Church in America* (New York: Schocken Books, 1975).

29. *Blackwater*, p. 41.

30. *Ibid.*, p. 7. Marable is correct in his view that there has always been a tension between accommodation and struggle, or what he calls "blackwater," in the history of the black church. Recognizing that both of these strands have often appeared in a single black religious leader in varying degrees, and that even the most conservative of these leaders may have within them the capacity to interject radicalism into their ministry, Marable makes the following observation in *How Capitalism Underdeveloped Black America* (1983): "When one surveys the single organization that is closest to the masses of Black people, the Black Church, one finds that the majority of Black religious leaders from the mid-nineteenth to late-twentieth centuries have been pragmatic or accommodationist in their politics, integrationists, and at times, profoundly

conservative. Few ministers would hold much credence in the exhortations of Thomas Sowell or Ronald Reagan, but not many would consider themselves the descendants of Nat Turner or Malcolm X." Yet Marable, still aware of the tension — aware that this is not descriptive of the whole of black experience — goes on to say that "the most conservative and accommodating Black itinerant preacher always has within him the capacity to become a Nat Turner" (pp. 181–182; 213). Howard Thurman makes a similar observation in his autobiography: "The view that the traditional attitude of the religion of black people was, or is, otherworldly, is superficial and misguided. 'Take all the world but give me Jesus is a false and simplistic characterization of our religion" (Thurman, *With Head and Heart* [New York: Harcourt Brace Jovanovich, 1979], pp. 17–18).

31. *Blackwater*, pp. 40–41.

32. *Black Religion and Black Radicalism*, p. xii.

33. *Ibid.*, p. x.

34. *Black Theology and Black Power*, p. 103.

35. *Ibid.*

36. *Ibid.*, p. 108.

37. Cone, "What Is the Church," in Cone, *Speaking the Truth* (Grand Rapids, Mich.: Eerdmans, 1986), p. 123. In his response to Jan Lochman's essay, "The Just Revolution," Cone described the church as "those people who have received God's revelation as liberation and who accept the risks of striving for freedom" (see *Christianity and Crisis*, July 10, 1972, p. 167).

38. *Black Theology and Black Power*, p. 106.

39. *Ibid.*, p. 104.

40. Historian Benjamin Quarles has written that the Klan had "a modest beginning" at Pulaski, Tennessee, in 1865, but by the spring of 1867 it was a highly organized group whose terrorist activities extended to many parts of the country. The primary goal was to instill fear into blacks in order to discourage them from protesting. See Quarles, *The Negro in the Making of America* (New York: Collier, 1968), p. 139.

41. Both Kenneth T. Jackson and Benjamin Quarles have written of the scare tactics and brutality of the Klan, and their effectiveness. See their respective texts: *The Ku Klux Klan in the City: 1915–1930* (New York: Oxford University Press, 1977), and *The Negro in the Making of America*.

42. *Black Theology and Black Power*, pp. 104–105.

43. *Ibid.*, p. 105.

44. *Ibid.*

45. *Ibid.*

46. *Ibid.*, p. 106

47. Joseph Washington, *Black Religion*, pp. 35, 37.

48. *My Soul Looks Back*, Chapter 3.

49. *Black Theology and Black Power*, p. 107.

50. *Martin & Malcolm & America*, p. 147.

51. *Ibid.*

52. Martin Luther King, Jr., *Where Do We Go from Here: Chaos or Community?* (Boston: Beacon Press, 1967), p. 124. See also p. 20, where King calls for active engagement on the part of more significant numbers of blacks.

53. Cited in *Martin & Malcolm & America*, pp. 75, 147.

54. *Black Theology and Black Power*, pp. 111, 112.

55. *Ibid.*, p. 109.

56. Cited in *Martin & Malcolm & America*, p. 75.

57. *Black Theology and Black Power*, p. 114.

58. *Black Religion and Black Radicalism*, p. x. It is important to observe that Cone seemed by the eighties to be more aware of this paradox. For example, in *For My People* he has written: "The black church has been radical, serving as the most important instrument of black liberation, but it has also been one of the most conservative institutions in the black community. This is the paradox. It has produced the Martin Luther King who creatively joined black religion with the struggle for justice; but it has also produced many Joseph H. Jacksons whose views on Christianity and politics were as conservative as King's were radical" (p. 100).

59. *Black Religion and Black Radicalism*, p. xiii.

60. *Blackwater*, pp. 45, 46.

61. *Ibid.*, p. 44.

62. *My Soul Looks Back*, p. 88.

63. *Ibid.*, pp. 79–80.

64. See *Black Theology and Black Power*, Chapter IV, and *A Black Theology of Liberation*, pp. 236–237.

65. Cone, "Black Theology and the Black Church...," p. 354. See also *For My People*, where Cone writes: "Without prophetic self-criticism, churches become self-serving institutions for their ministers, officers, and members" (p. 112). It is to their credit that black clergy radicals of the sixties avoided this and other mistakes "by creating a theology of the black church that offered negative and positive criticisms of it so that it could become a more effective instrument of liberation. If they had attacked racism without criticizing the opiate character of their own churches, their attack on the white church would have had little credibility" (*ibid.*).

66. *For My People*, p. 107.

67. *Black Theology and Black Power*, p. 114.

68. *My Soul Looks Back*, p. 88.

69. *Ibid.*, p. 89.

70. *Ibid.*

71. In a recent major publication, C. Eric Lincoln and Lawrence Mamiya document this phenomenon in their ten year study of 2,150 urban and rural churches of the seven historically black denominations: National Baptist Convention, National Baptist Convention of America, Progressive National Baptist Convention, African Methodist Episcopal Church, African Methodist Episcopal Zion Church, Christian Methodist Episcopal Church, and Church of God in Christ (the largest of the black pentecostals). Also, since their study was published a schism has occurred in the National Baptist Convention of America that has produced an eighth black denomination: the National Missionary Baptist Convention of America. Lincoln and Mamiya referred to what appeared to be an impending split (see Lincoln and Mamiya, *The Black Church in the African American Experience* [Durham, N.C.: Duke University Press, 1990], p. 36, chapters 5, 6).

72. *Ibid.*, pp. 90, 91.

73. Cone, "Black Ecumenism and the Liberation Struggle," in *Speaking the Truth*, p. 145.

74. Breitman, ed., *Malcolm X: By Any Means Necessary* (New York: Pathfinder Press, 1970), p. 13. See also Breitman, ed., *Malcolm X Speaks* (New York: Grove Press, 1965), pp. 21–22. See also *The Final Speeches: Malcolm X* (New York: Pathfinder, 1992), pp. 38–41.

75. The late Willie White was the lone African American on the faculty of Christian Theological Seminary in Indianapolis in the mid-seventies. Although I did not have the honor of meeting him it was he who cultivated the ground for my later arrival on that faculty in the early eighties where I was the only African American for seven years before the arrival of Karen and Garth Baker-Fletcher.

76. Cited in "Black Ecumenism and the Liberation Struggle," pp. 147–148.
77. This is Maya Angelou's term.
78. "Black Ecumenism...," p. 149.
79. *Ibid.*, p. 150.
80. *My Soul Looks Back*, p. 91.
81. *Black Theology and Black Power*, p. 114.
82. "Black Ecumenism...," p. 150.
83. *Ibid.*, p. 152; see also *My Soul Looks Back*, p. 92.
84. "Black Theology and the Black Church...," p. 358.
85. *Ibid.*, p. 359.
86. *Black Theology and Black Power*, p. 33.
87. "Black Theology and the Black Church...," p. 356.
88. *Black Theology and Black Power*, pp. 113, 114, 115.
89. "Black Theology and the Black Church...," p. 355.
90. *For My People*, p. 106.
91. *Martin & Malcolm & America*, p. 273.
92. *Black Theology and Black Power*, p. 115.
93. *Ibid.*, pp. 112–113. See also "Black Ecumenism...," p. 148. Here Cone writes of how good the history of the black church looks when compared with "the sick history of the white church." His primary concern, however, is not how good the black church looks when compared with its white counterpart, but how it looks through the eyes of black youths and others in the black community who view it as an irrelevant, bloodsucker institution concerned not about the black masses, but only with sustaining itself. "We may rightly claim that our separation from the white church is due to white racism, but what is the reason for continued separation from each other?" (p. 149). In a similar vein Cone writes of how black and white Methodism differs. "The central difference between black and white Methodism was and is the refusal of black people to accept racism and social injustice as reconcilable with the experience of conversion and new birth. We do not believe that it is possible to be sanctified and racist at the same time. If conversion and new birth mean anything at all, they must mean the historical actualization of the experience of salvation in works of piety and mercy on behalf of the oppressed of the land" (Cone, "Sanctification and Liberation in the Black Religious Tradition," in *Speaking the Truth*, pp. 30–31). Other black scholars have also written of the differences between the black and white church as far as their commitment to the ideals of their faith. Marable writes approvingly of DuBois's view in this regard: "DuBois understood that the shortcomings of the Black Church were small in comparison to the massive hypocrisy and blatant racism evident within white denominations. ... DuBois believed that all white Christian churches expressed 'a double standard of truth' towards the Negro, professing the highest ideals while carrying out 'the most selfish and self-seeking' practices of race hatred and oppression. For these reasons, DuBois argued, the Black Clergy had no other alternative except to become an active agent for social justice and political transformation" (Marable, *How Capitalism Underdeveloped Black America*, p. 199.
94. *My Soul Looks Back*, p. 92.
95. *For My People*, p. 117.
96. *My Soul Looks Back*,, p. 64.
97. "Black Theology and the Black Church...," p. 354.
98. Cone, "What Is the Church," in *Speaking the Truth*, p. 114.
99. Cited in W. J. Weatherby, *James Baldwin: Artist on Fire* (New York: Donald Fine, 1989), p. 228. See also Baldwin and Margaret Mead, *A Rap on Race* (New York: Lippincott, 1971), where Baldwin says, "I have to hang out with publicans and sinners,

whores and junkies, and stay out of the temple where they told us nothing but lies anyway" (p. 89).

100. *My Soul Looks Back*, p. 80.

101. "Black Ecumenism...," p. 148.

102. *My Soul Looks Back*, p. 15.

103. Bill Adler et al., eds., *The Wisdom of Martin Luther King, Jr.* (New York: Lancer Books, 1968), p. 128.

104. Baldwin, *Notes of a Native Son*, p. 6.

105. *Black Theology and Black Power*, p. 4.

106. Reinhold Niebuhr, *Leaves from the Notebook of a Tamed Cynic* (New York: Willett, Clark & Colby, 1929), p. xii.

107. Francis J. McConnell, *Borden Parker Bowne* (New York: Abingdon, 1929), p. 18.

108. *Narrative of the Life of Frederick Douglass*, p. 120.

109. Douglass, *The Life and Times of Frederick Douglass*, p. 85.

110. Cited in Cone, "Violence and Vengeance: A Perspective," in *Speaking the Truth*, p. 71.

Chapter 7

1. June Bingham, *The Courage to Change: An Introduction to the Life and Thought of Reinhold Niebuhr* (New York: Scribner's, 1961).

2. Reinhold Neibuhr, "Intellectual Autobiography," Charles W. Kegley, ed., *Reinhold Niebuhr: His Religious, Social, and Political Thought* (New York: Pilgrim Press, 1984), p. 3. Here Niebuhr himself writes: "I cannot and do not claim to be a theologian. I have taught Christian Social Ethics for a quarter of a century and have also dealt in the ancillary field of 'apologetics.'"

3. Calvin E. Bruce and William R. Jones, eds., *Black Theology II* (Cranbury, N.J.: Associated University Presses, 1978), p. 18.

4. *Ibid.*

5. *Ibid.*, p. 19.

6. *Ibid.*

7. *Ibid.*; see the essays by William H. Becker, "Vocation and Black Theology," and Clyde A. Holbrook, "Black and White Theologies: Possibilities for Dialogue," pp. 27–49 and 189–211, respectively.

8. Bruce and Jones, eds., p. 172.

9. *Ibid.*, p. 171.

10. *Ibid.*, p. 222.

11. *Ibid.*, p. 221.

12. William R. Jones, *Is God a White Racist?* (New York: Anchor Press/Doubleday, 1973).

13. Renita Weems, *Just a Sister Away* (San Diego: Lura Media, 1988); and Theodore Walker, Jr., *Empower the People: Social Ethics for the African American Church* (Maryknoll, N.Y.: Orbis, 1991).

14. See C. Eric Lincoln and Lawrence Mamiya, *The Black Church in the African American Experience* (Durham, N.C.: Duke University Press, 1990).

15. J. DeOtis Roberts, *A Black Political Theology* (Philadelphia: Westminster, 1974), p. 236.

16. Roberts, *Black Theology in Dialogue* (Philadelphia: Westminster, 1987), p. 115.

17. Ferm, *Contemporary American Theologies*, p. 56.

18. Letty Russell, "A Feminist Looks at Black Theology," Bruce and Jones, eds., *Black Theology II*, p. 257.

19. *Ibid.*, pp. 257–258.

20. Bruce, p. 171.

21. I extend gratitude to Beth Meyerson for this observation.

22. Rudolph Outlaw, "A Prisoner's View of Black Theology," Wilmore, ed., *Black Men in Prison: The Response of the African American Church* (Atlanta: ITC Press, 1990), p. 72.

23. *Ibid.*, p. 74.

24. *Ibid.*, p. 74.

25. *Sister Outsider*, p. 60.

26. *The Autobiography of Malcolm X*, p. 498.

27. Karen Baker-Fletcher, "There Is a River: The Black Church, Black Women, and Regeneration." Unpublished manuscript.

28. *Ibid.*, p. 4.

29. *Sister Outsider*, p. 120.

30. *Ibid.*, p. 65.

31. Andrew Hacker, *Two Nations: Black and White, Separate, Hostile, Unequal* (New York: Ballantine Books, 1992), p. 218.

32. *Sister Outsider*, p. 117.

33. I am grateful to both of these students, Seana Murphy (African American) and Rachel Metheny (European American) for their challenges and their own willingness to remain in the thick of battle even as they work their way through seminary.

34. Karen Baker-Fletcher, "There Is a River: The Black Church, Black Women, and Regeneration."

35. Jawanza Kunjufu, *Countering the Conspiracy to Destroy Black Boys* (Chicago: Afro-Am Pub. Co., 1985).

36. See Elsa Tamez, ed., *Against Machismo* (Oak Park, Ill.: Meyer-Stone, 1987), pp. 107, 108.

37. Baldwin, *The Price of the Ticket* (New York: St. Martin's/Marek, 1985), p. 667.

38. Baldwin, *The Fire Next Time* (New York: Dial Press, 1963), p. 108.

39. Jean Smith, "I Learned to Feel Black," Floyd Barbour, ed., *The Black Power Revolt* (New York: Collier, 1968), p. 217.

40. Vincent Harding recounts W.E.B. DuBois's story of how blacks are like would-be passengers on a train. "DuBois said that blacks were like passengers who had spent all of their time and energies trying to prove to their fellow passengers and to the conductor that they had a right to be on the American train. Indeed, he said that we had given so much of our attention to this task that we had never bothered to ask about the train's destination. Finally, said DuBois, after a few seats had been commandered and some of the immediate attacks had died down, a few black persons began to ask [and he was surely foremost among them]: 'Where, by the way, is this train going?' 'What is its destination?' Most often no one knew. When answers were supplied some of us began to wonder if we really wanted to go, especially if our destination would always be determined by the people who had fought for centuries to keep us off, or confined to the Negro car" (see Harding, "Beyond Chaos: Black History and the Search for the New Land," John A. Williams and Charles F. Harris, eds., *Amistad I* [New York: Vintage Books, 1970], pp. 269–270).

41. Linda Brent, *Incidents in the Life of a Slave Girl*, ed. by L. Maria Child (New York: Harcourt Brace Jovanovich, 1973), p. 163.

42. King, "Showdown for Nonviolence," James Washington, ed., *A Testament of Hope* (New York: Harper, 1986), p. 71.

43. "Conversation with Martin Luther King," *Conservative Judaism*, Volume 22, Number 3, Spring, 1968, pp. 8, 9.

44. Cited in Sister Jeanne Rollins, "Liberation and the Native American," Torres and Eagleson, eds., *Theology in the Americas*, p. 205.

45. *Martin & Malcolm & America*, p. 75.

46. Steve Clark, ed., *The Final Speeches: Malcolm X* (New York: Pathfinder Press, 1992), p. 22.

47. Nannie H. Burroughs, "Unload Your Uncle Toms," Gerder Lerner, ed., *Black Women in White America: A Documentary History* (New York: Vintage, 1973), p. 552.

48. Maulana Ron Karenga, from *The Quotable Karenga*, Barbour, ed., *The Black Power Revolt*, p. 164.

49. *The Price of the Ticket*, p. xix.

50. Cited in Foner, ed., *America's Black Past*, p. 100.

51. Greenlee, *The Spook Who Sat by the Door*, p. 113.

52. *Malcolm X Speaks*, p. 145.

53. Burroughs, p. 552.

54. William Loren Katz, *Black Indians: A Hidden Heritage* (New York: Atheneum, 1986), p. 13.

55. *Ibid.*, p. 14.

56. Virgil Elizondo, "Toward an American-Hispanic Theology of Liberation in the U.S.A.," Fabella and Torres, eds., *Irruption of the Third World*, p. 50.

57. Theodore Cross, *The Black Power Imperative* (New York: Faulkner Books, 1987), p. 706.

58. Leo D. Nieto, "Toward a Chicano Theology of Liberation," Anderson and Stransky, eds., *Mission Trends No. 4: Liberation Theologies*, p. 278.

59. Andrés G. Guerrero, *A Chicano Theology* (Maryknoll, N.Y.: Orbis, 1987), pp. 46-50.

60. A Chicano Reflection Group, "The Chicano Struggle," Torres and Eagleson, eds., *Theology in the Americas*, p. 209. Virgil Elizondo has also pointed to this concern about the identity problem in the Latino community, or what he calls "a limbo of nonidentity." See *Irruption of the Third World*, p. 52.

61. Nieto, p. 279. See also Elza Tamez, ed., *Against Machismo*. This book consists of taped interviews with fifteen male Catholic and Protestant Latin American liberation theologians on the issue of machismo.

62. *Ibid.*, p. 280.

63. Cross, p. 705.

64. Manning Marable develops the concept of the racist-capitalist state in *How Capitalism Underdeveloped Black America*, but would now add sexist as well. Blacks, Latinos, and Native Americans are among the chief victims of the racist-sexist-capitalist state.

65. Cross, p. 708.

66. *Ibid.*, p. 706.

67. *Ibid.*

68. Nieto, p. 281.

69. Thistlethwaite and Engel, p. 3.

70. Quoted in Robert L. Allen, *Black Awakening in Capitalist America* (New York: Anchor Books, 1970), pp. 6, 7.

71. Wilmore and Cone, eds., *Black Theology*, p. 511.

72. *Ibid.*, p. 514.

73. J. Russell Chandran, "A Methodological Approach to Third World Theology," Fabella and Torres, eds., *Irruption of the Third World,* p. 80.

74. This is a cumbersome term, but at this juncture the idea of retaining the dialectical tension between the universal and the particular is what is important, and for our purpose the phrase Two-Thirds World Theology-in-Black is at least suggestive.

75. Elizondo, pp. 54–55.

76. Vine Deloria, Jr., "A Native American Perspective on Liberation," Anderson and Stransky, eds., *Mission Trends No. 4: Liberation Theologies,* p. 262. Although Deloria insists on the need for particularity, he is not, in this particular selection, sympathetic with liberation theology. For him there can be no authentic liberation theology that does not seek to destroy completely the white Western way of perceiving things. He seems to be demanding a radically different epistemology and metaphysics. It may be this concern which prompted his writing of *The Metaphysics of Modern Existence* (New York: Harper & Row, 1979).

77. See Theodore Walker, Jr., "Theological Resources for a Black Neoclassical Social Ethics," *The Journal of Religious Thought,* Volume 45, Number 2, Winter-Spring, 1989, pp. 21–39; Henry J. Young, "Process Theology and Black Liberation: Testing the Whiteheadian Metaphysical Foundations," *Contemporary Philosophy,* Volume 12, Number 9, May 1989, pp. 26–30; *Hope in Process: A Theology of Social Pluralism* (Minneapolis: Fortress Press, 1990); and Archie Smith, Jr., *The Relational Self* (Nashville: Abingdon, 1982); "Black Liberation and Process Theologies," *Process Studies,* Volume 16, Number 3, Fall 1987, pp. 174–188.

78. Major J. Jones, *The Color of God* (Macon, Ga.: Mercer University Press, 1987), p. 43.

79. *God of the Oppressed,* p. 163.

80. *Ibid.* Similarly, Cone writes that Martin Luther King, Jr., "rejected Brightman's concept of the finite God as an explanation for the existence of evil. King's commitment to the faith of the Negro church was too strong to allow him to embrace a limited God" (*Martin & Malcolm & America,* pp. 29–30).

81. *Ibid.*, pp. 267–268n.

82. Cone, "God Is Black," Thistlethwaite and Engel, eds., *Lift Every Voice,* p. 93.

83. See *God of the Oppressed,* p. 163, and *Martin & Malcolm & America,* pp. 29–30.

84. *Ibid.*

85. Edgar S. Brightman, *Person and Reality,* ed. Peter A. Bertocci (New York: Ronald Press, 1958), p. 9.

SELECT BIBLIOGRAPHY
of Literature
by and about James H. Cone*

Books

Cone, James H.
  1969 *Black Theology and Black Power*. New York: Seabury Press.
  1970 *A Black Theology of Liberation*. Philadelphia: Lippincott.
  1972 *The Spirituals and the Blues*. New York: Seabury Press.
  1975 *God of the Oppressed*. New York: Seabury Press.
  1982 *My Soul Looks Back*. Nashville: Abingdon.
  1984 *For My People*. Maryknoll, N.Y.: Orbis Books.
  1986 *Speaking the Truth*. Grand Rapids, Mich.: William B. Eerdmans.
  1991 *Martin & Malcolm & America*. Maryknoll, N.Y.: Orbis Books.
Wilmore, Gayraud, and Cone, James H., eds.
  1979 *Black Theology: A Documentary History, 1966–1979*. Maryknoll, N.Y.: Orbis Books.
  1993 *Black Theology: A Documentary History, 1980–1992*. Maryknoll, N.Y.: Orbis Books.

Articles and Essays

Cone, James H.
  1968 "Christianity and Black Power," in *Is Anybody Listening to Black America?* ed. C. Eric Lincoln (New York: Seabury Press, 1968), pp. 3–9.
         "What Is the Church?" Essay presented at a pastor's conference on the church at Emory University (1968); rewritten for a conference on Jesus and Justice at Philander Smith College (1985).
  1969 "Toward a Constructive Definition of Black Power." *Student World* 62, 3-4:314–33.
         "In Search of a Black Christianity." *Time* 94:57–8, July 4.
         "Black Theology: We Were Not Created for Humiliation." *Ladies' Home Journal* 86:132, December.
  1970 "Black Consciousness and the Black Church: A Historical-Theological Interpretation"; *Annals of the American Academy of Political Science* 387:49–55, January; *Frontier* 13:87–90, June; *Christianity and Crisis* 30:244–50, November 2–16.

Compiled with the assistance of the Rev. Tyrone Eugene Fisher.

"Black Power, Black Theology, and the Study of Theology and Ethics." *Theological Ethics* 6:202–15, Spring.

"Christian Theology and the Afro-American Revolution." *Christianity and Crisis* 30:123–5, June 8.

"Toward A Black Theology." *Ebony* 25:113–6, August.

"Black Theology and Black Liberation." address il. *Christian Century* 87:1084–8, September 16.

1971 "Christ in Black Theology." *Thesis Theological Cassettes* 2, 2.

"An Introduction to Black Theology." *Enquiry*, March-May, pp. 51–80.

1972 "Black Spirituals; A Theological Interpretation." *Theology Today* 29:54–69, April.

"Response [to J.M. Lochman]." *Christianity and Crisis* 32:166–7, July 10.

1973 "Social Context of Theology; Freedom, History and Hope." *Risk* 9, 2:13–24.

"Social Context of Theology; Freedom, History and Hope." *The Journal of Interdenominational Theological Center* 1:55–64, Fall.

"Theological Reflections on Reconciliation." *Christianity and Crisis* 32:303–8, January 22.

"Black Theology on Revolution, Violence and Reconciliation." *Dialog* 12:127–33, Spring.

"Freedom, History, and Hope." *The Journal of the Interdenominational Theological Center* 1:55–64, Fall.

1974 "Negro Churches (in the United States)." *Encyclopaedia Britannica*, 15:926–42.

"Schwarze Theologie im Blick auf Revolution, Gewaltanwendung und Versohnung; ubers. von F. Herzog." *Evangelische Theologie* 34:4–16, January-February.

"Schwarze Theologie und Ideologie; eine Antwort an meine Gesprachspartner; ubers. von B. Link-Ewert [rejoinder to C. Eric Lincoln, and others]." *Evangelische Theologie* 34:80–95, January-February.

"White and Black [interview]." *The Other Side*, May-June.

"Biblical Revelation and Social Existence." *Interpretation* 28:422–40, October.

"The Dialectic of Theology and Life or Speaking the Truth." *Union Seminary Quarterly Review* 29:75–89, Winter.

1975 "Christian Theology and Scripture as the Expression of God's Liberating Activity for the Poor." Essay presented at the annual meeting of the Society for the Study of Black Religion (1975). Later appeared as "What Is Christian Theology?" *Caribbean Journal of Religious Studies* 3:1–12, September; *Encounter* 43:117–28, Spring 1982.

"Black and African Theologies: A Consultation." *Christianity and Crisis* 35:50–2, March 3.

"Who Is Jesus Christ for Us Today?" *Christianity and Crisis* 35:81–5, April 14.

"The Story Context of Black Theology." *Theology Today* 32:144–50, July.

"Black Theology on Revolution, Violence, and Reconciliation." *Union Seminary Quarterly Review* 31:5–14, Fall.

"Black Theology and Ideology: A Response to My Respondents." *Union Seminary Quarterly Review* 31:71–86, Fall.

"The Content and Method of Black Theology." *The Journal of Religious Thought* 32:90–103, Fall-Winter.

1976 "Black Worship: A Historical-Theological Interpretation." Essay presented at a workshop on black worship sponsored by Black Methodists for Church Renewal (Detroit, 1976).

"Black Theology and the Black College Student." *Journal of Afro-American Issues* 4, 3-4:420-31, Summer-Fall.

"'God Our Father, Christ Our Redeemer, Man Our Brother': A Theological Interpretation of the AME Church." *The Journal of the Interdenominational Theological Center* 4:25-33, Fall.

1977   "Sanctification and Liberation in the Black Religious Tradition, with Special Reference to Black Worship." Essay presented to the Sixth Oxford Institute on Methodist Theological Studies, Lincoln College, Oxford, England, July 18-28, 1977; *Sanctification and Liberation*, ed. Theodore Runyon (Nashville: Abingdon Press, 1981), pp. 174-92.

"Christian Faith and Political Praxis." Essay presented at a conference on the Encounter of Theologies (Mexico, October 1977); *Praxis Cristiana y producción teológica*, ed. Jorge V. Pixley and Jean-Pierre Bastian (Salamanca: Ediciones Sigueme, 1979), pp. 75-88; *Bulletin de théologie africaine* 2, 4:205-18, July-December 1980; *Encounter* 43:129-41, Spring 1982.

1978   "Black Ecumenism and the Liberation Struggle." Essay presented at the "Black Ecumenism and the Liberation Struggle" Conference at Yale University, February 16-17, 1978; presented at the Quinn Chapel African Methodist Episcopal Church on their 131st anniversary, May 22, 1978; *The Journal of the Interdenominational Theological Center* 7:1-10, Fall 1979.

"Black Theology: Tears, Anguish and Salvation." *The Circuit Rider*, May, pp. 3-6.

"Black Theology and the Black Church: Where Do We Go from Here?" *Mid-Stream* 17:267-77, July.

"Sanctification, Liberation, and Black Worship." *Theology Today* 35:139-42, July.

"A Black American Perspective on the Future of African Theology." *Africa Theological Journal* 7, 2:9-19.

1979   "Asian Theology Today: Searching for Definitions." *Christian Century* 96:589-91, May 23.

"A Critical Response to Schubert Ogden's *Faith and Freedom: Toward a Theology of Liberation*." *Perkins School of Theology Journal* 33:51-5, Fall.

"A Black American Looks at African Theology." *Worldview* 22:26, 36-8, December.

1981   "Black Theology and Third World Theologies." *Thesis Theological Cassettes* 12, 12.

"Left Strategies Must Deal with Racism." *Witness* 64:8-9, January.

"The Gospel and the Liberation of the Poor: How My Mind Has Changed; 16th in a Series." *Christian Century* 98:162-6, February 18.

1982   "Evangelization and Politics: A Black Perspective." *Bulletin de théologie africaine* 4, 7:5-15, January-June.

"My Soul Looks Back [excerpt]." *Sojourners* 11:26-30, September.

"Sanctification, Liberation and Black Worship." *Nexus* 24, 1-2, 2-12.

1983   "What Is the Church: A Black Perspective." *Bulletin de théolgie africaine* 5, 9:21-33, January-June.

"A Theological Challenge to the American Catholic Church." Essay presented at the Voices for Justice Conference at the College of Notre Dame in Baltimore (July 1983).

"Black Theology and Third World Theologies." *Chicago Theological Seminary Register* 73, 1:3-12, Winter.

1984   "Martin Luther King, Jr., Black Theology — Black Church." *Theology Today*

40:409–20, January; *Martin Luther King, Jr.: A Profile*, ed. C. Eric Lincoln (New York: Hill and Wang, 1984), pp. 243–59.

"Toward the Morning: A Vision for a New Social Order." *Sojourners* 13, 9:13–6, October.

"Violence and Vengeance: A Perspective." Essay prepared for the National Conference on Religious Community's Roles in Breaking the Cycle of Violence and Vengence, Indianapolis, Indiana, November 2-5, 1984.

1985   "Martin Luther King, Jr., Black Theology, and the Black Church. *The Drew Gateway* 56, 2:1–16.

"Ecumenical Association of Third World Theologians." *Ecumenical Trends* 14, 8:119–22, September [history].

"Black Theology in American Religion." *Journal of the American Academy of Religion* 53, 4:755–71, December [American Academy of Religion, 75th, 1984, Chicago].

1986   "Black Religious Thought in American History Part I: Origins [and] Part II: More Recent History." Essay written for inclusion in the *Encyclopedia of Religion in America*, eds. Charles H. Lippy and Peter Williams (New York: Scribner's, 1986).

"The Theology of Martin Luther King, Jr." *Union Seminary Quarterly Review* 40, 4:21–39.

"Martin Luther King, Jr.: January 15, 1929–April 4, 1968." *Union Seminary Quarterly Review* 40, 4:3–68 [thematic issue].

"A Dream or a Nightmare: Martin Luther King, Jr., and Malcolm X — Speaking the Truth About America." *Sojourner* 15, 1:26–30, January [photos].

"Black Theology in American Religion." *Theology Today* 43, 1:6–21, April.

Cone, James H., and Hordern, William
1971   "Dialogue on Black Theology." *Christian Century* 88:1079–80, September 15.
1990   "God Is Black." In *Constructing Christian Theologies from the Underside*, ed. Susan Brooks Thistlethwaite & Mary Potter Engel (New York: Harper & Row, 1990), pp. 81–94.

Articles about James H. Cone

Bennett, Robert A.
1976   "Biblical Theology and Black Theology." The *Journal of the Interdenominational Theological Center* 3:1–16, Spring.

Berenbaum, Michael
1976   "Women, Blacks, and Jews: Theologians of Survival." *Religion in Life* 45:106–18, Spring.

Biehl, João Guilherme
1986   "Teologías negra e feminista: um dialogo critico com a teología da libertação Latino-Americana." *Estudos Teológicos* (Brazil) 26, 1:9–36.

Bosch, D.J.
1974   "Currents and Crosscurrents in South African Black Theology." *Journal of Religion in Africa* 6, 1:1–22.

Boshoff, Carel W.H.
1981   "Christ in Black Theology." *Missionalia* 9:107–25, November.

Brown, Charles S.
1975   "Present Trends in Black Theology." *The Journal of Religious Thought* 32:60–8, Fall-Winter.

Bucher, Glenn R.
   1974   "Liberation in the Church; Black and White." *Union Seminary Quarterly Review* 29:91–105, Winter.
   1976   "Theological Method in Liberation Theologies: Cone, Russell, and Gutiérrez." *American Academy of Religion. Philosophy of Religion and Theology Proceedings*, pp. 118–21.
Burrow, Rufus, Jr.
   1993   "James H. Cone: Father of Contemporary Black Theology." *Asbury Theological Journal.* Fall.
Chapman, G.C., Jr.
   1974   "Black Theology and Theology of Hope: What Have They to Say to Each Other?" *Union Seminary Quarterly Review* 29:107–29, Winter.
Edwards, Herbert O.
   1975   "Black Theology: Retrospect and Prospect." *The Journal of Religious Thought* 32:46–59, Fall/Winter.
Grant, Jacqueline
   1985   "Black Christology: Interpreting Aspects of the Apostolic Faith." *Mid-Stream: An Ecumenical Journal* 24:366–75, October [reply to G. S. Wilmore, pp. 357–65].
Hefner, P.J.
   1974   "Theology Engagé; Liberational, Political, Critical." *Dialog* 13:188–94, Summer.
Herzog, Fredrick, ed.
   1975   "Special Issue on Black Theology." *Union Seminary Quarterly Review* 31:3–86, Fall.
James, R.B.
   1974   "Tillichian Analysis of James Cone's Black Theology." *Perspectives in Religious Studies* 1:15–28, Spring.
Jones, William R.
   1971   "Theodicy and Methodology in Black Theology; A Critique of Washington, Cone, and Cleague." *Harvard Theological Reivew* 64:541–57, October.
LeFevre, Perry D.
   1982   "Liberation Theology: Black." *Chicago Theological Seminary Register* 72, 2:30–2, Spring [reprint from *Radical Prayer*].
Long, Charles H.
   1983   "Freedom, Otherness, and Religion: Theologies Opaque." *Chicago Theological Seminary Register* 73, 1:13–24, Winter.
McBeth, H. Leon
   1981   "Images of the Black Church in America." *Baptist History and Heritage* 16, 3:19–28 + , July.
McDaniel, Jay
   1985   "The God of the Oppressed and the God Who Is Empty." *Journal of Ecumenical Studies* 22, 4:687–702, Fall [3rd Annual "God Conference," Puerto Rico, Jan. 1984].
McWilliams, Warren
   1979   "Theodicy According to James Cone." *The Journal of Religious Thought* 36:45–54, Fall-Winter.
   1980   "Divine Suffering in Contemporary Theology." *Scottish Journal of Theology* 33, 1:35–53.

Molla, Serge
 1982 "Au pay de la *Black Theology* [J. H. Cone and G. S. Wilmore, eds. 1979]."
   Revue de théologie et de philosophie 114 (3d ser 32), 3:277–83 [review article].
 1984 "James H. Cone, théologien noir américain." *Revue de théologie et de philosophie*
   116 (3d ser 34), 3:217–39 [includes bibliography].
Moore, David O.
 1980 "Black Theology, a Tentative Exploration." *The Modern Churchman* 23, 3:172–9
   [includes bibliography].
Morrison, Roy D.
 1982 "The Emergence of Black Theology in America." *The AME Zion Quarterly
   Review* 94, 3:2–17, October [Harlem Renaissance].
Motlhabi, Mokgethi
 1984 "The Historic Origins of Black Theology." *Bulletin de théologie africaine* 6, 12,
   211–26, June-December [United States; South Africa].
Oglesby, E.H.
 1974 "Ethical and Educational Implications of Black Theology in America." *Religious Education* 69:403–12, July-August.
Peters, Ted
 1983 "Methode und System in der heutigen amerikanischen Theologie; ubers.
   von R. Slenczka." *Kerygma and Dogma* 29:2–46, January-March.
Potter, Ronald C.
 1984 "A Comparison of the Conceptions of God in Process and Black Theologies." *The Journal of the Interdenominational Theological Center* 12:50–61, Fall-
   Spring.
Premnath, D. N.
 1985 "Comparative and Historical Sociology in the Old Testament Research: A
   Study of Isaiah 3:12–15." *Bangalore Theological Forum* 17, 4:19–38, October-
   December [includes bibliography].
Ruether, Rosemary Radford
 1971 "Black Theology of James Cone." *Catholic World* 214:18–20, October.
 1986 "Re-contextualizing Theology." *Theology Today* 43, 1:22–7, April [feminism
   and Christian commitment].
Rogers, C.
 1971 "James Cone and the Methodists." *Christian Century* 88:1340, November 17.
 1972 "James Cone and the Methodists: Discussion." *Christian Century* 89:201–2,
   February 16.
Sontag, Fredrick E.
 1979 "Coconut Theology: Is James Cone the 'Uncle Tom' of Black Theology." *The
   Journal of Religious Thought* 36:5–12, Fall-Winter [reply, A. Smith].
Stewart, Carlyle F.
 1983 "The Method of Correlation in the Theology of James H. Cone." *The Journal
   of Religious Thought* 40:27–38, Fall-Winter [includes figures].
Weddle, David L.
 1980 "The Liberator as Exorcist: James Cone and the Classic Doctine of Atone-
   ment." *Religion in Life* 49:477–87, Winter.
Williams, A.R.
 1971 "A Black Pastor Looks at Black Theology." *Harvard Theological Review*
   64:559–67, October.
Williams, Preston N.
 1972 "James Cone and the Problem of a Black Ethic." *Harvard Theological Review*
   65:483–94, October.

1981 "American Black Theology and the Development of Indigenous Theologies in India." *The Indian Journal of Theology* 30:55–68, April-June.
Williams, Robert C.
1973 "Moral Suasion and Militant Aggression in the Theological Perspective of Black Religion." *The Journal of Religious Thought* 30, 2:27–50.
Yancey, William L.
1981 "Books Worth Dicussing: James H. Cone, God of the Oppressed." *Currents in Theology and Mission* 8:178–80, June.

Reviews of Books by James H. Cone

Black Theology and Black Power
1969 Johson, R.P. *Social Progress* 60:40-3, September-October.
　　　Richards, D.R. *Bibliotheca Sacra* 126:356-7, October-December.
1970 Dickinson, Richard. *Encounter* 31:387-92, Autumn.
　　　Felder, C.H. *Union Seminary Quarterly Review*, 25:543-6, Summer.
　　　Herhold, R.M. *Lutheran World* 17, 4:388-90.
　　　Relyea, H.C. *Theology Today* 27:369-71, October.
1972 Davis, J.H. *Review of Religious Research* 13:154-5, Winter.
　　　Washington, Joseph R., Jr. *Journal for the Scientific Study of Religion* 11:310-1, September.
1979 Simmons, P.D. *Review and Expositor: A Baptist Theological Journal* 76:125-6, Winter.

Black Theology of Liberation
1971 Elliot, C. *Frontier* 14:85-8, May, C. Elliott.
　　　Reuther, Rosemary. *The Journal of Religious Thought* 28, 1:74-7.
　　　Wilmore, Gayraud S. *Union Seminary Quarterly Review* 26:413-9, Summer.

Spirituals and the Blues: an Interpretation
1972 Rogers, C. *Christian Century* 89:928-9, September 20.
　　　Reuther, Rosemary R. *The Journal of Religious Thought* 29, 2:98-9.
1973 Maura, S. *Theology Today* 29:446-8, January.
　　　Mays, B.E. *Union Seminary Quarterly Review* 28:255-6, Spring.
　　　Lacy, N., Jr. *Religion in Life* 42:271-2, Summer.
　　　Rookmaker, H.R. *Christian Scholar's Review* 3, 1:72-3.
1975 Keeley, Benjamin J. *Review of Religious Research* 16:151 Winter.
　　　Williams, Robert C. *Journal of the American Academy of Religion* 43:363-5, June.

Ich bin der Blues und mein Leben ist ein Spiritual ubers. von W. Luck
1974 Lehman, T. (Berlin) *Theologische Literaturzeitung* 99:234-6, March.

Teologia nera de la liberazione e black power
Trad. de B. Corsani et M. Corsani (Turin, Claudiana, 1973)
1974 Brun, M.A. *Revue d'Histoire et de philosophie religieuses* 54, 4, 581-3.

God of the Oppressed
1975 Mitchell, Henry H. *Review of Books and Religion* 5:5-6, September.

Roberts, J. DeOtis, Jr. *The Journal of the Interdenominational Theological Center* 3:58-63, Fall.
1976   Bucher, Glenn R. *Theology Today* 33:116, 118-9, April.
Burkle, Howard R. *Currents in Theology and Mission* 3:126, April.
Campbell, Ernest T. *Religion in Life* 45:256-7, Summer.
Manker, Raymond G. *Christian Century* 93:203, March 3.
Pinder, Nelson W. *The St. Luke's Journal of Theology* 19:222-3, June.
Taylor, Hycel B. *Union Seminary Quarterly Review* 31:302-4, Summer.
Tinney, James. *Christianity Today* 20:32-4, March 26.
Weber, Theodore R. *Theological Studies* 37:360-1, June.
1977   Becker, W.H. *Interpretation: A Journal of Bible and Theology* 31:214-6, April.
Fraser, I.M. *The Scottish Journal of Religious Studies* 30, 2:184-6.
Jones, L.N. *Christian Scholar's Review* 7, 1:68-9.
Reid, S. *The Drew Gateway* 48, 1:53-6.
Wright, O. *The Journal of Religious Thought* 34:50-3, Spring-Summer.
1978   Archibald, H.A. *Review of Religious Research* 19:219-20, Winter.
Davies, J.G. *The Expository Times* 89:125, January.
Robertson, E.H. *Theology* 81:136-8, March.
1980   Tutu, D. *Journal of Theology for Southern Africa* No. 31:73-4, June.

——— and Wilmore, Gayraud S., eds. *Black Theology:*
A Documentary History, 1966–1979
1980   Carey, J.J. *Theological Studies* 41:607-8, September.
Earl, R.R. *Journal of Ecumenical Studies* 17:697-8, Fall.
Herzog, F. *Christian Century* 97:415-8, April 9.
Newbold, R.T. *The Princeton Seminary Bulletin* 3 No. 1:111-2.
1981   Bennett, R.A. *Anglican Theological Review* 63:211-2, April.
Maimela, S.S. *Missionalia* 9:131-2, November.
Tinney, J.S. *Sojourners* 10:32-3, May.
1982   Conn, H.M. *Journal of the Evangelical Theological Society* 25:238-40, June.
Molla, S. *Review de théologie et de philosophie* 114 (3d ser 32), 3:277-83.

Gott der Befreier: Eine Kritik der weissen Theologie (Stuttgart, Kohlhammer, 1982)
1984   Waldenfels, H. *Zeitschrift für Missionswissenschaft und Religionswissenschaft* 68:249, July.

My Soul Looks Back
1983   Molla, S. *Revue de théologie et de philosophie* 115 (3d ser 33), 3:314.
Moore, A.J. *Christianity and Crisis: A Christian Journal of Opinion* 42:452-4, January 24.

For My People
1985   Anon. *Journal of Theology for Southern Africa* 51:84, June.
Burrow, Rufus. *Encounter* 46:187-90, Spring.
Fields, Bruce. *Trinity Journal* 6:94-7, Spring.
Molla, Serge. *Revue de théologie et de philosophie* 117 (3d ser 35), 4:328.
Van Rooy, J.A. *Missionalia* 13, 2:90-1, August.
Walker, Theodore. *The Journal of Religious Thought* 42:88-9, Spring-Summer.

Dissertations
(in Chronological Order)

Cone, Cecil Wayne
  1974   *The Identity Crisis in Black Theology: An Investigation of the Tensions Created by the Efforts to Provide a Theological Interpretation of Black Religion in the Works of Joseph Washington, James Cone, and J. DeOtis Roberts.* Ph.D. Dissertation, Emory University.
Jones, Amos, Jr.
  1975   *In Defense of the Apostle Paul: A Discussion with Albert Cleage and James Cone.* D. Min. Dissertation, Divinity School, Vanderbilt University.
Phillips, Steven
  1978   *The Use of Scripture in Liberation Theologies: An Examination of Juan Luis Segundo, James H. Cone, and Jürgen Moltmann.* Ph.D. Dissertation, Southern Baptist Theological Seminary.
Stewart, Carlyle Fielding III
  1982   *A Comparative Analysis of Theological-Ontology and Ethical Method in the Theologies of James H. Cone and Howard Thurman.* Ph.D. Dissertation, Northwestern University.
Townes, Emile Maureen
  1982   *The Kingdom of God in Black Preaching: An Analysis and Critique of James H. Cone.* D. Min. Dissertation, University of Chicago.
Wilson, Richard Francis
  1982   *Human Liberation and Theology: An Examination of the Theology of Gustavo Gutiérrez, James H. Cone, and Mary Daly.* Ph.D. Dissertation, Southern Baptist Theological Seminary. [A Latin American, a black, a feminist.]
Parker, Aaron Larry
  1983   *Theological Perspectives on the Nature of Jesus Christ in the Black Church.* Ph.D. Dissertation, Emory University.
Walker, Theodore D., Jr.
  1983   *God of the Oppressed: A Metaphysical and Ethical Analysis.* Ph.D. Dissertation, University of Notre Dame.
Buama, Livingstone Komla
  1985   *The Relevance of Professor James Cone's Black Theology for the Ghanaian Context.* Ph.D. Dissertation, Drew University.
Rossitter, Marion Larkin, Jr.
  1985   *A Reconstruction of John Rawls' Theory of Justice in Light of Selected Themes of Liberation Theologians.* Ph.D. Dissertation, Southern Baptist Theological Seminary.
Young, Josiah Ulysses, III
  1985   *Black and African Theologies: Siblings or Distant Cousins? A Critical Examination from a Black North American Perspective.* Ph.D. Dissertation, Union Theological Seminary.
Bolton, Keith A.
  1986   *The Theological Method of James Cone.* Ph.D. Dissertation, Fuller Theological Seminary.
Fulkerson, Mary McClintock
  1986   *Ecclesial Tradition and Social Praxis: A Study in Theological Method.* Ph.D. Dissertation, Vanderbilt University. [Liberation; feminism.]

Shippey, Robert Clifford, Jr.
  1986   *The Problem of Violence in the Writings of Rosemary Radford Reuther and James H. Cone*. Th.M. Thesis, Southern Baptist Theological Seminary. [Just war theory, feminist theology, justifiable revolution, black theology.]
Yancey, William Lee
  1986   *Hearing Means Death: James H. Cone's Black Theology as a Resource for Confronting the Modern Problem of Death*. Ph.D. Dissertation, Lutheran School of Theology at Chicago.
Sorge, Sheldon Warren
  1987   *Karl Barth's Reception in North America: Ecclesiology as a Case Study*. Ph.D. Dissertation, Duke University. [Cone; Carl Henry; Bloesch; Barmen declaration.]
Brown, Kelly Delaine
  1988   *"Who Do They Say That I Am?" A Critical Examination of the Black Christ*. Ph.D. Dissertation, Union Theological Seminary.
Englebrecht, Edgar
  1988   *The Pattern of Religion in the Black Theology of James Cone*. D.D. Dissertation, University of Pretoria (South Africa).
Kunnie, Julian Edward
  1990   *Bridges Across the Atlantic: Relating Black Theologies in the United States and South Africa, Focusing on Social Analytical Methodologies and Utilizing James Cone and Desmond Tutu as Respective Symbolic Symbols*. Th.D. Dissertation, Graduate Theological Union.

APPENDIX:
Some Samples of James H. Cone's Use of Scripture*

Black Theology and Black Power

Page		Scriptural Passages
35	....	Luke 4:18–19; Mark 1:14–15
36	....	Luke 7:22; Matthew 20:16; 21:31
39	....	Galatians 5:1
40	....	I John 3:8; Luke 4:1–13; Mark I:12ff.; Matthew 4:1–11; Mark 3:27; II Timothy 1:10; Ephesians 1:22; Hebrews 2:8; 10:13
44	....	Exodus 19:4–6
45	....	Psalms 10:14; 72:12; Amos 2:6, 7; Luke 6:20
51	....	John 3:16; Romans 5:8; Matthew 22:34–40; Luke 27:7ff.
57	....	John 3:8
59	....	Isaiah 45; Matthew 25:31ff.; 25:37–39; 25:40
60	....	Galatians 4:6
63	....	Genesis 1:27–28
64	....	Exodus 9:27
65	....	Matthew 5:11
70	....	Ephesians 2:14
99	....	Mark 15:34
124	....	Matthew 5:10–12
125	....	Romans 3:20, 23; Galatians 3:22
147	....	II Corinthians 5:19

A Black Theology of Liberation

Page		Scriptural Passages
2	....	Exodus 19:4–5a
3	....	Luke 4:18–19
23	....	I John 3:2a
47	....	Exodus 15:1b–3

*Compiled with the assistance of the Rev. Tyrone Eugene Fisher.

Page		Scriptural Passages
61	....	Mark 2:22
69	....	John 3:16; I John 4:8, 16
79	....	Romans 8:28
80	....	Romans 8:18
114	....	Luke 2:7
115	....	Mark 1:11; Luke 4:3–12
116	....	Mark 1:14–15; Matthew 27:57; Luke 23:50
117	....	Luke 11:20; Hebrews 2:14ff.
125	....	Matthew 18:4–9; Luke 15:7, 10; Matthew 13:44–46
128	....	I Samuel 14:45; 4:3; 7:8; 9:16; Job 26:2; Galatians 5:1; II Corinthians 3:17; I John 4:18
131	....	Matthew 28:19–20; 25:31ff.

God of the Oppressed

Page		Scriptural Passages
13	....	John 14:6
34	....	Colossians 1:15–16
47	....	Luke 4:18
61	....	Luke 24:32
63	....	Exodus 2:24–25; 6:6; 15:1, 2
64	....	Exodus 19:4–5; 20:2; 20:3; 22:21; cf. 23:9
65	....	Exodus 22:23–24
66	....	Amos 2:10; 3:2
67	....	Isaiah 31:1; Amos 4:2, 8:4; Hosea 13:5–6; 5:11; Hosea 13:7–8; 12:6; Amos 6:12; 8:6–8; 9:7–8
68	....	Jeremiah 5:26–28; Micah 6:8; Isaiah 37:35; II Samuel 7
70	....	Isaiah 3:13–15; Proverbs 19:7; 14:13; 23:10–11
71	....	Psalms 137; Jeremiah 31:31–34; Ezekiel 36:26
72	....	Isaiah 40:1–2; Matthew 5:17
73	....	John 1:1; Luke 1:49–53
74	....	Mark 1:10; cf. Matthew 3:16f.; Luke 3:21f.; Mark 1:11; Matthew 3:17; Luke 3:22; Psalms 2:7; Isaiah 42:1
75	....	Luke 4:1f; Matthew 4:1f.; cf. Mark 1:12–13; Luke 4:18–19; Isaiah 61:1–2
76	....	Luke 7:22f.; Matthew 11:5f.; Isaiah 35:5f.; Isaiah 29:18–21
77	....	Luke 11:20; 10:18
78	....	Matthew 11:28–30; Luke 18:22; 9:59f; Matthew 25:1f.; Luke 14:26
79	....	Matthew 5:3; Mark 2:17; Luke 6:20; 10:21; cf. Matthew 11:25; Mark 10:14; Matthew 21:31
80	....	Matthew 18:10; 15:30; Mark 10:45
85	....	I John 4:1f.
93	....	Exodus 14:11–12; 14:13; Luke 18:18
94	....	Luke 18:22; 10:29f.; 10:36
95	....	Mark 2:17
99	....	Exodus 6:5–7a

Page		*Scriptural Passages*
100	. . . .	Romans 12:19; cf. Deuteronomy 32:35
109	. . . .	Isaiah 40:4–5
110	. . . .	Acts 10:38–43
111	. . . .	John 1:13–14; I Timothy 3:16; Philippians 2:6, 8
113	. . . .	Romans 1:16–17
119	. . . .	Genesis 12:3; Exodus 19:6; I Corinthians 5:19
120	. . . .	Hebrews 2:17–18
121	. . . .	Acts 1:8; 2:1f.
134	. . . .	Isaiah 42:6–7
136	. . . .	Matthew 25:45; Luke 4:18f.
139	. . . .	Mark 15:34
144	. . . .	Exodus 3:14
150	. . . .	Mark 40:35–38; 10:39; 10:42–45
151	. . . .	Mark 10:45
154	. . . .	Exodus 5:24
158	. . . .	I John 3:2
161	. . . .	Exodus 14:11
164	. . . .	Exodus 15:3; Psalms 41:1–2; 147:3; 95:3; 136; Psalms 95:3; 94:6; 94:3
165	. . . .	Isaiah 3:10–11
166	. . . .	Proverbs 10:27; Jeremiah 12:1; Habakkuk 1:13
167	. . . .	Habakkuk 2:3–4; Psalms 37:16–17; Jeremiah 31:31; cf. Proverbs 24:19f.
168	. . . .	Ecclesiastes 1:2; 7:13; 9:2, 11–12
169	. . . .	Job 1:1; 27:5–6; 31:35; 38:4
170	. . . .	Job 42:3, 5–6; 1:6–12; Gen. 22:1–19; 42:10; Isaiah 53:11
171	. . . .	Isaiah 47:6; 41:17; 40:2; 40:28; 40:27; 49:14; Isaiah 49:3; 41:8
172	. . . .	Isaiah 42:1; 53
173	. . . .	Isaiah 63:9; Mark 1:1–3; Isaiah 40:3; Matthew 3:1–3; Luke 3:1–6; John 1:19–23; Isaiah 42:1; Psalms 2:7; Luke 3:21f.; Matthew 3:16f.; Mark 1:9f.; 9:7; Matthew 17:5; Luke 9:35; Luke 7:22; Matthew 11:5; Isaiah 61; Luke 4:18f.; Mark 10:45; Isaiah 53; John 1:29, 36; cf. Isaiah 53:4f., 7, 11
174	. . . .	I Corinthians 15:3; Isaiah 53:3
175	. . . .	Isaiah 53:4–5; 53:7
176	. . . .	I Corinthians 15:14; Galatians 5:1
178	. . . .	Romans 8:28
181	. . . .	Romans 8:28; 8:18
183	. . . .	Romans 8:18
184	. . . .	Psalms 46:1
195	. . . .	Matthew 5:39
225	. . . .	I Corinthians 1:26
227	. . . .	Ephesians 2:14–15
228	. . . .	II Corinthians 5:19; Ephesians 1:10
229	. . . .	Deuteronomy 26:5–10
230	. . . .	Luke 2:7
233	. . . .	Galatians 5:1; Exodus 19:5
234	. . . .	Ephesians 2:8; 2:10; Matthew 25:31ff.; 25:44, 45
241	. . . .	Matthew 13:44

INDEX

absolute pacifism 214
Acts 249
Adrian College xiv, 15, 93, 218
Allen, Richard 11, 151, 161, 225
Amos 247, 248
Anderson University xi
anger 78–79, 87
antebellum black church 148–53
Anthony, Susan B. 134, 135
Aptheker, Herbert 5
Ashanti 4
Assmann, Hugo 38, 129, 222
authentic Christianity 172

Baker, Ella 132
Baker, Theodore xi
Baker-Fletcher, Garth xi, 181, 230
Baker-Fletcher, Karen ix, 18, 138,
   181–82, 184, 199, 226, 230, 233
Balasuriya, Tissa 32, 48
Baldwin, James xx, 36, 47, 68, 70,
   170, 171, 186, 189, 197, 207, 231–32
Baldwin, Lewis ix, xviii
Baraka, Imamu Amiri 144
beaten Christs 18, 78
Benin 9
Benjamin, T. Garrott, Jr. 179
Bennett, John C. 125, 222
Berry, Mary 9
bifurcation of reality 12
black clergy radicals 88, 98, 109, 121
Black Manifesto xiv, 90, 94, 96
Black Methodists for Church Renewal
   170
Black Panthers xiv
black power 10
Black Power Statement 3, 13

black radicalism 8, 149, 172
Black Theology Project 18, 63,
   131
black womanist theologians 31
Black Women's Conference 18
blackwater 149, 151, 152–53, 159, 172,
   228
Blassingame, John 7, 10, 12, 152
Boesak, Allan 19, 27, 29
Boff, Clodovis 212
Boff, Leonardo 52, 212
Boggs, Grace 186
Boggs, James 186
Bonino, José Miguez 38
Bosnia 75
Bowne, Borden Parker 120, 171
Brawley, Benjamin 4
Brent, Linda 187
"bridge house" 183
Brightman, Edgar S. 198, 235
Brookins, H.H. 165
Brooks, Harriet xi
Brotherhood 4
Brown, Dee 211
Brown, John 214
Brown, Kelly 18, 226
Brown, Robert McAfee 22, 34, 43,
   46, 208–9, 211
Bruce, Calvin 174–75, 178
Bultmann, Rudolph 112
Bucher, Glen 222
Burks, Mary Fair 132
Burnley, Lawrence x
Burroughs, Nannie H. 184, 189, 190,
   234
Burrow, Eugena xi
Burrow, Fannie xi
Burrow, Rufus, Sr. xi
Burrow, Sheronn xi

Cannon, Katie 18, 226
Carmichael, Stokley 16, 195
Cayton, Horace 69
Chandran, J. Russell 196
Christian Church (Disciples of
  Christ) xiv
Christian Theological Seminary xi,
  178
Clark, Kenneth 80, 108
Clark, Septima 132
class analysis 83
classism 112, 128–31
Cleage, Albert 174, 176
Cole, Nat 144
Collins, Virginia 138
Colossians 248
commitment 26, 32–36
Compromise of 1877 154
Cone, Cecil 71, 106, 123, 222
Conean 1
Conference on Research and the Black
  Church 179–80
conjurors 8, 9
context 30
contextual 66
contextual dialectical method 51–52
Cooper, Anna Julia ix, 11, 37, 118,
  127, 135, 138, 225, 226
Cooper, J. California 184
Cooper-Lewter, Nicholas 151
Corinthians, I 249
Corinthians, II 247, 248, 249
Coser, Lewis 39
Cotton, Dorothy 132
Couch, Beatriz Melano 52–53
Counts, William P. xi
Cox, Oliver Cromwell 41
Craig, Richard xi
Cross, Theodore 192, 194
Cunningham, Mary x–xi

Dahomey 4, 9
Dahrendorf, Ralf 220
Davidson, Basil 6
Davis, Angela Y. 134, 222, 225
Davis, Ossie 181
Delany, Martin 76
Deloria, Vine 33, 37, 211, 235
Deuteronomy 249

DeWolf, L. Harold 209
Douglass, Frederick 25, 75, 133, 135,
  137, 149, 172, 214, 225
DuBois, W.E.B. 25, 88, 89, 112, 133,
  148, 206, 228, 231, 233

EATWOT 18, 53
Ecclesiastes 249
ecumenism 162–64, 168, 227
Elaw, Zilpha 137, 225
Ephesians 247, 249
epistemological break 34
equality 217
Equiano, Olauda 5, 205
Esther 72
Evans, James, Jr. 226
Exodus 247, 248, 249
Ezekiel 248

Ferguson, Jane x
Ferm, Deane 63–67, 85, 121, 122, 123,
  178
Foner, Eric 19–20
Foote, Julia A.J. 137, 225
Forbes, James 180
Forman, James xiv, 90, 94, 96
Foulkes-Montgomery, L. Joyce v
frame of reference 44–47
Frazier, E. Franklin 130, 148, 152, 228
Freire, Paulo 129

Galatians 247, 248, 249
Garnet, Henry Highland 11, 75, 151
Garrett Evangelical Theological Semi-
  nary 18, 136
Garrison, William Lloyd 75
Garrow, David 216
Garvey, Marcus 21
Genesis 247, 249
Gift of God 4
Gilder, George 40
Gilkes, Cheryl 18, 226
God, finite 235
God-concept 197, 198
Goldman, Peter 220

Goode Kenneth 6
Grant, Jacquelyn 18, 136, 137, 138, 224–25, 226
Greeley, Andrew 87
Greenlee, Sam 190
Grenada 75
Grimke, Angelina 120
Grimke, Sarah 120
Guerrero, Andrés G. 193
Gutiérrez, Gustavo 18, 21, 27, 28, 29, 33, 34, 35, 42, 44, 46, 53, 131

Habakkuk 249
Hacker, Andrew 182–83
Hamer, Fannie Lou 132
Hannah, William W. ix, xiii
Hardin, Kenny xi
Harding, Vincent 4, 8, 90, 96, 233
Harper, Francis Ellen Watkins 137
Harvey, Louis-Charles 114, 139–41, 194, 196, 226
Hebrews 247, 249
hermeneutic mediation 52
hermeneutic of suspicion 47–48, 211
hermeneutic of trust 46–49, 211
Herskovits, Melville 148, 228
historical praxis 27, 54
historical subject 44
Holmer, Paul 125
Holmes, Reginald Carl x
Hood, Robert 178
hooks, bell 134, 220, 224, 226
Hordern, William 31, 113, 207, 221
Hosea 248
Hough, Joseph 86, 215
Humbert, William 150

Iberian peninsula 3
identity crisis 222
inclusive language xxi, 18
insurrection 8
Integrity 4
Interdenominational Theological Center 94, 179
internationalists 132, 165, 216
Iraq 75

Isaiah 247, 248, 249
Isasi-Díaz, Ada María 46

Jackson, Kenneth T. 229
Jackson, Reubenia xi
Jacobs, Harriet Brent 187
Jeremiah 248, 249
Jesus 4
Job 248, 249
John 247, 248, 249
John, I 247, 248, 249
John the Baptist 4
Jones, Absalom 151, 161
Jones, Major 2, 15, 63, 64, 65, 85, 115, 122, 174, 176, 197, 199
Jones, William A. 99, 143, 227
Jones, William R. 174–76, 197, 198
Jordan, June 187
Justice 4

Karenga, Maulana Ron 189
Kaunda, Kenneth 75
King, Martin Luther, Jr. xviii, 2, 14, 16, 17, 34, 50, 58, 66, 71, 74, 76, 82, 83, 88, 91, 100, 105, 106, 110, 113, 121, 132, 133, 140, 144, 156, 157, 158, 164, 165, 167, 171, 186, 187–88, 216, 230
Kirby, James L. x
Ku Klux Klan 154–55
Kunjufu, Jawanza 185

Lee, Jarena 137, 225
Lewis, Dennis xi
Lexington Theological Seminary ix, x
Liberty 4
Lilly Endowment 179
Lincoln, C. Eric xiii, 177, 230
Logan, Rayford 49
Long, Charles 71, 106
Lorde, Audre 107, 117, 135, 182, 183, 220
Luckmann, Thomas 28
Luke 247, 248, 249

McConnell, Francis J. 171
McKissick, Floyd 16
Macquarrie, John 200
macrocharity 101
Malcolm, Livingston x
Malcolm X xviii, 2, 14, 15, 16, 17, 21,
    24-25, 57, 58, 59, 66, 67, 71, 74,
    76, 79, 80, 82, 83, 85, 86, 90-91,
    96, 100, 105, 106, 108-110, 113, 121,
    132, 133, 144, 147, 157, 160, 164, 165,
    167, 172, 181, 186, 187-88, 190, 216,
    220, 227, 229
Malemba 8
Mamiya, Lawrence xiii, 177, 230
Mannheim, Karl 39
Marable, Manning 8, 76, 130, 149,
    152, 153, 159, 186, 217, 228, 231, 234
Mark 247, 248, 249
Marx, Karl 42, 82, 87, 92, 101-102, 216
Marxism 18, 83, 87, 91-93, 128, 131,
    165, 217, 220, 223
Marxist social analysis xviii
Matthew 247, 248, 249
May, L. Susan ix
Means, Saderia x
mediation of pastoral action 52
medicine men 9
Meredith, James 16
Metheny, Rachel 233
Meyerson, Beth ix, 233
Micah 248
microcharity 101
Middle Passage 6, 7, 183
Midwest Christian Training Center 179
Mitchell, Henry 151
Morrison, Toni 184
Moss, Annie Pearl xi
Moynihan Report 133
Muelder, Walter G. 112, 210
mujerista theologies 31
Murphy, Seana ix-x, 233
Murray, Pauli 132
musicians 8
mutiny 7
Muzorewa, Gwinyai H. 203-4
Myrdal, Gunnar 10, 11

Naipaul, Shiva 195
National Committee of Black Church-
    men xiv, 13

National Committee of Negro Church-
    men xiv, 3, 16
National Council of Churches 80, 162
new earth 12, 13
new heaven 12, 13
Newby, Robert xi
Niebuhr, Reinhold 89, 93, 94, 102,
    171, 173, 219
Nieto, Leo D. 192, 194
nihilism x, 183, 184

Oates, Stephen 215
Ogden, Schubert 31, 32
Oglalas 37
ontological blackness 66, 113, 114-125
orthodoxy 30
orthopraxis 30
Outlaw, Rudolph 180, 233

Paris, Peter 178
Parks, Rosa 132
particularistic dimension 66
passionate language 50-51
Paul, Nathaniel 11
Payne, Daniel 11
Payton, Benjamin 95, 97
Pennington, James 11
personalism 201
personalistic metaphysics 200
Pfafflin, Ursula ix, x
Philippians 249
physiological blackness 113, 114-25
Plato, Ann 11
Ponnath, Heimo x
Poor Peoples' Campaign 140
Poussaint, Alvin 80
praxis 41-44, 48
pride 219
priests 8
process philosophy 197
Prosser, Gabriel 12
Proverbs 248, 249
Psalms 247, 248, 249
Puebla Conference 186

Quarles, Benjamin 229

race man 143, 227
racism 53, 112, 117
Rauschenbusch, Walter 219
Reagan administration 40
reason 42, 51, 211
reconciliation 63–65
recovering sexists 181, 182
"relentless surge toward freedom" 7
reparations 90, 94, 96
resistance 3–6, 7–10
retaliatory violence xviii
Ricks, Willie 16
Roberts, J. DeOtis xiii, 1, 15, 63, 64, 65, 85, 115, 122, 125, 146, 176, 177–78
Robinson, Jo Ann 132
Romans 247, 248, 249
Russell, Letty 178
Rustin, Bayard 108

sacredness of persons 226
Samuel, I 248
Samuel, II 248
Sartre, Jean Paul 104
Schmoller, Gustav 108
Scott, Nathan 218
Segundo, Juan Luis 34, 38, 47
self-inflicted genocide 182–83
self-worth 16
sexism 53, 112, 117, 132–39, 168, 180–82
shifts 106
Shockley, Grant 23
sin 219
Sioux 37
slave-holding religion 149
slave rebellions 9
Sleeper, C. Freeman 86, 215
Sloan, Fredeane xi
Smith, Amanda Berry 11
Smith, Archie, Jr. 197, 235
Smith, Frederick Douglass xi
Smith, Jean 186
Sobrino, Jon 34, 43, 65
social analysis xviii, 93–97, 98–105, 219
social ethics 22
social location 30
social sciences 38–41, 47, 210

social scientists 40, 41
socioanalytic mediation 52
socioeconomic analysis xviii, 105–110
solidarity 46–47
Society for the Study of Black Religion 17
sociology of knowledge 28, 39
solidarity with the oppressed 34
somebodyness xi, 16
South Africa 19, 30, 119
Sowell, Thomas 229
Stanton, Elizabeth Cady 134, 135
Stark, Werner 28
"Statement on Black Theology" 17, 94, 95–96, 99
Steele, Shelby 210
Stewart, Carlyle 203
Stewart, Maria ix, 151
subject 33
suicide 8, 183–84
symbol 115–17

Tamez, Elsa 234
Tate, Gloria J. xiii
theistic absolutism 197
Theology in the Americas 18, 73, 130
Theology in the Americas II 18
Third World people 129, 143
Third World Theology 223, 224
Thistlethwaite, Susan Brooks 23, 118, 195
Tillich, Paul 115
Timothy, I 249
Timothy, II 247
Togo 9
transitions xv
Truth, Sojourner 11, 118, 137, 138, 151, 225
Tubman, Harriet 11
Turner, Henry McNeal 11, 165
Turner, Nat 11, 151, 229
Two-Thirds World Theology 195

universal 63, 209
universal dimension 209
University of Pennsylvania x, 88

Vesey, Denmark 11
Vietnam 104
view from below 44

Walker, David 11, 149, 151
Walker, Theodore, Jr. 177, 197, 235
Wallace, Michelle 138
Washington, Joseph 2, 14, 85, 123,
   156, 174
Weaver, Carroll x
Weems, Renita 177
West, Cornel 97, 180, 215, 217, 220
West Africa xix, 3
West Indies 3
White, Willie 163, 230
Whitehead, Alfred North 2, 204
whiteness 61

Whydah 8
Williams, Delores 18, 226
Williams, Preston 224
Wilmore, Gayraud xiv, xx, 2, 11, 13,
   17, 18, 71, 94, 95, 97, 106, 114,
   142-43, 148, 149, 153, 158, 159, 174,
   180, 204, 206, 208
Wilson, William J. 210
Winn, Albert C. 22-23
Witvliet, Theo 2, 10, 33, 38, 55,
   81-82, 89
womanist theology ix, 18, 226
World Council of Churches 80, 162
Wortham, Anne 20

Young, Henry J. 10, 197, 206, 235
Young, Josiah 204, 224